For the Cause
of the
Son of God

*The Missionary Significance of the
Belgic Confession*

Wes Bredenhof

Reformation Media & Press
Fellsmere, Florida

For the Cause of the Son of God
The Missionary Significance of the Belgic Confession
   by Wes Bredenhof

Copyright © 2011 Wes Bredenhof

Published by Reformation Media & Press

Book number 1 in the *Reformed Mission History* series under the editorial oversight of:
   Dr. Jeffery K. Boer
   Dr. Wesley Bredenhof
   Rev. Geoffrey W. Donnan
   Dr. Richard Knodel
   Dr. Stephen Westcott

Cover and interior layout design by Luis Lovelace
Cover illustration colorized by Luis Lovelace

Cover Description: The Countess du Roeulx visiting Guido de Brès (with hand extended) in the prison in Tournai (now Belgium) in early April 1567 who is imprisoned with fellow Reformed pastor Peregrin de la Grange (to de Brès' right). The Countess asked de Brès how he could sleep, eat or drink with such heavy chains. De Brès answered, "My lady, the worthy cause that I uphold and the good conscience which my God has given me, makes me sleep, eat, and drink better than those who wish me harm." The worthy cause was "the cause of the Son of God" of which he so often spoke. He went on to say that the sound of his chains was like the sound of sweet music in his ears. [Woodcut taken from J. A. Wylie's *The History of Protestantism*, Vol. 2, Book iii, p. 61, originally published by Thymme & Jervis in the 1920s and republished in facsimilie by Mourne Missionary Trust, Co. Down, No. Ireland, 1990.]

ISBN: 0-9773442-5-8

Endorsements

True biblical Christianity has always faced two imperatives: a) to remain doctrinally sound, and b) to propagate that genuine, saving, faith, as widely as possible. Church history demonstrates how often these two foundational requirements have drifted apart, to the great detriment of the faith. In the centuries since the great Reformation it had often been the case that theology has been the preserve of the learned and the scholastic, whilst those with a zeal for missions have pressed ahead 'without tarrying for any', and often with a very defective understanding of the faith they wished to share. Dr. Bredenhof reminds us that this was not always the case, and indeed, should never have been the case, for it is far from the vision of the Reformers. In the fiery heat and battle to re-establish Biblical Christianity the Reformers forged a two-edged sword: true Bible doctrine, and an urgent desire to spread that saving truth to all to whom it might be presented. This is the strength of the Belgic Confession (true Bible Doctrine) and the vision of its prime author Guido de Brès (that truth for evangelism and missions), in a day when men faced the daily possibility of being called to die for their faith. In this magnificent study Dr. Bredenhof employs the Belgic Confession and its history to call the church back to its Reformation vision, its Reformation zeal, and its Reformation commitment. May 'For the Cause of the Son of God' be widely read, for it has a message desperately needed by the Church today!

DR. STEPHEN P. WESTCOTT, Author, Professor and Doctoral Chair at Reformation International Theological Seminary

Wes Bredenhof has composed the best study of Reformed missions (both missiology and missions) in print. It is quite simply essential reading, and puts to bed (hopefully forever) the claim that the reformed church has been deficient in its evangelical activity. Bredenhof's scope is very broad so that one is sure to discover new things about the Reformation and its advance. Yet he focuses sharply on *missions* and the advance of Christ's church from an originally Protestant and Reformed perspective. No one will regret purchasing this book!

DR. RICHARD E. KNODEL, JR., Church Planter, Reformed Presbyterian Church of North America, Cincinnati, Ohio; Adjunct Professor and Doctoral Committee member of Reformation International Theological Seminary; former missionary to Scotland; former Orthodox Presbyterian Church pastor.

Endorsements

Though often decried as an inward looking church document, Dr. Bredenhof proves clearly, both from internal evidence and contemporary sources that this confession by Guido de Brès was written as a 'martyr' document in the double sense of the word. In the first place, it is a clear missionary witness (*martyria*) to those who needed the pure light of the gospel of grace; besides that, conceived in a time of much persecution, the author himself became a martyr and died by hanging because he preached the simple Word of God. Very soon after its publication, this pamphlet in 37 articles was embraced by many believers in the Low Countries and adopted as the confession of all Reformed churches in that region. Their leaders had a clear vision of their mission task for the sixteenth-century world around them: to spread the gospel. As a retired missionary of those churches, I do hope and pray that this profound study of their oldest Reformed confession may serve to refocus the mission vision of our churches for a biblical witness of the pure gospel of our Savior Jesus Christ to our twenty first-century needy world.

Dr. Frans L. Schalkwijk, author of *The Reformed Church and Its Mission in Dutch Brazil (1630-1654)*

It would be an understatement to say that Dr. Wes Bredenhof has chosen a *neglected* topic for this book by studying the missiological relevance of the Belgic Confession. Many missiologists would consider this to be an *impossible* topic! In our days the idea is widespread that the Belgic Confession has no missiological relevance at all. Yet, Dr. Bredenhof succeeds admirably in arguing that the Belgic Confession has definite missiological strengths even though it does not set forth a global approach to mission work. Written during a time of persecution, the Belgic Confession aimed to defend *and promote* the Reformed faith — an evangelistic purpose! In addition, Dr. Bredenhof shows that much of the content of the Belgic Confession, with its emphasis on justification by faith and its Christological focus, is surprisingly relevant for teaching in missionary situations today. What makes reading of Dr. Bredenhof's book all the more interesting are various excursions into historical and contemporary developments, ranging from the mission work of Johannes Megapolensis among the Mohawks to the Christian Reformed Church's endeavour to formulate a Contemporary Testimony.

Dr. Arjan de Visser, professor of mission at Canadian Reformed Theological Seminary, Hamilton, ON, Canada.

Endorsements

For the Cause of the Son of God by Dr. Wes Bredenhof gives the following definition of "Mission": "Mission is the official sending of the church to go and make disciples by preaching and witnessing to the good news of Jesus Christ in all nations through the power of the Holy Spirit."

Dr. Bredenhof does a masterful job of demonstrating, through careful historical study, that the Reformed confession of faith known as the *Belgic Confession*, derived from the Scriptures, not only sets forth the proper *content* of the Gospel that is to be preached, but also provides a primary *motivating force* behind the missionary outreach of Reformed churches. Both of these factors are necessary if the Reformed churches of our day are to continue to fulfill the Great Commission properly.

Dr. Jeffrey K. Boer, Pastor of Sharon Orthodox Presbyterian Church, Hialeah, FL (USA), former member of the OPC Committee on Foreign Missions; Board member and Doctoral Committee member of Reformation International Theological Seminary.

In this study Bredenhof has broken new ground. Using newer Reformation research methods he has reopened the discussion on the link between the Reformers and mission. He has rightly left behind the obsolete idea that the Reformation was lacking in missionary character. Bredenhof demonstrates how the Belgic Confession emerges from a perspective in which its author and original adherents believed that they were witnessing to an unbelieving world. Moreover, he argues that the Confession's missionary character has to be considered in close connection with the phenomenon of martyrdom. Guido de Brès and his fellow Reformed believers could have avoided martyrdom by keeping silent, but they chose to speak and their model is instructive for us today too. The study goes on to show how the Belgic Confession can be an instrumental part of developing a Reformed missiology. Both its strengths and weaknesses in that regard are taken into consideration. We live in a time in which many Christians want to move away from Scripture and our creeds. We need to have our thoughts developed in a confessional way, also when it comes to mission. *For the Cause of the Son of God* will be a great help in moving us in that direction, bringing us to a faithful summary of the Bible's teachings so that we can be more effectively engaged in the task to which Jesus has called us.

Dr. Leen Joosse, retired pastor of the Reformed Church of Groningen-West, the Netherlands.

Endorsements

For the Cause of the Son of God provides a well-researched, respectful and timely answer to the claim that predestinarian, creedal theology is detrimental to missions. As the author demonstrates, this nagging complaint against Reformation theology certainly finds no support in Guido de Brès' *Belgic Confession*. De Brès' life beat to a missionary pulse, his martyr's death sealed the authenticity of his ministry and his great confessional contribution to Christian thought abides as a summary of the kind of religion that inspires and enables men to do great things for God. In shedding much-needed light upon the relationship between Reformed theology and God-honoring missions the author has done a service to both. No one who is serious about theology or missions will want to be without Rev. Bredenhof's weighty contribution to the church.

WILLIAM BOEKESTEIN, Pastor, Carbondale, Pennsylvania; Author of *Faithfulness under Fire: The Story of Guido de Bres*

It is somewhat embarrassing to admit that as a missionary since 1976, it never occurred to me to think of a Confession of Faith as a missionary statement. My mind has been given a serious and well-needed course correction after reading *For the Cause of the Son of God* by Dr. Wes Bredenhof. My hope is that many others who may suffer from this same malady will also be enlightened by this profound work. Its reading and study should prove additionally useful in rectifying the thoughtless addiction of many who mistakenly consider the Reformed and Presbyterians as late-comers to the outreach of missions. They will now be able to see more clearly that the same Son of God who was the center of focus and force behind the Reformation was also the same force that spearheaded what we now call modern day missions initially through the early Reformed and Presbyterian churches. He must remain so today in today's missions and missionaries.

REV. GEOFFREY W. DONNAN, President, Reformation Christian Ministries; Co-Pastor, King's Reformed Presbyterian Church, Palm Bay, Florida (USA)

Seal of Massachusetts (or Salem) Colony Translation of seal: Seal of the Governor and Colony of the Massachusetts Bay in New England.[1]

Reformed Mission History

Series Preface

The impression is often given that strong support for the missionary cause has never really come from those who hold to Reformed convictions. Writers such as Kenneth Scott Latourette and Stephen Neill have minimized or neglected the contributions of Reformed figures in the history of Christian mission. Sometimes explanations are offered as to why the Reformation produced no missionary fervour. These explanations range from the theological ("Calvinism kills missionary motivation") to the political ("Their governments would have prevented them from being engaged in missionary endeavours"). Our contention is that these explanations are at least unnecessary because the phenomenon itself does not exist. It is simply not true that the Reformation had nothing or little to do with mission.[2] Neither is it true

---

1. Nehemiah Adams, *The Life of John Elliot: with an Account of the Early Missionary Efforts among the Indians of New England* (Massachusetts Sabbath School Society, Boston, 1847), 6.
2. We use the singular "mission" advisedly since there is one mission given by Jesus Christ to the church in such passages as Matthew 28:18-20. However, we do recognize a justifiable common parlance in which churches and missionaries speak about their mission in several ways: 1) their particular work of missions as a more specific application of the overall mission given to the church by Jesus Christ, and 2) the organizational structure under whose auspices they do their work, be it under a church committee or some "para-church" organization which oversees or supervises their work. In that manner of speaking one could speak of "missions" in the plural.

that the descendants of the Reformation cared little or nothing about missionary outreach.

This volume is one of a series of mission histories and biographies entitled "Reformed Mission History." This series will demonstrate that the Reformation was a missionary movement. We endeavour to put to rest the notion that the Reformation and its heirs disregarded those who are lost, whether at home or abroad. We want to show how there was a missionary emphasis from the beginning of the Reformation. This emphasis was found with its leaders and their actions and writings, and especially in the Reformed (including Presbyterian and other) confessions. Our focus in this series is on what is commonly called the "Calvinistic side" of the Reformation.

But long before Calvin was born, the seeds were being sown. Genuinely Christian missionary efforts were undertaken and bore fruit. For long centuries Europe lay under medieval spiritual darkness. While Christian in name, the vast majority had been deprived of the gospel and the Christ who saves. Around 1400, John Wycliffe's 'poor preachers' were missionaries to England and lowland Scotland. The followers of John Huss (1372-1415) and Jerome of Prague (1370-1416) performed the same work in central Europe, often paying the price with their blood. These "morning stars of the Reformation" already saw their work in missionary terms. With the appearance of Luther, Melanchthon, Zwingli, Farel, Calvin, and others, the true gospel began going out with increased vigour to the nations of Europe.

John Calvin's relationship to mission has received some attention in the last century or so.[3] Despite the claims of some, Calvin insisted that the church has an abiding call to bring the gospel to the nations.[4] In his extant congregational prayers, one can hear Calvin praying for

---

3. See "John Calvin and Missions," Wes Bredenhof, *Christian Renewal* 27:11 (February 25, 2009), 24-27; "Calvijn en de Zending," J. VanderLinden, *De Reformatie* 17:46 (August 13, 1937), 376-377; "The Missionary Dynamic in the Theology of John Calvin," Charles Chaney, *The Reformed Review* 17.3 (March, 1964), 24-38; "The Reformers and Missions," S.H. Rooy, in *Signposts of God's Liberating Kingdom: Perspectives for the 21st Century* (Vol.2) (Potchefstroom: Potchefstroomse Universiteit vir Christelike Hoër Onderwys, 1998), 187-224; "Calvin's Evangelism," Joel Beeke, *Mid-America Journal of Theology* 15 (2004), 67-86; "John Calvin in Mission Literature," James DeJong, *Pro Rege* 4.1 (September 1975), 6-17.

4. See *Commentary on a Harmony of the Evangelists*, John Calvin (Grand Rapids: Baker, 1984), 383-384; *Commentary on Isaiah*, John Calvin (Grand Rapids: Baker, 1984), 402-403.

the gospel to go out to those who are lost.⁵ One of the key things to recognize about Calvin's theology of mission is that he sees the objects of mission in broader terms than many would today. This was true of all sixteenth- and seventeenth-century Reformed believers. For Calvin, Europe under the sway of Roman Catholicism was essentially pagan, or at least sub-Christian. From his standpoint, the lost were certainly in far-off lands overseas. However, they were also close to home, wherever people still consistently held to Roman Catholic beliefs and practices. This led Fred Klooster to comment some years ago that the Reformation "deserves to be called one of the greatest home missionary projects in all history."⁶ The comment is anachronistic insofar as the Reformers themselves made no distinction between local evangelism and foreign mission. Calvin and other Reformers saw all gospel outreach as mission, whether local or otherwise, whether within a culture or cross-cultural.

That leads us to note that Calvin was not only a theorizer or theologian of mission, he was also a man of action. The Genevan academy under his leadership was recognized as a missionary training center. The missionaries in training there were mostly being equipped for ministry in Roman Catholic Europe. During Calvin's lifetime, at his direction, and having received his instruction, literally hundreds of men were sent out from Geneva to preach the biblical gospel to the lost and confused.

Furthermore, Calvin also had an eye for the lost abroad. In 1556, the Genevan church sent out two missionaries with a group of French Huguenots hoping to start a colony in Brazil.⁷ Arriving in March of 1557, they began working among the Tupinambas, an indigenous people. Unfortunately, this work was sabotaged when the leader of the colony apostatized back to Roman Catholicism. Three of the Huguenots were martyred for their faith, not by the Tupinambas, but by their fellow Frenchmen. It was a tragic outcome, but the entire event testifies that Reformed churches of the sixteenth century were concerned about what many today would call foreign mission.

---

5. *Tracts and Treatises Vol. 2: The Doctrine and Worship of the Church*, John Calvin (Grand Rapids: Eerdmans, 1958), 102.

6. "Missions — the Heidelberg Catechism and Calvin," Fred H. Klooster, *Calvin Theological Journal* 7.2 (November 1972), 187.

7. For fuller accounts, see Beeke, *op.cit.*, 79-82 and *Fulfill Your Ministry*, K. Deddens (Winnipeg: Premier, 1990), 158-160

Much more could be said about the first generations of Reformers. For instance, there were the successful efforts of William Farel and Anthony Saucier to bring the Waldensian movement into greater conformity with the biblical gospel.[8] Martin Bucer has been described as a "father of Reformed mission."[9] His writings are full of evidence of missionary fervour. Guido (or Guy) de Brès is another figure to whom we could draw your attention. The author of the Belgic Confession never went overseas to Brazil or any non-European nation, yet he regarded his work as missionary nonetheless. The Roman Catholics among whom he was evangelizing were not distant brothers in the Lord, but those who were lost in darkness and apart from Jesus Christ. In fact, the Belgic Confession may be considered as a missionary witness to a lost world.[10]

While this emphasis was present with the first two generations of Reformers, it only grew stronger with the coming generations. The first Protestant with a detailed theology of mission was Gisbertus Voetius (1589-1676). Voetius taught at Utrecht in the Netherlands and was zealous for the missionary cause at home and overseas.[11] In Voetius' day, the Reformed Church in the Netherlands was actively involved in missionary work in present-day Indonesia, Taiwan, Sri Lanka, Brazil, and the northeastern United States.[12] Later on, missionary work was also undertaken in present-day South Africa. The church sent out ministers to these places with the dual task of pastoring colonialists and discipling native peoples. This all took place in the context of cooperative arrangements between the Reformed church and the Dutch East and West India Companies. While the arrangement was less than ideal, it does reflect an ongoing missionary consciousness amongst Reformed believers in the seventeenth century.

---

8. *You Are My Witnesses—The Waldensians across 800 years*, Giorgio Tourn et al. (Torino: Claudiana Editrice, 1989), 69-73.

9. *Reformatie en zending, Bucer en Walaeus: vaders van reformatorische zending*, L. J. Joosse (Goes: Oosterbaan & Le Cointre B.V., 1988).

10. *For the Cause of the Son of God: the Missionary Significance of the Belgic Confession*, Wes Bredenhof (Fellsmere: Reformation Media and Press, 2011).

11. See "The Missiology of Gisbertus Voetius: the First Comprehensive Protestant Theology of Missions," Jan Jongeneel, *Calvin Theological Journal* 26:1 (April 1991): 47-79; *De zendingsleer van Gisbertus Voetius*, H. A. Van Andel (Kampen: J. H. Kok, 1912).

12. On Brazil, see *The Reformed Church and her Mission in Dutch Brazil (1630-1654)*, Frans Schalkwijk (Fellsmere: Reformation Media and Press, 2011); also see *Mission in Chains*, David Kpobi (Fellsmere: Reformation Media and Press, 2011).

This was not only taking place on the European continent. Those with Reformed convictions in the British isles were also reflecting on Christian mission **and** participating in it. Already in 1560, the Scots Confession evidenced missionary awareness when it bore on its title page the words of Christ in Matthew 24:14, "And this glad tidings of the Kingdom shall be preached through the whole world for a witness to all nations; and then shall the end come." With the advent of the Reformation, the church in Scotland dedicated its energies to the great task of evangelizing the northern reaches of Britain.[13] This was the church taking its missionary calling seriously.

The seventeenth century saw further developments in the British isles and their colonies. The classic work in this regard is still Sidney Rooy's *The Theology of Missions in the Puritan Tradition*.[14] Rooy researched some English Puritans and concluded that mission theology and practice was alive and well in this period. Richard Sibbes, for instance, stressed the communicative nature of faith, recapitulating an emphasis from the sixteenth-century Reformation. Richard Baxter was more practically oriented in his development of mission principles, especially in his discussions of the role of the church. John Eliot famously put mission principles into practice in his labours among the native inhabitants of New England. Cotton Mather stressed how the missionary cause could be furthered through printed literature. And then there was Jonathan Edwards. He too not only wrote about mission theology, but also served as a missionary in colonial New England. These were but representative figures — not the exception, but the norm. Rooy's study is important for it reveals that Puritan Calvinism, growing out of the Reformation, held to a "theology of redemption for the world."[15] This theology went on to bear fruit at home and overseas and laid the foundations upon which others, such as Zinzendorf and Carey later built.

A moment ago we mentioned the cooperative arrangement between the Dutch Reformed Church and the trade companies. The Church of England sought a similar arrangement with the British West and East India Companies.[16] However, due to concerns over the stability of econom-

---

13. *The Missionary Ideal in the Scottish Churches*, D. Mackichan (London: Hodder and Stoughton Publishers, 1927), 64-65.

14. *The Theology of Missions in the Puritan Tradition: A Study of Representative Puritans: Richard Sibbes, Richard Baxter, John Eliot, Cotton Mather, and Jonathan Edwards*, Sidney H. Rooy (Delft: W.D. Meinema, 1965).

15. *The Theology of Missions*, 11.

16. Robert Boyle (1627-1691), a Protestant Irishman, was perhaps one of the leading lights under some influence from the Puritans. He was one of the direc-

ic opportunities, the Companies were reluctant. Where missionary work was permitted, it was only under stringent restrictions. Nevertheless, oftentimes dedicated chaplains and ministers accompanying colonists worked "under the radar" to reach out to local indigenous communities. It took until the nineteenth century for allowances to be made for legal outreach in places like India.

We might also mention the early history of the colonies in what is today the United States. The Mayflower Compact stated the purpose of the new colony being established. It was to be "for the glory of God and advancement of the Christian faith." The advancement of the faith was why men like John Eliot came to the new world and established mission efforts among indigenous Americans. The original seal of the Colony of Massachusetts Bay portrayed a Native American with these words proceeding from his mouth, "Come over and help us." This reveals that the colony regarded themselves as foreign missionaries to North America.

This was also the case with their brethren in the Plymouth Colony, who had arrived eight years previous. Before they had departed from the Netherlands, Governor Bradford had spoken of their motivations. Among them were: "From an inward zeal and great hope of laying some foundation or making way for propagating the kingdom of Christ to the remote ends of the earth, though they should be but as stepping stones to others."[17]

Many others could be mentioned. Basically, by the time William Carey arrived on the scene, Reformed, Presbyterian, and Congregational Calvinistic churches had already been serious about mission since the Reformation. Not only was there missionary action, there had also been serious missiological reflection. To be sure, there were inconsistencies and there were lulls, but no one who has done meaningful research can claim that Protestant missions effectively began with Carey, or perhaps slightly earlier, the Moravian Zinzendorf. We do not deny that Carey's work introduced a new era in the history of mission. His context was characteristically lackadaisical when it came to mission. Yet this was not

---

tors of the British East India Company. Desiring to spread Christianity throughout the East, he made large donations made from his estate (acquired during Cromwell's conquest in the Irish war (1649-1653) for the establishment of many missionary societies.

17. *The Life of John Eliot: with an Account of the Early Missionary Efforts among the Indians of New England*, Nehemiah Adams (Boston: Massachusetts Sabbath School Society, 1847), 6-9.

because of any inherent defect in Protestantism, nor because of the Calvinistic convictions held by Carey or others.

Our goal in this series is to revive interest in the great history of Reformed mission. We aim to bring God glory with what he has done through great men and events of the past. Moreover, we endeavour to demonstrate that orthodox Reformed convictions are not merely compatible with missionary zeal; in fact, such convictions inevitably must result in such zeal. In fact, the evidence demonstrates that William Carey and others caught the age-old biblical vision from their Reformed forebears and heard the call to mission and the rest, as they say, is history. Those gripped by the doctrines of grace and the beauty of the gospel as best expressed in Reformed theology, cannot but be passionate about bringing the good news of Jesus Christ to those yet in darkness.

Dr. Wesley Bredenhof,
Dr. Stephen Westcott,
Rev. Geoffrey Donnan

FUTURE TITLES COMING SOON:

The Reformed Church and its Mission in Dutch Brazil (1630-1654) by Dr. Frans L. Schalkwijk
(EXPECTED MID 2011)

Mission in Chains — The life, theology and ministry of the ex-slave Jacobus E. J. Capitein (1717-1747) with a translation of his major publications by Dr. David Nii Anum Kpobi
(EXPECTED LATE 2011)

To be advised of future books in this series, contact Reformation Media & Press by email at *president@reformation.edu*.

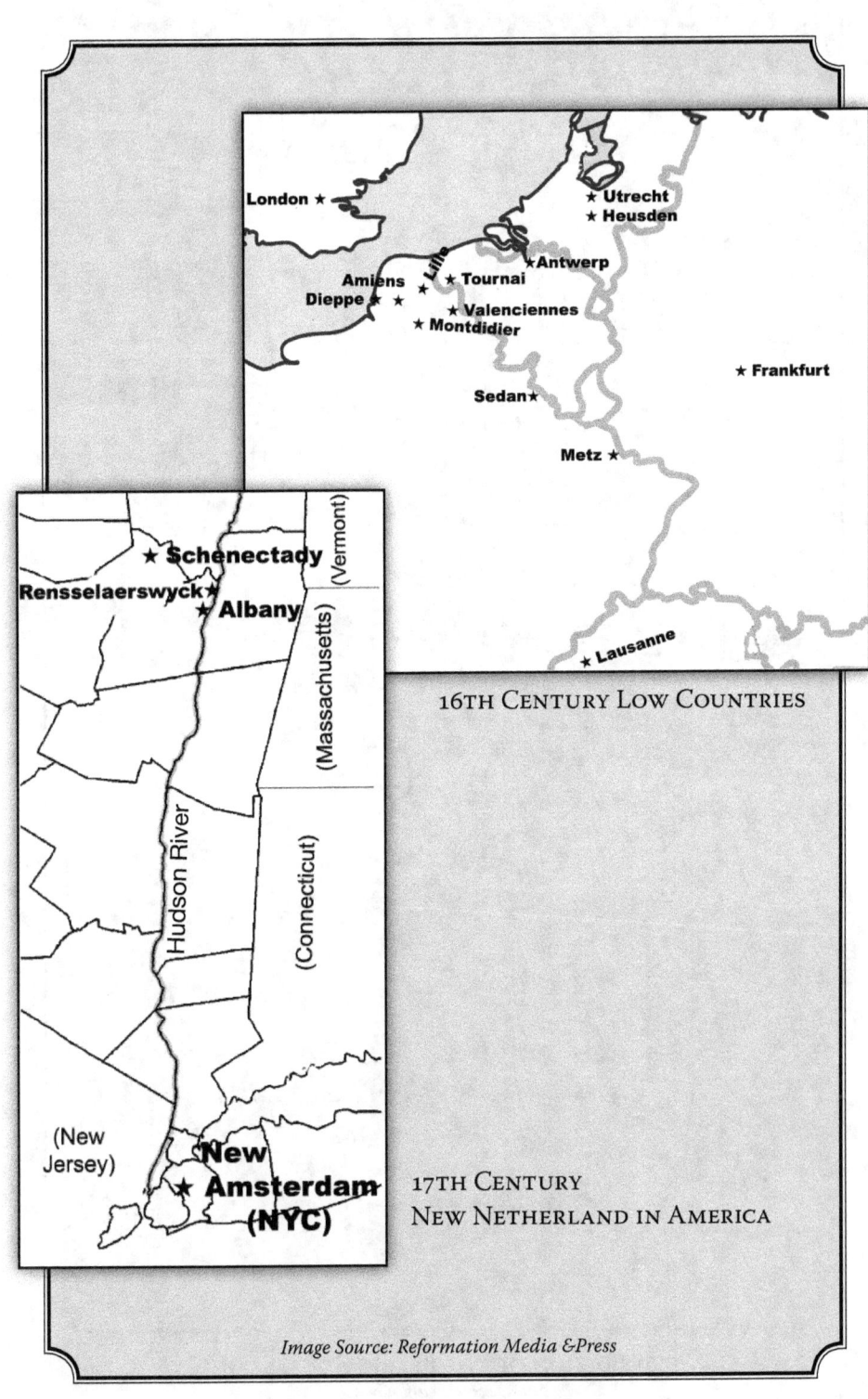

16TH CENTURY LOW COUNTRIES

17TH CENTURY
NEW NETHERLAND IN AMERICA

Image Source: Reformation Media &Press

CONFESSION DE FOY,

Faicte d'un commun accord par les fideles qui conuersent és pays bas, lesquels desirent viure selon la pureté de l'Euangile de nostre Seigneur Iesus Christ.

I. PIER. III.

Soyez tousiours appareillez à respondre à chacun qui vous demande raison de l'esperance qui est en vous.

M.D.LXI.

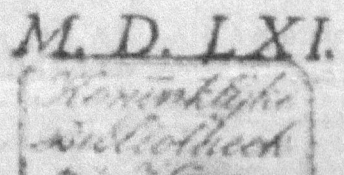

1561 EDITION OF THE BELGIC CONFESSION
Image source unknown

Contents

Acknowledgements — ix

Introduction — 1

CHAPTER 1 — BRIEF HISTORY AND BACKGROUND — 7

- 1.0 Introduction — 7
- 1.1 The Broader Context — 7
  - 1.1.1 Locating the Belgic Confession Historically — 7
    - 1.1.1.1 A Sixteenth-Century Confession — 7
    - 1.1.1.2 A Sixteenth-Century (Reformed) Protestant Confession — 9
    - 1.1.1.3 A Confession of the Lowlands — 11
      - 1.1.1.3.1 The Dutch Revolt — 11
      - 1.1.1.3.2 Brief History of the Reformation in the Lowlands — 13
  - 1.1.2 Locating the Belgic Confession Socio-Politically: Interplay between Religion and Politics — 15
  - 1.1.3 Sixteenth-Century Understanding of the Relationship between the Gospel, the Church and the World — 17
- 1.2 The Narrower Context — 21
  - 1.2.1 Authorship of the Confession — 21
  - 1.2.2 Influences and Sources — 22
  - 1.2.3 The Writing of the Confession, Provenance and Text History — 23

CHAPTER 2 — THE DEFINITION OF MISSION(S) — 27

- 2.0 Introduction: A Question of Exegesis — 31
- 2.1 Biblical Data — 31
  - 2.1.1 The Old Testament — 31
  - 2.1.2 The New Testament — 34
    - 2.1.2.1 John 20:21 — 34
    - 2.1.2.2 Matthew 28:18-20 — 36
    - 2.1.2.3 Mark 16:9-20 — 38
    - 2.1.2.4 Luke 24:46-49 — 42
    - 2.1.2.5 Acts 1:8 — 43
    - 2.1.2.6 Romans 10:14-15 — 44
- 2.2 Defining Mission — 45
- 2.3 Distinguishing Mission and Evangelism — 47
- 2.4 Mission and Missions — 48
- 2.5 Missiology and Missiological — 50
- 2.6 The Concept of Mission in the Sixteenth Century — 50

2.6.1 Martin Bucer ... 51
2.6.2 Adrian Saravia ... 56
2.7 Conclusion ... 59

CHAPTER 3 — ORIGINAL MISSIONARY NATURE AND INTENT ... 63

3.0 Introduction ... 63
3.1 The Belgic Confession, Martyrdom and Mission ... 63
  3.1.1 Martyrdom and Persecution in Scripture and History ... 63
  3.1.2 Martyrdom and Mission ... 66
    3.1.1.1 Kevin Vanhoozer ... 68
    3.1.1.2 John Piper ... 71
    3.1.1.3 Missiological Foundation of Martyrdom and Suffering ... 75
    3.1.1.4 Missiological Message of Martyrdom and Suffering ... 76
    3.1.1.5 Missiological Result of Martyrdom and Suffering ... 77
  3.1.3 Martyrdom as Metanarrative for the Belgic Confession ... 78
  3.1.4 The Belgic Confession as Μαρτυς ... 90
3.2 Missionary Perspective: Antithetical Religions ... 91
  3.2.1 Magisterial Protestant Reformers ... 91
  3.2.2 Reformed Churches in the Lowlands ... 99
  3.2.3 Guido de Brès ... 102
  3.2.4 The Belgic Confession ... 110
3.3 Missionary Perspective: The Non-European World ... 118
3.4 Conclusion ... 119

CHAPTER 4 — RELATING STRUCTURE TO NATURE AND INTENT ... 121

4.0 Introduction ... 121
4.1 The French Confession and The Institutes: Structural Models ... 122
  4.1.1 The French Confession ... 122
  4.1.2 The Institutes ... 123
  4.1.3 Structural Model for Calvin: Locus Method ... 124
4.2 Structure of the Belgic Confession — Sixteenth-Century Contextualization ... 128
  4.2.1 Contextualization ... 129
  4.2.2 Options for Confessional Structures in Sixteenth-Century Europe ... 138
  4.2.3 Intention and Effect: Rationale for Locus Method in Belgic Confession ... 139
4.3 Conclusion ... 140

CHAPTER 5 — MISSIOLOGICAL STRENGTHS AND WEAKNESSES — 143

- 5.0 Introduction — 143
- 5.1 Missiological Strengths — 145
  - 5.1.1 Confession of a Church Under the Cross — 145
  - 5.1.2 An Elenctic Confession — a Confession of the Antithesis — 148
  - 5.1.3 A Catholic Confession — 152
  - 5.1.4 Redemptive Historical Framework — 155
  - 5.1.5 A Confession Providing a Doctrinal Foundation for the Further Development of Reformed Missiology — 158
- 5.2 Missiological Weaknesses — 185
  - 5.2.1 A European Confession Over 400 Years Old — 185
  - 5.2.2 Limited Perspective on World Religions — 188
  - 5.2.3 The Holy Spirit — 190
  - 5.2.4 Role of the Civil Government — 191
- 5.3 Conclusion & Evaluation — 195

CHAPTER 6 — SEVENTEENTH-CENTURY USES — 197

- 6.0 Introduction — 197
- 6.1 The First Reformed Missiologist: Gisbertus Voetius — 197
  - 6.1.1 Overview of Voetius' Missiology — 199
  - 6.1.2 Use of the Belgic Confession — 202
  - 6.1.3 Evaluation — 206
- 6.2 The Belgic Confession in New Netherland & Johannes Megapolensis — 208
  - 6.2.1 Overview of Dutch Reformed Mission Work in New Netherland — 208
  - 6.2.2 Johannes Megapolensis: Pioneer Reformed Missionary to the Mohawks — 210
  - 6.2.3 Use of the Belgic Confession — 215
  - 6.2.4 Evaluation — 220
- 6.3 Conclusion — 223

CHAPTER 7 — LATE TWENTIETH-CENTURY JUDGMENTS — 225

- 7.0 Introduction — 225
- 7.1 Robert Recker — 225
  - 7.1.1 "An Analysis of the Belgic Confession as to its Mission Focus" — 225

7.1.2 Evaluation 232
7.2 The Christian Reformed Church in North America 235
   7.2.1 Background: 1950s & 1960s 236
   7.2.2 Development of "Contemporary Testimony: Our World Belongs to God." 242
   7.2.3 Reception of "Contemporary Testimony: Our World Belongs to God." 258
   7.2.4 Evaluation 261
7.3 Conclusion 266

CHAPTER 8 — CONFESSION AND REFORMED MISSIOLOGY — 269

8.0 Introduction 269
8.1 The Confession and Reformed Theology 269
8.2 The Confession and Reformed Missiology 272
8.3 Status Confessionis 275
   8.3.1 Abraham Kuyper: Confessional Revision 278
   8.3.2 Robert Bertram: A New Confession? 282
   8.3.3 Evaluation 285
8.4 Conclusion 290

BIBLIOGRAPHY — 293

INDICES

People and Places 317
Subject 322

PHOTOS AND ILLUSTRATIONS:
All photos and illustrations not otherwise credited are taken from Wikipedia Commons.

Acknowledgements

What goes without saying must be said: I give thanks to my heavenly Father for the strength, health, and resources to complete this study. The Father of Guido de Brès and my other Reformed brothers and sisters of the sixteenth-century Low Countries has also proven to be my faithful Father and through Christ I trust that he will continue to be. The Psalmist rightly says, " . . . I am continually with you; you hold me by my right hand" (Ps. 73:23). May this study be for the glory of our God, Father, Son, and Holy Spirit.

I am deeply grateful for the love and support of my wife Rose. You have always been my best friend and through these last years your help and encouragement have been invaluable. None of our children remember when their father began work on this project. But at the finish line, the three oldest are well aware and have been also among my greatest "cheerleaders." Josiah, Julie, Emeline, and Bethany: thank you!

My advisor, Dr. Leen Joosse, has been exceptional in providing helpful feedback, advice, encouragement and insights. Thank you also for the wonderful hospitality you and your wife provided as I visited with you in Groningen in 2004.

The staff of Reformation International Theological Seminary are also to be thanked. Rev. Geoff Donnan was among those who encouraged me to enter the RITS doctoral program and he made it feasible. During a visit to his home in Weston-Super-Mare, Dr. Stephen Westcott provided not only superb hospitality, but also excellent advice.

When I set out to write this book as my doctoral dissertation, I was a missionary of the Smithers Canadian Reformed Church. Together with the Home Mission Board, the Council of the Smithers church was supportive of this endeavour and I thank them. I must also express similar sentiments for the support of the Langley Canadian Reformed Church and the Providence Canadian Reformed Church of Hamilton, Ontario. Their willingness to give me extra time off for study was much appreciated and my prayer is that the fruit of this study will prove beneficial for the churches in the fulfillment of their missionary calling.

The research for this project took place at several libraries across North America and Europe. Among others, I am grateful for the person-

Acknowledgements

nel and material resources of the library at the Rijksuniversiteit in Groningen, the Netherlands; the Norma Marion Alloway Library at Trinity Western University in Langley, BC; the Hekman Library at Calvin College and Seminary in Grand Rapids; and the Hiebert Library at Fresno Pacific University. I would like to single out Margaret Van der Velde of the library of the Theological College of the Canadian Reformed Churches in Hamilton, Ontario. Your assistance was above and beyond the call of duty, and I am sincerely grateful.

I am also very thankful for the good advice and counsel of numerous friends and colleagues. As one of my seminary professors, Dr. N.H. Gootjes first instilled in me an interest in the Belgic Confession and modelled theological and historical care and precision. Rev. Ted VanRaalte encouraged me to pursue further studies and also provided helpful advice along the way. Dr. James Visscher was my close colleague in Langley for over four years and always a willing and thoughtful conversation partner. I appreciate your support, good advice, and willingness to read and provide feedback on some of the material in this study. Dr. R. Scott Clark was also willing to engage me on several issues and I'm glad for your friendship and input. Rev. Daniel Hyde has shared my enthusiasm for the Belgic Confession and I have enjoyed and benefitted from our discussions about it. Todd Rester and Albert Gootjes, presently Ph.D. students at Calvin Theological Seminary, were also very helpful in obtaining and managing the use of primary sources. Thank you, brothers! Finally, there is a nameless cloud of friends out in cyberspace who helped at various stages. I think here especially of those on the Reformed Missions discussion list and the Puritan Board.

Francine Van Woudenberg-Sikkema and Mary Montague did the final editing and proof-reading. They did wonderful work and I thank them. The standard disclaimer about any remaining errors naturally applies.

A word of gratitude also goes to Danika Schoof. She was kind enough to help with the preparation of the maps.

Last of all, a word of loving appreciation to my father and step-mother who were not only encouraging all through the writing of this dissertation, but also helped along in other ways. I could not have done this without you!

Wes Bredenhof
Hamilton, Ontario
March 2011

Introduction

This book was originally written as a Th.D. dissertation for Reformation International Theological Seminary. The project was conceived when I was serving as a missionary in the north-central region of the Canadian province of British Columbia. During and after my seminary studies, I had a special interest in three areas of research: the Belgic Confession, church history, and missiology. I was interested in writing a thesis that would bring these three areas together.

Right from the beginning, I was convinced that it had to focus on the significance of the Belgic Confession for the study and practice of mission. There were three phenomena that I observed that led me in that direction. First, in my church federation (the Canadian Reformed Churches) there was and is a growing emphasis on the importance of missionary outreach/evangelism. Of course, this is a development to be welcomed and encouraged! Second, there are a number of people in my federation who view the confessions of the church as a liability. They are a minority, but they also tend to be the ones who place a lot of stock in mission. Third, there is a notion among some Reformed folk (including among some in my own federation) that being missionary-minded and being confessional are to some degree antithetical. It almost seems to be a given that you cannot be a missionary and love the Reformed confessions — and a Reformed missionary is certainly not going to use the Reformed confessions in any kind of conspicuous way.

Given these three phenomena, I concluded that it would not be long before someone comes along and lays our past lukewarmness about mission at the feet of the Belgic Confession. Why the Belgic Confession in particular? Because it is the preeminent defining confession in the Three Forms of Unity. The Heidelberg Catechism is primarily a teaching confession, focussed on teaching some key points of Christian doctrine. The Canons of Dort are a primarily a polemical confession, focussed on refuting the Remonstrants and explaining further the doctrines of grace found in the other two confessions. Even if individuals are not familiar with these categories, if there is a problem to be found with the confessions and mission, the blame will intuitively be laid at the feet of our defining symbol, the Belgic Confession. This book is therefore a pre-emptive effort to address those who might be tempted to see the Belgic Confession as a hindrance for the mission of the church to reach the lost with the gospel of Jesus Christ.

Let me also say something here to my Presbyterian brothers and sisters. You are more familiar with the Westminster Standards than the Three Forms of Unity. That is to be expected — of course, the situation is reversed for me. However, I am familiar enough with the Westminster Standards to be able to say that I think this study may have interest and relevance for you as well. It is true that the Westminster Confession and Catechisms emerged from a completely different context than the Belgic Confession. Peace and stability allowed a group of theologians to work on these confessional standards for several years in the 1640s. The Belgic Confession, as will be elaborated upon in chapter 3, comes out of the fires of persecution and an unsettled ecclesiastical world. Nevertheless, it may be said that the faith expressed in the Westminster Standards is largely that found in the Belgic Confession. Of course, the Westminster Standards are much later and so one can expect to see further theological developments, but at the roots, both share a common confessional heritage. So, for instance, some of what is said about article 36 of the Belgic Confession in chapter 5 can be applied also to what the Westminster Confession affirms in chapter 23.3 (particularly in the original unaltered text).

Unfortunately, very little has been written on the missiological significance of the Westminster Standards. In his brief missiological study of WCF 14, Valdeci Santos did not identify any other works, other than to mention some comments of B. B. Warfield on the 1903 American revision of the WCF. Warfield affirmed that "the Confession, as it was originally written, disclosed a missiological concern."[1] However, it does not appear that much has been done to systematically outline that concern in any comprehensive way. Perhaps this is the appropriate place then to encourage one or more of our Presbyterian brethren to undertake such a study. It could surely be of mutual benefit and serve the advancement of the gospel in our countries and overseas.

---

[1] Valdeci S. Santos, "A Missiological Analysis of the Westminster Confession of Faith — Chapter 14," in *The Westminster Confession into the 21st Century* (Vol. 3), ed. J. Ligon Duncan (Ross-shire: Christian Focus Publications, 2009), 329.

Introduction

That brings us back to the Belgic Confession and its missiological relevance. The question is not a new one. In fact, this might be considered a question that has already received a decisive judgment. In 1972, Christian Reformed missiologist Robert Recker concluded that "the Belgic Confession projects an image, in the main, of a church talking with itself rather than a church before the world."[2] He went on to write:

> If I were to construct a missiology today, or if I would hope to be inspired with missionary passion, I would reach for the Bible and not for the Belgic Confession. Reading this Confession with analytical care impressed me with the fact that it is partial. And when I read it to discern the missionary focus of the whole Word of God, then I can only say it is inadequate.[3]

Recker's opinion is by no means idiosyncratic or unexpected. Many contemporary missiologists and church historians see the Reformation in general as a movement lacking in missionary zeal and character.[4] This view has a lengthy pedigree, going back at least to Gustav Warneck.[5] If this view is true, we would also reasonably expect the confessional documents of the Reformation to reflect a lack of missionary zeal and consciousness.

This book will argue that past judgments on the missiological relevance of the Belgic Confession have not done it justice. In the past, missiologists and church historians have simply worked with the received dogma that the Reformation was not in any sense a missionary movement. This in turn has affected how they regarded the Belgic Confession. In more recent times, new scholarship is bringing a fresh and more accurate contextual understanding of the Reformation, particularly of how the Reformers viewed themselves.[6] This new scholarship impacts our assess-

---

2. R. Recker, "An Analysis of the Belgic Confession As To Its Mission Focus," *Calvin Theological Journal* 7.2 (November 1972): 179.

3. Recker, "An Analysis," 180.

4. For a recent example, see A. Scott Moreau, Gary R. Corwin, and Gary B. McGee, *Introducing World Missions: A Biblical, Historical, and Practical Survey* (Grand Rapids: Baker, 2004), 120-121.

5. Gustav Warneck, *Outline of a History of Protestant Missions from the Reformation to the Present Time* (New York: Fleming H. Revel Company, 1901), 19.

6. See Scott H. Hendrix, *Recultivating the Vineyard: The Reformation Agendas of Christianization* (Louisville: Westminster John Knox, 2004); Hans-Werner Gensichen, "Were the Reformers indifferent to missions?," *Verbum SVD* 25.1 (1984): 3-10.

ment of the Reformation and mission and consequently also our assessment of the confessional documents of the Reformation.

I will examine the relevance of the Belgic Confession for contemporary Reformed missiology. The history and background of the Confession will be investigated to determine its original missionary intent and nature. I will explore how and why it was organized in relation to its intent and nature. The missiological strengths and weaknesses of the Confession will be outlined. I will also consider its relationship to the study and practice of mission in the Dutch Reformed churches of the seventeenth century. Finally, this study will interact with those who have already rendered their judgments on whether the Belgic Confession has missiological relevance for today.

As I noted above, this study is intended to be church historical, symbolic, and especially missiological in nature. From a church historical perspective, I am interested in describing the milieu from which the Belgic Confession emerged and in which it later functioned, particularly in the seventeenth century and last half of the twentieth century. From a symbolic perspective, I want to study and identify the content, form and structure originally given to the Belgic Confession and evaluate how that might relate to mission. The perennial issue of status confessionis (being in a state of having to make a confession) also requires description and evaluation, and again specifically relating that issue to the study and practice of mission. From a missiological perspective, I am interested in developing a formulation of the missionary mandate from Scripture and describing and evaluating the understanding of that mandate in the Belgic Confession and its historical context. I am also concerned with exploring questions regarding contextualization and communication pertaining to the Confession in its original context, in some historical uses, and today. Given the diversity of fields involved, various methods have been employed, some of which have just been mentioned. Others will be noted at the appropriate places in the body of the study.

With those methods and broad purposes in mind, chapter 1 will provide a brief history of the Confession, noting the salient points for the purposes of this book. In a parallel (though obviously much briefer) discussion on John Calvin's missiological relevance, James DeJong has pointed out that the definition of mission is crucial.[7] Therefore, chapter 2 will

---

7. James DeJong, "John Calvin in Mission Literature," *Pro Rege* 4.1 (September 1975): 10.

develop the definition of mission. Chapter 3 will consider the original missionary nature and intent of the Belgic Confession. Chapter 4 will analyze the structure of the Confession with an eye to its missionary intent and nature. In chapter 5, we discuss the missiological strengths and weaknesses of the Confession. Historical missiological/missionary uses of the Confession in the seventeenth century receive attention in chapter 6. In the next chapter, more recent judgments on the missionary significance of the Confession are described and evaluated. Finally, chapter 8 offers concluding thoughts and considers the issue of status confessionis and the relationship between confessions (in general) and the study and practice of mission.

As far as literature is concerned, this study will utilize primary sources in their original language where necessary and possible. With regard to secondary sources, the focus will be primarily on those available in English. However, in a number of places, resources available in Dutch, German, and French have also been referenced.

Does the Belgic Confession have anything to say to the mission of the Church of Jesus Christ today? Twenty-first century Christians appear to consider mission as the "Cause of the Son of God" par excellence. The question before us is whether this Reformation confession has a similar orientation. Please join me now as we begin investigating that question....

Philip II of Spain (1527-1598)

Margaret of Parma,
Governor of the Netherlands (1522-1586)

Chapter One
Brief History and Background

1.0 Introduction

In this chapter, the stage is set for the more intensive look at the Belgic Confession which follows in later chapters. Before we can properly assess its missiological relevance, it should be placed in its proper historical and social context. It will also prove helpful to survey the immediate context of the Confession in order to ascertain its authorship, influences and sources, and provenance.

1.1 The Broader Context

1.1.1 Locating the Belgic Confession Historically

From what sort of era does this Confession emerge? What are the notable and relevant features of this era that may influence how this Confession should be understood? In this section, we will explore those questions.

1.1.1.1 A Sixteenth-Century Confession

As already noted earlier, the Belgic Confession was first published in 1561, placing our document just a little over half way into the sixteenth century. At this point, we want to consider some of the central features of this era and how they may relate to our study. To narrow the focus more, we need to specifically give attention to sixteenth-century *Europe*.

In his contribution to the Fontana History of Europe, G. R. Elton mentioned several commonly recognized features of this era.[1] One of the most obvious is the wide-spread use of the printing press. Though an invention of the fifteenth century, there can be little question that it was the sixteenth century in which the printing press really came into

---

1. G. R. Elton, *Reformation Europe, 1517-1559* (London: Fontana, 1963).

its own. The perfection of a cost-effective manufacturing of paper was also responsible for the proliferation of literature on the eve of the Reformation.[2] As we shall see, it was these developments that allowed for the rapid and widespread dissemination of the Belgic Confession.

Related to printing were two other major developments. Humanism is universally recognized as a contributing force to the monumental changes of the sixteenth century. With its excellence in philology, emphasis on ancient languages, careful study of documents and the establishment of accurate ancient texts, the humanist movement laid a scholarly foundation for the Reformation.[3] As Quirinus Breen and others have argued, John Calvin was a child of French humanism.[4] While the influence of humanism on the author of the Belgic Confession, Guido de Brès, is something that apparently remains to be studied, we do know for certain that Calvin was a highly influential figure in the life of de Brès and his influence is detectable in the Confession (we shall look at this in 1.2.2). Moreover, we know from his writings that de Brès capitalized on humanism's gains through his expansive reading of the Church Fathers — many of whose writings were edited by the preeminent humanist Desiderius Erasmus.

The other related development mentioned by Elton is the explosive growth of vernacular literature in this era. He notes that while there was little prose fiction, "there was plenty of serious writing both in Latin and in the vernaculars. The bulk of it touched religion and theology."[5] While most scholarly work continued to be in Latin, the growing demand for translations reflected "the development of national self-consciousness."[6] In the area of religion, of course, the publication of writings in vernacular languages also served the widest possible dissemination of ideas. This naturally ties into the Belgic Confession insofar as it was first published, not in Latin, but in French in 1561. A Dutch translation followed the year after, but it was not until 1566 that the first Latin translation appeared.

---

2. Steven Ozment, *The Age of Reform, 1250-1550: An Intellectual and Religious History of Late Medieval and Reformation Europe* (New Haven: Yale UP, 1980), 201.

3. Ozment, *the Age of Reform*, 290.

4. Quirinus Breen, *John Calvin: A Study in French Humanism* (Hamden: Archon Books, 1968).

5. Elton, *Reformation Europe*, 289.

6. Elton, *Reformation Europe*, 297.

Finally, we can note that sixteenth-century Europe found itself in an "Age of Expansion." Not only were there increases in population and trade, but European powers were steadily adding empires in the Americas, Asia and Africa.[7] It was an era in which the borders of the world were rapidly changing. There was a growing realization that the world was bigger and its peoples far more numerous and diverse than thought in previous centuries. The question remains to be answered whether the author and original recipients of the Belgic Confession were sensitive to or involved with this realization. Did they see this document as having any bearing on the bringing of the gospel to new lands and nations? In due time (see 3.3), we will come back to this question.

1.1.1.2 A SIXTEENTH-CENTURY (REFORMED) PROTESTANT CONFESSION

At this point, we will briefly survey some of the main features of the history of Reformed Protestantism in Europe as they pertain to this study. Though there are many factors that could be considered here, four have been selected that seem to be most pertinent to the history of the Belgic Confession and its missiological relevance. As mentioned previously, this section works with the secondary sources, but applies those findings to our subject matter.

A. G. Dickens and countless others have noted that the Reformation was primarily an urban event.[8] Euan Cameron elaborates on this:

> The point, however, is not that cities were the only, the most important, or even always the first places to become reformed: rather that they above all else possessed the concentration of people, the literary awareness, and the political sophistication to propel the ideas of preachers and pamphleteers to the forefront of the political agenda in the early 1520s. It was much easier for city tradesmen to learn about the Reformation, become enthusiasts for it, and then press reform measures upon the city fathers living a few streets away, than for farmers or villagers even to hear a reforming preacher, let alone to lobby a distant prince or king on that preacher's behalf.[9]

---

7. Elton, *Reformation Europe*, 318-319.
8. A. G. Dickens, *The German Nation and Martin Luther* (New York: Harper & Row, 1974), 182.
9. Euan Cameron, *The European Reformation* (Oxford: Clarendon Press, 1991), 210.

In other words, it was only natural that the Reformation would be centered on urban areas. This has relevance for our subject matter in that the milieu of the preparation, production, and dissemination of the Belgic Confession is urban. It is a confession of the city rather than of the countryside and this factor allowed for maximum impact.

Next we consider that, as a movement, its appeal stretched across class lines. Though there were differences in distribution from region to region, and from Calvinists to Lutherans to Anabaptists, the total picture was of a movement that included peasants, artisans, nobility and royalty. Closer to our subject matter, it was Calvinism that was especially broadly inclusive and this is reflected in Calvin's correspondence with individuals of varying stature. According to James Tracy, Calvinism was successful in some rural areas, especially those "marked by cottage industry and unusually high rates of literacy."[10] But he goes on to note that around twenty German princes converted from Lutheranism to Calvinism between 1520 and 1620, taking their territories with them. In France, "it is estimated that around 1560 some 10 percent of the population were Calvinist but 50 percent of the nobles were." The same appears to have been true in the Lowlands, though not after 1572.[11] All of this fills in an important aspect of the background of the Belgic Confession. The Confession was intended as an appeal to Philip II (the king of Spain), since Spain had control of the Lowlands during this time. It was not unheard of for European nobility or royalty to change their religious allegiances. The Belgic Confession could be promulgated with the hope that it would accomplish its desired end, even if that was a comparatively rare happenstance in Spain, France, and the Lowlands.

Another relevant factor is the geographic limitation of the Reformation. By the end of the sixteenth century, most of southern Europe remained Roman Catholic. While there were some pockets of Huguenots in southern France, the countries of Italy, Spain and Portugal remained Roman Catholic, present-day Greece and much of Hungary remained Orthodox and present-day Albania was Muslim. Even in northern Europe, the situation often appeared to be one of pockets of Calvinist or Lutheran (and more rarely Hussite) churches surrounded by Roman Catholicism.[12]

---

10. James D. Tracy, *Europe's Reformations, 1450-1650* (Lanham: Rowman and Littlefield, 1999), 262.
11. Tracy, *Europe's Reformations*, 262.
12. Ulinka Rublack, *Reformation Europe* (Cambridge: Cambridge UP, 2005), 105.

The only exceptions were in the northern Netherlands and German/Scandinavian/Baltic regions, where Calvinism and Lutheranism reigned respectively. While the religious hegemony of Rome had been broken in this century, it was by no means complete. This is important to note for our study because, as we shall see in greater detail in chapter 3, for the Reformed it meant that large swaths of Europe remained unconverted, and therefore a mission field.

Lastly, we need to briefly note that the Reformation was a diverse movement. Lutheranism, Calvinism, and Anabaptism are usually (rightfully) identified as the major players, though the Anabaptists are sometimes separately identified as the "Radical Reformers." Within each of these there were variations, and then additionally we have Hussites, Zwinglians, Melanchthonians, and others. The end result is that the Reformation is a complex whole of many parts. The Belgic Confession emerged in this context as the expression of one understanding of what it means to be "re-formed" according to Scripture. Some of the other understandings were explicitly excluded and this exclusion placed their proponents outside of the Christian faith. With other understandings, however, there was meaningful overlap and their proponents could rightly be regarded as brothers in the Lord.

1.1.1.3 A Confession of the Lowlands

To rightly place the Belgic Confession in its historical context, we need to spend a moment surveying the political and religious highlights of the Lowlands from whence this confession originates. Specifically, we want to investigate the Dutch Revolt of the sixteenth century and its relevance for the Confession and then also explore the history of the Reformation in this region and its significance for our study.

1.1.1.3.1 The Dutch Revolt

A combination of political and religious factors led to strife in the Low Countries in the middle of the sixteenth century.[13] On the one hand, there were tensions between the king of Spain (Charles V and later Philip II) and the territorial states and towns, between the hereditary nobility and the officials of the king, and between the financial needs of the monarchy

---

13. The Low Countries/Lowlands are also sometimes called the Netherlands, but in this period consisting of the modern-day Netherlands, Belgium, and small parts of modern-day France and Germany.

and the reluctance of local officials to institute higher levels of taxation.[14] On the other hand, there was palpable strain on the unity of the Roman Catholic Church in this region with the introduction of what appeared to be new ideas and practices. The introduction of the Reformation (which we shall examine more closely in the next section) complicated a volatile situation. However, as Israel notes, up until the 1550s, "it appeared that the Habsburg government was succeeding in uniting the Netherlands, expanding and refining the apparatus of central government, and containing, if not eliminating Protestantism."[15]

The question of what to do about Protestantism was the catalyst for the turmoil of the 1550s and 1560s. It began with an edict of Charles V in 1550 which threatened death for those promoting Protestantism, even to the point where one could be executed merely for the possession of heretical books. Despite this edict, both the Anabaptists and the Reformed were making gains in the Low Countries. Additionally, not only was popular opinion against persecution of the Anabaptists and the Reformed, but also the magistrates and courts were reluctant to enforce the wishes of the king. In fact, a number of territorial governors vociferously protested to Philip II regarding this edict; however, it had no effect. In October 1565, Philip II wrote his "letters from the Segovia Wood" in which he demanded strict enforcement of the edicts regarding heresy. Parker comments, "There was no disguising the fact that the letters from the Segovia Woods constituted a direct challenge to the nobles and their supporters." They could either obey and persecute the heretics (Reformed and Anabaptists) or they would "become guilty of gross disobedience, if not treason."[16]

The disobedience of several governors marked the beginning of the revolt. In the spring of 1566, a large group of lesser nobility presented a petition to Margaret of Parma (governess-general of the Low Countries) asking that the persecution be abated. With the help of some political intrigue on the part of some territorial governors (such as William of Orange), a reprieve was granted and leniency towards "heretics" was authorized.[17]

---

14. Much of this (unless otherwise noted) is based on Juliaan Woltjer, "Revolt of the Netherlands," in *The Oxford Encyclopedia of the Reformation* (Vol. 3), ed. Hans J. Hillerbrand (New York: Oxford UP, 1996), 426-428.

15. Jonathan Israel, *The Dutch Republic: Its Rise, Greatness, and Fall, 1477-1806* (Oxford: Clarendon Press, 1995), 130.

16. Geoffrey Parker, *The Dutch Revolt* (New York: Penguin, 1979), 67.

17. Parker, *The Dutch Revolt*, 71.

Exiled men and women returned to their homes, open-air preaching took place, and the Reformed began more fully organizing their churches. The darker side of this new freedom was in widespread iconoclasm and other provocative behaviour, including the public singing of Psalms (*chanteries*) and coming to the huge open-air meetings bearing arms.[18]

All of this was bound to provoke a reaction from Margaret and the Habsburg Empire, and it did. She demanded a focused and aggressive response to the crowds, but the governors refused unless she would promise freedom for preaching. In August of 1566 she made that promise and order was restored in most places. However, Margaret was not finished with the rebels and heretics. The *chanteries* continued and these provoked Margaret to the point where she laid siege to the city of Valenciennes. In March 1567, Valenciennes fell to her forces and she was again able to enforce the ban on Reformed preaching everywhere in the Low Countries. Following this, Philip appointed the Duke of Alva (Fernando Alvarez de Toledo) to be governor of the region and he proved to be passionate about the eradication of heresy.

The revolt continued until 1581, but it is the early part of the revolt described above that is particularly relevant so we will leave off here. One of the most significant features of the Dutch Revolt is the passionate hatred of Philip II, Margaret of Parma and the Duke of Alva for any non-Roman Catholic religion. In their view, the Reformed faith of Calvin, de Brès, and others was rank heresy, and heretics were to be dealt with through the most severe means. Persecution, therefore, stains this region in this era and, as we shall see in chapter 3, also left its mark on the character of the Belgic Confession.

1.1.1.3.2 The History of the Early Reformation in the Lowlands

Unlike in Germany and Switzerland, the Reformation in the Low Countries began with blood. Tracy notes that this region was connected with Germany through quite a number of different trade routes. "Thus Wittenberg theology could travel west as readily as Flemish cloth or Brabantine retables traveled east."[19] Travel it did and very quickly. The prior of an Augustinian monastery in Antwerp, Jakob Propst, was advocating the teachings of Luther already in 1519. Luther's writings were being dis-

---

18. Parker, *The Dutch Revolt*, 73.
19. James D. Tracy, "Netherlands," in *The Oxford Encyclopedia of the Reformation* (Vol.3), 136.

tributed in the Netherlands already in 1518, and by 1525, there were more than eighty editions and translations.[20]

It was not long before the Habsburg empire took note, and the first martyrs died. In July 1523, Heinrich Voes and Johann Esch were burned at the stake in Brussels. In the northern part of the Netherlands, the taste for persecution was poorly developed and hence martyrdom was comparatively rare. However, the southern regions were under the supervision of Pieter Titelmans, underinquisitor for Flanders, Lille, Douai, Orchies and Tournai between 1545 and 1566. Titelmans was zealous for his work and under his oversight, an average of one hundred heresy cases per year were prosecuted.[21] Government edicts forced the nascent Reformed movement underground. They would meet in houses, fields and even local taverns to do Bible study, give and receive doctrinal instruction and sit under biblical preaching.[22]

While not properly part of the Reformation movement, the rise of Anabaptism also plays a significant role in its history in the Netherlands. Melchior Hoffmann came to East Friesland in 1530. His message spread rapidly through the region and he appears to have gained many converts. In 1534, John Matthijs and John of Leiden seized Munster, justifying the widespread feeling (especially among governing officials) that the Anabaptists were not only religiously dangerous, but also politically.[23] This becomes extremely important for the writing of the Belgic Confession because one of its explicit aims is to distance the Reformed from the Anabaptists.

One final event that requires mention is the rise of Calvinism in the Low Countries in the 1540s. The Reformed faith spread directly from Geneva and also via France. In fact, the history of the Reformed churches in the Low Countries is very much intertwined with the Huguenot churches. The borders were very fluid and, sharing a common language, the French Reformed strongly influenced the doctrine and organization of the Reformed churches in the Low Countries.

---

20. Carter Lindberg, *The European Reformations* (Oxford: Blackwell Publisers, 1996), 298.
21. Tracy, "Netherlands," 136.
22. Lindberg, *The European Reformations*, 301.
23. Joke Spaans, "Reform in the Low Countries," in *A Companion to the Reformation World*, ed. R. Po-Chia Hsia (Malden: Blackwell Publishing, 2004), 121.

The Reformed faith took hold in both large towns and cities throughout the Netherlands, centered in the south around Antwerp and in the north around Emden.[24] The Reformed movement grew quickly in these areas, appealing to a broad cross-section of society including artisans, labourers, merchants, and men of learning.[25] However, persecution forced many to choose between exile and martyrdom. The vast majority chose the former and spent several years in the refugee congregations of places such as London, Sandwich, Emden and Wesel. Hence the underground life that characterized the early Reformation in the Netherlands continued to exist in the period in which the Belgic Confession emerged. Nevertheless, some of the Reformed leaders were in favour of taking a more public stance since, they argued, persecution was only facilitated by secrecy. It would be more difficult for the Spanish authorities to intervene with or restrain a Reformed church community which carried out its affairs in public.

1.1.2 Locating the Belgic Confession Socio-Politically: Interplay Between Religion and Politics

At this point, we need to consider briefly the socio-political milieu as it bears on our subject. In particular, what was the sixteenth-century understanding of the relationship between religion and politics?

In the centuries leading up to the Reformation, there were often struggles between the church and the state. History tells many stories of intrigue, suspicion and outright warfare between kings and popes in the Middle Ages. In the late medieval period, three views competed for dominance: church over state, state over church, and state and church as equals. However, by the early sixteenth century, the state had decisively taken the upper hand both in principle and in practice.[26]

The rise of anticlerical sentiment is a significant part of this development. Beginning in the twelfth century, a gradual separation took place between the clergy and the laity. The priesthood claimed a higher level of spiritual attainment and a condition of perfection that qualified them to mediate salvation to the laity. However, moral failure, legal immunity, economic activity, legalism and a host of other weaknesses and failings led to the rise of resentment, rejection, and even outright rebellion among the laity.[27]

---

24. Lindberg, *The European Reformations*, 303.
25. Tracy, "Netherlands," 137.
26. Ozment, *Age of Reform*, 178.
27. Hans-Jürgen Goertz, "Anticlericalism," in *The Oxford Encyclopedia of the*

During the late Middle Ages, this anticlericalism combined with factors such as nationalism and a growing respect for monarchs, rulers, and magistrates to produce a situation where secular rulers achieved a stronger position of power.[28] The church became dependent on the state for its survival. Ozment notes that the pre-Reformation church was an institution very much on the defensive against spiritual and political forces — this continued into the era of the Reformation.[29] Additionally, the influence of humanism led to an increasing understanding of political authorities as representatives of those under their rule. These representatives would also place the church in a more defensive position.

Recognizing these realities in the early sixteenth century, Reformers appealed to civil magistrates not only to seek their protection, but also their conversion. There were varying degrees of success. For example, beginning in 1520, Luther often called upon secular authorities to become involved with ecclesiastical matters. While he was not able to persuade Charles V, he was successful with Frederick the Wise of Saxony and other territorial rulers. By the middle of the sixteenth century, "*cuius regio, eius religio*" ("of whom the region, his the religion") had become a defining feature of the relationship between religion and politics in much of Europe, particularly in the Holy Roman Empire.

During the period in which the Belgic Confession was written, religion and politics continued to be inseparable. The Roman Catholic Church continued to depend on secular magistrates for its survival. For their part, throughout Europe, magistrates often continued to be loyal sons and daughters of the church — with the difference that, in certain areas, "the church" was being re-formed and redefined. Ann Ramsey notes that, in this era, "The legitimacy of rulers depended upon their efficacy in defending the faith."[30] Civil rulers felt an obligation to actively and publicly defend the faith, and this sometimes took sinister forms. In the Lowlands of Western Europe, under the leadership of Philip II, many magistrates respected and enforced the Inquisition. One factor in this was

---

Reformation. Ozment, *Age of Reform*, 211.

28. James D. Tracy, "Church and State," in *The Oxford Encyclopedia of the Reformation*. For a full account of the strengthening of state power in pre-Reformation Europe, see Ozment, *Age of Reform*, 135-181.

29. Ozment, *Age of Reform*, 180.

30. Ann W. Ramsey, *Liturgy, Politics and Salvation: The Catholic League in Paris and the Nature of Catholic Reform, 1540-1630* (Rochester: University of Rochester Press, 1999), 18.

Philip's self-understanding that he was a pillar of the church on a divine mission to eradicate heresy.[31] Additionally, there was the belief that religious revolution necessarily engendered political revolution.[32] The Belgic Confession was written partly to demonstrate that, from the perspective of the Reformed Churches, this did not follow.

While political revolution was not on the agenda of the Belgic Confession, political responsibility was. The Confession asserts that civil rulers have the task to remove and destroy idolatry, to promote the kingdom of Jesus Christ, and to further the preaching of the gospel everywhere (article 36). This is one of the more controversial statements of the Confession and it has often been deleted in modern renditions. Obviously it does have a bearing on the topic at hand and in due time we will return to this article for further investigation and evaluation (see 5.2.4).

1.1.3 Sixteenth-Century Understanding of the Relationship between the Gospel, the Church, and the World

The relationship between the gospel, the church and the world in this era is significant because it goes to the heart of mission. However, since the sixteenth century is a lengthy time period, and since it is impossible to survey every conception of this relationship, we will focus briefly on two influential figures in Protestantism: Martin Luther and John Calvin. Surveying their understanding of the relationship between gospel, church, and world may allow us to approximate typical Protestant understandings around the time of the Belgic Confession.

According to Luther, "the church owes its birth to the Word, [and] is nourished, aided and strengthened by it."[33] As Althaus rightly observes, in its context, "the Word" here means the same thing as the gospel.[34] The gospel is the foundation for the church, but also sustains it and gives it the means to grow and continue. In his Larger Catechism, when he deals with the sec-

---

31. Robert Collinet, *La Réformation en Belgique au XVIme Siècle* (Brussels: Editions de la Librairie des Eclaireurs Unionistes, 1958), 68.
32. W. Stanford Reid, "Calvin and the Political Order," in *John Calvin: Contemporary Prophet*, ed. J. T. Hoogstra (Grand Rapids: Baker, 1959), 252; Phyllis Mack Crew, *Calvinist Preaching and Iconoclasm in the Netherlands: 1544-1569* (Cambridge: Cambridge UP, 1978), 152.
33. Martin Luther, *Luther's Works* (Vol. 40) (Philadelphia: Fortress Press, 1958), 37.
34. Paul Althaus, *The Theology of Martin Luther* (Philadelphia: Fortress Press, 1966), 288-289.

ond petition ("Your kingdom come") Luther builds on this with respect to the world: "All this is simply to say, 'Dear Father, we pray Thee, give us Thy Word, that the Gospel may be sincerely preached throughout the world and that it may be received by faith and may work and live in us."[35] The gospel is the foundation of the church, strengthens the church, and is given to the church so that the church may preach it sincerely throughout the world.

Paul Drews drew out more of the contours of Luther's understanding of this relationship.[36] Through the church, the gospel preaching is universal and continues until the last day. Luther believed that the preaching of the gospel to the heathen was essentially finished, but still ongoing. He also asserted that, while the gospel would be preached throughout the world, one ought not to expect a universal embracing of Jesus Christ. When it comes to the definition of the world to which the gospel goes out, there is no clear dividing line between "Christendom" and the "non-Christian world." According to Luther, the world exists as much in Europe as it does elsewhere on the globe. Finally, Luther maintained that where the gospel is not cherished by the church, it will be lost and given to others.

There is continuity and overlap between Luther and John Calvin on this matter. Commenting on Isaiah 12:5, Calvin says, "it is our duty to proclaim the goodness of God to every nation."[37] Elsewhere he writes, "God has deposited the teaching of his salvation with us, not for the purpose of our privately keeping it to ourselves, but of our pointing out the way of salvation to all mankind."[38] In his commentary on Matthew 28:19, Calvin writes, "...

---

35. *The Book of Concord: The Confessions of the Evangelical Lutheran Church*, trans. and ed. by Theodore G. Tappert (Philadelphia: Fortress Press, 1959), 427.

36. Paul Drews, "Die Anschauungen reformatorischer Theologen über die Heidenmission," in Zeitschrift für praktische Theologie 19 (1897): 1-26. Cited in James A. Scherer, *Gospel, Church & Kingdom: Comparative Studies in World Mission Theology* (Minneapolis: Augsburg, 1987), 58.

37. John Calvin, *Commentary on the Book of the Prophet Isaiah* (Grand Rapids: Eerdmans, 1948), 403.

38. John Calvin, *A Commentary on Daniel* (London: Banner of Truth Trust, 1966), 377. Admittedly, there is some ambiguity here for, in the preceding sentence, Calvin writes, "No one of God's children ought to confine their attention privately to themselves, but as far as possible, every one ought to interest himself in the welfare of his brethren." And in the following sentence, "This, therefore, is the common duty of the children of God — to promote the salvation of their brethren." Who are the "brethren"? They could be Christian brothers, or there could be some notion of the brotherhood of man here. "All mankind" would suggest the latter.

the Lord commands the ministers of the gospel to go to a distance, in order to spread the doctrine of salvation in every part of the world."[39] Like Luther, Calvin understood that the gospel had been entrusted to the church and the church was expected to take that gospel to all mankind, viz., to the world. As Charles Chaney concludes, "Calvin had a gospel that was offered to all the world. He was participating in the extension of a kingdom that would include people from every language and land."[40]

Sidney Rooy elaborates and indicates that, for Calvin, the church was entrusted with the gospel, and the means for the church to grow and expand throughout the world is the preaching of that very gospel "especially by ministers as instruments appointed by the Church itself, and through her, called by God."[41] Van den Berg for the most part concurs, but adds a disclaimer: "It appears that with Calvin the thought that the Gospel has to spread throughout the world and has to take its course to the ends of the earth is very clear; less clearly, however, does he see in what manner this must happen; and the practical application of the missionary ideal is almost completely lacking."[42]

Without straying too far from the path, it should be noted that Rooy provides an outline of the way in which Calvin envisions the spreading of the gospel:

1. Evangelize by the Sword of the Spirit (Comm. on Is. 53:2).

2. To this end send laborers (builders) to the harvest, according to Matt. 9:38 (Comm. on Is. 49:17).

3. Use a gentle manner and persuasive methods to draw inquirers so that they come freely and voluntarily (Comm. on Micah 4:3, Comm. on Philemon 10).

4. Never use exterior force or soldiers to impose faith (Comm. on Micah 4:3).

---

39. John Calvin, *Commentary on a Harmony of the Evangelists, Matthew, Mark and Luke* (Vol. 3) (Grand Rapids: Baker, 1979), 384.
40. Charles Chaney, "The Missionary Dynamic in the Theology of John Calvin," in *The Reformed Review* 17.3 (March, 1964): 31.
41. S. H. Rooy, "The Reformers and Missions," in *Signposts of God's Liberating Kingdom: Perspectives for the 21st Century* (Vol.2) (Potchefstroom: Potchefstroomse Universiteit vir Christelike Hoër Onderwys, 1998), 203.
42. J. Van den Berg, "Calvin's Missionary Message: Some Remarks About the Relation Between Calvinism and Missions," *The Evangelical Quarterly* (Vol. 22, 1950): 176.

5. "…the riches of the Spirit…are not to be kept by us to ourselves, but everyone must communicate to others what he has received…according to the measure of each (Comm. on 2 Cor. 1:4).

6. The duty of every believer is to show concern for the well-being of his neighbor and so procure his salvation, and to give testimony to our love by godly prayers (Comm. on 1 Tim. 2:4).

7. God uses his people to overcome the racism of the past to establish one people (Comm. on Is. 66:20).

8. "…believers, instead of addressing to their brethren the command, Go up, rather lead the way by their own example. This is the true method, therefore, of profitable teaching, when, by actually performing what we demand, we make it evident that we speak with sincerity and earnestness (Comm. on Is. 2:3).[43]

Rooy thus provides an answer to Van den Berg's assertion that Calvin did not envision the practical means for carrying out his missionary ideals. The assertion that Calvin did not put this into practice goes to the heart of the question of the definition of mission, something we will consider in the next chapter. Suffice it to say that Vandenberg's definition appears to be too narrow and imposes an unrealistic expectation upon Calvin.[44]

There are many more nuances in both Luther's and Calvin's conception of the relationship between the gospel, the church, and the world, but we are simply interested in the general contours of their position. For

---

43. Rooy, "The Reformers and Missions," 212-213.
44. Contra DeJong, "John Calvin in Mission Literature," 12. DeJong sees Van den Berg as agreeing that it is anachronistic to apply contemporary definitions of mission to Calvin. However, while the seeds for this thought are there, it does not bear fruit in Van den Berg as it does in DeJong. Van den Berg still does not get to the point where he sees the self-understanding of the Reformation as a missionary movement (a point argued in the next chapter), a movement reaching out to the unconverted of Europe. He does not see the non-Reformed areas of Europe as being "the non-Christian world." See J. Van den Berg "Calvin and Missions," in *John Calvin: Contemporary Prophet, A Symposium* (Philadelphia: Presbyterian and Reformed, 1959), 168. For more recent assessments of Calvin and missions, see Richard A. Muller, "'To Grant this Grace to All People and Nations:' Calvin on Apostolicity and Mission," in *For God So Loved the World: Missiological Reflections in Honor of Roger S. Greenway*, ed. Arie C. Leder (Belleville: Essence Publishing, 2006), 211-232; D. McKay, "The Missionary Zeal of Calvin," *Lux Mundi* 27.4 (December 2008): 83-89; Wes Bredenhof, "John Calvin and Missions," *Christian Renewal* 27.11 (February 25, 2009): 24-27.

these Reformers, the gospel is the foundation of the church, which has been gathered out of the world through the gospel. The gospel has been entrusted to the church for the church to grow from within and from without. Especially because of the influence of Calvin on Guido de Brès, the understanding of this relationship forms part of the theological/missiological background to the Belgic Confession and will have a bearing on how we evaluate its missiological relevance. This also ties into the question of the concept of mission during this time period, something we will consider in the next chapter.

1.2 THE NARROWER CONTEXT

1.2.1 AUTHORSHIP OF THE CONFESSION

The first edition of the Belgic Confession did not give any indication as to who the author was, and subsequent sixteenth-century editions did not either. It was simply the confession "made with common agreement by the faithful who live in the Netherlands, who desire to live according to the purity of the Gospel of our Lord Jesus Christ." Nicolaas Gootjes notes that no one claimed authorship during the sixteenth century, nor was the identity of the author generally known. The question did not begin receiving attention until the following century during debates about the confession's authority.[45]

Adrian Saravia wrote in a letter that the Belgic Confession "was first written in the French language by the servant of Christ and martyr Guido de Brès."[46] Gootjes assesses this information as being trustworthy.[47] Other seventeenth-century sources (Thysius, Uytenbogaert, Trigland, Schoock) which deal with authorship rely on Saravia.

Besides Saravia, there is another reliable sixteenth-century source on the authorship of the Confession: a 1582 letter from Thomas Van Tielt to Arent Cornelisz. In this letter, Van Tielt says, "I have spoken with Taffin about the confession, which he says was made by Guy de Brès and presented in French to his Majesty."[48] Jean Taffin was a minister in the Reformed church at Antwerp, and his family members were known as

---

45. Nicolaas H. Gootjes, *The Belgic Confession: Its History and Sources* (Grand Rapids: Baker Academic, 2007), 33-34.
46. Gootjes, *The Belgic Confession*, 36.
47. Gootjes, *The Belgic Confession*, 39.
48. Gootjes, *The Belgic Confession*, 47.

strong supporters of de Brès in Doornik/Tournai.[49] Gootjes judges this information to be reliable. There is no longer any doubt whatsoever that the main author of the Belgic Confession was Guido de Brès. One question that does remain open (and which may never be solved) is whether or not any others directly contributed to its writing. Saravia indicated that de Brès had consulted other ministers, but it is unknown as to whether they actually had a hand in the formulations found in the Confession.[50]

1.2.2 INFLUENCES AND SOURCES

Scholars of the Confession have identified a number of influences and sources. One of the most obvious in terms of language, structure, purpose and provenance is the French (or Gallican) Confession of 1559. The first draft of this confession came from the hand of John Calvin at the request of François de Morel. De Morel had written to Calvin indicating that a Synod of the French Reformed churches was going to prepare a confession of faith. Calvin brought forward the draft of this confession and the Synod of Paris (1559) used this draft as its plumb line, making several changes and edits where they felt necessary.[51] In turn, Guido de Brès used this confession as his starting point when preparing a confession for the churches of the Lowlands. Faber goes so far as to call the Genevan Reformer the "ghost author" of the Belgic Confession.[52]

The Belgic Confession bears the influence of John Calvin via the French Confession, but also via his *Institutes of the Christian Religion*. Strauss and others have noted that the structure of the Belgic Confession follows the *Institutes*, three books classified according to the three persons of the Trinity and then a fourth regarding the church.[53] There is not only a structural similarity, but also a similarity in content, particularly in the way certain doctrines are expressed. For instance, in article 27, de Brès wrote that "Christ is an eternal king who cannot be without subjects." This is almost a verbatim quote from Calvin's prefatory address in the *Institutes* to Francis I.[54]

---

49. "Doornik" was the Dutch name of Tournai. Since the city is today widely known as Tournai, I have chosen to use this name from here on.
50. Gootjes, *The Belgic Confession*, 48.
51. Gootjes, *The Belgic Confession*, 62-64.
52. J. Faber, "De Brès Versus Calvin? Early History of the Belgic Confession," in *Clarion* 8.17 (August 25, 1979): 355.
53. S. A. Strauss, "John Calvin and the Belgic Confession," in *In Die Skriflig* 27.4 (December 1993): 507.
54. Strauss, "John Calvin and the Belgic Confession," 512.

It is undeniable that Calvin was one of the strongest influences behind the Belgic Confession. This can be accounted for in the influence that Calvin had upon Guido de Brès. As we shall see in chapter 3, de Brès did much traveling and it is possible that they met at some point, either in Strasbourg or Geneva. There is solid evidence that de Brès had read at least one book by Calvin as well as evidence that he owned at least one of his books. There was also at least one letter (no longer extant) written by Calvin to de Brès. While Calvin was not the only influence on de Brès (his library did contain works by other notable Reformers, including Luther), it is clear that his influence was substantial.[55] Furthermore, we can note that the Belgic Confession was sent to Calvin and the other ministers of Geneva and met with their approval.[56]

The 1559 Confession of Theodore Beza has also been identified as a secondary source. The most obvious place where de Brès relied on Beza was in article 37, regarding the last judgment. However, expressions of Beza find their way into many other articles of the Belgic Confession as well, although they are often rephrased. While the French Confession is definitely the most influential source, Gootjes asserts that Beza's Confession cannot be ignored. He concludes, "Guido de Brès probably wrote an outline for a confession based on the Gallican Confession and then decided to include material from Beza's confession as well. This is why many of Beza's statements were rephrased to fit existing articles."[57]

1.2.3 The Writing of the Confession, Provenance and Text-History

The Belgic Confession was written by Guido de Brès in early 1561, with its first printing likely on May 25 of that year.[58] It appears to have been written during de Brès' ministry in Tournai. Before and especially after this time, de Brès was a fugitive from the Spanish authorities in the Netherlands. While much is known about the circumstances surrounding the production of the Confession (which we shall explore in some detail in chapter 3), precious little is known about its actual writing. We know that de Brès lived in secret with his family in the rooms at the back of a house in the neighbourhood of St. Brice (or Brixe) and that his study

---

55. Gootjes, *The Belgic Confession*, 61-62.
56. Gootjes, *The Belgic Confession*, 67-70.
57. Gootjes, *The Belgic Confession*, 89.
58. Gootjes, *The Belgic Confession*, 30.

was nearby, close to the walls of Tournai.[59] We may assume that his study was the place where the Confession was drafted. As mentioned above, it appears likely that de Brès did the lion's share (if not all) of the work in writing this confession. He then likely shared it with his colleagues who may have made editorial contributions towards the final product. Gootjes also notes some mistakes in the two editions of 1561 that indicate that the Confession was printed hastily, without first being carefully checked over by the author or the printer.[60] Aside from these details, little is known about the actual writing.

Although the Confession was not made public until later in 1561, it appears that it was already officially adopted by the Reformed Churches of the Lowlands in the early months of that year. Godfried Van Wingen mentions a meeting of ministers in a letter dated February 14, 1561, and it appears that it was officially sanctioned at this meeting. This would account for the subtitle of the Confession, which indicates that it was made "in common agreement by the faithful" of the Lowlands. In other words, this was not a personal confession of faith which was later adopted by the churches, but was from the beginning an official ecclesiastical confession of faith.[61]

The Confession became publicly known during the autumn of 1561. It was thrown over the castle wall in Tournai on November 1. However, prior to this, a copy of the Confession had been discovered by the authorities in the home of Jean du Mortier, a leader in the Reformed church. This had taken place on October 15, 1561.[62]

As mentioned above, the Belgic Confession was printed twice in 1561. Two more printings appeared in 1562. A second revised edition was published in 1566, the result of a careful review by the Synod of Antwerp. Most of the changes were of a cosmetic nature; however, there were a few more significant revisions, but even these did not alter the substance of the Confession.[63]

---

59. Gootjes, *The Belgic Confession*, 49.
60. Gootjes, *The Belgic Confession*, 32.
61. Gootjes, *The Belgic Confession*, 114-115.
62. Gootjes, *The Belgic Confession*, 17.
63. Gootjes, *The Belgic Confession*, 117-131.

Martin Bucer (1491-1551)

Chapter Two

The Definition of Mission(s)

2.0 Introduction: A Question of Exegesis

Having reviewed the history and background of the Belgic Confession, our next stop must be a detailed consideration of the definition of mission(s). In order to inquire meaningfully about the missiological relevance of the Belgic Confession, we need to consider what we mean by the words 'mission,' 'missions,' 'missiology,' and 'missiological.' Building on our discussion of the sixteenth-century understanding of the relationship between the gospel, the church, and the world in the last chapter, we also need to consider how the concept of mission was understood in the sixteenth century. Therefore, this chapter explores those important issues.

The definition of mission is not presently a significant issue in missiological circles, particularly in North America. A survey of recent volumes of missiological journals reveals that many missiologists appear to assume a working definition and never take pains to make it explicit. It appears that, especially in evangelical circles, issues of mission praxis (especially contextualization) receive most of the attention, while more basic issues, perceived by some as rather abstract (such as the definition of mission), have been for the most part forgotten or left to the introductory textbooks. Even in the introductory textbooks, a definition is often given without any significant development or defense.[1] Part of the reason for this lacuna likely rests with the fact that the issue is one on which unanimity may never be found. However, another reason could be that missiology has not fully appreciated the significance of this issue.

---

1. This is especially true in the English literature. See the recent textbook of Moreau, Corwin, and McGee, *Introducing World Missions*, 9, 17. In the recent Dutch literature C. J. Haak does spend a lot of time developing his definition; see his *Gereformeerde Missiologie & Oecumenica: Beknopt overzicht aan het begin van de 21e eeuw A.D.* (Zwolle: De Verre Naasten, 2005), 31-42.

In this chapter, it will be argued that the definition of mission is crucially important, not only for our consideration of the missiological relevance of the Belgic Confession, but also for missiology in general. It is not something that can be taken for granted. Even if complete agreement on the definition is not forthcoming, we can examine the Scriptures (the normative foundation for missiology) and determine some basic common denominators for a definition. Since it would take us too far afield, we will lay aside a diachronic accounting of the definition; rather, a definition will be developed based on exegesis of key Scripture passages. We will also briefly examine two issues directly related to the definition and then explore two influential figures from the sixteenth century and their position on this issue.

To say that the issue is not presently regarded as significant is not to say that it has not received attention. Numerous scholars have ventured definitions ranging from the all-inclusive to the very narrowly restricted. As an example of the former, consider John Stott's definition: "Mission describes everything the church is sent into the world to do. 'Mission' embraces the church's double vocation of service to be 'the salt of the earth' and 'the light of the world.'"[2] The problem with these sorts of definitions is that they are vulnerable to Stephen Neill's trenchant criticism: if everything is mission, then nothing is mission.[3] Broad definitions threaten to make the term "mission" meaningless — in which case, Neill argued, another word will have to be found to describe the Church's obligation to reach out to those without Christ.

On the other end of the spectrum, we find definitions like this one from a currently authoritative work on short-term missions: Christian mission is "sending messengers (missionaries) away from their 'normal' home culture as soon as possible, and into another culture and people (intended receptors), for the express purpose of proclaiming with word and deed (the intended activity) the Good News that sets any person free from anything that binds them."[4] One problem with these kinds of definitions is that mission is cross-culturally restricted. Missionaries from India working in their own culture in India are not technically mission-

---

2. John R. W. Stott, *Christian Mission in the Modern World* (Downers Grove: IVP, 1975), 30.
3.. Stephen C. Neill, *Creative Tension* (New York: Doubleday, 1959), 81-82.
4. Roger Peterson, Gordon Aeschliman, and R. Wayne Sneed, *Maximum Impact Short-Term Mission: the God-commanded Repetitive Deployment of Swift, Temporary, Non-professional Missionaries* (Minneapolis: STEMPress, 2003), 52.

aries with these types of definitions. The time factor ("as soon as possible") is also problematic as it ties into the being sent away from a home culture. Finally, "anything that binds them" is troublesome since it is not concretely defined. For instance, in the final analysis, one could be bound by legitimate obligations to one's family.

Of course, historically speaking, we are not the first ones to discuss this issue. Speaking out of the continental Reformed tradition, the definition of mission was discussed at several synods in the Netherlands. At the Synod of the Liberated (*Vrijgemaakte*) churches in 1948, for example, numerous reports were presented on the matter of mission. New approaches were being considered on a number of fronts. Specifically, a "Mission Order" that had been adopted by the Reformed Churches in the Netherlands in 1902 was under intense scrutiny. This Mission Order was a special church order specifically dealing with mission. Included with this Mission Order was provision for the institution of *hulpdiensten* (auxiliary services); these included schools (theological and general) and medical services. In this context, some of the reports to Synod 1948 dealt directly or indirectly with the matter of the definition of mission. One of these reports was particularly concerned with whether or not *hulpdiensten* should be included under the notion of *zending* (mission) — something for which J. H. Bavinck had advocated.[5] The fact that the deputies who penned the report could not reach a consensus is indicative of the complexities inherent in the discussion.

Scholars do not debate an issue unless they believe it is important. Why does the definition of mission matter? Among other reasons, a definition of mission is helpful for circumscribing the discipline of missiology — the science of mission. That reason serves the purpose of this book. However, David Bosch was correct when he wrote that there is "much more than mere academic gymnastics at stake here."[6] The basic issue here is not a definition per se, but the obedience to Christ that

---

5. *Rapport over de verhouding van den zendingsarbeid tot medischen en onderwijs-arbeid op de zendings-terreinen (kwestie 'hoofd' —en 'hulp-diensten') uitgebracht door de Deputaten, benoemd vanwege de Generale Synode te Amersfoort 1948 tot herziening van de K.O. (art.52) en Z.O. volgens art. 65 and 129 der Acta, aan de Kerken voorgelegd* (Kampen: Drukkerij Ph. Zalsman, 1950). *Zending in een wereld in nood*, J. H. Bavinck (Wageningen: N.V. Gebr. Zomer en Keuning's Uitgeversmij, 1948), 58-61.

6. David J. Bosch, "Mission and Evangelism: Clarifying the Concepts," *Zeitschrift für Missionswissenschaft und Religionswissenschaft* 68 (1984): 161.

flows from a grateful heart. It is safe to assume that everybody involved with this debate will agree that mission is about doing something. Before ascending into heaven, Christ sent his followers to do something.[7] When we search for a definition of mission, we are inquiring about what that "something" is. If we are to follow Christ, we have to know what it was he was saying.

In other words, we arrive at a question of exegesis. In his book *Christian Mission in the Modern World*, John Stott endeavoured to explore the Scriptures to reach a definition of mission. As already indicated, his end product leaves much to be desired, but his approach is praiseworthy since Stott takes the authority of Scripture seriously. So, we too should ask the question: what do the Scriptures say to the question of "What Is Mission?" As we ask this question, we should remember that the broader issue here is not a definition per se, but obedience growing out of gratitude and love. Hence, in general, we can be satisfied with common denominators and not necessarily agree on a rigidly delineated definition. Nevertheless, an attempt will be made to provide such a definition in this chapter, especially with a view to the purposes of this study.

Before proceeding, we need to briefly lay out the exegetical presuppositions and method that guide this investigation. The Word of God should be approached on its own terms, and its inspiration and divine authority taken seriously. The Belgic Confession clearly and correctly states in articles 3 and 5:

> We confess that this Word of God did not come by the impulse of man, but that men moved by the Holy Spirit spoke from God, as the apostle Peter says…
>
> We receive all these books [the 66 canonical books mentioned in article 4], and these only, as holy and canonical, for the regulation, foundation and confirmation of our faith.[8]

This is the historic Protestant (Reformed) position on the character of Holy Scripture.[9] Hermeneutically, the older (but still valuable) approach

---

7. In the Vulgate the word used is a form of *mitto, mittere, misi, missum*, 'to send.'
8. Belgic Confession, Articles 3 and 4, *Book of Praise (Anglo-Genevan Psalter)*.
9. For an older defense of this position, see Edward J. Young, *Thy Word Is Truth: Thoughts on the Biblical Doctrine of Inspiration* (Grand Rapids: Eerdmans, 1957). For a more recent defense, see Dr. Robert L. Reymond, *A New Systematic Theology of the Christian Faith* (Nashville: Thomas Nelson Publishers, 1998), especially "Part One — A Word From Another World."

The Definition of Mission(s)

of Seakle Greijdanus is built upon biblical presuppositions and forms part of my method.[10]

With respect to exegesis, I follow the grammatical-historical method.[11] It is important to work with the original languages of Scripture, paying close attention to grammar and syntax. Moreover, responsible exegesis also carefully examines the context (literal, historical, and otherwise) of any given passage. It is also critical to consider the manner in which key words and phrases are employed. Finally, the manner in which a passage has been understood by other exegetes needs careful consideration before reaching a definitive exegesis.

2.1 Biblical Data

2.1.1 The Old Testament

Even though we are examining something Christ told his followers to do before he ascended into heaven, the Old Testament is not irrelevant. The Old Testament provides important background for the development of mission in the Scriptures. Therefore, one cannot properly understand Christ's command without considering earlier revelation.

The first two chapters of Scripture provide us with the context for the greatest tragedy in the history of the world. Through Genesis 1 and 2, we learn of a creation good in every respect. With his Word, *ex nihilo*, God brought forth light and every other good thing, including humanity. From the beginning, it was God's purpose that this humanity would fill the earth with peoples and nations bringing glory to him.[12]

Prior to the fall into sin, it is possible to speak of a form of mission given to humanity. When God commanded Adam and Eve to be fruitful

---

10. Dr. S. Greijdanus, *Schriftbeginselen ter schriftverklaring: en historisch overzicht over theorieen en wijzen van schriftuitlegging* (Kampen: Kok, 1946). An English summary is available at www.bredenhof.ca

11. For two representatives of this method, see L. Berkhof, *Principles of Biblical Interpretation* (Grand Rapids: Baker, 1950) and Walter C. Kaiser, Jr., *Toward an Exegetical Theology: Biblical Exegesis for Preaching and Teaching* (Grand Rapids: Baker, 1981).

12. J. Geertsema, "The Scriptural Foundation of Mission in its Biblical History and Normative Direction," in *Missionary Preaching: Papers Presented at the First Reformed Missions Conference*, ed. Wes Bredenhof (Hamilton: Theological College of the Canadian Reformed Churches, 2005), 5-6. Geertsema argues that the command to be fruitful and multiply implies God's intention to fill the earth with nations and peoples.

and multiply (Genesis 1:28), he included a mandate to fill the earth. This implies a being sent out into the earth — a form of mission. G. K. Beale describes it this way: "we can speak of Genesis 1:28 as the first 'Great Commission' that was repeatedly applied to humanity. The commission was to bless the earth, and part of the essence of this blessing was God's salvific presence. Before the fall, Adam and Eve were to produce progeny who would fill the earth with God's glory being reflected from each of them in the image of God."[13] At the beginning, then, a good humanity was entrusted with a divine commission.

It was the fall of this good humanity and the universal brokenness it engendered which led to the reconfiguring of mission into a salvific mode. The ultimate goal of mission (i.e. the glory of God over all the earth) remains, but the means by which that goal is reached now involves the salvation of sinful men. While it is difficult to link it etymologically to the notion of mission (connected as it is with "sending"), the earliest pages of the Old Testament portray a God who seeks out that which is lost. There is no question that God is concerned for the salvation of his sin-stained creation, particularly the crown of that creation — man.

As the Old Testament slowly unfolds, we see God working towards the fulfillment of his plan for redemption. At certain points, God provides hints that his plans are broad and universal. We see this particularly in the relationship God established with Abraham. The well-known passage of Genesis 22:18 illustrates this beautifully: "In your seed all the nations of earth shall be blessed..."[14] This is comparable to Psalm 87 which speaks prophetically of Rahab (Egypt), Babylon, Philistia, Tyre and Ethiopia as being regarded as native-born in Zion, indicating a broader purpose of God among the nations. However, the bulk of the Old Testament is taken up with God's interaction with the one people directly descended from Abraham. As he relates to that one people, on occasion we can hear notes that sound like the music of mission. When God brings his initial commission to the prophet Jeremiah, it is clearly a matter of God "sending" (Jeremiah 1:7) the prophet. This sending was mostly focused on the one people of God, but it included messages concerning the nations. Most of these messages were prophetic judgments, but occasionally there are positive notes as well, particularly with Moab, Ammon, and Elam.

---

13. G. K. Beale, *The Temple and the Church's Mission: A Biblical Theology of the Dwelling Place of God* (Downers Grove: IVP, 2004), 117-118.

14. All passages are NKJV, unless otherwise noted.

Some of the Old Testament's most anticipatory passages, missiologically speaking, are the section of servant songs in Isaiah. Here we read of a servant being sent by the LORD (Isa. 42:19). However, unlike with Jeremiah, it is clear that this servant is ultimately sent with good news. He impacts not only the affairs of God's people, but also the affairs of the nations. This servant has often been seen as a metaphor for the people of Israel and, more proleptically, as a prophecy of Jesus Christ. With this in mind, it is clear that the root idea of the sending of a messenger or servant with God's Word was present in the Old Testament.

We can see this also with the Psalter. Psalm 87 was already mentioned, but many other Psalms exhort God's people to announce his glorious kingship to the nations. In Psalm 96, the people of God are told to "[s]ay among the nations, 'The LORD reigns...'" This can be understood as a prototypical call to mission in the Old Testament. However, this call was not taken very seriously by Israel in the old covenant. Though there was some proselytism in later Old Testament Judaism (cf. Matt. 23:15), it was not comparable to the scale and intensity of the early Christian mission.

The Old Testament people's lack of mission-mindedness was most clearly evidenced in the account of Jonah. Jonah was sent to Nineveh — the clearest approximation of a missionary in the Old Testament. Jonah's reluctance as a missionary prophet is not merely a personal indictment of the prophet, but a vivid portrayal of Israel's ethnocentric understanding of God's plans for the world — their failure to understand the scope of God's promises to Abraham, David, and others. Of course, we also acknowledge that it was God's will to generally let the nations go their own way in this era. He had a plan for redemption and all these pieces fit together as parts of that plan.[15] Because of these redemptive-historical factors, there could be nothing more than an incipient mission in the Old Testament. This mission was relatively undefined. It seems to consist of announcing God's kingship over and judgment on the nations. Beale points out that the temple (and related concepts throughout the Old Testament) also give a picture of the expectation of mission among God's people, but again, this could only be incipient.[16] Finally, it was not only relatively undefined, it was also not taken seriously in its execution. That would have to wait until the Spirit-filled era of the new covenant. The most we can say is that

---

15. Geertsema, "The Scriptural Foundation of Mission," 13-14. Geertsema cites Acts 14:16; 17:30; and Romans 3:25.

16. Beale, *The Temple and the Church's Mission*, passim.

Christ's sending of the apostles was latent in the Old Testament messianic promises and prophecies.[17]

2.1.2 THE NEW TESTAMENT

The mission which was incipient and rudimentary in the Old Testament becomes full-blown and animated in the pages of the New Testament. It starts with the Son of God himself being sent into the world to seek and save that which was lost. It continues with the same Son of God sending out his followers. Our task at this point becomes identifying the purpose of this sending out. Why did the Lord Jesus send out his followers? What were they being sent out to do?

2.1.2.1 JOHN 20:21

This question is really the focus of what some claim to be the most important "Great Commission" passage in the New Testament, viz., John 20:21. Some argue that John's version of Christ's words is the crucial one.[18] But is it true that any one passage is more crucial than the others? Rather, is it not the case that they belong together as a coherent whole? Indeed, together they give us a complete picture of Christ's sending out of the apostles.

The passage in John 20:21 reads, "So Jesus said to them again, 'Peace to you! As the Father has sent Me, I also send you.'" John quotes the Lord Jesus with similar words in John 17:18, "As You sent Me into the world, I also have sent them into the world." The context there is the time prior to the crucifixion and resurrection — at this point, the Lord Jesus is praying. Interestingly, in John 17:18, we find the verb Ἀποστελλω (*apostellō*) in the aorist with both clauses, whereas in John 20:21, the first verb is ἀποστελλω and the second is πεμπω (*pempō*), the first being perfect, and the second being present. The verb πεμπω (*pempō*) is not used by John prior to 20:21 with the apostles as object. Ἀποστελλω (*apostellō*) is used in this manner only in John 4:38, referring to the Lord Jesus sending out the apostles to reap what they have not worked for. When ἀποστελλω is used here with respect to Christ, the difference between the aorist in 17:18 and the perfect in 20:21 is striking. The switch to the perfect could be explained by the post-resurrection context in which the redemptive

---

17. Samuel M. Zwemer, *Into All the World, The Great Commission: A Vindication and an Interpretation* (Grand Rapids: Zondervan, 1943), 9.
18. Stott, *Christian Mission in the Modern World*, 23.

work is virtually completed.[19] With ἀποστελλω and πεμπω used with respect to the apostles, the difference between the aorist and the present is not striking on its own. It is only striking when put in contrast with what these texts say about Christ. For while the lexicological evidence suggests that ἀποστελλω and πεμπω are virtually synonymous and thus the sending of Christ and his apostles have a close analogy, the grammar suggests that there is an important difference.

Indeed, this difference has not always been appreciated. Consequently, some draw strong parallels between Christ being sent into the world and believers being sent out.[20] However, Christ's sending into the world was a unique event and facile comparisons are in danger of devaluing the unique character of the incarnation. Furthermore, as D. A. Carson points out: "John's gospel does not set forth our going as an 'incarnation.' The observation is more than a narrow point of picky exegesis: under the guise of the 'incarnation' model of Christian mission some now so focus on 'presence' and identification with those being served that the proclamatory, kerygmatic, 'good news' elements are largely suppressed."[21]

John 20:21 (and John 17:18) does imply a *limited* analogy between the mission of Christ and the mission of the apostles. However, the grammar demonstrates that this is not a direct identity. This is an important point: the Lord Jesus Christ was sent into this world with a very unique and specific task. That task is the redemption of his elect, and it was virtually completed at the time of John 20:21. No one else ever has nor will perform the same task. But the Lord Jesus sends out his apostles, and by extension, his church, to gather the fruits of what he has accomplished. This involves the work of the Holy Spirit, as is evident by Christ's words in verse 22, "Receive the Holy Spirit." J. DeJong aptly summarizes the passage: "He now sends His apostles in the power of the Spirit in order to gather the harvest, that is to bring forth the fruits of His task . . . He sends

---

19. "The redemptive mission of Jesus is now finished; this is the sense of the extensive perfect, 'has sent me,' denoting an act now complete." R. C. H. Lenski, *The Interpretation of St. John's Gospel* (Columbus: Lutheran Book Concern, 1942), 1370.

20. "The special Johannine contribution to the theology of this mission is that the Father's sending of the Son serves both as the model and the ground for the Son's sending of the disciples." Raymond E. Brown, *The Gospel According to John* (Anchor Bible) (New York: Doubleday, 1970), 1036.

21. D. A. Carson, "Christology," in *Evangelical Dictionary of World Missions (EDWM)*, ed. A. Scott Moreau (Grand Rapids: Baker, 2000), 191.

the Spirit into the world to work with the Word for the completion and fruit of His Work."[22]

The important point in the passage is this: Christ is the one who sends out his apostles in the power of the Holy Spirit. The passage is deliberately brief and its message rather simple. It could be paraphrased like this: "I was sent by the Father. Now I am sending you." Such a paraphrase captures the essential difference between the tenses in the two clauses and also maintains the overlap in semantic domains between ἀποστελλω and πεμπω. To accomplish this, the paraphrase works with a lesser-known meaning of καθως (*kathōs*), namely "since" or "on account of." Thus, a more literal translation would read, "Since the Father has sent me, I am sending you."

Rather than providing a base for all manner of theologizing about the parallels between the mission of the Son and that of the apostles, the intent of the passage seems to be to invite the reader to ask: "Sent to do what?" What are the apostles sent to do? To answer those questions, we are forced to the broader context of the book of John. From John 17:18, we know that the "sending" or "mission" was "into the world." In the following context, in John 17:21,23, it is evident that there was an element of being sent into the world so that others would believe the message embodied by Jesus Christ. In the immediate context of John 20:21, we see that this message includes the forgiveness of sins as a significant feature (verse 22). All of that fits with the broader purpose of the Fourth Gospel, as given in John 20:31. However, the answer at this point is still rather nebulous. Hence, to gain more clarity, we need to examine the broader Scriptural context, particularly the parallels in the Synoptics.

2.1.2.2 MATTHEW 28:18-20

Matthew 28:18-20 provides the most well-known version of the Great Commission: "And Jesus came and spoke to them, saying, 'All authority has been given to Me in heaven and on earth. Go therefore and make disciples of all the nations, baptizing them in the name of the Father and

---

22. J. DeJong, "Even So I Send You — Some Reflections on the Current Missionary Task of the Church — (2)" *Clarion* 45.21 (October 18, 1996): 473. For other critiques of "incarnational ministry," see J. Todd Billings' articles, "Incarnational Ministry and the Unique, Incarnate Christ," *Modern Reformation* 18.2 (March/April 2009): 19-22 and "'Incarnational Ministry': A Christological Evaluation and Proposal," *Missiology: an International Review* 32.2 (April 2004): 187-201.

of the Son and of the Holy Spirit, teaching them to observe all things that I have commanded you; and lo, I am with you always, even to the end of the age.' Amen." Though formerly much of the emphasis fell upon the participle πορευθεντες (*poreuthentes*) ("Go"), it is generally recognized today that the imperative μαθητευσατε (*mathēteusate*) ("make disciples") is the key to understanding this version of the Great Commission.[23] The command in this passage is to "make disciples." To be sure, that may involve some kind of movement, though the duration and distance of that movement is left unspecified. This discipling will also entail triune baptism and a teaching of all that Christ has commanded. Already at this point, we have some idea of what μαθητευσατε (*mathēteusate*) involves, or at least something of the way in which it is to be accomplished.

Nevertheless, it would be helpful to reflect further on the content of this command. The verb μαθητευω (*mathēteuō*) is, surprisingly, rarely used in the New Testament. Aside from three uses in Matthew, it is used once in Acts. In Matthew 13:52, the Lord Jesus says, "Therefore every scribe instructed (μαθητευω) concerning the kingdom of heaven is like a householder who brings out of his treasure things new and old." This seems to indicate some kind of educational activity done by the Lord Jesus akin to what the Jewish scribes had been doing.[24] In Matthew 27:57, Joseph of Arimathea is described as someone that the Lord had discipled. Finally, in Acts 14:21, Luke describes Paul and Barnabas as having not only preached the gospel in Derbe, but also as having made many disciples. From this overview of the use of this verb, it can be said that the verb μαθητευω (*mathēteuō*) expresses something that the Lord Jesus did and something that Paul and Barnabas were likewise engaged with. Matthew 13:52 contains an implied imperative or invitation for Jewish scribes to be the objects of μαθητευω, while our passage in Matthew 28 contains a direct imperative to be the subjects of the verb.

The limited usage of the verb forces us to cast a wider net and look at the related word μαθητης (*mathētēs*) (disciple). The usage of this term is distributed rather evenly over the four gospels and Acts, being found 252 times. As is to be expected, many of these usages describe the core group of twelve that the Lord Jesus gathered to himself. However, there is also

---

23. See J. Ronald Blue, "Go, Missions," *Bibliotheca Sacra* Vol.141, No. 564 (October/December 1984): 342-344.
24. Hans Kvalbein, "Go therefore and make disciples....The concept of discipleship in the New Testament," *Themelios* 13.2 (Jan./Feb. 1988): 49.

a wider use of this word to describe all those who follow the Lord. This usage was found already during Christ's earthly ministry, and it continued after his ascension. In fact, we find that before believers were known as Christians, they were known as disciples (Acts 11:26). Hence, the term μαθητης (*mathētēs*) defined what believers were about.

In its basic sense, μαθητης meant "learner" or "student." In Matthew 23:8-10, it becomes clear that the relationship between Christ and believers is one of a teacher with his students. The students are aiming to become like their master, as a student in a rabbinic school would aim to become as his rabbi. This replication of the master can be seen quite vividly in Christ's words in John 13:13-15. It can be said, therefore, that the aim is to become an obedient follower, one who does exactly as his master does. In the New Testament, a disciple learns by hearing his master and doing exactly as his master does.[25]

From this brief word study we can conclude that what the Lord Jesus means in Matthew 28 is that he wants to see the apostles going and making obedient followers in all the nations. As a means to reach that end, Christ Jesus sends out his apostles to baptize and teach. Though the imperative is directly given in this passage, it can be seen as a natural development since making more disciples is something that disciples instinctively do. Nevertheless, the Holy Spirit has seen fit that what should be instinctive is underlined with a direct command: Jesus Christ sends out his apostles to all nations to make disciples. They are to be baptizing and teaching to reach that end.

2.1.2.3 MARK 16:9-20

When we come to Mark 16:9-20, we encounter a well-known text-preservation problem. The canonical integrity of these verses is brought into question or outright denied by most modern translations and commentators. In fact, the recent commentary of R. T. France maintains that the verdict is "virtually unanimous" that there is a broad consensus that these verses are not original to Mark's Gospel.[26] The same consensus appears to extend to missiological circles, though not quite as broadly.[27]

---

25. Kvalbein, "Go therefore and make disciples," 49.

26. R. T. France, *The Gospel of Mark: A Commentary on the Greek Text* (Grand Rapids: Eerdmans, 2002), 685.

27. Two examples of proponents for the longer ending's authenticity in missiology are Samuel Zwemer in *Into All the World*, 69-86; and, less forcefully, George W. Peters in *A Biblical Theology of Missions* (Chicago: Moody Press, 1972), 172.

The problem is that the verses are missing from codices Sinaiticus and Vaticanus, along with a fair number of other manuscripts. From this external evidence and the internal evidence (lexicological and stylistic), following mainstream presuppositions and canons of textual criticism, many New Testament scholars have excised the longer ending. However, if one does not accept those mainstream presuppositions and canons, a different conclusion can be reached.

The critiques of J. Van Bruggen and others of the mainstream presuppositions and canons are compelling.[28] Negatively, Van Bruggen argued that the Byzantine text was originally dismissed on the faulty arguments advanced by Westcott and Hort. For instance, Westcott and Hort argued that the Byzantine (majority) text has little value because all these manuscript types can be traced back to a single recension, that of Lucianus of Antioch (d. 312 AD). However, VanBruggen points out that it is "not possible to prove historically that Lucianus of Antioch offered a revised text of the New Testament."[29] Further, he interacts with the "internal evidence" proposed by Metzger (following Hort) for generally dismissing the Byzantine text. Metzger argued that the Byzantine text is "characterized chiefly by lucidity and completeness. The framers of this text sought to smooth away any harshness of language, to combine two or more divergent readings into one expanded reading (called conflation), and to harmonize divergent parallel passages."[30] Responding to this, VanBruggen maintains that this position is simply impossible to prove. Furthermore he says, "After all, one could without much difficulty give a large number of examples from the Byzantine text to support the proposition that this text does *not* harmonize and does *not* smooth away."[31]

Positively, VanBruggen argued that the "codicology and the history of text-corruption and text-preservation plead in favour of the antiquity of the so-called Byzantine text-type."[32] This text was ac-

---

Two examples of opponents are Mortimer Arias and Alan Johnson in *The Great Commission: Biblical Models for Evangelism*, (Nashville: Abingdon Press, 1992), 36-37; and Joel F. Williams in "Mission in Mark," in *Mission in the New Testament: An Evangelical Approach* (Maryknoll: Orbis, 1998), 146-147.

28. J. VanBruggen, *The Ancient Text of the New Testament* (Winnipeg: Premier, 1976).
29. Van Bruggen, *The Ancient Text*, 17.
30. Van Bruggen, *The Ancient Text*, 30.
31. Van Bruggen, *The Ancient Text*, 30-31.
32. Van Bruggen, *The Ancient Text*, 29.

cepted by the Church for centuries. "The person who thinks he knows better than those who preserved and transmitted the text in the past should come along with proof."[33] VanBruggen specializes in questioning and dismantling the presuppositions of those who favour the so-called eclectic text. However, in his statement of the positive position, he also reflects a biblical presupposition (cf. Isaiah 59:20-21) whereby the place of the church in preserving the Word of God is fully accounted for.[34]

Therefore, we need not a priori accept the superiority of codices Sinaiticus and Vaticanus. The fact that the longer ending is missing from these codices requires explanation, but it does not automatically void the canonicity of this passage. Moreover, the internal evidence argument is also based on mainstream canons which are vulnerable to critique. For instance, arguments are presented on the basis of diction, style and contents to prove that Mark did not write verses 9-20.[35] However, none of these arguments disprove the thesis that these verses are part of the inspired canon; they might merely disprove Markan authorship and even that is relatively insignificant since the book itself does not claim to have Mark for its author. Therefore, we are not compelled to dismiss this passage from the canon on the basis of the internal linguistic and contextual evidence.

In conclusion, the totality of the arguments are not convincing to exclude Mark 16:9-20 from the canon. There is nothing to drive one inescapably to the dismissal of this passage. Without belaboring the point any further, it remains possible to assent to the concluding words of John Burgon: "that not a particle of doubt, that not an atom of suspicion, attaches to the last twelve verses of the Gospel According to St. Mark."[36]

---

33. Van Bruggen, *The Ancient Text*, 36.

34. This position (i.e. providential preservation) is also that of the Westminster Confession of Faith 1.8. Contra Daniel B. Wallace, "The Majority-Text Theory: History, Methods and Critique," *Journal of the Evangelical Theological Society* 37/2 (June 1994): 185-215. Wallace argues that "a theological a priori has no place in textual criticism" (204). He proceeds from the presupposition that so-called textual criticism is a neutral, scientific endeavour — a position I do not find compelling.

35. For a summary of these arguments see *New Testament Commentary: Exposition of the Gospel According to Mark*, William Hendriksen (Grand Rapids: Baker, 1975), 683-687.

36. John W. Burgon, *The Last Twelve Verses of the Gospel According to S. Mark*

The Definition of Mission(s)

We can now proceed to examine the passage itself. The relevant verse for our purposes is verse 15: "And He said to them, 'Go into all the world and preach the gospel to every creature.'" As in Matthew, there is one main command. However, this time it is κηρυξατε (*kēruxate*), "preach the gospel." Only one participle accompanies the imperative in the Markan version, viz., πορευθεντες (*poreuthentes*). Again, movement is indicated but the distance of the movement is left unspecified. The important verb in this verse is the imperative of κηρυσσω (*kērussō*).

The Lord Jesus sends out the apostles to preach the good news. The word κηρυσσω (*kērussō*) indicates that this preaching is of an official character; it is the message of a herald who has been appointed by an authority figure. In antiquity, a κηρυξ (*kērux*) was required to be faithful in delivering the message exactly as it had been given to him. With this condition being fulfilled, it could be known for certain that a higher authority stood behind the message.[37] Moreover, there is also a connection with mission here, for the κηρυξ (*kērux*) was not only appointed, but also *sent* to deliver his message.[38] Jesus Christ sends the apostles as heralds with the specific message of the ευαγγελιον (*evangelion*), "the good news."

What is the good news mentioned here? It is defined most obviously by what we read in the immediate context. In verse 16, the Lord Jesus speaks of belief, baptism, and salvation. But in the broader context of the gospel, the ευαγγελιον is what the whole book of Mark is about. Mark 1:1 frames the ευαγγελιον christologically with an emphasis on Jesus being the Son of God. Mark portrays Jesus Christ in his divine activity.[39] Elsewhere in the gospel, we hear that Jesus Christ is Lord and Saviour. The fact that he is Lord comes through with the theme of discipleship in the gospel. The fact that he is Saviour comes through not only with the weighty emphasis on the passion narrative in the gospel, but also Mark's attention to the many healing miracles performed by Jesus. Mark's gospel is holistic in that it includes the whole person, body and soul. Hence, we can say that the gospel includes the good news that Jesus Christ takes hold of and transforms the entire life by his saving power. From here, we can

---

(Ann Arbor: Sovereign Grace Book Club, 1959), 334.

37. Gerhard Friedrich, "κηρυξ" in *Theological Dictionary of the New Testament* (hereafter *TDNT*), Vol. 3, ed. Gerhard Kittel (Grand Rapids: Eerdmans, 1965), 687-688.

38. Friedrich, "κηρυξ," 713.

39. Donald Guthrie, *New Testament Introduction* (Revised Edition) (Downers Grove: IVP, 1990), 63.

draw the following conclusion for Mark 16:15: Jesus Christ sends out his apostles to preach, to officially herald the good news that he is divine Lord and Saviour all over the world.

2.1.2.4 LUKE 24:46-49

Luke 24:46-49 presents us with a slightly different but not incompatible picture. Unusually, the only direct imperative in this passage comes from verse 49: "stay in the city." The Lord Jesus commands the disciples to wait in Jerusalem until the promise of the Father comes upon them, a reference to the coming of the Holy Spirit on Pentecost. It is worth noting that, like John (but unlike Matthew and Mark), the command is given here with reference to the Holy Spirit. The mission command is carried out in the power of the Holy Spirit. With this command, there is an accompanying implication indicated by the ἕως (heōs). The implication is that once the Holy Spirit gives them "power from on high," that will be the right time to go and leave the city. "Wait now and go later in the power of the Spirit," seems to be the essence here in this Lukan version of the Great Commission.

But what are they supposed to do when they go at a later time? We find evidence of that in verses 46 and 47. In verse 46, the Lord Jesus speaks of what was written regarding the necessity of the Christ suffering and rising from the dead on the third day. In verse 47, he goes further and says that Scripture (here, the Old Testament) had prophesied that repentance and the forgiveness of sins would be preached to all nations in his Name, starting at Jerusalem. This passage affirms that not only the New Testament, but also the Old Testament has an all-inclusive view of the salvation of the nations.[40] The words of the Lord Jesus in this passage also lay out a divine-human effort to carry this out. The divine Word prophesied that it would be accomplished and ultimately, under God's sovereign power, so it will be. At the same time, the prophecy concerning the nations also lays a burden upon the hearts of the apostles, not merely to be witnesses in some passive sense, but also to be active participants. Verse 48 indicates that not only have the disciples been witnesses in the past, they are going to be witnesses in the future.

There is one similarity here with Mark's version. We find that in verse 47 with the use of the verb κηρυσσω (kērussō). Again we have here the of-

---

40. "...both Old and New Testament proclaim a *Christ for all the nations.*" William Hendriksen, *New Testament Commentary: The Gospel of Luke* (Grand Rapids: Baker, 1978), 1075.

ficial preaching, the word of a herald bringing a message from one higher up. The official character is here underlined by the addition of "in his name." Further, that official preaching consists of repentance and the forgiveness of sins. It seems that in Luke the content of the herald's message is defined much more precisely than in Mark and it fits with the emphasis on repentance and forgiveness found throughout Luke's writings.[41] From Luke's gospel we can conclude that Christ, in fulfillment of the Old Testament, sent out his apostles in the power of the Spirit to witness to his suffering and resurrection and to preach officially repentance and the forgiveness of sins in his name to all nations.

2.1.2.5 ACTS 1:8

Luke gives the Great Commission in another form in Acts 1:8: "But you shall receive power when the Holy Spirit has come upon you; and you shall be witnesses to Me in Jerusalem, and in all Judea and Samaria, and to the end of the earth." The key idea is that the apostles will receive power from the Holy Spirit. As in Luke's gospel, the Great Commission is given here with an accent on the work of the Spirit. As a result of the pouring out of the Spirit, the apostles are to be witnesses for Jesus Christ, starting in their immediate vicinity and slowly working outward. Interestingly, the Lord Jesus is quoted as using the future rather than the imperative. The words may therefore appear at first glance to be merely predictive. However, even though the future is used here, it is most likely an imperatival future, having a "universal, timeless and/or solemn force to it."[42] This understanding also makes the most sense given the parallels in the gospels.

As in Luke 24:46-49, the apostles are not so much sent out as commissioned with a task. To be sure, there is a geographic locale attached to the commission, implying both a sending out and a going. However, the emphasis is not on the sending and going here. Rather, it is on the fact that

---

41. "Its content corresponds with Luke's emphasis on repentance and forgiveness in the teaching and ministry of Jesus...Apart from Mark 1:4 this form of words is confined to Luke-Acts in the NT, and it governs the presentation of the church's mission in Acts." C. F. Evans, *Saint Luke* (London: SCM, 1990), 923.

42. "Evidence that the imperative is used for such commands can be demonstrated by Synoptic parallels (in which one Gospel has the imperative while the other has the future indicative) and textual variants (in which the imperative is found in some MSS, the future indicative in others." Daniel B. Wallace, *Greek Grammar Beyond the Basics: An Exegetical Syntax of the New Testament* (Grand Rapids: Zondervan, 1996), 569.

Christ commissions his apostles to be witnesses (μαρτυρες; *martures*). The New Testament idea of a witness comes with a legal connotation. A witness gives sound testimony to the truth of something, and this sound testimony could stand up under legal scrutiny. A witness speaks about what he or she has seen and heard (cf. Acts 4:20). The apostles, therefore, were commissioned in the power of the Holy Spirit to bring a sober word of truth about Jesus Christ that could convince a doubtful world that he is truly the Saviour of all mankind, the Saviour whose work is sufficent to redeem all.

Going through the book of Acts, this is exactly the picture that we see of the early Christian church. The church goes out from Jerusalem into the whole world and witnesses for Jesus Christ, giving sound testimony that he is the Saviour of the whole world. When we look at the church in Acts, there are certainly acts of mercy and kindness, but the emphasis always falls on the verbal heralding of the good news of Jesus Christ. Going through Acts, one cannot help but notice the numerous sermons and speeches. Kerygmatic speech makes up 20 to 30 percent of the book.[43] The spoken proclamation of the church is front and centre. It seems that the apostles and other early Christians understood very well what it was that Jesus Christ had commissioned them to do.

2.1.2.6 ROMANS 10:14-15

Another New Testament passage that explicitly ties being sent with the verbal proclamation of the gospel is Romans 10:14-15, "How then shall they call on Him in whom they have not believed? And how shall they believed in Him of whom they have not heard? And how shall they hear without a preacher? And how shall they preach unless they are sent? As it is written, 'How beautiful are the feet of those who preach the gospel of peace, who bring glad tidings of good things." In this passage, κηρυσσω (*kērussō*) is connected with ἀποστελλω (*apostellō*), possibly invoking the words of the Lord Jesus himself in the gospel accounts of the Great Commission. In this passage, the sender is not explicitly identified. However, in the immediate context of Romans 10, particularly with the quotes from

---

43. Steve Walton, "Acts: Many Questions, Many Answers," in *The Face of New Testament Studies: A Survey of Recent Research* (Grand Rapids: Baker Academic, 2004), ed. Scot McKnight and Grant R. Osborne, 238. Just a cursory survey reveals gospel proclamation reproduced in chapters 2-4, 7, 10, 13, 17, 20, 22, 24, 26, and 28. This does not include the instances where gospel proclamation is described but not reproduced.

The Definition of Mission(s)

the Old Testament, it is evident that God is the one who sends prophets and preachers. In three of the quotes, God's words come through the prophets.[44] In the broader context of Scripture, particularly of the New Testament passages examined thus far, it is Jesus Christ who does the sending. Jesus Christ sends men to herald or preach the gospel. When this happens, it is Christ speaking through them, and this places an obligation to obedience upon the hearers. This passage makes it very clear that the missionary task is about kerygmatic speech.

2.2 Defining Mission

Given the brief survey of the Scripture passages above, it is possible to formulate an answer to the question, "What is Mission?" Several elements have been isolated in the passages examined. Our study of the usage of κηρυσσω (*kērussō*) has indicated that we are looking at something official — it has to do with a solemn office or duty. Furthermore, κηρυσσω is indicative of a verbal act, as are the verbs μαρτυρεω (*martureō*) and μαθητευω (*mathēteusate*) The content of this speaking is captured in the use of the noun εὐαγγελιον (*evangelion*). Moreover, all of the passages either speak of or imply a going out. Three of the passages we surveyed placed some emphasis on the power of the Holy Spirit, so this should be accounted for in the definition. Finally, the ones who are targeted by this command are identified as παντα τα ἐθνη (*panta ta ethnē*) or, τον κοσμον ἁπαντα (*ton kosmon apanta*). The target audience is the broadest conceivable.

Putting those elements together, we arrive at this definition:

> Mission is the official sending of the church to go and make disciples by preaching and witnessing to the good news of Jesus Christ in all nations through the power of the Holy Spirit.

Several elements of this tentative definition deserve further comment. First, mission is the official sending *of the church*. Jesus Christ sent out his apostles, and we understand from elsewhere in Scripture that those apostles stood as representatives of the entire church.[45] Therefore, mission belongs with the church. Through the apostles, the church has been sent out by Jesus Christ.

---

44. In verse 19 with Deut.32:21, in verse 20 with Isa. 65:1, and in verse 21 with Isa. 65:2.

45. This is made clear by the fact that the Lord Jesus, in Matt. 28, spoke of "even to the end of the world." See J. I. Packer, *Evangelism and the Sovereignty of God* (Downer's Grove: IVP, 1961), 74.

The second thing we want to note with this proposed definition is that it is an *official* task. In other words, it is closely connected to office. In many Reformed churches there are special office bearers who are sent out to be missionary ministers. Through their verbal preaching and witnessing, they are ambassadors and heralds of Jesus Christ. They are standing in for Christ. When unbelievers accept them, they are accepting Christ. When unbelievers reject them, they are rejecting Christ. Unbelievers may reject the message, but they are not allowed to. Since it comes from the *Lord* Jesus, there is an obligation to obey the gospel call.

However, that is not to say that believers who are not office bearers cannot be regarded as missionaries under certain conditions. We recognize that all believers have a general office that includes being a prophet, confessing the name of Christ.[46] All believers can witness to the good news of their Saviour. However, when it comes to mission, we should keep things tied as closely as possible to the church. Working under the meaningful supervision of a church, unordained believers can legitimately claim the title of "missionary."

The geographical location of this task is also worth noting. In our proposed definition, it says, "in all nations." This captures the biblical data accurately. "In all nations" means that it makes no difference whether the outreach is done cross-culturally, in our own country or overseas. To further clarify, in this definition, "nation" is not to be identified with a "country." Many countries contain a multitude of nations or "people-groups." The borders of nations often transcend the borders of countries. This understanding of the term fits better with the biblical usage of the term τα ἔθνη (*ta ethnē*).[47]

Finally, we also note that this definition accounts for the "power of the Holy Spirit." Without his endowment, missions would be futile, both from the side of those sent out and from the side of those who receive. He provides the message preached, he creates the means by which the message is brought (the church), he guides the missionary enterprise, he calls the individual messengers and energizes them, he convicts of sin and he regenerates.[48] Apart from the Holy Spirit, the missionary cause would not even exist.

---

46. Heidelberg Catechism, Lord's Day 12.
47. See Karl Ludwig Schmidt, "ἔθνης" in *TDNT*, Vol. 2, 369.
48. Robertson McQuilkin, "The Role of the Holy Spirit in Missions," in *The Holy Spirit and Mission Dynamics*, ed. C. Douglas McConnell (Pasadena: William Carey Library, 1997), 23-31.

2.3 Distinguishing Mission and Evangelism?

This brings us into a brief discussion of whether there is any difference between mission and evangelism. Traditionally, many Reformed missiologists have maintained a distinction between the two concepts. Among others, J. Verkuyl follows this distinction: "Evangelism (*evangelistiek*) has to do with the scientific study of communicating Christian faith in Western society, while missiology centers on communicating it in the regions of Asia, Africa, Latin America, and the Caribbean."[49] However, with the advent of globalization, this formulation of the distinction has lost any usefulness. The peoples and cultures of Asia, Africa, Latin America, and the Caribbean are now increasingly found in Western society. In similar fashion, Western society is increasingly distanced from the Christian influences which formerly made its position unique. Therefore, it is no longer viable to formulate a distinction between mission and evangelism based on the place where the Christian faith is communicated.

David Bosch made a different proposal, arguing that "[m]ission is a much wider concept than evangelism. It is the total task which God has set the Church for the salvation of the world. Mission therefore has to do with crossing of frontiers between Church and world, frontiers of all kinds: geographical, sociological, political, ethnic, cultural, economic, religious, ideological . . . Mission means being sent by God to love, to serve, to preach, to teach, to heal."[50] To support this understanding, Bosch appealed to Luke 4:18-19. However, this passage speaks only of the task of the Lord Jesus and says nothing about the mission of the church. In the same article, Bosch defined evangelism with the words of Emilio Castro, "Evangelism is . . . 'our opening up the mystery of God's love to all people inside that mission, the linking of all human lives with the purpose of God manifested in Jesus Christ.' As such evangelism is the heart of mission."[51] Bosch went on to state that evangelism "consists in the proclamation of salvation in Christ to non-believers, in announcing forgiveness of sins, in calling people to repentance and faith in Christ, in inviting them to become living members of Christ's earthly community, and to begin a life in the power of the Holy Spirit."[52]

---

49. Johannes Verkuyl, *Contemporary Missiology* (Grand Rapids: Eerdmans, 1978), 9.
50. Bosch, "Mission and Evangelism," 169.
51. Bosch, "Mission and Evangelism," 170.
52. Bosch, "Mission and Evangelism," 170.

With the 1991 publication of his magnum opus, *Transforming Mission*, Bosch had slightly changed the equation. The meaning of mission was no longer clear: "We may, therefore, never arrogate it to ourselves to delineate mission too sharply and too self-confidently. Ultimately, mission remains undefinable; it should never be incarcerated in the narrow confines of our own predilections. The most we can hope for is to formulate some *approximations* of what mission is all about."[53] This change in approach to the definition of mission may be related to Bosch's view on the relationship of Scripture to missiology. Regardless, Bosch maintained his 1984 definition of evangelism in *Transforming Mission*. Similarly, he maintained that mission is wider than evangelism, but moved away from regarding evangelism as the heart of mission, preferring to describe it as "an essential dimension of the total activity of the Church."[54]

Since Bosch is off the mark on the definition of mission, his formulation of a distinction between mission and evangelism is also problematic. At the heart of this disagreement is a difference of methodology — Bosch did not seem to regard the exegesis of the Scriptures as a valid method to determine one's definitions.[55] In the approach taken here, evangelism and mission are closer than Bosch would have allowed. In fact, they are nearly to be identified with one another. If we understand evangelism as a communication of the εὐαγγέλιον (*evangelion*), then evangelism is what the church has been sent to do: "preaching and witnessing to the good news of Jesus Christ." In other words the mission of the church is evangelism.[56]

2.4 Mission and Missions

Another oft-used distinction with which we have to reckon is the one between *mission* in the singular and *missions* in the plural. Bosch tied this distinction into the difference between the *missio Dei* (the mission of God) and *missiones ecclesiae* (the missions of the church). Mission is the *missio Dei* and missions are the *missiones ecclesiae*. He wrote, "'Mission' singular, remains primary; 'missions' in the plural, constitutes a derivative."[57] Bosch's distinction is predicated upon an acceptance of the concept of *missio Dei*.

---

53. David J. Bosch, *Transforming Mission: Paradigm Shifts in Theology of Mission* (Maryknoll: Orbis, 1991), 9.
54. Bosch, *Transforming Mission*, 412.
55. Bosch, *Transforming Mission*, 9.
56. See Haak, *Gereformeerde Missiologie & Oecumenica*, 34. When Haak provides his definition, he equates mission and evangelism.
57. Bosch, *Transforming Mission*, 391.

He elaborated on the concept, "In the new image mission is not primarily an activity of the church, but an attribute of God. God is a missionary God."[58] Insofar as God is the one who seeks out that which is lost, there is a kernel of truth in this concept. However, J. DeJong argued that the notion of *missio Dei* is inadequate, as it "tends to blur the specific mandate given by Christ to his church."[59] David Hesselgrave offered a similar criticism, pointing out that in ecumenical circles "the effort to carry out *missio Dei* came to be divorced from obedience to God's Great Commission."[60] Though mission begins with the eternal decree of the Father, it is historically executed through the mandate of the Son given to the church. In this picture, there is one mission. The church carries out the one mission given to her by Jesus Christ. While the *missio Dei* notion does underscore the Triune God's involvement as the author and primary agent of mission (specifically through the work of the Holy Spirit), it cannot be used to make a meaningful distinction between mission and missions.

Others have taken a different approach to the question. In the evangelical world, George Peters argued that mission was a more comprehensive term, referring to the total task of the church in the world: "It is the church as 'sent' (a pilgrim, stranger, witness, prophet, servant, as salt, as light, etc.) in this world."[61] Peters maintained that missions are the actual work and "the practical realization of the mission of the church."[62]

Biblically speaking, the distinction between "mission" and "missions" is groundless and indefensible. There is one mission given by Jesus Christ to the church. Nevertheless, we recognize a common parlance in which missionaries speak about their mission, i.e. the organization under which they do their work. This comes close to the manner in which Peters expressed the distinction. The historical development of disparate churches or organizations involved with mission work is the only defensible explanation for the continuing use of the plural "missions."

2.5 Missiology and Missiological

This brings us to briefly consider our use of two other words: "mis-

---

58. Bosch, *Transforming Mission*, 390.
59. DeJong, "Even So I Send You," 473.
60. David J. Hesselgrave, *Paradigms in Conflict:10 Key Questions in Christian Missions Today* (Grand Rapids: Kregel, 2005), 323.
61. Cited by A. Scott Moreau, "Mission and Missions," in *EDWM*, 637.
62. Moreau, "Mission and Missions," 637.

siology" and "missiological." Missiology is simply the science or study of mission in all its various aspects. Missiology has the task of delineating the what and how of mission — and to be obedient to Christ, the task has to be undertaken entirely in submission to the Scriptures. Missiological is the adjectival form.

For the purposes of this study, therefore, we understand that when we speak about the missiological relevance of the Belgic Confession, we are inquiring about the precise relevance of the Confession for the study of mission in all its various aspects. Given the definition outlined above, what does the Belgic Confession say to the study of "the official sending of the church to go and make disciples by preaching and witnessing to the good news of Jesus Christ in all nations through the power of the Holy Spirit"? When we say "study," we mean to include not only the more academic or theoretical aspects of this field, but also the practical and concrete. With a nod to Robert Recker, we could ask: what does the Belgic Confession have to say to the construction of a contemporary Reformed science of mission? Does the Belgic Confession inspire us to missionary passion, and if so, how?

2.6 THE CONCEPT OF MISSION IN THE SIXTEENTH CENTURY

Before proceeding further, we also need to give attention to the understanding of mission in the sixteenth-century Western European milieu. Here we need to shift from considering a precise definition to a broad conception or understanding of mission. This shift is required because the notion of a precise definition of mission is tied to the development of missiology as a discipline and that development does not take place in the sixteenth century. In the last chapter, we explored sixteenth-century conceptions of the relationship between the gospel, the church, and the world. Exploring Luther and Calvin, we came to a general picture of this relationship. Similarly, we can outline certain contours of a definition of mission in the conceptions of some of the contemporaries of Guido de Brès and the Belgic Confession. This will be done by briefly examining one of the early Reformers, Martin Bucer (1491-1551), and a slightly later figure, Adrian Saravia (1532-1612).

2.6.1 MARTIN BUCER

Martin Bucer was born in Selestat, an Alsatian city in modern-day France. Though it is impossible to know for sure, it is generally thought that he was born in 1491.[63] Entering the Dominican Order in 1506, he was eventually sent to Heidelberg for further studies. While in Heidelberg, he converted to the Reformed faith and later became a pastor, first in the German region of the Palatinate and then in Strasbourg in 1523. In 1549, Bucer took up an invitation to assist in the reformation of the Church of England and was appointed as a professor at Cambridge. He died in 1551 and his remains were later exhumed and burned by Queen Mary. Bucer is remembered primarily as an irenicist who worked tirelessly for the unity of magisterial Protestantism in Western Europe.

Several scholars have also described Bucer as a "father of Reformed mission."[64] In the same vein, Bosch describes him as one of the Reformers who "propounded an essentially missionary theology."[65] Acknowledging Walter Holsten's contribution to the study of the Reformation and mission, Scott Hendrix describes Bucer as one of three Reformers (Luther and Calvin are the others) who "conceived of reformation as mission."[66] We shall now proceed to examine the evidence for these claims.

Though Bucer was a prolific author, only one of his major works has been translated, and even this translation is an abridgement. The book in question is *De Regno Christi*, translated in 1969 by Wilhelm Pauck.[67] This was his last book and he wrote it in 1550 for Edward VI "in the hope that during his reign and under his own auspices, the Reformation would be established in England in such a way that it would shape and penetrate the entire life of the nation."[68] We can consider this book a product of a mature theologian and a likely place to encounter whatever conceptions of mission he may have held.

---

63. The definitive modern biography on Bucer is: Martin Greschat, *Martin Bucer: A Reformer and His Times*, trans. by Stephen E. Buckwalter (Louisville: Westminster John Knox, 2004).

64. The expression comes from L. J. Joosse, *Reformatie en zending, Bucer en Walaeus: vaders van reformatorische zending* (Goes: Oosterbaan & Le Cointre B.V., 1988).

65. Bosch, *Transforming Mission*, 245.

66. Hendrix, *Recultivating the Vineyard*, 86. The reference is to Walter Holsten, "Reformation und Mission," *Archiv für Reformationsgeschichte* 44 (1953): 1-32.

67. *De Regno Christi* (DRC) is found in the Library of Christian Classics volume *Melanchthon and Bucer*, ed. Wilhelm Pauck (Philadelphia: the Westminster Press, 1969), 153-394.

68. DRC (Editor's Introduction), 157.

It is especially in Book One of *De Regno Christi* that we find Bucer speaking about the extension of Christ's kingdom (which he identifies at certain points with the Church). One of the first things that he notes is that this kingdom is ruled by a king who is ever present and ever active. He writes: "But our heavenly King, Jesus Christ, is, according to his promise, with us everywhere and every day, 'to the consummation of the world' (Matt. 28:20). He himself sees, attends to, and accomplishes whatever pertains to the salvation of his own."[69] While he does not need representatives, he has chosen to "use ministers and certain specific kinds of offices for his work of salvation."[70] This includes ministers who are sent by Christ to Christian kings and magistrates, for, as Bucer notes, "...the Lord sends his ministers as the Father has sent him (John 20:21)."[71] Along the same trajectory, towards the end of chapter 2, Bucer writes: "According to his infinite goodness and mercy, he also offers salvation to all and he obviates the excuse of ignorance for anyone. As once he commanded all the sons to be circumcised, whether freeborn or slaves (Gen. 17:12), in order that they should observe all his religious laws, so he wills now that all should be baptized (Matt. 28:19) and then be taught under the discipline of the Church whatever he has commanded."[72] At this point already, we can note that Bucer takes the commission given by Christ to the apostles and carries it over into his own day.

Chapter 3 consists of a survey of Bible passages which more fully explain Bucer's program for the establishment of the Kingdom of Christ. One of the striking features in the first pages is his attention to Isaiah 2:2-5, a passage which (according to Bucer) makes several references to the expansion of the Kingdom of Christ in all the nations. Again he indicates that Matthew 28:18-20 highlights the need for Christian ministers, enabled by the Lord, to recommend God's ways from the Scriptures. He notes that the apostles gave an example of obedience to this command on the day of Pentecost.[73]

Further into chapter 3, Bucer considers the prophecy found in Isaiah 11:6-9. He gives special attention to the words of verse 9: "They shall not hurt or harm in all my holy mountain, for the earth is filled with the knowledge of the Lord, like the all-covering waters of the sea." From this passage,

---

69. DRC, 179.
70. DRC, 180.
71. DRC, 187.
72. DRC, 190.
73. DRC, 193.

he deduces that "[o]ne must note carefully how great a knowledge of God is here promised to the Church, to be spread to all, far and wide."[74] While at this particular place he applies that especially to "every baptized person," he goes on momentarily to apply this in a much broader way.

He does this in the context of Isaiah 11:10, which says, "At that time, the root of Jesse shall stand as a sign for the people, and the nations shall seek it, and its repose will be glorious." Bucer explains: "Here the prophet foretells that the gospel much be preached effectively to all nations so that as many people as possible from all nations will go to Christ as a saving sign and find in him a glorious rest for their souls, both in this and in the future life, according to his promise (Matt.11:28-30)."[75] He goes on to state that Christ must be made known to all men and he emphatically states that the church which does not make the "clear and constant preaching of the gospel" a high priority can only vainly boast about being the church of Christ.[76] A few paragraphs further, he makes the same bold claim: "Churches, therefore, where that voice is silent, call themselves in vanity churches of Christ."[77]

Genuine churches of Christ, according to Bucer, will present the Son of God as the fount of all blessing and the one in whom the forgiveness of sins may be found. Furthermore, this message is to be preached indiscriminately, not only to the members of the church, but also to those outside. Says Bucer, "Any true church of Christ should preach and proclaim this indefatigably and as clearly as possible, not only to its own members but also to whatever peoples and manner of men it can: 'Behold your God.'"[78]

Bucer sees this proclamation of the gospel to all the nations as the responsibility of the King and the citizens of the kingdom, but it comes especially to a certain cadre. He writes that "the proclamation of the gospel is the main task of Christ the King and all his citizens, and most especially of those who have received a particular calling for this in his Church."[79] Later, with a quote from Rom. 10:15, he notes that those particularly called to this task should be ministers of the gospel with a special

---

74. DRC, 196.
75. DRC, 197.
76. DRC, 197.
77. DRC, 199.
78. DRC, 199.
79. DRC, 201.

calling to be evangelists.[80] Romans 10:14-17 was an important text for Bucer's missionary perspective because it highlighted the fact that Jesus Christ speaks through the preaching.[81] In all this, it is evident that Bucer's mission concept was ecclesio-centric and involved a high view of ecclesiastical office.

Next, we can observe Bucer's slightly more extended treatment of Matthew 28:18-20 in chapter 4. His words here are worth quoting in full:

> Here the Lord teaches, first that he has received power from the Father over all, both men and spirits, and even over all creatures. Next, that his Kingdom ought to be offered to all nations. Further, that all the citizens of his kingdom ought to be incorporated into himself in Holy Baptism and to be dedicated to the communion and discipline of his Church. In this regard, it is the function of the ministers of his Kingdom to teach all the baptized to observe whatever he has commanded, to teach them diligently, perseveringly, and in every way both to care about the precepts of Christ and wholly to consecrate themselves day by day to be more fully perfected in all things.[82]

It should be noted again that Bucer clearly sees the Great Commission as applicable to the church of his day.

This brings us to consider briefly what may appear to be a contradiction in Bucer's thought. Harry Boer alleges that, while he did have a missionary concern, Bucer "did not free himself from the conception that the Great Commission was limited to the apostles."[83] He quotes from Bucer's 1538 work, *Von der waren Seelsorge* where he says that the elders of the church "do not have an apostolic call and command to go to strange nations."[84] Perhaps the explanation for this apparent contradiction rests in the fact that *De Regno Christi* is a later work, having been published in 1550. It is not unusual for men to change their minds as they mature. Alternatively, the explanation may also be found in the fact that *Von der waren Seelsorge* is speaking about the elders of the church whereas *De*

---

80. DRC, 226-227.
81. Joosse, *Reformatie en Zending*, 63.
82. DRC, 222.
83. Harry R. Boer, *Pentecost and Missions* (Grand Rapids: Eerdmans, 1961), 20.
84. Boer, *Pentecost and Missions*, 20. The quote is from M. Bucer, *Von der waren Seelsorge* (Straszburg, 1538), 46. Presumably this is Boer's own translation.

Regno Christi speaks of men who are ordained as minister-evangelists. At any rate, the allegation of Boer is difficult to maintain in light of Bucer's repeated quotations from various formulations of the Great Commission in *De Regno Christi*, his emphasis on Romans 10:14-17, and his application of those passages to the church of his day.[85]

Finally, we can note that Bucer exhorted Edward VI to encourage the sending out of evangelists throughout his realm. These evangelists would be sent to the churches and they "must announce assiduously, zealously and in a timely fashion to the people everywhere the good news of the Kingdom."[86] As noted before, these men were to be ministers of the church, trained and chosen especially for this evangelistic calling. The invocation at the end of *De Regno Christi* expresses Bucer's hope that this would extend also beyond the realm of Edward VI. Bucer prayed that God would "give him success in all things, for the increase of His own glory and for the wonderful consolation and salvation of all the people who are his, in this and other realms."[87]

All of the foregoing evidence points to the fact that Bucer did in fact have a mission-concept, even if he did not use the word or provide an explicit definition. Hendrix comments that the agenda laid out in *De Regno Christi* was "manifestly a missionary venture; indeed, he made it sound as if he had landed in the heart of heathenism."[88] Moreover, his eyes were not only set on the subjects of Edward VI — there is ample evidence in *De Regno Christi* to demonstrate that Bucer also recognized a scriptural responsibility with respect to those of other nations. To use a modern distinction, Bucer saw the necessity and obligation of both home and foreign mission.

In conclusion, we can state that Bucer conceived of mission as being the extension and consolidation of the Kingdom of Christ through the preaching of the gospel. He believed that the Church has a responsibility to go into all the nations and bring the gospel so that more and more people are brought under the reign of Christ. He saw this primarily as the responsibility of those called to the office of minister/evangelist. Through these men, the voice of Jesus Christ himself would be heard. Moreover, Bucer conceived of mission as belonging to the essence (*esse*) of the

---

85. Besides those passages already mentioned, see also DRC, 228 and 260.
86. DRC, 269. Cf. 390.
87. DRC, 394.
88. Hendrix, *Recultivating the Vineyard*, 85.

Church. A unique feature of Bucer's mission-concept was the involvement of the civil magistrate. *De Regno Christi* was addressed to Edward VI, and Bucer thought that the king had a responsibility to ensure that the gospel is proclaimed, not only in his own realm, but also in others.

2.6.2 Adrian Saravia

Adrian Saravia was born in Flanders in 1532, making him nearly 30 years old when the Belgic Confession was written and published. Saravia is an important figure in our study for he spent much of his life and some of his ministry in the Lowlands where the Belgic Confession first appeared. As mentioned in the previous chapter, in later life, in a 1612 letter to Uytenbogaert (a Remonstrant leader), Saravia showed familiarity with the origin and authorship of the Confession. While he was an early promoter of the Confession, it is certain that he was not involved with its writing.[89]

Saravia's adult life featured many moves between England and the Netherlands.[90] He had been a Franciscan friar. By 1557 he was converted to the Reformed faith and then spent time in Paris, Geneva, and England. A couple of moves later, he was back in the Netherlands, serving as a pastor of the Walloon church in Antwerp (1562). The following year he moved to Guernsey to become a headmaster of a school and a minister in St. Peter's Church. This officially signalled his change of sentiments regarding church polity from Reformed/Presbyterian to Episcopalian. This change had taken place some time earlier, but it took some time before Saravia acted on his new beliefs. However, he returned to the Netherlands upon accepting a position as a professor in Leiden in 1584, becoming rector of that university the following year. Because of political troubles between England and the Netherlands (which included the church at Leiden), Saravia was forced to flee to England in 1588, where he remained for the rest of his life.

Bosch describes Saravia as a Reformation-era champion "of the idea that the 'Great Commission' continued to be binding on the church and had to be understood in the sense of going out to those beyond the boundaries of Christendom."[91] Thomas asserts (wrongly, as we have seen with

---

89. Gootjes, *The Belgic Confession*, 35-39.

90. The only biography that appears to exist on Saravia is: Willem Nijenhuis, *Adrianus Saravia (1532-1613): Dutch Calvinist, First Reformed Defender of the English Episcopal Church Order on the Basis of the Ius Divinum* (Leiden: E. J. Brill, 1980).

91. Bosch, *Transforming Mission*, 247.

The Definition of Mission(s)

Bucer) that Saravia was the only Reformation period theologian who "was able to emancipate himself completely from the dominant Lutheran and Calvinist view that the Great Commission was fulfilled by the apostles."[92] In this way, says Thomas, Saravia was a precursor to William Carey. J. H. Bavinck likewise (again, wrongly) identifies Saravia as the first Protestant theologian to argue that the command of Matthew 28:19-20 is meant for the church of all ages.[93] Let us now move on to consider briefly the mission conception of this unique figure.

Saravia's writings on mission cannot be separated from his agenda for the justification of Episcopalian polity. When he argues for the abiding validity of Matthew 28:19-20, he does so on the basis that the bishops of the church are the appointed successors of the apostles. This is evident in several of his writings, but it is most fully developed in his 1590 work *De Diversis Ministrorum Evangelii Gradibus*.[94]

Two chapters of that work (17 and 18) are particularly devoted to mission, but the concept already emerges on the first page when Saravia writes: "The preaching of the Gospel is Christ's mission to all peoples."[95] We can note already the use of the word "mission," something we did not encounter in Bucer's *De Regno Christi*. According to Nijenhuis, Saravia insisted that this mission is valid for "unlimited time and knows no boundaries."[96] Saravia wrote, "The command of preaching the gospel and the sending to every nation are precepts to be understood of the apostles, but are also understood to obligate the church. For the command of announcing the gospel to unbelieving nations referred not only to the age of the apostles, but to all peoples which might exist until the end of the world."[97] We can note here that Saravia understands the preaching of the gospel to be at the heart of mission.

Further in that same chapter, Saravia goes on to argue that the continuing validity of the Great Commission hangs on the successors of the apostles. He explained, "If the apostolic authority had been temporary, a purely personal and peculiar gift, and not intended for their associates and helpers, they would be present for the Lord's work for which they

---

92. Thomas, *Classic Texts*, 41.
93. Bavinck, *Zending in een wereld in nood*, 34-35. Cf. Warneck, *Outline of a History of Protestant Missions*, 20-22.
94. Nijenhuis, *Adrianus Saravia*, 240.
95. Nijenhuis, *Adrianus Saravia*, 240.
96. Nijenhuis, *Adrianus Saravia*, 241.
97. Thomas, *Classic Texts*, 42.

were destined. Yet since they knew their ministry and those things for which they enjoyed authority rather to have been given to the church than to persons, they understood the making of companions in their apostolic power, whom they also understood as their successors."[98] Thus, in the thinking of Saravia, the abiding validity of the mission imperative is not something given to individuals but to the church, and specifically to the successors of the apostles. Moreover, because mission was a matter of the whole church, Saravia argued that it was necessary to entrust this task to more than a local ministerial office.[99]

Like Bucer, Saravia also conceived of mission in terms of the kingdom of Christ. This is evident when he writes: "The fact that at the present no one is sent by the churches of Christ to the nations who do not know him, does not count against the authority for mission but proves a lack of persons fit to be sent, or certainly a want of enthusiasm for the spread of Christ's kingdom."[100] Saravia therefore equated the spreading or propagation of Christ's kingdom with the mission of the church and noted the lack of zeal for such in his day.

There are two more important features of Saravia's mission-conception. Dealing with the question of whether the gospel has indeed come to every nation (as many in his day alleged), Saravia writes: "Is it necessary to parade examples of the fathers from the primitive church? With what application, with what labor, and with what blood of martyrs have not the churches been planted and irrigated? The story is so well known that simply to rehearse it would not be profitable."[101] Saravia went on to write that in spite of all those efforts over 1500 years, much of the world remained unevangelized. From these words, we can note (as Nijenhuis does) that Saravia believes that the abiding mission imperative applies to both the preservation and strengthening (irrigation) of existing churches and the planting of new churches.[102] A second important feature is that he connects the blood of martyrs with the mission of the church in antiquity. Though he does not appear to develop this, this is suggestive, and this notion will be explored more fully in the next chapter.

---

98. Thomas, *Classic Texts*, 42.
99. Nijenhuis, *Adrianus Saravia*, 242.
100. Nijenhuis, *Adrianus Saravia*, 241.
101. Thomas, *Classic Texts*, 42.
102. Nijenhuis, *Adrianus Saravia*, 241.

Saravia's writings on this subject were not widely accepted and, in fact, created controversy, especially with Calvin's successor in Geneva, Theodore Beza. Beza could not accept Saravia's interpretation of Matthew 28:19-20, and his aversion can perhaps be attributed to the fact that this interpretation was closely tied to Saravia's polemicizing for Episcopalian polity. A sort of hermeneutical suspicion made it difficult for some to separate the abiding validity of the Great Commission from arguments for the abiding validity of apostleship in the Church of Christ.

In summary, we can note that Saravia was indeed a sixteenth-century scholar with a mission-conception whose contours are readily identifiable. We discovered that Saravia used the word "mission," and by it he understood the Christ-mandated preaching of the gospel to the nations — a command which is permanently valid for the church of all times and places. However, he also included in that the strengthening of existing churches and the planting of new ones. Further, he conceived mission to be the spreading of the kingdom of Christ. Historically, that has taken place through preaching *and* through martyrdom. Finally, he conceived of mission as being the responsibility of the whole church and particularly of the apostolic successors in the episcopacy.

2.7 CONCLUSION

It has been noted that the word "mission" often carries with it a negative connotation in our modern era. For that reason, some have considered whether it is necessary to retain the word in the life of the church. After all, some might argue, the word itself is not found in the Scriptures — though ἀποστελλω (*apostellō*) comes close. Furthermore, the word has become worn out and unduly multivalent.[103] Despite all this, it is clear that the word is here to stay. Moreover, even if the word is not expressly used, the concept is no less derived from God's Word than the doctrine of the Trinity. Just as the doctrine of the Trinity required clear definition for the sake of purity and truth in the church, so also there is a strong need to be clear about the definition of mission.

We have seen that while attempts at clarity on the definition did not emerge until the formation of missiology as a discipline, various conceptions of mission have long existed. These testify to the perspicuity of God's Word, also on this matter. We noted that these conceptions of mission

---

103. Klauspeter Blaser, "Should we stop using the term 'mission'?" *International Review of Mission* 301 (January 1987): 68-71

also existed during the sixteenth century, during the time of the writing of the Belgic Confession. It remains for our study to discover whether the document reflects any familiarity with those conceptions. We will begin to do that in the next chapter.

Going outside the framework of our immediate discussion, we must insist that the definition of mission ultimately matters because it involves thankful obedience to Christ and love for him. Having received such a great salvation, we cannot be slack in our obedience; rather, out of gratitude and love we must exert ourselves to understand first what Christ would have us do, and second, how he would have us do it. This is the task of missiology, the science of mission. Missiology has the task of delineating the what and how of mission — and to be obedient to Christ, the task has to be undertaken in submission to the Scriptures. Having investigated these preliminary matters, we can now proceed to determine whether the Belgic Confession speaks to that discipline in a meaningful way.

CONFESSION
DE FOY, FAICTE D'VN
COMMVN ACCORD PAR LES

Fideles qui conuersent és pays Bas, lesquels desirent viure selon la pureté de l'Euangile de nostre Seigneur Iesus-Christ.

Auec vne remonstrance aux Magistrats de Flandres, Braban, Hainault, Artois, Chastelenie de l'Isle, & autres regions circonuoisines.

I. PIERRE 3.

Soyez tousiours appareillez à respondre à chacun qui vous demande raison de l'esperance qui est en vous.

LVC 12. 7. 9.

Quiconque me confessera deuant les hommes, le fils de l'homme le confessera aussi deuãt les Anges de Dieu.

Mais qui me reniera deuant les hommes, il sera renié deuant les Anges de Dieu.

1562.

Chapter Three
Original Missionary Nature and Intent

3.0 Introduction

The preliminary matters of context and definitions having been dealt with, we can now proceed to explore the relationship between mission and the Belgic Confession in some detail. In this chapter, we do that by first exploring the potentially fruitful area of the relationship between mission and martyrdom and how this bears on the missiological relevance of this symbol. Synthesizing and building on material from the last two chapters, we will also explore the missionary perspective of the magisterial Protestant Reformers, the Reformed Churches of the Lowlands, Guido de Brès and the Belgic Confession.

3.1 The Belgic Confession, Martyrdom and Mission[1]

Among the confessions of Reformed Churches of a Dutch background, the context of the Belgic Confession is unique. Only the Belgic Confession was forged in the furnace of intense persecution. The Heidelberg Catechism and Canons of Dort emerged out of completely different circumstances that may or may not have their own bearing on their missiological significance. Persecution and suffering molded the Belgic Confession and should also mold how we understand its relevance for mission.

3.1.1 Martyrdom and Persecution in Scripture and History

Martyrdom and persecution have to be carefully defined. Especially with the word "martyrdom" (and its cognates), the word can have slightly different nuances depending on the historical context. Our English word

---

1. An earlier version of this section first appeared as my article "Martyrdom, Mission, and the Belgic Confession," *The Confessional Presbyterian* 4 (2008): 109-121.

"martyr" is, of course, derived from the Greek μαρτυς (*martus*). The root word has a historical development which will be helpful to outline briefly.

Μαρτυς and its cognate forms (especially μαρτυρεω (*martureō*) and μαρτυρια (*marturia*)) were originally used in secular Greek with two slightly different senses. It either denoted an eyewitness to an event, or it could be used to "describe a witness to the facts in the legal sphere."[2] Much the same usage was found in the Septuagint, although the latter meaning was definitely coming to the fore. We also find this meaning on a number of occasions in the New Testament. Both μαρτυς (*martus*) and μαρτυρεω (*martureō*) are used in several contexts with a legal connotation, directing readers to the idea of a courtroom.[3] This courtroom has God as judge and various witnesses, including Christ and the apostles, are present to testify against the accused. It is this usage we find in the Lukan versions of the Great Commission in the gospel (Luke 24:48) and in Acts (1:8). However, these words can also be used in a less concrete way to refer to those who have seen or heard something and are simply reporting the truths of what they saw. This is the usage most often applied to the apostles.

In the New Testament there is also a development towards these terms referring to one who dies for his faith. We find such a usage in Acts 22:20 where Stephen is referred to as a martyr. The term μαρτυς (*martus*) is also used in this way in Revelation 17:6. In that passage, Scripture speaks of "the blood of the martyrs of Jesus" — a clear reference to those who have died for their faith. However, on these usages, Strathmann makes this cautionary comment: "Not every committed Christian who dies for his faith is called μαρτυς. The name is reserved for those who are at work as evangelical witnesses... The name is reserved for those who prove the final seriousness of their witness by suffering death."[4]

Moving along chronologically past the New Testament, we find that the word group moves more in the direction of one who suffers death because of his witness.[5] This increasingly happens until the two are basically identified in patristic Greek and, through the use of the church, into

---

2. H. Strathmann, "Μαρτυς," in *TDNT* 4:476.
3. Cf. Matthew 18:16, 26:65; John 8:12-20; 1 Timothy 5:19; 6:12; 1 Peter 5:1, etc.
4. Strathmann, "Μαρτυς," 495.
5. See Allison A. Trites, "Μαρτυς and Martyrdom in the Apocalypse: A Semantic Study," *Novum Testamentum* 15.1 (January 1973): 72-73.

Latin as *martyr*.⁶ Strathmann notes that *The Martyrdom of Polycarp* is the first work to have all the words of this group found with the "fixed martyrological sense."⁷ By the middle of the second century, this usage became firmly established, particularly through the experiences of the church in Asia Minor.⁸

As already noted, the word group passed into ecclesiastical Latin, most likely through the influence of the Vulgate. Via Latin, we find the word "martyr" appearing in numerous other European languages, including English. Its earliest appearance in English is traced to circa 900 in Bede's *Ecclesiastical History* and a reference to St. Alban, the first British martyr.⁹ The sense is clearly that of the "fixed martyrological" variety. With the passage of time, "the events of the Reformation caused the word to be popularly associated esp. with death by fire."¹⁰

By way of conclusion, in its original sense μαρτυς and its cognates initially referred to the act of witnessing in a trial. This sense is found in the New Testament as well. Most of the usages refer to a simple act of observing either by sight or by sound. However, it eventually began to refer to the act of witnessing to the truth of something through suffering and especially death. As we noted, this sense is also found in the New Testament, but it comes to fuller expression in later times in patristic Greek, ecclesiastical Latin and then in all European languages.

The concept of persecution also receives attention in the Scriptures. Among other places, the verb διωκω (*diōkō*) is used by the Lord Jesus in Matthew 5 with respect to the covenant people. In verse 10, he speaks in one of the Beatitudes of those who "are persecuted for righteousness' sake." In verses 11 and 12, he notes that this persecution is the same pattern as that experienced by the Old Testament prophets. In verse 44, he encourages his followers to pray for those who persecute them. In John 15:20, the Lord Jesus notes that if his enemies persecuted him, they will also persecute his followers. Being a follower of the Lord Jesus and facing persecution are often associated in the New Testament. The Lord warns

---

6. From what I can tell, the word was not used in classical Latin. I did a concordance search with the Vulgate and could only find the word used in the passage from Revelation 17:6.
7. Strathmann, "Μαρτυς," 505.
8. Strathmann, "Μαρτυς," 506.
9. *Oxford English Dictionary* (New York: OUP, 1971), s.v. "martyr."
10. *Oxford English Dictionary* (New York: OUP, 1971), s.v. "martyr."

his followers repeatedly that they will face stiff opposition — often from the covenant people.

If we attempt to define it, persecution is simply the pattern of opposition faced by the Lord Jesus in his earthly ministry. This pattern of opposition is re-enacted in the lives of his disciples then and now. This pattern involves attacks, subtle and not so subtle. When we look to what the Lord experienced, then we are reminded that persecution includes the various forms of suffering.

This overview of the history of the concepts of martyrdom and persecution gives us some helpful background as we begin looking at the relationship between the Belgic Confession and mission. In any case, the Belgic Confession cannot be properly understood apart from its original intent and context. However, it remains necessary first to give ample attention to the question of the relationship between martyrdom/persecution and mission.

3.1.2 Martyrdom and Mission

The connection between martyrdom and mission has not been explored in any great depth. There have been several recent examinations of the phenomenon of martyrdom in general, but these do not explore any possible correlation with mission. For instance, the book *Martyrdom: The Psychology, Theology and Politics of Self-Sacrifice* does not even mention the concept of mission. In the chapter on "the Theology of Martyrdom," only the Jewish and Islamic conceptions of martyrdom are explored theologically.[11] Lacey Baldwin Smith's *Fools, Martyrs, Traitors* traces the concept of martyrdom in a very general way. Christian martyrdom is considered, but not as a phenomenon related in any way to mission.[12] Finally, a recent anthology of writings related to martyrdom also considers the Christian variety but does not provide any direction on a possible relationship to the missionary enterprise.[13]

Historically, Christian writers, while writing a lot about martyrdom, have not really written about martyrdom as a phenomenon of mission.

---

11. Rona M. Fields ed., *Martyrdom: The Psychology, Theology and Politics of Self-Sacrifice* (Westport, Conn.: Praeger, 2004).
12. Lacey Baldwin Smith, *Fools, Martyrs, Traitors: the Story of Martyrdom in the Western World* (New York: Alfred A. Knopf, 1997).
13. Jan Willem Van Henten and Friedrich Avemarie, *Martyrdom and Noble Death: Selected Texts from Graeco-Roman, Jewish and Christian Antiquity* (London: Routledge, 2002).

Original Missionary Nature and Intent

One of the earliest examples of someone who did is the church father Tertullian. In his most important writing, *The Apology*, Tertullian provided a defense of the Christian faith to the provincial governors of the Roman Empire. Towards the end of the document, Tertullian makes the memorable statement: "The oftener we are mown down by you, the more in number we grow; the blood of Christians is seed."[14] Now it is true that there is some variation in how these words are translated in the different English editions. Many translators felt compelled to add some words to explain what the seed is going to produce: faith, a greater harvest, the church, or a new life. Regardless, the context makes it clear enough. Tertullian believed that God uses martyrdom and persecution in some mysterious way to cause the Christian faith to grow in strength and numbers.

In more modern times, martyrdom has mostly received attention as an historical phenomenon. This is especially true in missiological circles. Missiologists give some attention to martyrdom, but mostly because so many missionaries were martyred. The history of mission is filled with accounts of suffering and blood shed unto death for the faith. Yet this aspect of mission does not receive as much attention as it deserves. A survey of leading textbooks from different backgrounds illustrates that martyrdom is usually considered by missiologists to be a mere historical fact rather than a component or facet of the Christian mission worthy of deeper thought and reflection.[15] This lacuna led missiologist William D. Taylor to reflect in his closing address at the Iguassu Consultation, "How can the church around the world best prepare to grapple with the increasing waves of persecution and suffering? What does it mean to be

---

14. "Plures efficimur quotiens metimur a vobis; semen est sanguis Christianorum." Apol. 50.13. (accessed at www.tertullian.org/latin/apologeticus.htm on February 13, 2008); the English translation is from the Ante-Nicene Fathers.

15. J. H. Bavinck's *An Introduction to the Science of Missions* (Phillipsburg: P&R, 1960) does not appear to have any discussion apart from mentions of the historical fact of martyrdom. Paul J. Visser in *Heart for the Gospel, Heart for the World: The Life and Thought of a Reformed Pioneer Missiologist, Johan Herman Bavinck [1895-1964]* (Eugene: Wipf and Stock, 2003), likewise makes no mention of martyrdom in the missiological thought of Bavinck. While noting that "mission never has progressed without suffering and martyrdom," Moreau, Corwin, and McGee also essentially treat martyrdom as an historical phenomenon (*Introducing World Missions*, 146). David J. Bosch in his treatment of "Luke's missionary paradigm" follows the same trajectory: "...mission, of necessity, encounters adversity and suffering." (*Transforming Mission*, 121-122).

the global body of Christ in these contexts? Where is our theology of martyrdom?"[16]

3.1.2.1 KEVIN VANHOOZER

Let us now look at two recent authors who have made efforts at setting forth something of a "theology of martyrdom" in connection with mission.[17] Kevin Vanhoozer takes a specialized approach to the subject, looking at mission and martyrdom in connection with "the epistemology of the cross." This fits with the theme of the book in which his essay is found: *To Stake a Claim: Mission and the Western Crisis of Knowledge*.

Vanhoozer begins with a recognition of the dual sense of the word "martyr." On the one hand, it refers to "giving witness," and on the other hand to "giving one's life for the truth." He wants to argue that martyrdom is the ultimate sine qua non for staking a theological truth claim. It is this, he contends, because it "ultimately communicates truth claims about the way of wisdom." In turn, the witness of a martyr speaks to the postmodernist critiques of "traditional modes of justification," as well as to the typically postmodern coldness towards the very notion of truth.[18] We should note at this point that Vanhoozer's introduction of a response to postmodernism does indicate his intent to speak to the contemporary situation. Whether or not this is rel-

---

16. William D. Taylor, "Drawing to a close: inviting reflective, passionate, and globalized practitioners," in *Global Missiology for the 21st Century: The Iguassu Dialogue*, William D. Taylor ed. (Grand Rapids: Baker Academic, 2001), 552.

17. Other treatments (of varying helpfulness) include Georg Evers, "The Problem of Martyrdom in Missionary Countries," in *Rethinking Martyrdom — Concilium 2003/1*, ed. Teresa Okure, Jon Sobrino, and Felix Wilfred (London: SCM Press: 2003), 87-95; Hans von Campenhausen, "Das Martyrium in der Mission," in *Kirchengeschichte als Missionsgeschichte Band I: Die Alte Kirche*, ed. Heinzgunter Frohnes and Uwe W. Knorr (Munich: Chr. Kaiser Verlag, 1974), 71-85; Andras Koranyi, "Mission as Call to Metanoia and Witness to Hope: A Historical Survey, in *International Review of Mission* 88 (July 1999): 267-279; Dirk van der Merwe, "Perseverance Through Suffering: A Spirituality for Mission," in *Missionalia* 33.2 (August 2005): 329-354; Thomas Schirrmacher, *The Persecution of Christians Concerns Us All: Towards a Theology of Martyrdom*, (Bonn: VK/Idea, n.d.); Craig Hovey, *To Share in the Body: A Theology of Martyrdom for Today's Church* (Grand Rapids: Brazos Press, 2008).

18. Kevin J. Vanhoozer, "The Trials of Truth: Mission, Martyrdom and the Epistemology of the Cross," in *To Stake a Claim: Mission and the Western Crisis of Knowledge*, ed. J. Andrew Kirk and Kevin J. Vanhoozer (Maryknoll: Orbis, 1999), 134.

Original Missionary Nature and Intent

evant for our investigation of the Belgic Confession is something that deserves further research.

Vanhoozer "reclaims" the category of martyr in its dual sense of witnessing and suffering. He then defines witnessing: *"Witnessing is the way to put others in the position of coming to know (i.e. to believe and to understand) evangelical truth."*[19] This definition is not incompatible with the definition developed previously in this study from Scripture. In fact, this definition also characterizes the relationship between witnessing (martyrdom) and mission; witnessing is an instrument by which mission is executed.

Further on, Vanhoozer develops the relationship between discipleship and suffering. He notes that suffering follows on the heels of discipleship. In fact, he argues, the truth is bound to suffer. Disciples do not seek suffering, but they inevitably face it because the world persecutes the truth. The cross of Christ illustrates the reality of this. Vanhoozer goes on to ask, "Why should this be so? Because the truth is ultimately not of this world. It is eschatological, not immanent, and cannot be contained within a worldly framework . . . Those who stake theological truth claims, then, should not oppress, but rather suffer oppression."[20] This last statement particularly applies to imperialistic and colonial paradigms of mission. In other words, the relationship between discipleship and suffering/martyrdom implies that mission can never be done in an oppressive fashion, imposing truth on those who do not believe and do not wish to believe. As we shall see, this consideration is extremely relevant as we consider the missiological significance of the Belgic Confession in its historical context.

Vanhoozer parses the revelatory character of martyrdom by noting that "Martyrdom can be a powerful form of truth-disclosing action."[21] Martyrs for the Christian faith disclose the truth about God's love and Jesus Christ's Lordship. When a Christian martyr suffers and dies, he speaks volumes about these convictions which are foundational for the Christian life. Martyrdom discloses these truths in a powerful way. It must be said that martyrdom, by itself, does not do this. Martyrdom accompanied by the witness of words is what is effective. A silent martyr is

---

19. Vanhoozer, "The Trials of Truth," 138 — italics are the author's.
20. Vanhoozer, "The Trials of Truth," 147-48.
21. Vanhoozer, "The Trials of Truth," 148. Contra Hovey, *To Share in the Body*, 142-143.

no real martyr and does not really disclose any truth about God's love and Christ's lordship. Vanhoozer does go on to recognize that "speaking the truth in love is tied up with bearing witness."[22] It is important to emphasize that, just as in all aspects of Christian mission, word and deed belong together in martyrdom.

Of course, people have been martyred for a variety of causes throughout world history. Some of them were overtly religious, others political, and others philosophical. Vanhoozer compares the death of Socrates with the death of Jesus. At 70 years of age, the Greek philosopher was put on trial for corrupting the youth of Athens and for refusing to recognize the gods of the state. Socrates was found guilty and sentenced to drink poison hemlock. Vanhoozer concludes that, unlike Jesus, Socrates was merely half a martyr. He died the death of a misunderstood genius, but not the death of a witness and certainly not the death of an apostle for some cause. According to Vanhoozer, Socrates "dies for a question, not an answer."[23] Consequently, we can make a judgment on the value of Socrates' truth claims. Socrates did not testify to hope, but to open-ended uncertainty. Christian martyrs, following in the steps of their Master, are entirely different — they testify "in concrete terms to hope."[24] This leads Vanhoozer to conclude that "witnessing is the epistemologically correct way of staking a theological truth claim."[25]

Vanhoozer's analysis is valuable, for it lays out the correlation between the suffering Christ and the suffering Christian. As the Christ sends out his people (mission), they can expect to face suffering as their Master did. Their suffering and martyrdom says something powerful about the truth for which they stand. However, if there is one gap in Vanhoozer's discussion it is the reality that competing Christian traditions have often persecuted one another.[26] Given that fact, is it always the case that truth is on the side of the oppressed? He comes close to this point when he writes that those who make theological truth claims should not oppress, but rather suffer oppression. Nevertheless, he does not draw this out into a theoretical framework or in a concrete church-historical context. We will do this a bit further on in this chapter.

---

22. Vanhoozer, "The Trials of Truth," 149.
23. Vanhoozer, "The Trials of Truth," 152-53.
24. Vanhoozer, "The Trials of Truth," 155.
25. Vanhoozer, "The Trials of Truth," 156.
26. See Schirrmacher, *The Persecution of Christians*, 24-26.

3.1.1.2 JOHN PIPER

Another writer who has analyzed the connection between martyrdom/suffering and mission is John Piper. His popular book *Let the Nations Be Glad* has a chapter entitled "The Supremacy of God in Missions through Suffering."[27] Piper begins with a reference to Matthew 13:44, in which the Lord Jesus compares the kingdom of heaven to a treasure hidden in a field. "When a man found it, he hid it again, and then in his joy went and sold all he had and bought the field" (NIV). In this similitude, Piper sees the worth that this man puts on the treasure of God. It is worth a great sacrifice and gives a deep joy. Says Piper, "Loss and suffering, joyfully accepted for the kingdom of God, show the supremacy of God more clearly in the world than all worship and prayer . . . This is why the stories of missionaries who gladly gave their all have made God more real and precious to many of us."[28] Throughout this chapter, Piper gives concrete examples of such missionaries. However, our interest is more in the lines that Piper draws between martyrdom/suffering and mission.

He notes that the calling of every believer is to experience some suffering, but those called to bear the gospel to the unreached can especially expect this. For whatever reason, Piper does not fully draw out this thought but moves right away to the general passages (Mark 8:34-35; Luke 14:33,26; John 12:25) which quote the Lord Jesus speaking about taking up the cross and hating or losing one's own life. These passages sufficiently prove his assertion about the calling of every believer, but do not provide any basis for arguing that it is especially missionaries who can expect to suffer. Nevertheless, this can be supported from other passages that Piper mentions later on. At this point, Piper does prove the case that the Christian life in general is one of taking up the cross and suffering loss for the gospel.

Piper goes on to note that any discussion about martyrdom is dangerous because of the ascendancy of a certain variety of terrorism in the twenty-first century. As Vanhoozer did with Socrates and Jesus, he gives a comparison between terrorist "martyrs" and Christian martyrs. This comparison speaks quite pointedly to our discussion. Piper writes, "First, the life of a Christian martyr is taken by those whom he wants to save. He

---

27. John Piper, *Let the Nations Be Glad: the Supremacy of God in Missions* (Second Edition, Revised and Expanded) (Grand Rapids: Baker, 2003), 71-107.
28. Piper, *Let the Nations Be Glad*, 71.

does not fall on his own sword, and does not use it against his adversary."[29] Taken as a rule, this may be true. Yet, one could envision a situation where one's life is taken by one already saved. Granted, these situations may be rare, but it is not impossible. Nevertheless, it is a valid point that in *many* instances of Christian martyrdom, the ones who are carrying out the violence would not claim to be regenerated. Conscientious and faithful believers would naturally desire the salvation of their oppressors — a missionary impulse, one could say.

Piper's second point regards the aim of martyrs and their method: "Christian martyrs do not pursue death; they pursue love. Christians do not advance the gospel of Christ by the use of the sword."[30] He follows this up with appropriate references to several Scripture passages.[31] The important thing here is that the gospel advances by a certain approach that is non-violent and does not involve the shedding of blood. Piper maintains that Christianity advances "by suffering to bring life, not suffering to cause death."[32] This is close to Vanhoozer's position that those who make theological truth claims should not oppress, but be oppressed.

From here, Piper proceeds to draw out in more detail the implications that follow from the believer's union with Christ. He mentions the passages that speak of the believer having being crucified with Christ and notes that this does involve a spiritual transaction, but there is more involved.[33] Piper asserts that "the point of this spiritual death is not that it takes the place of a real, practical application of Jesus' teaching to physical suffering and death but that it makes that application possible."[34] In this way, Christ's suffering and death are appropriated in the life of the believer in the fullest possible manner. Piper develops this further when he points to Christ's words in John 15:20: "If they persecuted me, they will persecute you." 1 Peter 2:20-21 establishes Christ's suffering and death both as a substitution and a pattern for believers to follow. Piper draws out the same thought with a slightly different nuance from Hebrews 13:12-14, a passage which speaks about believers going to the Christ who suffers

---

29. Piper, *Let the Nations Be Glad*, 74.
30. Piper, *Let the Nations Be Glad*, 74-75.
31. Matthew 26:52; John 18:36; Mark 10:45; and Colossians 1:24.
32. Piper, *Let the Nations Be Glad*, 75.
33. The passages he mentions are Galatians 5:24; Galatians 2:19-20; Romans 6:6; and Colossians 3:2-3.
34. Piper, *Let the Nations Be Glad*, 76.

outside the gate, bearing the reproach which he endured. Piper writes, "This is above all a missionary text. Outside the camp means outside the borders of safety and comfort. Outside the camp are the 'other sheep' that are not of this fold. Outside the camp are the unreached nations. Outside the camp are the places and the people who will be costly to reach and will require no small sacrifice. But to this we are called: 'Let us go and bear the reproach he endured.' It is our vocation."[35] Thus, union with Christ and the pattern he set for us figures prominently in Piper's reflections. He fills this out with more concrete examples, including incidents in the life of the Apostle Paul.

Piper moves on to consider the question of whether or not God allows or appoints this suffering to take place. Based on such passages as Philippians 1:29, Piper answers that it is indeed God's appointment for his people: "The suffering that missionaries meet is not something unforeseen by the Lord. He saw it clearly, embraced it for himself, and sent his disciples into the same danger."[36] The question is: why? Piper gives six reasons.

First, he argues that, in the biblical perspective, suffering gives a greater depth to faith and holiness. This argument is easy enough to support with reference to biblical passages such as 2 Cor.1:8-9.

The second reason is "suffering makes your cup increase." By this, Piper means to say that when we endure suffering on earth, we can expect a greater reward of God's glory in heaven. Because of the controversial nature of the claim that there are varying degrees of reward in heaven, Piper exerts some effort to lay it out biblically. His appeals to Scripture and the accompanying interpretations are convincing and lie within the pale of orthodoxy.[37]

Third, he argues that the suffering of missionaries is something that God uses to encourage others who might be timid or otherwise lethargic. He makes a reference to Paul's words in Philippians 1:14 that God used his imprisonment and suffering to embolden the other believers.

Piper's fourth reason is captured with Paul's words in Colossians 1:24: "I rejoice in my sufferings for your sake, and in my flesh I am filling up what is lacking in Christ's afflictions for the sake of his body, that is, the

---

35. Piper, *Let the Nations Be Glad*, 80.
36. Piper, *Let the Nations Be Glad*, 85.
37. He discusses passages such as 2 Corinthians 4:17-18; Romans 8:18; and Matthew 5:11-12. He also gives a lengthy quotation from Jonathan Edwards on this matter. See Piper, *Let the Nations Be Glad*, 88-89.

church." Piper explains that this does not refer to any lack in the substitutionary atonement of Christ; rather it points to the fact that Christ's sufferings "are not known and felt by people who were not at the cross."[38] Through the suffering of the body of Christ, unbelievers are confronted with the suffering of Christ himself.

Fifth, Piper asserts that "suffering enforces the missionary command to go." When the church suffers, her outreach is extended to places where she might not otherwise go. "If you see things with the eyes of God, the Master strategist, what you see in every setback is the positioning of troops for a greater advance and a greater display of his wisdom, power, and love."[39] Piper refers to two passages in Acts that affirm this perspective: Acts 8:1 and Acts 11:19. In these passages we read about the persecution which began after the martyrdom of Stephen and how this resulted in the church being spread to such places as Phoenicia, Cyprus, and Antioch. This gets developed further when we discover from Scripture that "Jesus told the disciples to expect arrest and imprisonment as God's deployment tactic to put them with people they would never otherwise reach."[40] Indeed, Luke 21:13 very explicitly says, "This will result in your being witnesses to them."

Finally, Piper maintains that it is in the suffering of believers that Christ's supremacy is made manifest. When believers suffer and die for their faith, they demonstrate in a very concrete way that Christ is of inestimable value to them. They witness to the supremacy of God's worth. In fact, says Piper, this is "the reason for suffering running through and above all the other reasons. God ordains suffering because through all the other reasons it displays to the world the supremacy of his worth above all treasures."[41]

Piper's discussion of this subject is comprehensive and grounded firmly in exegesis of the Scriptures and therefore extremely helpful. Vanhoozer presents a theological/philosophical approach to the relation between martyrdom and mission, whereas Piper is more interested in providing a direct summary of scriptural teaching. Vanhoozer works with the concept of martyrdom extensively, while Piper focuses on the broader category of persecution/suffering. In the next three sections, we will explore a synthesis of their approaches while adding some other insights.

---

38. Piper, *Let the Nations Be Glad*, 92.
39. Piper, *Let the Nations Be Glad*, 94.
40. Piper, *Let the Nations Be Glad*, 96.
41. Piper, *Let the Nations Be Glad*, 99.

3.1.2.3 MISSIOLOGICAL FOUNDATION OF MARTYRDOM AND SUFFERING

As we concluded in the last chapter, the origin of the mission of the New Testament church rests with the command of the Lord Jesus to his apostles in Matthew 28:16-20 and the parallel passages. The Lord Jesus was sent into this world as the Redeemer and he in turn sends out his followers (John 20:21). The New Testament is amply clear that these followers stand in a special relationship to their Lord. The New Testament Scriptures describe this relationship succinctly with the expression ἐν Χριστῷ (*en Christo*) and similar expressions.

The missiological foundation of martyrdom and suffering is to be found in this union with Christ the sender. Jesus Christ was the "man of sorrows and [was] acquainted with grief" (Isaiah 53:3). His entire life on earth was characterized by suffering. The paradigm of attaining glory through suffering finds its archetype with him. While believers are on earth, because of and through their mystical union with him, they share in his sufferings with the hope of glory to come. Naturally, they do this in a limited way, for the sufferings of Christ and particularly his experience of God's wrath were unique.[42] Nonetheless, there is a sense in which believers can and sometimes do share the sufferings of their Lord (cf. Philippians 3:10).

Vanhoozer comes closest to incorporating this when he speaks about believers following in the steps of Jesus their Master. As he who sends them out experienced suffering, so also his people can expect the same. However, Vanhoozer does not develop the thought to any significant degree, leaving the matter at more of the level of an example than of something rooted in a mystical union. To be sure, there is a level at which the Lord Jesus left his followers an example to be followed, also when it comes to his suffering (1 Peter 2:21). Yet, this level is also incorporated into the union with Christ. Those who are "in Christ" look to his example to discover what it means to live as such. The example is the means by which the union is realized in day-to-day living. So, also with the example of the sufferings of the Lord Jesus, they become a part of the missiological foundation of believers' suffering and martyrdom through the mystical union.

Of course, John Piper is much more explicit on this matter of the union with Christ. Piper ties it initially into the death of the old nature and the coming to life of the new. He says that it is because we share in

---

42. "...Christian crosses differ from the cross of Christ." Hovey, *To Share in the Body*, 104.

Christ's resurrection and victory over death that we can in turn take risks, suffer pain, and even die a martyr's death.[43] Like Vanhoozer, Piper also speaks of the example or pattern of Christ's sufferings in such passages as 1 Peter 2. However, he could have strengthened his point by tying it into the believers' union with Christ.

Without Christ and his suffering, Christians would never suffer. Had Christ never sent out his apostles with the gospel, Christians would not suffer for their faith. Apart from their union with the Christ who suffered in his ministry on earth, believers would not — and indeed could not — suffer even to the point of dying for their faith. One cannot help but think of the words of Revelation 14:13a, "Then I heard a voice from heaven saying to me, 'Write: "Blessed are the dead who die *in the Lord* from now on."'" (italics added).

3.1.2.4 MISSIOLOGICAL MESSAGE OF MARTYRDOM AND SUFFERING

As others have noted (especially Vanhoozer), the phenomena of martyrdom and suffering communicate a message. The message is being communicated by the one who suffers to the one who causes the suffering (and to others who may witness it as well). The message consists of at least three parts.

First of all, it is a message about the one who suffers. The martyr communicates that he or she is so firmly rooted in the faith that apostasy is not an option. Is this a testimony to truth, as Vanhoozer claims? We can distinguish between two senses. In the broad sense, those who suffer for Christian faith demonstrate a commitment to the absolute nature of truth. They realize that Christian faith is not grounded in relativism. This is absolutely true, and martyrs of every Christian tradition communicate this message — one which obviously carries great missiological import. Nevertheless, there is a narrow sense in which some Christian martyrs were firmly convinced of "the truth," but yet were wrong. We think particularly here of Anabaptist and Roman Catholic martyrs. They died for their commitment to certain doctrines which cannot be supported from Scripture.

Second, there is a message about the one who causes the suffering. Historically speaking, persecution and martyrdom have come from two directions. First, from the unbelieving world, and then second, from those who call themselves followers of the Lord Jesus. To the first group,

---

43. Piper, *Let the Nations Be Glad*, 76.

martyrdom communicates the radical antithesis between faith and unbelief. Unbelief is without an apologetic (Romans 1:20), and so it sometimes resorts to blunt force. In this sense, martyrdom and persecution tell us something about the desperation of unbelief. It also reflects the deep animosity of the unbelieving world. Martin Luther captured this when he wrote, "The clearer the Church recognizes Christ and testifies of him, the more certain it will encounter the contradiction, the confrontation, and the hatred of the Antichrist."[44]

Things become more complicated when Christian believers are on both the giving and receiving end of persecution and martyrdom. In such a situation, the reality of persecution and martyrdom may reveal something about the real spiritual condition of the persecutors. Will those who truly have union with Christ persecute and oppress others? It hardly seems possible. On the other hand, perhaps there have been regenerate persecutors. In such cases, persecution and martyrdom communicates something about the maturity and consistency of their commitment to Christ. Even this may not be satisfactory for every situation. Venturing outside the realm of theory places one in the real world where people and their motivations are complex and cannot always be fully explained.

Finally, martyrdom and suffering communicate something about the one for whom believers suffer. Their tribulations reveal the message of the cross. In some sense, martyrs share in the sufferings of Christ and portray them to the world. Where words lose their edge and meaning, the graphic picture of believers suffering for Christ can be a powerful missionary message.

3.1.2.5 MISSIOLOGICAL RESULT OF MARTYRDOM AND SUFFERING

Martyrdom and suffering have an impact on the execution of the church's missionary task. As noted earlier, this was recognized already by Tertullian. There are two particular ways in which we can draw this out. First of all, speaking historically, martyrdom and suffering have usually resulted in the growth of the church. This growth has been both in quantitative and qualitative terms. Whether during the history of the early church, during the days of the Great Reformation, or during contemporary persecutions in Asia, the church has often appeared to grow numeri-

---

44. Martin Luther, *Sämtliche Schriften* (Vol. 5) (Groß Oesingen: Verlag der Lutherischen Buchhandlung H. Harms, 1986), 106. Cited (in translation) by Schirrmacher, *The Persecution of Christians*, 27.

cally during times of persecution.⁴⁵ Moreover, although this is a more subjective aspect, the church also often grows in maturity and commitment through persecution. Believers hunger for the Word of God, and those whose commitment is less than whole-hearted tend to fall away in the face of suffering. As Piper noted from Phil. 1:14, persecution usually (but not always) strengthens God's people. It prepares and equips them to be God's instruments to continue reaching out to the lost.

All of this serves for the ultimate result: the glory of God. As John Piper emphasizes, the whole enterprise of Christian mission is pointed in the one direction of the glory of God. "Missions exist because worship doesn't."⁴⁶ Worship is about God's glory. When believers suffer death and physical pain for their faith, other believers are led to call upon God. They ask for deliverance, but they also give him glory and praise for strengthening his people. They give him glory when they see how the suffering of the church results in the advance of God's kingdom. They worship the God who sovereignly controls history and will bring it to its glorious end, doing so also through the sufferings of his people.

3.1.3 Martyrdom as Metanarrative for the Belgic Confession

Having laid out the framework, we can move ahead to consider the connection between martyrdom and the Belgic Confession. This will be done under the rubric of martyrdom as a metanarrative for this document. We are using the word "metanarrative" in the sense of a dominant theme that can be put in a narrative form, an overarching integrative story. Metanarrative is thus more specialized than context. Both metanarrative and context are tools by which historians can draw meaning out of the past, but metanarrative is grounded on a particular metaphysical foundation (in this case, union with Christ) and is oriented more towards an integrative and diachronic accounting of the facts.⁴⁷

---

45. See Koranyi, "Mission as Call to Metanoia"; Robert Kolb, "God's Gift of Martyrdom: The Early Reformation Understanding of Dying for the Faith," *Church History* 64.3 (September 1995): 399-412. Also see Schirrmacher, *The Persecution of Christians*, 38: "Persecution does not automatically lead to church growth or to a purer, stronger faith." Schirrmacher notes the example of the German church under the Third Reich and under communism.

46. Piper, *Let the Nations Be Glad*, 17.

47. See Justin A. Irving and Karin Klenke, "Telos, Chronos and Hermeneia: The Role of Metanarrative in Leadership Effectiveness through the Production of Meaning," *International Journal of Qualitative Methods* 3 (September 2004):

Original Missionary Nature and Intent 79

In chapter 1, we concluded that the authorship of the Confession rests with Guido de Brès. We also noted that de Brès relied quite heavily on other confessional writings, particularly the French Confession of 1559. In some instances, the wording of de Brès' confession is very similar to these earlier works, especially to the French. Among the significant differences between the Belgic and the French is the emphasis in the Belgic on persecution and martyrdom. De Brès' language on this count is entirely original. Among the articles on the church, for instance, the French does not explicitly mention the false church or its persecution of the godly. Furthermore, the French does not have an article regarding eschatology. Finally, even in the introductory letter of the French, while persecutions are acknowledged, they do not receive the same emphasis as in the work of de Brès. Insofar as this goes, the Belgic Confession is in a class all by itself. There is no Reformation confession as oriented to this subject as the work of de Brès. Let us now consider the story of his life and the writing of the Confession.

Guido de Brès was born in 1522, a native of Mons in the present-day region of southwestern Belgium. He was the fourth son of devout Roman Catholic parents. Owing especially to the influence of his mother, the environment of his upbringing was profoundly religious.[48] Through what appears to have been a drawn-out process of reflection and careful consideration, de Brès was converted to the Reformed faith in 1547.[49] This was no small matter. De Brès lived in the Low Countries, the same area which William Monter tells us was the "epicentre of heresy executions in Europe" since the 1530s.[50] According to Alastair Duke, the distinctive feature of the Reformation in the Low Countries was persecution.[51] One can be sure that the author of the Belgic Confession had counted

---

5; Anna Green and Kathleen Troup, *The houses of history: A critical reader in twentieth-century history and theory* (Manchester: Manchester UP, 1999), 204.

48. E. M. Braekman, *Guy de Brès, I. Sa Vie* (Brussels: Editions De La Librairie Des Esclaireurs Unionistes, 1960), 35.

49. Braekman, *Guy de Brès*, 40-41.

50. William Monter, "Heresy Executions in Reformation Europe, 1520-1565," in *Tolerance and Intolerance in the European Reformation*, ed. Ole Peter Grell and Bob Scribner (Cambridge: Cambridge UP, 1996), 57. Cf. Philip Benedict, *Christ's Churches Purely Reformed: A Social History of Calvinism* (New Haven: Yale UP, 2002), 176.

51. Alastair Duke, "The Netherlands," in *The Early Reformation in Europe*, ed. Andrew Pettegree (Cambridge: Cambridge UP, 1992), 163.

the cost before making the commitment to be Reformed. He was deeply aware that martyrdom was a real possibility for him, as it was for other Reformed believers of his era.[52]

Following his conversion, it appears that de Brès may have done evangelistic work in his hometown.[53] However, persecution made the life of Reformed believers in this area very difficult. As a result, in 1548, one year after his conversion, de Brès fled to England.[54] While in London, de Brès provided assistance to other exiles, including the Polish Reformer John a Lasco. He also developed a sense of calling to the ministry and received some training to that end.[55] De Brès remained in England for five years, a time in which he grew as a Reformed believer, but also a time in which the atmosphere of persecution elsewhere in Europe could not be forgotten.

In 1552, the tide turned in England with the death of Edward VI. De Brès returned to the Low Countries and took up a pastorate in Lille, a city which had a Reformed contingent very early on.[56] It was also a city which had offered up more than her share of martyrs.[57] De Brès' ministry here was powerful. Moreover, his influence spread far and wide through his itinerant preaching and teaching. While in Lille, he also wrote his first published work, *Le baston de la foy chrestienne* (1555). This was written as a retort to an earlier popular Roman Catholic work by Nicolas Grenier, *La Bouclier de la Foy* (1547). As a retort, it is composed mostly of Scripture passages that contradict specific Roman Catholic teachings, along with quotes from the early fathers. The first edition was dedicated to his church in Lille, that they would "perpetually persevere in the knowledge of the gospel of the Son of God."[58] De Brès' first (very popular) work thus emerges out of an environment where the Reformed faith was struggling to exist because of persecution.

---

52. In his final letter to his wife, de Brès says that in the years before and after their marriage, he was a man "uncertain of life." *Procedures Held With Regard To Those of the Religion of the Netherlands* (1568), author, translator, and publisher unknown, 136.

53. Braekman, *Guy de Brès*, 42.

54. Braekman, *Guy de Brès*, 48.

55. Braekman, *Guy de Brès*, 59.

56. Braekman, *Guy de Brès*, 63.

57. Braekman, *Guy de Brès*, 79.

58. Quoted in Braekman, *Guy de Brès*, 87. Translation mine.

Though he does not appear to have been involved with the first edition, it was during de Brès' years in Lille that the first Reformed martyrology was published. Jean Crespin published the first edition of his *Histoire des Martyrs* in Geneva in 1554. The significance of this event should not be underestimated. The rediscovered genre of martyrology contributed enormously to sixteenth-century attitudes towards persecution and martyrdom.[59] Music also made a significant contribution, for during the same period, Huguenot songs about persecution and endurance in suffering were becoming so popular that they were printed and widely distributed.[60]

Persecution and suffering continued to impact de Brès' life. Several members of his congregation were martyred for their faith.[61] Eventually, his popularity became his undoing in Lille. After a crackdown on the Reformed believers, the authorities were soon on de Brès' trail, and in 1556 he was forced to flee into exile once again, this time to Frankfurt in Germany. He was only there for a short time before moving on again to Lausanne, where he studied under Pierre Viret. Lausanne was a veritable training ground for Reformation preachers. It shared this distinction, of course, with Geneva, and before long, de Brès had also spent time there.[62] Among other subjects, de Brès had given special attention to the early church fathers in his studies and his facility in this area is reflected in his recorded debates.[63]

By 1559, the atmosphere was such that de Brès could return to the Lowlands. It was at about this time that he married Catherine Ramon, a native of Tournai, where de Brès was ministering.[64] At the time of de Brès' arrival, Tournai was sympathetic to the cause of the Reformation and a

---

59. See A. G. Dickens and John Tonkin, *The Reformation in Historical Thought* (Cambridge: Harvard UP, 1985), 39-57.

60. Brad S. Gregory, *Salvation at Stake: Christian Martyrdom in Early Modern Europe* (Cambridge: Harvard UP, 1999), 170.

61. Braekman, *Guy de Brès*, 98-99.

62. According to Crew (*Calvinist Preaching*, 86), de Brès spent three years in Geneva. Gootjes (*The Belgic Confession*, 61-62) is less certain about the extent of de Brès' sojourn there. The only source is Jean Crespin's martyrology and with that in hand, the most we can say is that de Brès was in Geneva some time between 1556 and 1559.

63. *Procedures*, 4.

64. Braekman, *Guy de Brès*, 118.

relatively safe place for a Protestant pastor to live and minister.[65] While he lived and did most of his pastoral work in Tournai, he also carried out some itinerant work in other towns, particularly Lille and Valenciennes.[66]

Mention was made earlier of Jean Crespin, the author of the first Reformed martyrology. Crespin and de Brès had crossed paths during de Brès' sojourns outside the Lowlands. During de Brès' first year in Tournai, Crespin wrote to de Brès asking for information about Reformed martyrs in that area. De Brès responded, and this information was incorporated into the second edition of *Histoire des Martyrs*.[67]

After nearly two years of relative peace in Tournai, things began to deteriorate for de Brès. The public singing of psalms (*chanteries*) had been strictly prohibited, but in September of 1561 a good number of citizens ignored the prohibition. There was an ongoing debate among the Reformed believers about whether or not the authorities could be challenged in this fashion. De Brès took his stand and warned his parishioners against this practice, but to no avail. Before long, Margaret of Parma received news that the people of Tournai were openly violating the law. She sent a commission of noblemen to investigate and arrest the instigators. Consequently, the relative peace and safety of Tournai was compromised, and de Brès was again forced to live on the run.[68]

It was some months before this time that de Brès penned his *Confession de foy*, later known as the Belgic Confession.[69] The Confession was printed and consequently tossed over the castle wall at Tournai. It seems likely that it was the edition published by Abel Clemence of Rouen, though the Frellon edition published in Lyon is also a possibility.[70] The title page of both editions includes the subtitle: "Made with common agreement by the faithful living in the Lowlands who desire to live according to the

---

65. See Duke, "The Netherlands," (96-97) for some discussion on why this was so.

66. Braekman, *Guy de Brès*, 133. He also sometimes ministered in his hometown of Mons and in Douai.

67. Gerard Moreau, "Contribution à l'Histoire du Livre des Martyrs," *Bulletin de la Société de l'Histoire du Protestantisme Français*, 103 (1957): 196-199. Cited in Gregory, *Salvation at Stake*, 426.

68. See P. Y. DeJong, *The Church's Witness to the World* (St. Catharines: Paideia Press, 1980), 24-25; and Braekman, *Guy de Brès*, 151ff.

69. As noted in chapter 1, Gootjes suggests that it is quite probable that the Confession was already written at the end of May, 1561. Cf. Gootjes, *The Belgic Confession*, 30.

70. See Gootjes, *The Belgic Confession*, 19-25.

purity of the gospel of our Lord Jesus Christ."[71] With the Clemence edition, there is a seal with an abbreviated Latin translation of Psalm 102:26a, "All grow old, however the Lord will remain."[72] Finally, just above the date (1561) in the Clemence edition, there is a quote from 1 Peter 3:15, "Always be prepared to respond to anyone who demands from you a reason for the hope which is in you." For our purposes, it is especially this last quote which calls our attention again to the theme of persecution. The context in 1 Peter 3 is clearly one of persecution and suffering. Consequently, it was not difficult for these words to be applied to the particular situation the Reformed churches were facing in 1561 in the Lowlands.

After the title page, there is a poem (*sonnet*) most likely written by de Brès. In this little work, the author pleads for the ruling authorities to give the Reformed believers a fair hearing. It concludes by claiming that if the rulers would only read the Confession, they would know that to condemn the Reformed believers would be a very grave injustice.[73] The possibility of another kind of verdict looms in the background.

Then follows the Dedicatory Epistle to Philip II. This epistle follows somewhat the pattern of Calvin's dedication of the first edition of the *Institutes of the Christian Religion* to Francis I. The goal of both is the same: to persuade the ruling authorities that the Reformed believers pose no threat to the state and that the Reformed religion simply follows the Word of God. The theme of persecution and martyrdom permeates this epistle like no other writing of Guido de Brès.

Already in the first paragraph, we hear about the current state of affairs that the Reformed believers are facing: "But our enemies have stopped your ears with so many false accusations and reports that we are

---

71. "Faicte d'un commun accord par les fideles qui conversent és pays bas, lesquels desirent vivre selon la pureté de l'Evangile de nostre Seigneur Iesus Christ." Guy de Brès, *Confession de foy, faicte d'un commun accord par les fideles qui conversent és pays bas.* Rouen: Abel Clemence, 1561. Guy de Brès, *Confession de foy, faite d'un commun accord par les fideles qui conversent és pays bas.* Lyon: Jean Frellon, 1561. Translation mine.

72.. "Omnia veterascent, Dominus autem permanebit." De Brès, *Confession de foy* (Rouen: Abel Clemence, 1561). Translation mine.

73. " . . .Vous connaîtrez, lisant notre Confession, Que de nous condamner c'est trop grande injustice." The sonnet is found on the second page of both the Clemence and Frellon editions. It is also reproduced by Braekman, *Guy de Brès*, 162 and. J. N. Bakhuizen van den Brink, *De Nederlandse Belijdenisgeschriften* (Second Edition) (Amsterdam: Uitgeverij Ton Bolland, 1976), 60. This last source gives the older, original orthography.

not only prevented from appearing before you, but driven from your territories, murdered and burnt wherever we may be."[74] Further on in the epistle, de Brès makes it clear that the Reformed faithful are determined to hold to the faith they confess in this document. He writes:

> The banishments, prisons, racks, exiles, tortures and countless other persecutions plainly demonstrate that our desire and conviction is not carnal, for we would lead a far easier life if we did not embrace and maintain this doctrine. But having the fear of God before our eyes, and being in dread of the warning of Jesus Christ, who tells us that He shall forsake us before God and His Father if we deny Him before men, we suffer our backs to be beaten, our tongues to be cut, our mouths to be gagged and our whole body to be burnt, for we know that he who would follow Christ must take up his cross and deny himself.

The dedicatory epistle is not often quoted, but when it is, it is usually this remarkable passage. It speaks poignantly of the determination of de Brès and his fellow Reformed believers. Their martyrdoms (or potential martyrdoms) and persecution were interpreted and understood in the light of what they understood Christ to be saying to them in Scripture.

The blood of the martyrs is mentioned further on in the epistle, and de Brès makes amply clear that the Reformed believers are willing to seal this Confession with their blood. The dedication stands out for its boldness in the light of the contemporary circumstances. There can be little question that this early introduction to the Belgic Confession was framed under the shadow of persecution.

Finally, before the actual body of the Confession, de Brès included "Some passages of the New Testament in which the faithful are exhorted to render confession of their faith before men."[75] The first passage mentioned is Matthew 10:32-33: "Therefore whoever confesses me before men, him I will also confess before my Father who is in heaven. But whoever denies me before men, him I will also deny before my Father who is

---

74. This quote and all those that follow from the epistle are from the English translation of Alastair Duke found in appendix 1 of Hyde, *With Heart and Mouth*, 499-504. The French original can be found reproduced in Bakhuizen van den Brink, *de Nederlandse Belijdenisgeschriften* (hereafter BvdB), 62-68.

75. This is found on the twenty-second (unnumbered) page of the Clemence edition and the tenth (unnumbered) page of the Frellon edition. It is also found in BvdB, 68.

in heaven." The context of Matthew 10 is that of the Lord Jesus sending out the apostles and warning them of coming persecution and even martyrdom. This reference is followed by the parallel passages of Mark 8:38 and Luke 9:26, "For whoever is ashamed of me and my words in this adulterous and sinful generation, of him the Son of Man will also be ashamed when he comes in the glory of his Father with the holy angels." Here too, the context is one of suffering and persecution, with both passages making reference to the taking up of one's cross. Then follows a reference to a passage already mentioned, namely 1 Peter 3:15, and references to Romans 10:10 and 2 Timothy 2:12b. The last two passages excepted, the references here are almost entirely to be located contextually in persecution, suffering, and martyrdom.

At this point, one finally gets to the body of the Belgic Confession. Throughout the Confession, we find references to enemies, persecution, and martyrdom. In article 12, we read about the devils and evil spirits who "lie in wait like murderers to ruin the church and all its members."[76] They wait "to destroy everything by their wicked devices." In article 13, concerning the providence of God, de Brès writes about the consolation this doctrine provides: "In this we trust, because we know that He holds in check the devil and all our enemies so that they cannot hurt us without his permission and will."[77] Article 27 is perhaps the most pointed in this regard. De Brès writes about how God preserves the church "against the fury of the whole world." He makes a reference to the reign of Ahab during which "the Lord kept for himself seven thousand persons who had not bowed their knees to Baal."[78] Article 28 continues the theme when it speaks of believers joining the assembly of the church "wherever God has established it. They should do so even though the rulers and edicts of princes were against it, and death or physical punishment might follow."[79] In article 29, de Brès mentions the characteristics of the false church. Among these is the fact that "it persecutes those who live holy lives according to the Word of God."[80] Finally, in the last article, de Brès writes

---

76. English quotes from the Belgic Confession are from the *Book of Praise: Anglo Genevan Psalter* (Winnipeg: Premier, 1998) (hereafter BoP). BoP, 449. Critical text of the French original in BvdB, 88.
77. BoP, 450. BvdB, 90.
78. BoP, 462. BvdB, 120-122.
79. BoP, 463. BvdB, 122.
80. BoP, 464. BvdB, 124-126.

about the last judgment. He says that the righteous will be vindicated: "Their innocence will be known to all and they will see the terrible vengeance that God will bring upon the wicked who persecuted, oppressed, and tormented them in this world."[81]

The booklet containing the Confession was concluded with a remonstrance addressed to the magistrates of the Low Countries. In this remonstrance, de Brès called for them to carry out their God-given task of delivering justice. Not unexpectedly, this document also contains the themes of persecution and martyrdom.[82]

Moreover, we can also note that the entire package (including the Confession) was also an attempt by de Brès to reach the authorities with the true gospel — and then not only the authorities, but also the people under their rule. It was not merely an effort to allow for religious toleration; there was also a kerygmatic character to the package. In this way as well, the Confession and its accompanying documents held missionary significance.

The metanarrative of persecution and martyrdom continued as de Brès fled Tournai. Shortly after the confession was delivered, somebody gave the authorities a description of de Brès, who by this time had changed his appearance and was going by the name of Jerome. An order went out from Tournai that de Brès, should he be found, must be arrested. De Brès had fled, but the congregation he left behind was ravaged by persecution and martyrdom. De Brès himself was burned in effigy.[83]

This time, de Brès fled south to France and he served the Reformed churches there. From December 1561 to July 1566, de Brès served the churches in Dieppe, Amiens, Montdidier, Sedan and Metz.[84] During his time in Sedan, he also served as a chaplain for the Duke of Bouil-

---

81. BoP, 472. BvdB, 144.
82. Braekman, *Guy de Brès*, 171-174. Braekman quotes the remonstrance: "Si au milieu de la flamme en angoisses de la mort, tu ne peux arracher au fidèle martyr, la confiance qu'il a mise en Jésus Christ, ne confesseras-tu point que tu persécutes et crucifies derechef Jésus-Christ en ses membres, quand tu baignes et ton coeur et tes mains au sang de celui qui par foi vive tâche de se transformer en son image, et le vêtir par l'esprit de régénération?" (172) The original can be found on the sixty-second (unnumbered) page of the Clemence edition and page 27 of the Frellon edition.
83. Braekman, *Guy de Brès*, 179-180.
84. Braekman, *Guy de Brès*, 212-213.

lon, Henri-Robert de la Marck.[85] This period should have been a time of relative peace for de Brès personally since each of these cities was populated by large contingents of Reformed believers. However, that fact was not enough to prevent de Brès from being arrested and incarcerated in a French prison for a short time.[86] It appears that, from time to time, de Brès returned to Tournai. In fact, Braekman argues that de Brès again served as an informant for Crespin during this time, informing him of the events surrounding the martyrdom of Michel l'Aveugle.[87] It would appear that martyrdom and suffering continued to be on his mind and in his heart.

During his years in France, de Brès was responsible for the publication of three more works. *Oraison au Seigneur* was a small 24-page booklet containing a prayer for Reformed believers living in the midst of persecution.[88] Next, in 1565, de Brès translated a 255 page Dutch book regarding the imprisonment and martyrdom of Christopher Fabri.[89] Finally, in 1565, de Brès wrote and published his book dealing with Anabaptist teachings, *La racine, source et fondement des anabaptistes*.

De Brès returned to the Lowlands in July of 1566 after being pressured by the pastor of the Reformed Church at Valenciennes, "the Geneva of Flanders." De Brès joined Pérégrin de la Grange in pastoring not only this large church, but also the surrounding congregations in Lille and Tournai.[90] However, on August 24, 1566, iconoclastic fervour gripped Valenciennes — with devastating consequences. The ruling authorities, being Roman Catholic, were outraged. The city was declared guilty of rebellion and was eventually besieged for three months. After the capitulation of the city on

---

85. Braekman, *Guy de Brès*, 192. Cf. *Procedures*, 4.
86. Crew (*Calvinist Preaching*, 40) indicates that the period of imprisonment was six months. However, Braekman (*Guy de Brès*, 182-183) thinks it was probably only a month or two. He was arrested at an illegal worship service in someone's home in Amiens.
87. Braekman, *Guy de Brès*, 185-189.
88. C. Vonk, *de Voorzeide Leer* (Deel IIIb: de Nederlandse Geloofsbelijdenis, Art. 22-24 en 27-37) (Barendrecht: Drukkerij "Barendrecht," 1956), 590-596. Vonk provides a Dutch translation.
89. *Histoire notable de la trahison et emprisonnement de deux bons et fidèles personnages en la ville d'Annuers: c'est assavoir, de Christophe Fabri, Ministre de la parole de Dieu en la dite ville, et d'Oliuier Bouck, Professeur...* Cf. Gregory, *Salvation at Stake*, endnote 183 (427); and Braekman, *Guy de Brès*, 207-208.
90. Braekman, *Guy de Brès*, 223-224.

March 23, 1567, de Brès and de la Grange managed to escape but not for very long. On March 28, they were captured and imprisoned initially at Tournai (March 31 to April 11).[91] During this time, various visitors came to see de Brès and attempted to debate with him. Records of many of these debates are found in *Procedures*. On April 11, the prisoners were transferred to Valenciennes, to a dark and gloomy prison named Brunain. De Brès was held in the lowest place of the building where the sewage and filth ended up.[92]

Despite the ugliness of these living conditions, de Brès continued to write letters of encouragement to his congregation and others (including his wife and mother). In the extant letter to his mother, de Brès evokes Tertullian and speaks of how the ground will be watered with his blood and bear much fruit. Such a sentiment was expressed more often by Belgian Reformed martyrs. In his martyrology, Van Haemstede records some of the last words of Gillis Verdickt: "the ashes of my body shall be scattered through the town, and from it many Christians will spring up, for the blood of the martyrs is the seed of the faithful."[93] Though not a martyr himself, Jean Taffin also drew attention to the missionary value of martyrdom. When the poor and ignorant observe the martyrdom of believers, they "see that this doctrine for which people suffer must come from God, since divine strength is needed to endure all those slanders, difficulties, and cruelties so steadfastly and willingly. By this the proverb is established that the blood of the martyrs is the seed of the church."[94]

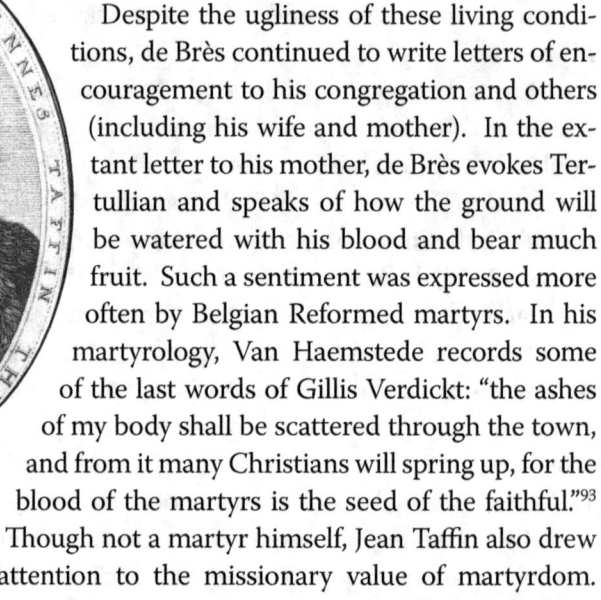

JEAN TAFFIN
(1529-1602)
Image source unknown

---

91. Braekman, *Guy de Brès*, 257.
92. Braekman, *Guy de Brès*, 260. Braekman quotes extensively from a letter written by de Brès to Pasquier de la Barre and Nicolas Soldoyer.
93. "The witness of Calvinist martyrs: Arnoud Diericx, Carolus de Koninck, Gillis and Antoon Verdickt, Adriaan [Coreman] de Schilder, Hendrik [Snoelacke] van Boekholt, 1557-1559" — an excerpt from Adriaen Van Haemstede, *De Geschiedenisse ende den doodt der vromer Martelaren* (1559), translated by Alastair Duke and available on-line at http://dutchrevolt.leidenuniv.nl
94. Jean Taffin, *The Marks of God's Children*, trans. Peter Y. De Jong, ed. James A. De Jong (Grand Rapids: Baker Academic, 2003), 123.

THE MARTYRDOM OF GUIDO DE BRÈS BY HANGING
AT VALENCIENNES ON THE 31ST MAY, 1567
Image source unknown

Eventually, on May 30, 1567, de Brès was martyred for his faith. He was hung for celebrating the Lord's Supper contrary to the commandment of the magistrates. Afterwards, his body was placed in a shallow grave and shortly thereafter desecrated by wild animals.[95]

De Brès died a martyr, but his *Confession de foy* lived on. By the time of his death, it had been widely accepted throughout the Lowlands. It went through numerous printings and was translated into Dutch already in 1562. Within a century, it had been translated into German, Latin, Greek, English and Spanish. It quickly became one of the most widely accepted Reformation confessions.

Finally, it should be noted that the 1570 edition of Crespin's *Histoire des Martyrs* included an abbreviated version of the Belgic Confession. Beginning in 1582, *Histoire des Martyrs* included the entire first edition of the Confession.[96] This tells us that from a very early date, the Belgic Confession was regarded as a document stained with the blood of martyrs. Therefore, it is entirely at home with the metanarrative of martyrdom and suffering in the Christian church.

---

95. *Procedures*, 150-152, 154.
96. Gootjes, *The Belgic Confession*, 33.

3.1.4 The Belgic Confession as Μαρτυς

We may now begin considering the missiological significance of the Belgic Confession. Does this document really portray a church dialoguing with itself? If we consider the metanarrative of martyrdom and persecution that surrounds this confession one could hardly reach that conclusion. After all, the phenomenon of martyrdom is inseparable from mission; it is an act of witness.[97] Furthermore, from the perspective of those giving the witness, this was not a witness to the Church, but to the non-Reformed world.

The Belgic Confession was formulated on the foundation of martyrdom and suffering, a theology of the cross. Those involved with its production, particularly Guido de Brès, lived in union with Jesus Christ and thus shared in his sufferings. The same can be said for those churches that first adopted this confession. They knew that being sent out with the gospel of Jesus Christ would result in suffering and possibly even death. Martyrdom was an intrinsic part of the trajectory of the life of a Reformed believer in this period.[98]

The Belgic Confession communicates the missiological message of martyrdom and suffering. The one who wrote it and those whose faith it expressed communicated very clearly through it that apostasy was not an option, at least in principle, if not always in practice. They were committed to the absolute and objective nature of the truth expressed in this confession. The Belgic Confession also communicates a witness about the desperation of the unbelieving world and those who claim to be Christians but whose lives do not conform to that claim. The Reformation was a missionary movement, and its strength caused grave concern to those in authority.[99] Finally, the Belgic Confession communicates to the world a powerful message about the cross. In fact, the churches which first adopted this confession often called themselves "Churches Under the Cross." They shared in the sufferings of Jesus Christ, and this is plain not only in the text of the Belgic Confession, but also in its literary and historical context.

The Belgic Confession and its rapid adoption throughout Western Europe had an enormous impact on the spread of the Reformation. The result of all the suffering and martyrdom was a rich harvest, not only in

---

97. See von Campenhausen, "Das Martyrium in der Mission," 71.
98. See Euan Cameron, *Interpreting Christian History: The Challenge of the Churches' Past* (Malden: Blackwell Publishing, 2005), 76.
99. Hendrix, *Recultivating the Vineyard*, 70-71.

terms of growth in numbers, but also in quality. At last, the Reformed churches of the Lowlands could rally around a confession they could call their own — a confession which not only reflected what they believed the Bible to be saying, but also one which grew out of their experiences.

3.2 Missionary Perspective: Antithetical Religions

As we turn to consider if there is a missionary perspective among the Reformers in this era, and especially de Brès and his confession, we need to distance ourselves from modern conceptions of mission. In many minds, mission is exclusively about bringing the gospel to heathen people who are unfamiliar with the Bible and who have never heard of, much less believed in, Jesus Christ. We concluded in chapters 1 and 2 that this was not the perspective of Reformers such as Luther, Calvin, and Bucer. Here we are going to build on that and explore the Reformers' (and de Brès') conception of the antithesis between the true and the false church, between true and false religion. Does this conception have a bearing on the question of the missiological relevance of the Belgic Confession?

3.2.1 Magisterial Protestant Reformers

Luther

When the library of Guido de Brès was seized by the authorities, books by Martin Luther were found in his possession.[100] Thus, no apology needs to be made for looking closer at the German Reformer and his views of the missionary character of the Reformation. Luther was hugely influential, and his influence stretched into the Netherlands.

Hendrix has described Luther's program to "Christianize" Europe in these words, building on a painting by Lucas Cranach the Younger: "As [Luther] saw it, the medieval church had planted the faith in the soil of pagan Europe but, after the faith had germinated, the bad husbandry of the papal church had neglected the field. Christianity had withered almost beyond recognition, and now the faith, in its genuine form, had to be replanted and cultivated."[101] From this perspective, it is entirely fitting to regard the Reformation as a sort of missionary movement. The Reformers were setting out to recover the gospel in a region where it had once been known, but then lost.

---

100. Gootjes, *The Belgic Confession*, 62. The original report of the discovery of de Brès' library is in Document 4 in the Appendix.
101. Hendrix, *Recultivating the Vineyard*, 65 .

A number of factors are integral to this perspective as it emerges in Luther and other Reformers. One is a reaction to the concept of "Christendom." Speaking generally, this is the notion that Europe comprised a Christian civilization. A precise definition of this concept is difficult, but for our purposes some of the most relevant contours include:

- the adoption of Christianity as the official religion of city, state, or Empire
- the assumption that all citizens (except Jews) were Christian by birth
- infant baptism as the symbol of obligatory incorporation into Christian society
- the development of a 'sacral society,' *corpus Christianum*, where there was no freedom of religion and political power was divinely authenticated
- division of the globe into 'Christendom' and 'heathendom' and wars waged in the name of Christ and the church
- there was no longer any significant distinction between 'church' and 'world'[102]

Essentially, the dominant perspective at the dawn of the Reformation was that Europe was Christian — "Christendom" was not in any sense a mission field.

Luther reacted to this notion, insisting that much of Europe had been infested by the sixteenth-century equivalent of the Canaanites: "Oh miserable people that we are, to live in these last times so securely and unperturbed among all these Baalites, Bethelites and Molechites, all of whom appear to be religious and Christian but who have nevertheless swallowed up the whole world and claim that they alone are the Christian church!"[103] According to Luther, the gospel was not being preached, and where the gospel is not preached, there can only be pagans.[104] That meant that, as far as Europe was concerned, there was a great deal of paganism. Writing in 1522, Luther insisted, "we are almost completely pagan and only

---

102. Stuart Murray, *Post-Christendom: Church and Mission in a Strange New World* (Waynesboro: Paternoster Press, 2004), 83-85.
103. *Luther's Works* (hereafter LW) 36:225-226.
104. *What Luther Says* (Vol. 1), comp. Ewald M. Plass (Saint Louis: Concordia Publishing House, 1959), 264.

Christian in name."[105] Through this assessment of the spiritual health of the continent, Luther was challenging the notion of Christendom and one of the assumptions that lay at the heart of it, viz., that Europe was not a mission field.

Closely connected with his challenge of the notion of Christendom was Luther's concept of the antithesis between true and false religion. Luther makes some strident comparisons between the Church of Rome and what he calls "the true church." He says that the Church of Rome is the bride of the devil.[106] He calls the papacy the kingdom of Babylon and anti-Christ.[107] He insists that the warfare between the seed of the woman and the seed of the serpent is recapitulated in the warfare between the Church of Rome and the true church.[108] He proves Rome to be the false church, "Satan's whore and synagogue," and a "heathen church."[109]

Nevertheless, despite all that harsh language, Luther's views of Rome were considerably more nuanced. He not only conceded that the Roman Church was part of Christendom (not a substantial concession), he also went so far as to say that "the church of Rome is holy."[110] He also granted that, while there was much of heathenism in her midst, "We do not regard you as Turks and Jews who are outside the church. But we say you do not remain in it but become the erring, apostate, whorelike church (as the prophets used to call it), which does not remain in the church, where it was born and brought up. You run away from this church and from your true husband and bridegroom (as Hosea says of the people of Israel [Hos. 1:2]) to the devil Baal, to Molech and Astaroth."[111] Luther insisted that the pre-Reformation church had its true Christians and through that church many of the essential elements of the Christian church and faith were preserved. As Hendrix rightly points out, there was both continuity and discontinuity.[112]

---

105. LW 36:264.
106. *What Luther Says* (Vol.1), 127.
107. *What Luther Says* (Vol. 2), 1010.
108. *What Luther Says* (Vol. 2), 1020.
109. LW 41:193-194, 199ff.
110. LW 26:24. This was written in 1535. However, cf. LW 41:271 where Luther in 1545 writes that Rome is not the holy church but a "school of scoundrels." Whether this is to be attributed to development or a tension in Luther's thought (or some other cause) is something that needs further investigation.
111. LW 41:207.
112. Hendrix, *Recultivating the Vineyard*, 45.

Nevertheless, by the sixteenth century there was much darkness over the land and, in Luther's mind, the Reformation was a missionary movement, bringing the gospel to Christendom. Writing to Philip Melanchthon in 1521 from Wartburg, Luther compares Wittenberg to Antioch and his colleagues to missionaries of a much earlier vintage:

> You lecture, Amsdorf lectures, Jonas will lecture. For goodness' sake, do you want the kingdom of God to be proclaimed only in your town? Don't others also need the gospel? Will your Antioch not release a Silas or a Paul or a Barnabas for some other work of the Spirit?
>
> I tell you: although I would be very happy to be with you all, yet I would not be disturbed if the Lord deigned to open to me a door for the Word either at Erfurt or Cologne or anywhere else, since you already have a surplus [of preachers and teachers]. Look how big a harvest there is everywhere — and how few are the harvesters! You all are harvesters. Certainly we have to consider not ourselves but our brethren who are spread out all over the country, lest we live for ourselves, that is, for the devil and not for Christ. Therefore be concerned that we are not drawn to one another too strongly and see the presence of the flesh more than the Spirit. I am ready to go where God wants me to go, either to Wittenberg or somewhere else.[113]

Considering the original biblical context of "You all are harvesters" in Matthew 9:37, Luther could just as well have said, "You all are missionaries." Reformation was mission.

Bucer

In chapter 2, we noted that Martin Bucer conceived of mission as being the extension and consolidation of the Kingdom of Christ through the preaching of the gospel. We also concluded that he had an eye for the necessity and obligation to both (what we would call) home and foreign mission. In this section, we want to build on that and briefly consider further Bucer's notion of the antithesis between true and false religion and how that relates to his missionary perspective.

Bucer is best known as the pre-eminent ecumenical theologian of the Reformation era. However, he is often portrayed as one whose ecumenic-

---

113. LW 48:262-263. Cf. Hendrix, *Recultivating the Vineyard*, 56-57.

ity only extended to the Reformation churches. This is a reasonable portrayal, for in his writings we find much of the same rhetoric as in Luther. Bucer describes the Roman Church as the "church of Antichrist."[114] He asserts that the church which lacks the marks of the true church (implicating the Roman Church) is not the body of Christ and is not the church of God.[115] In *De Regno Christi*, he complains that under the popes, the light of the gospel became virtually extinguished in Germany.[116] Like Luther, Bucer declares the Church of Rome to be the false church.[117] By the appearance of things, Bucer shared Luther's conception of a pagan Christendom in a Babylonian captivity.

As we saw in chapter 1, that perspective is definitely there in Bucer, and it contributes to his missionary outlook. Yet, quite remarkably, there is another Bucer. When it comes to the question of the Nicodemites, we find a Bucer who squares up against the other Swiss Reformers, including Calvin. There is the Bucer who "engaged in a prolonged flirtation with reforming Catholicism" at the Diet of Regensburg in 1541.[118]

Here we find a Bucer who still recognizes the darkness but proposes a different, more subversive strategy to address it. Interestingly, this proposal comes in the context of a Reformation debate between those who argued for the necessity of martyrdom and those who stood for a more subversive missionary strategy.[119] Under the influence of Luther, the Pope and the Roman Church were regarded by many Reformers as the forces of Antichrist who make martyrdom almost inevitable.[120] With this view, to compromise was to be complicit in idolatry. Matheson elaborates: "Discipleship was eminently overt. Dissimulation was to be abhorred. To confess the faith was to come out into the open about it,

---

114. *Common Places of Martin Bucer*, trans. and ed. D. F. Wright (Appleford: The Sutton Courtenay Press, 1972), 209.
115. *Common Places of Martin Bucer*, 206.
116. DRC, 211-212.
117. Martin Bucer, "Epistola Apologetica," in *Martini Buceri Opera Omnia I, series II: Opera Latina*, ed. F. Wendel et al. (Paris, Gütersloh, Leiden, 1955-), 104. Cited by Peter Matheson, "Martin Bucer and the Old Church," in *Martin Bucer: Reforming Church and Community*, ed. D. F. Wright (Cambridge: Cambridge UP, 1994), 5.
118. Matheson, "Martin Bucer and the Old Church," 11.
119. Peter Matheson, "Martyrdom or Mission? A Protestant Debate," *Archiv für Reformationsgeschichte* 80 (1989): 154.
120. Matheson, "Martyrdom or Mission?," 155.

to witness by propaganda, by exile, by martyrdom. Provocation became a principle."[121]

Bucer was on the other side of this debate. In 1540, he authored *Consilium Theologicum* in which he argued for a third way for Protestants living in Roman Catholic territories. Matheson describes the essence of Bucer's proposal:

> In Bucer's view the alternative to exile and martyrdom was the ultimately much more costly way of remaining within the Old Church, whether as layman, cleric or even bishop, if need be venerating the saints and even buying indulgences, but quietly spreading the true faith, waiting in longing for the day when 'Christ our Lord must reign everywhere.'...
>
> ... They saw the excellent prospects of Catholic bishoprics being drawn into the reformed orbit. They believed the religious colloquies would open up exciting possibilities for spreading Biblical faith and practice throughout a reunited Church. The missionary strategy they propounded, therefore, strikes some curiously contemporary notes, with its sensitivity to the problems of acculturation, and to the dangers of a 'foreign missions' mentality. Mission was not only to be conducted from a Protestant base, to which exiles could flee and in which potential martyrs could be trained. The key instrument of mission was the 'anonymous' individual working from within the situation, and exercising thus his God-given vocation.[122]

In Bucer's mind, the subversive way of reformation from within was to be preferred to the way of martyrdom. In the context of this study, it is worth pointing out that one of Bucer's opponents in this debate was Pierre Viret, the Lausanne Reformer under whom Guido de Brès studied for some time.[123] Finally, Matheson questions whether this strategy of Bucer was ever a real option to begin with.[124] With the failure of the Diet of Regensburg, hope faded for the possibility of reformation from within. All that was left was public confession, propaganda, exile, and martyrdom.

---

121. Matheson, "Martyrdom or Mission?," 157.
122. Matheson, "Martyrdom or Mission?," 163-164.
123. However, books by Bucer were also discovered in the library of de Brès. See Gootjes, *The Belgic Confession*, 62.
124. Matheson, "Martyrdom or Mission?," 171.

Calvin

In the first chapter we noted the enormous influence of John Calvin on de Brès and the writing of the Belgic Confession. Now we want to look more closely at Calvin and his missionary perspective. Particularly, we want to address this question: in Calvin's thinking, did Europe constitute a mission field? Is there continuity between Luther, Bucer and Calvin on this point?

In the preface to his commentary on the Psalms, Calvin provided a rare personal glimpse into his biography. He indicated his father had long planned for him to study theology, but as there was more money in law, the young Calvin was sent to study that instead. As he did so, something happened to him:

> To this pursuit I endeavoured faithfully to apply myself, in obedience to the will of my father; but God, by the secret guidance of his providence, at length gave a different direction to my course. And first, since I was too obstinately devoted to the superstitions of Popery to be easily extricated from so profound an abyss of mire, God by a sudden conversion subdued [*subita conversio*] and brought my mind to a teachable frame, which was more hardened in such matters than might have been expected from one at my early period of life. Having thus received some taste and knowledge of true godliness, I was immediately inflamed with so intense a desire to make progress therein, that although I did not altogether leave off other studies, I yet pursued them with less ardour.[125]

From this it would readily seem that Calvin considered his experience to be one of conversion to true Christianity. For Calvin, Roman Catholicism was sub-Christian at best.

The Prefatory Address to Francis I in Calvin's *Institutes* also demands our attention. According to Calvin, many of the French were hungering and thirsting for Christ, but very few had any degree of knowledge of him.[126] Under the Roman Church, "the light of divine truth had been ex-

---

125. John Calvin, *Commentary on the Book of Psalms* (Vol. 1) (Grand Rapids: Baker, 1979 reprint), xl.

126. *Institutes*, Dedicatory Epistle, 9. All references to the *Institutes* are to *Institutes of the Christian Religion* (2 volumes), ed. John T. McNeill; trans. Ford Lewis Battles (Philadelphia: the Westminster Press, 1960).

tinguished, the Word of God buried."[127] The papists may take the name of Christ upon their lips, but in reality they do not hold fast to him.[128] Calvin also adopts the view that the pope is Antichrist.[129] He not only denies that the Roman Church is the true church, but asserts that it is no church at all. In fact, he goes further than Luther, intimating that there is no difference between those in the Church of Rome and the Turks.[130] He starkly states the antithesis as being between Jerusalem and Babylon, between Christ's church and Satan's cabal.[131] The false church and those in it were the world and not really the church in any sense.

Muller has also drawn attention to Calvin's use of the term "labyrinth" in the *Institutes* to describe the problems of Roman Catholic theology. For instance, at one point Calvin writes that apart from looking straight to Christ we are left to "wander through endless labyrinths."[132] According to Muller, this is a patristic metaphor used by writers such as Jerome and Augustine to describe paganism and heresy.[133]

In Calvin's mind, Europe under the sway of Romanism was essentially pagan, or at least sub-Christian. This perspective raised questions when it came to practical matters such as marriage. In 1552, the pastors of Geneva received a letter from a Christian woman in France asking for marriage advice. She was a Reformed believer but married to a staunch Roman Catholic, "an idolater and persecutor of Christians." She asked if she could lawfully leave her husband. The reply, almost certainly written by Calvin, applies 1 Corinthians 7:10-16 (which speaks of a believing wife and an unbelieving husband) to the situation. She should make every effort to lead her husband to the way of salvation.[134]

There was one other question in this area: could a Christian (a Reformed believer) marry a Roman Catholic? This question arose in

---

127. John Dillenberger ed., *John Calvin: Selections from his Writings*, (Scholars Press, 1975), 102.
128. *Institutes*, 2.15.1.
129. *Institutes*, 4.2.11-12.
130. *Institutes*, 4.2.10.
131. *Institutes*, 4.2.4.
132. *Institutes*, 3.2.2.
133. Richard A. Muller, *The Unaccommodated Calvin: Studies in the Foundation of a Theological Tradition* (New York: Oxford UP, 2000), 83.
134. This letter and its reply can be found in *The Register of the Company of Pastors of Geneva in the Time of Calvin*, ed. and trans. Philip Edgcumbe Hughes (Eugene: Wipf & Stock, 2004), 193-198.

the context of debates with Faustus Socinus. He asked Calvin whether a Reformed believer ought to refrain from marrying a Romanist as one would refrain from marrying a Turk. Calvin replied that the adherents of the Roman Church were outside of Christ and that consequently there could be no marriage in the Lord, therefore marriage between Reformed believers and Romanists was unacceptable.[135] As far as Calvin was concerned, marrying a Roman Catholic was the same thing as marrying an unbeliever. This was not only Calvin's perspective, it was also that of the consistory of Geneva. In their estimation, one who would marry a Romanist would be renouncing Jesus Christ to go and worship idols.[136]

We can conclude that there was indeed agreement between the magisterial Reformers on the nature of sixteenth-century Europe as a mission field. Luther, Bucer, and Calvin, while sometimes disagreeing on the means by which this mission field should be Christianized, were in fundamental agreement on the spiritual state of the continent. Darkness and unbelief hung over the land like a dark cloud. In this state of affairs, Christ was hidden, the gospel was overthrown, and the worship of God had very nearly disappeared.[137]

3.2.2 Reformed Churches in the Lowlands

The ideals of the Protestant Reformation were not only propagated in the Netherlands by preachers and theologians. Artists, musicians, and actors were also key figures. In the Netherlands, and especially in Flanders, the Chambers of Rhetoric produced numerous dramatic productions reflecting a strongly held anti-clerical sentiment.[138] There were also poetry contests and pageants organized by the Chambers. Annual events were held at which awards and prizes were given for the best works.[139] During the 1560s, almost every play produced was anti-Roman. In at least one play, Roman Catholics were explicitly identified as being the heathen.[140] This sentiment existed in the popular mind as early as 1540. Crew cites a Flemish poem from that period:

---

135. Hendrix, *Recultivating the Vineyard*, 92.
136. Hendrix, *Recultivating the Vineyard*, 92.
137. *Institutes*, 4.3.12
138. See Collinet, *La Réformation en Belgique au XVIme Siècle*, 17-18.
139. Crew, *Calvinist Preaching*, 52.
140. Crew, *Calvinist Preaching*, 146.

> [The images] stand in the temple like house beams
> Rusted, dusty, covered with spider webs,
> Dirtied by birds, by cats, by mice.
> And in addition you must also acknowledge
> That they neither smell nor taste
> Nor have any sense of life; that is true.
> Those who love them, must be despised
> And they should not even be regarded as Christians.[141]

This poem alludes to the polemic against idolatry found in Psalm 115, and in so doing heightens the sense that the Romanists are truly the pagans in the land.

That sense was also there among the ministers of the Reformed churches in the Lowlands. Herman Moded insinuated that those in the Church of Rome were followers of Baal.[142] It was commonly held by the Reformed that the priests of Rome were sorcerers and magicians who practiced witchcraft.[143] In 1544, a delegation was sent from Tournai to Geneva, requesting that a Reformed missionary be sent because of the great paganism in the land.[144] In a poem, Jean Taffin expressed his understanding of the great antithesis between Rome and the Church:

> If the LORD is God, why not follow him?
> And if Baal is God, fall in with him, all of you.
> You cannot serve two masters at the same time,
> Nor can anyone acknowledge ministers and priests together:
> The Roman Mass and the Lord's Supper
> Can never walk hand in hand as equals.[145]

---

141. Crew, *Calvinist Preaching*, 29. The citation is from *Christelijcke en schriftuerlijcke referijnen* (publication information unknown), cited in turn from K. Pieter Aertzen Moxey, *Joachim Beuckelaer and the Rise of Secular Painting in the Context of the Reformation* (New York and London: Garland Press, 1977), 33.
142. Crew, *Calvinist Preaching*, 22.
143. Crew, *Calvinist Preaching*, 23, 25.
144. Crew, *Calvinist Preaching*, 53.
145. "Si l'Eternel est Dieu, sy ne le suivez vous?
    Et sy Baal est Dieu, rengez vous à luy tous.
    Vous ne pouvez server tout d'un coup à deux maistres,
    Ny advouer ensamble et ministres et prêstres:
    La Messe Romanesque et Cène du Seigneur
    Jamais ne marcheront d'une égale teneur."
Crew, *Calvinist Preaching*, 131. Cited from *Bibliophile Belge*, IV, 38. Translation mine.

Some of the last words of Gillis Verdickt were mentioned earlier in this chapter. While this minister was in prison, he was interrogated by an officer. At a certain point in the discussion, someone alleged that Verdickt thought that his opponents would all be eternally damned. Gillis replied, "No, my lord, you can repent and live."[146] His son Antoon was a deacon in the Reformed church and also a martyr. Van Haemstede relates that the younger Verdickt would encourage the minister during outdoor hedge preaching "so that the ignorant might be instructed and come to know the Lord and to fear him." He did everything in his power to plant the gospel in Flanders.[147] In a 1555 letter to the church at Emden, Gaspar vander Heyden wrote of Anabaptists who had been converted to the true faith. He also described a man who had become a Christian in Emden and vander Heyden's prayer was that the Lord would also open the eyes of his wife.[148] Guido Marnef notes that "Van der Heyden and the Antwerp consistory made a distinction between the children of God and the children of the World, according to which the former category consisted of those who made confession of their faith and accepted ecclesiastical discipline."[149] The continuity between the magisterial Reformers and these views is unmistakable.

In this mission context, the Reformed ministers of the Netherlands attempted to spread the gospel through a variety of means, the predominant of which was the use of public conventicles.[150] There were also secret conventicles held only for sworn members of the Reformed churches, but the public conventicles were open to all and were in fact intended to be an evangelistic tool. These events were held in a variety of places, from homes to wooded areas. They would consist of Bible reading and teaching, psalm-singing and prayers. Interestingly, the secret conventicles were usually led by elders and deacons, whereas the public conventicles would be led by ordained pastors.[151]

---

146. "The witness of Calvinist martyrs..." Crew, *Calvinist Preaching*, 6.
147. Crew, *Calvinist Preaching*, 9.
148. "The Minister of the Infant Reformed Congregation at Antwerp seeks the Advice of the Brethren at Emden, 17 December 1555." Translated by Alastair Duke and found at http://dutchrevolt.leidenuniv.nl
149. Guido Marnef, "Calvinism in Antwerp, 1558-1585," in *Calvinism in Europe: 1540-1620*, ed. Andrew Pettegree, Alastair Duke, and Gillian Lewis (Cambridge: Cambridge UP, 1994), 147.
150. Crew, *Calvinist Preaching*, 65.
151. Crew, *Calvinist Preaching*, 61.

One of those ordained pastors was the martyrologist Adrien van Haemstede. Van Haemstede ran into conflict with his consistory in Antwerp because of his desire to preach outside of the secret conventicles. He was of the opinion that public and open worship would make it more difficult for the Spanish to persecute the Reformed believers and that this would not only make life easier for the Reformed, but would also facilitate their evangelistic outreach. He desired to leave the ninety-nine sheep behind to go in search of the one who was lost, but the consistory maintained that his calling was to be a pastor of the flock and not to preach "hier ende daer."[152] Van Haemstede appears to have disobeyed the injunction of his consistory — and with dire consequences for the people of his city.[153] Nonetheless, with van Haemstede we do see a concern for the lost.

Crew's book (on which the above is dependent) raises more questions in this area. An important feature of the Reformation in this period is iconoclasm, especially that which took place in 1566. To what extent did iconoclasm function as part of the missionary perspective of the Reformed churches of this period? Another question grows out of the tension in this period between a quest for the toleration of Calvinism and a quest for the supremacy of Calvinism. There were ministers and other leaders whose goal was religious freedom for the Reformed churches. There were others whose goal was the complete eradication not only of the Romanists, but also the Anabaptists — their aim was nothing less than Reformed hegemony. Can these two quests be reconciled? Do these quests also grow out of a missionary perspective? These are questions that require further research.

3.2.3 Guido de Brès

We now consider the perspective of the author of the Confession as far as can be determined from his other writings. The writings to be considered here include a number of letters, records of debates held while he was in prison, and his major works, *Le baston* and *La racine*. Was the Belgian Reformer on the same page as his contemporaries when it came to how he viewed the context in which he lived and ministered?

As mentioned earlier, *Le baston de la foy chrestienne* was written in 1555 as a response to an earlier Roman Catholic work by Nicolas Grenier. It is essentially a collection of *loci communes* from Scripture

---

152. Crew, *Calvinist Preaching*, 71.
153. Crew, *Calvinist Preaching*, 81.

and the early church fathers. The title already gives evidence of the perspective of its author. De Brès is writing here about *the* Christian faith as distinguished from other faiths. This is underlined with the subtitle, "*pour s'armer contre les ennemis de l'Euangile & aussi pour cognoistre l'anciennete de nostre foy & de la vraye Eglise.*" With this subtitle, de Brès identifies the Roman church as an enemy of the gospel, comprised of those who have abandoned the ancient faith of the fathers, and which cannot be called the true church.

Interestingly, the 1558 edition has what appears to be a woodcut on the inside title page. The picture portrays one man planting and another man watering. Between the two of them a tree is growing, and over the tree is a cloud. In the midst of the cloud is the Tetragrammaton in Hebrew. On the fringes of the picture is a quote from 1 Corinthians 3:7: "So then neither he who plants is anything, nor he who waters, but God who gives the increase." The use of this passage is interesting because in its original context it speaks of the missionary efforts of Paul and Apollos in Corinth. It is impossible to know whether Guido de Brès had anything to do with the title page, but it does reflect the understanding of at least the publisher that this work is along the same lines of the apostolic mission.

While the content of the book is mostly dedicated to quotations from the fathers and from the Bible, there is a preface which contains the words of de Brès himself. He writes about the war and combat which exists with respect to guarding and maintaining the true and pure Christian doctrine and the ancient and true church of God.[154] According to de Brès, the Roman church does not possess the true doctrine, nor is it the church of God. Rather, it is an enemy of the gospel of the Son of God. Consequently, he identifies those under the yoke of Rome as pagans and idolaters.[155] Ironically, the children of God are zealously put to death by those who venerate the fathers, the very fathers whom de Brès proves to be in disagreement with the Roman Church.[156]

In the chapter on the church, de Brès discusses the marks of the church. He says that the church may be known by the marks given by Jesus Christ himself. According to de Brès, the marks are three: the Word of God, the Sacraments, and charity. Leaving aside the interesting discrep-

---

154. Guy de Brès, *Le baston de la foy chrestienne* (Geneva: Nicolas Barbier & Courtreau, 1558), 3.
155. Guy de Brès, *Le baston*, 4.
156. Guy de Brès, *Le baston*, 13.

ancy with that third point (and noting that the Belgic Confession speaks of discipline), for our purposes it is worthwhile to draw attention to de Brès' use of Matthew 28:18-20 under the heading of the Word of God as a mark of the church.[157] He comes back to this text (and its parallels in Mark 16 and Acts 1) in a subsequent section in which he argues that the authority of the church consists only in the preaching of the Gospel, the administration of the sacraments, and excommunication.[158] What this tells us is that de Brès' vision for the true church included what we call the Great Commission. He saw it as the continuing task of the church to spread the gospel everywhere, and that included the essentially pagan regions of Europe under the Roman yoke.

La racine may be considered the magnum opus of de Brès. This 1565 work of over 900 pages systematically exposed the weaknesses and falsehoods of Anabaptist teachings. The full title in translation is, "The Root, Source and Foundation of the Anabaptists, or the rebaptized of our time. With very ample refutations of the principal arguments by which they have been accustomed to trouble the Church of our Lord Jesus Christ and to seduce the simple."[159]

The mere size of this book indicates de Brès' concern with the influence of the Anabaptists in France and the Lowlands. In fact, it becomes clear that de Brès, like his contemporaries, regards Anabaptism as another religion.[160] Early in the work, he briefly describes the history of the gospel in Munster. He relates how Bernard Rotman began preaching the gospel in 1532 and that this preaching was very fruitful. In due time, a group of faithful ministers emerged and presented thirty articles of faith to the city magistrates. The city magistrates responded by calling the Romanist clergy to defend themselves with the Scriptures. Being

---

157. Guy de Brès, *Le baston*, 241.
158. Guy de Brès, *Le baston*, 244-245.
159. Guy de Brès, *La racine, source et fondement des anabaptistes ou rebaptisez de nostre temps. Avec tres ample refutations des arguments principaux, par lesquels ils ont accoustumé de troubler l'Eglise de nostre Seigneur Iesus Christ, & seduire les simples* (Rouen: Abel Clemence, 1565). A partial English translation was made by Joshua Scottow and published in Cambridge, MA in 1668 as *The Rise, Spring and Foundation of the Anabaptists*.
160. Crew (*Calvinist Preaching*, 116) relates that de Brès had several books by Menno Simons in his library (though Gootjes does not mention this, nor does document 4 in his appendix). If Crew is correct, then de Brès had direct access to Anabaptist thought.

unable to do so, the clergy were commanded to resign and give up their offices and churches to the Reformers. The result was that peace reigned in Munster. However, de Brès relates that the situation was soon greatly disturbed: "But Satan, the enemy of peace and of the truth, could not long endure the peace and publication of the Gospel; therefore, just as he had already done in other places, with might he worked to obstruct and overthrow the Gospel. He did this in order to establish in its place these seditious Anabaptists. He did just this at Munster, to the great damage of the faithful and the destruction and infamy of the Gospel."[161] While de Brès recognized the differences between Anabaptist groups (Munster was an extreme), it is clear that he saw at least some of them as being essentially sub-Christian or even pagan.

Later in *La racine*, de Brès interacts with the Anabaptist assertion that infant baptism was a Romanist invention. In this context, he puts as much distance as he can between the Reformed and the Roman Church. While infant baptism is something biblical that was preserved in the midst of much falsehood, according to de Brès there is no denying that the Roman Church is Antichrist.[162] He compares the situation to the people of Israel in the Old Testament. De Brès mentions the days of Jeroboam and the establishment of idolatrous worship at Dan and Bethel, worship offered to Baal and Molech, and the pointed prophecies of Ezekiel. He pays particular attention to Ezekiel 16 and the accusation that Israel had become more wicked than either Samaria or Sodom. During the days of Christ himself, the false prophets (and "the wicked ministers") ruled by force and tyranny — a parallel with the sixteenth-century context.[163] In this book, too, it is evident that de Brès regarded himself and his Church as being located in a missional context.

We now turn to some of de Brès' minor writings as collected in *Procedures*. As mentioned earlier, de Brès was imprisoned for several weeks in Valenciennes before his execution on May 31, 1567. We have a number of de Brès' letters from this period. One of them, dated April 18, 1567, was written to his church in Valenciennes. He relates how he was visited in prison by the Countess du Reu, accompanied by a group of women from the Reformed church. She expressed amazement at his heavy chains and

---

161. Guy de Brès, *La racine*, 19. Translation mine. As for Rotman, he succumbed to the teachings of Herman Staprede and became an Anabaptist.
162. Guy de Brès, *La racine*, 767. Cf. 773.
163. Guy de Brès, *La racine*, 768-770.

his ability to continue to sleep, eat, and drink. He responds by saying that it is the cause for which he is held that allows him to do these things. That cause is "the holy word of God."[164] The Countess then spoke of the fact that she had heard that de Brès "slandered the divine service of the Roman church" in his sermons. De Brès said, "I answered that I spoke as my text required and not otherwise, and when the doctrine that I preached required it, I did not disguise it. My charge required me to show the people the abuses and idolatries which led poor souls to perdition."[165] From this, we confirm that de Brès considered those under the yoke of the Roman church to be lost.

This is confirmed later in the same letter when de Brès looked back over his ministry, writing in Pauline tones: "It is well-known how I performed my duty of trying to lead those who were wrong to the right, and when men would not heed, God knew all about it. I proclaimed the Gospel, and instructed the people in the knowledge of the Son of God, and if I had a hundred thousand lives I would be willing to expose them all to death for the confirmation of that doctrine."[166] He bemoans the fact that so many have heard the preaching of the Gospel and yet so many continue to reject it. In fact, in his preaching he expressed his grief at this fact on many occasions.[167]

De Brès wrote another (much lengthier) letter to the Reformed church of Valenciennes sometime in the month of May. This letter is mostly taken up with providing a refutation of the Roman doctrine of the mass from Scripture and the early church fathers. Along the way, de Brès indicates the gravity of the situation in which the Reformed believers find themselves. Describing the Roman priests who turn bread into the body of Christ through five words ("*Hoc est enim corpus meum*"), de Brès exclaims, "I am surprised that the earth will hold such blasphemers."[168] He

---

164. *Procedures*, 7. I compared and corrected this (poor) English translation with the French found in *Procedures tenues a l'endroit de ceux la religion du pais bas* (Geneva: Jean Crespin, 1568) and the edition published by S. Cramer and F. Pijper. This consists of pages 491-643 of *Biblotheca Reformatoria Neerlandica* (Vol. 8) (hereafter BRN), 501.

165. *Procedures*, 8. BRN, 501.

166. *Procedures*, 12. BRN, 505.

167. *Procedures*, 12. BRN, 506. The English translation of *Procedures* leaves a sentence untranslated here: " . . . mon coeur est transpercé de douleurs. Helas ie voy auenir ce que plusieurs fois ie vous ay dit en mes preches."

168. *Procedures*, 53. BRN, 544.

insists that the Romanists hold forth the sophistries and fantasies of man, rather than the plain truth of God.[169] Those who seek the truth and the salvation of their souls will follow the teachings of Scripture, reaffirmed by the early church, and summarized by de Brès.[170] De Brès maintains that these matters are not light or indifferent, but matters of eternal salvation. Rome holds forth a "new doctrine" and a "new god," one who will not and cannot save.[171] As other Reformers, de Brès maintained the position that Rome was the Babylon described in Revelation 18.[172]

In the last paragraphs of this letter, de Brès exhorts the Reformed believers of Valenciennes to steadfastness. He reminds them that he preached to them the Gospel of their salvation and urges them to continue in it, again resorting to Pauline manners of expression, "So I admonish you with all my heart to walk in the holy doctrine which I have preached to you. And remember that I often exhorted you with tears and weeping, to do it publicly."[173] De Brès also speaks about those who have abjured as those who have renounced Christ and "revolted wickedly against the Son of God." He refers to Matt. 10:32-33 and directly implies that those who have left the Reformed faith are those who have denied Christ and who will consequently be denied by Christ before the Father in heaven.[174] In this letter, too, it is clear that de Brès regarded being Reformed as a matter of eternal welfare — those who were not Reformed, or who turned from being Reformed, were regarded as being under the wrath of God and thus, those who were in need of the gospel. This was what motivated de Brès to write this lengthy letter: "I will never forget you as long as I am in this world. I have written to you at great length about this matter of the Lord's Supper and the mass because they are the principal points on which those of the Roman church insist. And I have done that because of my concern for your salvation. I pray that you will receive this gladly as I present it to you."[175] Getting the doctrine of the Lord's Supper correct was, for de Brès,

---

169. *Procedures*, 56. BRN, 547.
170. *Procedures*, 58. BRN, 549.
171. *Procedures*, 65. BRN, 557.
172. *Procedures*, 96. BRN, 586.
173. "Et qu'ils vous souuienne que ie vous ay souuntesfois exhortez et admonnestez de ce faire publiquement, auec larmes et pleurs." *Procedures*, 102. BRN, 591.
174. *Procedures*, 102. BRN, 592.
175. *Procedures*, 103. BRN, 592.

an important part of the doctrine of the Son of God — so important that it was a matter of salvation.

In the beginning of May 1567, de Brès debated a Carmelite monk named Cordelier. At the beginning of their conversation, Cordelier said that he maintained the true religion and his prayer was that de Brès would do likewise. De Brès countered that he could not see that his visitor was maintaining the true religion.[176] Naturally, the conclusion is that this monk was following a false religion — something that was not truly Christianity.

Cordelier may have held similar sentiments about the Reformed faith. In 1302, Pope Boniface VIII issued his papal bull, *Unam Sanctam*. According to this bull, it is necessary for a Christian to be subject to the pope to be saved.[177] In 1516, the Fifth Lateran Council reaffirmed *Unam Sanctam* stating, "it is necessary to salvation that all the faithful of Christ be subject to the Roman pontiff."[178] It seems reasonable to assume that Cordelier was familiar with these deliverances from his church.

De Brès reports on an earlier conversation with Cordelier at a certain lady's home in Valenciennes. He says that Cordelier was accused by one of the people present as teaching that one's salvation depended on believing in both the corporeal and carnal body of Christ in the mass. Cordelier, however, denied going so far. The man replied that "the poor people who have listened to you preach believe that it is necessary to live and die in this faith."[179]

On May 22, 1567, a debate was held between François Richardot (the bishop of Arras) and de Brès. During the course of this debate, de Brès referred to the Roman Catholic faith as "your religion," thereby identifying it as something entirely different than the Christian faith which he believed.[180] At another point, de Brès referred to 1 Samuel 15 and, implicating Romanism, declared that humanly devised religion is idolatry and divination.[181]

---

176. *Procedures*, 126. BRN, 615.

177. Philip Schaff gives the bull in both English and Latin in his *History of the Christian Church* (Vol. 6) (Peabody: Hendrickson Publishers Inc., 2002 reprint), 25-28.

178. Schaff, *History*, 29.

179. *Procedures*, 134. BRN, 623.

180. "... si vous auez pensé de me gaigner à vostre religion ..." *Procedures*, 105. BRN, 594.

181. *Procedures*, 114. BRN, 603.

Two of the most touching letters of de Brès from this period are addressed to his wife and his mother. In the April 12, 1567, letter to his wife, Catherine, de Brès affirmed that he had preached "the doctrine of the Son of God" and encouraged her to honour that doctrine with word and deed.[182] On May 19, he wrote a letter to his mother in which he asserted that his cause had been "the cause of the Son of God" and for him to capitulate would be to "leave his God and give up eternal life."[183] God had heard the prayers of his mother and he had been "called to the holy ministry, not to preach the doctrines of man, but the pure and simple Word of Jesus and his Apostles." He maintains that he fulfilled this calling with a clear conscience, "seeking only the salvation of men."[184] He was confident that the large number of people that he had won to Christ would be his glory and crown on the last day.[185] Underlining his self-understanding as an evangelist/missionary, he claimed to have procured the salvation of many.[186] He was certain that he had sowed much good seed and that now that seed was about to be watered with his blood.[187]

FRANÇOIS
RICHARDOT
(1507-1574)

So it was on May 31, 1567. The report of his martyrdom tells us that he testified to the other prisoners and preached to them "the doctrine of the Son of God." He encouraged them to stand fast in that doctrine. He also said at least twice that he was being executed for "the doctrine of the Son of God."[188] In the mind of de Brès, he was a martyr, not for a tradition of the Christian faith, but for *the* Christian faith itself. He was not being martyred for what he believed, but for *the* faith as handed down by the Son of God himself. As far as he was concerned, those who were putting

---

182. *Procedures*, 139. BRN, 627.
183. *Procedures*, 140. BRN, 628.
184. *Procedures*, 141. BRN, 629.
185. "Et certes i'espere que le grand people que i'ay gaigné à mon Seigneur Iesus par l'Euangile, sera ma gloire et ma couronne au iour dernier." *Procedures*, 142. BRN, 630.
186. "I'ay procuré le salut de tous hommes . . ." *Procedures*, 144. BRN, 633. This is a strange expression and it may either be hyperbole or perhaps the meaning of "tous" has narrowed since the sixteenth century.
187. *Procedures*, 141. BRN, 630.
188. *Procedures*, 148-149. BRN, 636-637.

him to death were of the world. They were to be evangelized; they were those among whom it was necessary to sow the seed of the gospel.

3.2.4 THE BELGIC CONFESSION

Turning now to the Confession itself, it should not surprise us to find continuity. First of all, we note that the title indicates that it is the confession made by those who desire "to live according to the purity of the Gospel of our Lord Jesus Christ." This immediately sets the confessors apart from others around them. This is further emphasized by the quote from 1 Peter 3:15. Peter was clearly writing to Christians living in a pagan world, encouraging them to be always ready to offer a defense for their faith. The appropriation of these words on the title page of the Confession would seem to indicate the self-awareness of living in a pagan world in need of the gospel.

That self-awareness is also evident in the Dedicatory Epistle to Philip II. One would think that, given Philip's religious allegiance, there would be some restraint in this epistle on this score. However, while there is ample respect for Philip as a monarch, that restraint regarding the Roman Catholic context is simply not there. Referring to the blood of the Reformed martyrs shed thus far, de Brès writes that it was not for the cause of the brethren so much as "for the cause [or quarrel] of Jesus Christ."[189] Here too, de Brès speaks about abjuration as a denial of Christ before men, alluding once again to Matthew 10:32-33.[190] Attempting to assuage any concerns about the possibility of open rebellion, de Brès refers to one hundred thousand men who "hold and follow the religion" expressed in the Confession.[191] De Brès briefly outlines how the gospel was lost before and denied during the Reformation:

> From this Confession we trust that you will see that we are wrongly called schismatics, promoters of disunity, rebels and heretics, for we not only uphold and profess the chief heads of the Christian faith, comprehended in the Symbol and Common Creed [the Apostles' Creed], but also the whole teaching, revealed by Jesus Christ, for our life, justification and salvation, proclaimed by the evangelists and apostles, sealed with the

---

189. Hyde, *With Heart and Mouth* (hereafter WHM), 500. "... *pour la querrelle de Iesus Christ.*" BvdB, 64.
190. WHM, 500.
191. WHM, 501. BvdB, 64.

blood of so many martyrs and preserved true and complete by the primitive Church until at length it was perverted through the ignorance, greed and ambition of the ministers, who have corrupted it with human inventions and traditions contrary to the purity of the gospel, by which our adversaries deny that it is the power of God for the salvation of all believers...[192]

Moreover, de Brès identifies the broader context in which he ministers as "the world." He respectfully reminds Philip that "the world has always hated the light and rebelled against the truth" and, instead of receiving the Gospel with gratitude, sets itself against it.[193]

After the Dedicatory Epistle, the first editions of the Belgic Confession contained a number of passages "wherein the faithful are exhorted to give confession of their faith before men." We surveyed those passages above (3.1.3) with an eye to the metanarrative of martyrdom, but now we can look at those passages with an eye to missionary self-awareness. The first passage is Matthew 10:32-33 and this passage comes up repeatedly in the writings of de Brès, as we have seen. The use of this passage indicates a particular understanding of the Reformed faith as the only path to salvation; to abjure is to be lost. Concomitantly, not to confess this same faith is also to be lost. Next, de Brès quotes Mark 8:38, referencing also the parallel in Luke 9:26. In this passage, the Lord Jesus speaks about those who are ashamed of him "in this adulterous and sinful generation." Christ says that he in turn will be ashamed of them and in so saying implies that confession is a matter of eternal salvation. 1 Peter 3:15 is found next (this text has already been discussed above). Finally, de Brès cites 2 Timothy 2:12b: "If we deny him [Jesus Christ], he also will deny us." There is nothing new in that; it serves to emphasize the serious consequences of abjuring the faith. From this selection of texts, it is apparent that the faithful of the Lowlands confessed their faith with the self-awareness that they were living in the midst of an "adulterous and sinful generation." They, like the recipients of Peter's first letter, were the "pilgrims of the Dispersion," a sixteenth-century Christian diaspora.

Before getting into the body of the Confession, there is one final preliminary item to consider. The Confession in its earliest editions contained an additional title immediately before the text: "Truly Christian

---

192. WHM, 502. BvdB, 66. I have revised the translation of Duke here in some places to more faithfully reflect the French.
193. WHM, 503-504. BvdB, 66.

Confession, Containing the Eternal Salvation of the Soul." There is a reason why virtually all modern editions of the Belgic Confession drop these words.[194] There is a self-understanding implied here that does not comport well with modern ecumenical sensitivities. The understanding is that the faith expressed in this Confession is the one and only true faith. Not that other Confessions have not expressed the same content in different words and languages, but that the content of this Confession, i.e. the Reformed faith, is *the* Christian faith.

Following the confession of the "only one God" in article 1, the Confession turns to the matter of the revelation of this God. Article 6 expresses the difference between the canonical and apocryphal books. First, the Confession lists the books and then the following is asserted:

> The church may read and take instruction from these [apocryphal books] so far as they agree with the canonical books. They are, however, far from having such power and authority that we may confirm from their testimony any point of faith or of the Christian religion; much less may they be used to detract from the authority of the holy books.[195]

This is a remarkable statement for a number of reasons. First, the Roman Catholic Church takes a different perspective on these books, treating them as canonical. This raises the possibility that, when de Brès wrote, "The church may read…", he was implying that the Roman Catholic Church is not "the church." Second, this is also the effect of asserting that the apocryphal books may not be used to confirm "any point of faith or of the Christian religion."[196] The true Christian religion does not stand on the foundation of any teachings found only in the apocryphal books. Third, de Brès himself does, in fact, refer to the apocryphal books in a number of his writings and even the first edition of the Belgic Confession contained two citations from apocryphal books (in articles 12 and 37).[197]

---

194. The only one that I could find was the *Book of Praise*. The *Book of Praise* has slightly altered the words to: "True Christian Confession, Containing the Summary of the Doctrine of God and of the Eternal Salvation of Man."
195. BoP, 444. BvdB, 76.
196. There does not appear to be any significant difference here between "faith" and "the Christian religion." I believe the terms are used here nearly synonymously, perhaps in apposition.
197. In all his writings, de Brès quotes from 9 apocryphal books 48 times. Of those 48 times, only once is it in a negative context. 20/48 (42%) of the references

After one more article on the doctrine of Scripture (article 7), the Confession begins a section dealing with the doctrine of the Trinity (articles 8-11). Article 8 provides the statement of the doctrine, and then article 9 lays out the scriptural proofs. At the conclusion of this article, de Brès asserts that this doctrine of the Trinity has always been maintained by the true church though various efforts have been made to assail it. Among those assailants are "false Christians and heretics" such as Marcion, Mani, Praxeas, Sabellius, Paul of Samosata, and Arius. The article concludes with an affirmation of the three ecumenical creeds: that of the Apostles; the Nicene; and the Athanasian.[198] The mention of the last is especially noteworthy because of its anathemas upon those who deny the orthodox teachings of the Trinity and of the two natures of Christ. According to the Athanasian Creed, "false Christians and heretics" cannot be saved if they deny "the Catholic faith." We shall come back to this point momentarily.

Articles 12-14 lay out the biblical teachings on creation and providence. The providence of God is the subject of article 13, and it concludes with a denunciation: "We therefore reject the damnable error of the Epicureans, who say that God does not concern Himself with anything but leaves all things to chance."[199] Using the background of Calvin's publications, Gootjes has identified the term "Epicureans" in this article as a sixteenth-century pejorative, referring to a broad school of thought which minimized or denied God's involvement in the world.[200] This error was "damnable" because all things are left to chance ("*adventure*") and that includes things pertaining to salvation. The Epicureans were those who, according to Calvin, trample the gospel, make it into a joke, and "despise the blood of Christ, the eternal truth of God and the light of life."[201] From the perspective of Calvin (and de Brès), this was a movement in darkness and the fact that the Belgic Confession mentions it demonstrates that the churches were self-consciously aware of the lost in their context. They were compelled to witness for the truth of God's providence.

---

are to Wisdom. 16/48 (33%) are to Ecclesiasticus. Together they make up 75% of the apocryphal references in de Brès' writings.

198. BoP, 447. BvdB, 84.

199. BoP, 450. BvdB, 90-92.

200. Nicolaas H. Gootjes, "Calvin on Epicurus and the Epicureans: Background to a Remark in Article 13 of the Belgic Confession," *Calvin Theological Journal* 40.1 (April, 2005): 33-48.

201. Quoted in Gootjes, "Calvin on Epicurus," 47.

Likewise, they were compelled to witness for the truth of Christ's incarnation. Following articles on original sin, election, and man's rescue, article 18 outlines the Reformed confession on the incarnation of the Son of God. A familiar pattern emerges: first the doctrine is stated positively, followed by the rejection of an error (or errors). In this case, the Anabaptists are identified as heretics, as those who "deny that Christ assumed human flesh of his mother."[202] To place this statement in its proper context, we need to briefly consider the sixteenth-century understanding of heresy. The word "heresy" was not casually used; rather, it refers to an error of significant proportions, an error which is a matter of salvation.[203] This is illustrated with Calvin when he deals with the Anabaptist Christology. Calvin does not even deign to mention Menno Simons and his followers by name; instead he calls them Marcionites.[204] As mentioned above, the Marcionites were recognized by the Reformed churches as having been justly condemned by the early fathers — they denied the Catholic faith. In other words, to be a Marcionite was to remain outside of Jesus Christ. This is the reason why the longest chapter of de Brès' massive *La racine* is taken up with the Anabaptist Christology — this was the most serious of the Anabaptist errors, an error which was a dangerous heresy. Read in this light, article 18 of the Confession is another testimony regarding the self-awareness of the Reformed Churches that they were living on what we would call a mission field.

Christology forms the heart of the Belgic Confession (articles 18-26). Article 22 affirms the Reformation doctrine of justification by faith alone. True faith does not seek anything besides Jesus Christ — all we need for our salvation is in him. If someone has Jesus Christ, he or she has complete salvation: "It is, therefore, a terrible blasphemy to assert that Christ is not sufficient, but that something else is needed besides Him, for the conclusion would then be that Christ is only half a Saviour."[205] This raises the question of where one might locate blasphemers in the sixteenth cen-

---

202. BoP, 453. BvdB, 100.

203. See "Heresy," in *Encyclopedia of the Reformed Faith*, ed. Donald K. McKim, (Louisville: Westminster John Knox Press, 1992), 172; Harold O. J. Brown, *Heresies: The Image of Christ in the Mirror of Heresy and Orthodoxy from the Apostles to the Present* (Grand Rapids: Baker, 1984), 310.

204. *Institutes*, 2.13.1.

205. "De dire donc que Christ ne suffit point, mais qu'il y faut quelque aultre chose avec, c'est un blaspheme trop enorme contre Dieu. Car il s'ensuivroit, que Iesus Christ ne seroit que demy Sauveur." BoP, 456-457. BvdB, 106.

tury. We have seen above (3.2.3) that, according to de Brès, blasphemy is a feature of the world, not of the church. To deny justification by faith alone is to blaspheme, to be on the dark side of the antithesis.

This comes back in article 26, dealing with the intercession of Christ. De Brès outlined the mediatorial work of Christ in heaven, especially as it pertains to the prayers of God's people. Then, again looking Rome-ward, he adds, "Therefore it was pure lack of trust which introduced the custom of dishonouring the saints rather than honouring them, doing what they themselves never did nor required."[206] This is an ingenious way of addressing the Roman Catholic veneration of the saints. De Brès identifies such veneration as dishonour for the saints, but goes even further and identifies it as a pure lack of trust (*la seule deffiance*) in Christ. In other words, honouring the saints reflects an entire mistrust with regard to Jesus Christ — where the saints are honoured, there can be no true faith in Christ and consequently no salvation.

Articles 27 to 32 express the ecclesiological understanding of the Reformed churches. Article 27 alludes to the persecution experienced by the believers in the Lowlands and classifies that persecution as being "the fury of the whole world." In article 28, the false church is recognized by, among other things, its persecution of "those who live holy lives according to the Word of God and who rebuke the false church for its sins, greed, and idolatries."[207] Either the false church is in collusion with the world, or it is to be identified as part of the world. The body of evidence considered so far favours the latter conclusion.

This is confirmed by the manner in which the Belgic Confession appropriates the patristic teaching that "There is no salvation outside of the church" in article 28. This is the church from which one may (but is not allowed to) withdraw, the church which every believer is obliged to join and unite with. This is the church which exists in local communities and, in the context of the Belgic Confession, is to be strictly identified with the Reformed church. In the Lowlands, the Reformed church was where one would find the pure preaching of the gospel, the pure administration of the sacraments, and the exercise of church discipline (the marks of the true church outlined in article 29). In this framework, to say "there is no salvation outside of it" is to say that life in the Netherlands for the Reformed believers was a situation of the church against the world. Outside

---

206. "Pure lack of trust" = "*La seule deffiance.*" BoP, 460. BvdB, 118.
207. BoP, 464. BvdB, 126.

of the church is the world of unbelief, of which the false church and sects are a part. If one desires salvation, he must be where the marks of the church are found, especially the pure preaching of the gospel.[208]

Article 28 also says that, with regard to the true catholic church, everyone "must submit themselves to its instruction and discipline, bend their necks under the yoke of Jesus Christ, and serve the edification of the brothers and sisters..."[209] Bending the neck under the yoke of Jesus Christ is, of course, an allusion to the words of Jesus in Matthew 11:28-30. This statement here in the Confession qualifies the unity of the true church, insisting that it is determined by Jesus' teaching and discipline. Those who submit to those share true unity, whereas those who do not are implied to be objects of the mission of the church. This expression first received ecclesiological attention from Martin Bucer.[210] Building on his exegesis of Ezekiel 34 in *Von der waren Seelsorge*, Bucer started to categorize peoples within and outside the church.[211] Similarly, as noted above, in article 9, the Belgic Confession speaks of unbelievers (Jews, Muslims) and heretics. Later on, the unbelieving world would be categorized by Reformed theologians into infidels (Gentiles, Jews, Muslims), heretics (e.g. Roman Catholics) and schismatics (e.g. Lutherans).[212] The first two groups would be regarded as objects of mission.

---

208. This is not to say that de Brès and other Reformed theologians did not allow for the possibility that individual Roman Catholic, Anabaptists or others would be saved. As Hyde comments, "The ordinary, promised means by which God saves sinners is his visible church, because there is a necessary link between salvation in Christ and his body, the church..." Hyde, WHM, 379.

209. BoP, 462-463. BvdB, 122.

210. For more on the background and meaning of this expression, see W. van't Spijker, "'Den Hals Buygende Onder Het Jock Jesu Christi..', Oorsprong en zin van een uitdrukking in art. 28 and 29 van de Nederlandse Geloofsbelijdenis" in *Bezield Verband: Opstellen aageboden aan prof. J. Kamphuis*, J. Douma (ed.) (Kampen: Van den Berg: 1984), 206-219. For an English summary of van't Spijker, see G. Van Rongen, *The Church: Its Unity in Confession and History* (Neerlandia: Inheritance Publications, 1998), 96-100.

211. Joosse, *Reformatie en zending*, 57ff.

212. Philippe Du Plessis Mornay, *De Veritate Religionis Christianae Liber; Adversus Atheos, Epicureos, Ethnicos, Judaeos, Mahumedistas, et caeteros Infideles* (Antwerp: Christopher Plantin, 1583); see also Leendert Jan Joosse, *Geloof in de Nieuwe Wereld: Ontmoeting met Afrikanen en Indianen (1600-1700)* (Kampen: Uitgeverij Kok, 2008), 81.

Following the articles on the church, the Confession deals with the sacraments. Then follows an article on the civil government (article 36) and one on the last judgment (37). Article 36 has been extensively discussed in the Reformed churches in the last century and a half because of the role that it assigns to the civil magistrate. A General Synod in the Netherlands in 1905 deleted a number of words originally penned by de Brès and held by the Reformed churches for over three centuries. The relevant section reads as follows (the deleted words are in italics):

> Their task of restraining and sustaining is not limited to the public order but includes the protection of the church and its ministry in order that *all idolatry and false worship may be removed and prevented, the kingdom of Antichrist may be destroyed,* the kingdom of Christ may come, the Word of the gospel may be preached everywhere, and God may be honoured and served by everyone as He requires in His Word.[213]

As we have noted previously, in the sixteenth-century context, "the kingdom of Antichrist" was to be identified with the Roman church and others regarded as enemies of the gospel. "The Kingdom of Christ," on the other hand was regarded as the church of Christ and the progress of the gospel. We will discuss this matter of the role of the civil government in chapter 5, but for now we note that here the Confession continues to evidence awareness of a missional environment. The kingdom of Antichrist exists, and the way to suppress it and advance the kingdom of Christ is through the preaching of the gospel.

Article 37 expresses the main contours of the eschatology of the Reformed believers in the Lowlands. For our purposes, it is worth noting that the Confession holds out hope for vindication at the last judgment. In this world, the wicked persecute, oppress, and torment the righteous elect. Here again, the enemies of the Reformed are classified on the black side of the antithesis — they are "the wicked and evildoers." On the bright and righteous side of the antithesis are the Reformed: "God will wipe away every tear from their eyes (Rev. 21:4), and their cause — at present condemned as heretical and evil by many judges and civil authorities — will be recognized as the cause of the Son of God."[214] With that, the Reformed churches again reflect their self-identity as the ones

---

213. BoP, 470-471. BvdB, 140.
214. BoP, 472. BvdB, 144.

who have been entrusted with the gospel and sent out into the world for a witness to unbelief.

We can therefore conclude this section by affirming that there is indeed continuity between the magisterial Reformers, the Reformed churches of the Lowlands, Guido de Brès, and the Belgic Confession. All recognize that the Reformed churches exist in a context of darkness and unbelief, even virtual paganism. In sixteenth-century Reformed thinking there is a strict antithesis between belief and unbelief. Roman Catholicism, Anabaptism and other sects/philosophies fall on the unbelief side of this antithesis, whereas the Reformed fall on the side of belief. This antithesis undeniably shapes the Reformed understanding of sixteenth-century Europe as a mission field.

3.3 Missionary Perspective: The Non-European World

Earlier (1.1.1.1) we noted that sixteenth-century Europe found itself in an "Age of Expansion." Many European powers were steadily adding empires in the Americas, Asia, and Africa. The borders of the world were quickly changing. It could be questioned, however, whether the author and original recipients/patrons of the Belgic Confession were sensitive to this realization. Did the Confession lead them to consider their task in bringing the gospel to newly discovered lands and nations?

This is not a question that needs to occupy our attention for long. In the middle of the sixteenth century, discovery and colonization required powerful naval capabilities. Such capabilities were only available to well-established nations such as Spain or Portugal. Moreover, the Reformed believers in the Low Countries would have had only a meagre knowledge of distant lands. Their political and social situation was such that very little (if any) thought would have been given to the newly discovered regions of the world.

Richard Muller has quite rightly drawn attention to the singular failure of much missionary historiography in its analysis and evaluation of sixteenth-century Reformed churches. He noted that while "modern practitioners of mission consistently argue the need to contextualize — their historiography fails to do so."[215] Sixteenth-century Reformers were, by and large, citizens of lands with no pretensions to achieving global dominance through discovery and colonization. Therefore, it is anachronistic to assume that they would be looking for ways and means to spread

---

215. Muller, "To Grant this Grace," 217.

the gospel beyond Europe.[216] The same conclusion can be made with regard to the Reformed churches of the Low Countries in this era.

Conclusion

In chapter 2, we explored the definition of mission and noted that the contours of this definition were in place already in the sixteenth century. In this chapter, we have explored the original missionary nature and intent of the Confession. The Confession was the witness of churches "under the cross." It developed in a context where martyrdom was understood to have a powerful missionary effect. Its author and many of his brothers in the faith were put to death for the doctrines contained therein. Their deaths and the confession for which they died were regarded as a witness.

Being a witness leads one to inquire as to the object of this witness. This is what we considered in more detail in the second half of this chapter. Our conclusion must be that P. Y. DeJong was exactly right when he titled his commentary on the Confession, *The Church's Witness to the World*. Amongst its original confessors, the Belgic Confession was regarded as a testimony to the unbelieving masses outside the (Reformed) church.

So we can say that, speaking historically, the Belgic Confession did have missiological relevance. But what about for today? We will explore this in more detail in chapter 5, but for now we can note that the Belgic Confession speaks in article 27 about "The Catholic Christian Church." The Church's catholicity is socio-cultural, temporal, and geographic. The Belgic Confession reminds believers of the sufferings of the Church both in ages past and today. Even if believers in a given locale do not suffer for their faith, the Belgic Confession reminds them that there are multitudes of believers elsewhere who are giving (or who are prepared to give) the ultimate witness to and for Jesus Christ. Part of the contemporary missiological significance of the Belgic Confession rests in its unique witness to the sufferings of the Church in the past, present, and future. The church which gives up this Confession for one emerging from a more comfortable milieu is impoverishing itself and its witness.

The Confession also has missiological relevance in the way it continues to challenge us with respect to the antithesis. Our age has very keenly developed ecumenical sensitivities, but these have often developed at the expense of the antithesis. Do we still understand the difference between the true and false church? Do we still see the false church as being part

---

216. Muller, "To Grant this Grace," 215.

of the world — as a mission field? Recovering the antithesis in mission also tempers any sort of missionary triumphalism. Especially in certain circles, missiologists have a fascination with statistics and the story that these allegedly tell about the progress of the gospel. A distinction is often made between reached and unreached peoples. Yet, the Belgic Confession challenges us: can we really consider an area that is predominantly Roman Catholic as an area that has been reached with the gospel? We will also evaluate and explore this in more detail in chapter 5.

So, when we ask the question as to whether the Belgic Confession had an original missionary nature and intent, the answer must be in the affirmative. We can also begin to see that this original nature and intent has a relevance for the present day. Now it remains to be investigated whether its organization supports this nature and intent. We will look at that in the next chapter.

Chapter Four
Relating Structure and Organization to Nature and Intent

4.0 Introduction

The structure and organization of the Confession often receives attention in the literature, but this attention is typically superficial. A survey of commentaries reveals that the structure of the Confession is generally well-recognized. However, it is difficult to locate any serious discussion on the rationale for the structure.[1] Therefore, in this chapter, we will investigate not only the structure but also its background and rationale, doing so with an eye to missiological relevance.

TStructure ofhe Belgic Confession consists of 37 articles of faith. The 1561 original divided the confession according to these 37 articles, but added no other structural indicators. Also, headings were not added to the articles until later editions. As a result of these factors, there is (predictably) some variation in the way commentators view the structure. The following is one helpful way to divide the articles:

    Articles 1-11   The Triune God and Scripture
    Articles 12-15 Creation and Fall
    Articles 16-26 Redemption through Jesus Christ
    Articles 27-35 The Church and Its Ministry
    Article 36   The Civil Government
    Article 37   The Last Judgment

Hyde prefers a different structure, following the organization of modern systematic theologies:

---

1. The commentaries surveyed were: Hyde, WHM; DeJong, *The Church's Witness to the World*; J. Van Bruggen, *The Church Says Amen: An Exposition of the Belgic Confession*, (Neerlandia: Inheritance, 2003); and Clarence Bouwman, *The Overflowing Riches of My God: Revisiting the Belgic Confession* (Winnipeg: Premier, 2008).

Articles 1-13	The Doctrine of God
Articles 14-15	The Doctrine of Man
Articles 16-21	The Doctrine of Christ
Articles 22-26	The Doctrine of Salvation
Articles 27-36	The Doctrine of the Church
Article 37	The Doctrine of the End[2]

Such an organization may also be defensible, and one can note the overlaps indicating a general sense of structure to this Confession regardless of how one defines the details. Now it remains for us to determine whether there is a reason for this particular structure and the relation that might have to the original missionary nature and intent of the Confession as determined in the last three chapters.

4.1 THE FRENCH CONFESSION AND THE *INSTITUTES*: STRUCTURAL MODELS

As indicated earlier, there are two main sources for the Belgic Confession: the French Confession of 1559 and John Calvin's *Institutes of the Christian Religion*. These sources have also contributed to the structure/organization of the Confession. Thus, when we examine this aspect of the Confession, we also need to carefully consider this aspect of these sources.

4.1.1 THE FRENCH CONFESSION

The French Confession traces its origins to 1557 and a period of persecution among the Reformed believers in France. Around this time, an eighteen-article statement of faith was sent to Calvin for his input. Likely collaborating with Theodore Beza and Pierre Viret, Calvin sent back a revised draft consisting of thirty-five articles. In May of 1559, a Synod of the Reformed Churches was held in Paris, and after several days of discussion and revision, the French Confession was adopted. The adopted text differed from the text sent by Geneva in that it featured forty articles, rather than thirty-five. The first two articles had been expanded into six.[3]

---

2. Hyde, WHM, 26-29.
3. See Arthur C. Cochrane ed., *Reformed Confessions of the Sixteenth Century* (Louisville: Westminster John Knox Press, 2003), 137-138.

The structure of the French Confession is very similar to that of the Belgic:

	French	Belgic
Triune God and Scripture	1-7	1-11
Creation and Fall	8-11	12-15
Redemption	12-24	16-26
Church	25-38	27-35
Civil Government	39-40	36
Last Judgment	None	37

Not only is the structure similar; so is the format. It consists of a number of articles of faith dealing with certain topics, preceded by a letter addressed to a monarch. It is a genre very common among the churches of the Reformation, both Calvinist and Lutheran.

For our purposes, the noteworthy feature is the influence of John Calvin. Though his influence does not become explicit until his reception of the eighteen articles, it is very likely that his fingerprints were all over this document also in its early stages. Research into Calvin's correspondence during this period reveals that the most frequent destination for the Genevan Reformer's letters was France.[4] Moreover, P. Y. De Jong observed that the French Confession is, in fact, a summary of Calvin's *Institutes*.[5] That being true, Calvin's disciples in France summarized the *Institutes* and then sent that summary back to him for his own input. So, if we are to investigate the structure of the Belgic Confession, we also need to give attention to the structure of the *Institutes*.

4.1.2 THE INSTITUTES

Many authors have noted the parallels in content and structure between the Belgic Confession and the *Institutes*. For instance, the structural parallels have been observed by Hyde: "...the Confession follows the structure of the *Institutes*: God the Father (articles 1-15; book 1), God the Son (articles 16-21; book 2), God the Holy Spirit (articles 22-26; book 3),

---

4. Benedict, *Christ's Churches Purely Reformed*, 111. During 1559, Calvin sent over 20 letters to northern France, between 10 and 14 to Paris, 1 to 4 to central France, and 4 to 9 to southern France.

5. De Jong, *Church's Witness to the World*, 29. Cf. C. Vonk, *De Voorzeide Leer (Deel IIIa: De Nederlandse Geloofsbelijdenis Art.1-21 en 25-26)* (Barendrecht: Drukkerij "Barendrecht," 1955), 103.

and the church (articles 27-36 [article 37 is on eschatology]; book 4)."⁶ In general, this is a helpful observation.

However, can we insist on such parallels? How much value can we place on them? After all, the Confession dates from 1561 and prior to 1559, Calvin's *Institutes* was not divided into books. If we trace the lineage of the Belgic Confession through the French Confession, we do well to remember that the final 1559 edition of the *Institutes* was not published until after August, whereas the French Confession was adopted by the Synod of Paris in late May.⁷ Nevertheless, Calvin probably had been working on the revisions when he contributed to the drafting of the French Confession. Furthermore, while the division into books took place in 1559, the basic final structure was already in place with the 1550 edition. An additional consideration is that there are places in which de Brès departs from the structure of the French Confession to follow the structure of the 1559 *Institutes* instead.⁸

To understand the structure of the Belgic Confession, we need to get behind the rationale for the structure of the *Institutes*. In the 1559 edition, the work was divided into four books:

Book 1: The Knowledge of God the Creator

Book 2: The Knowledge of God the Redeemer in Christ, First Disclosed to the Fathers Under the Law and Then to Us in the Gospel

Book 3: The Way in Which We Receive the Grace of Christ: What Benefits Come to Us From It and What Effects Follow

Book 4: The External Means or Aids By Which God Invites Us into the Society of Christ and Holds Us Therein

But what are the origins of this structure? As we shall see in the next section, Calvin was not an innovator on this score, and consequently, neither was Guido de Brès.

---

6. Hyde, WHM, 20-21. Cf. Strauss, "John Calvin and the Belgic Confession," 507-508.
7. W. de Greef, *The Writings of John Calvin: An Introductory Guide* (Expanded Edition) (Grand Rapids: Baker, 2008), 129, 188.
8. For instance, in the doctrine of the church. See C. Vonk, *De Voorzeide Leer (Deel IIIb)*, 105.

4.1.3 STRUCTURAL MODEL FOR CALVIN: LOCUS METHOD

In the last decades a number of Reformation scholars have made significant efforts to relate John Calvin and the other Reformers to the preceding medieval context. One of those is David Steinmetz. He has evaluated Calvin in light of the scholastic theologians of the late Middle Ages and noted several surprising continuities. While there are important differences in the content and emphasis of Calvin's theology, there are also formal similarities. For instance, Steinmetz has noted that the Latin of Calvin in the *Institutes* is comparable to that of Gabriel Biel. He also noted the structural similarities between the *Institutes* and the *Sentences* of Peter Lombard.[9]

Richard Muller shares these observations and develops them further. In his book *The Unaccommodated Calvin*, Muller has argued that the *Institutes* have to be understood in relationship with medieval theology. From the beginning of his career, Calvin was concerned with proper structure and organization, with *ordo recte docendi*. In his first published work, a commentary on Seneca's *De Clementia*, Calvin criticized the Roman author for his lack of orderly arrangement.[10] Throughout the development of the *Institutes* (from 1536 to 1559), Calvin himself was obsessed with a proper structure for this work.

According to Muller, a number of medieval structural streams converge in the development of the *Institutes*. In the first place, we find the use of the *locus* method found with Lombard and other medieval scholastic theologians. As mentioned, Muller sees the parallels between the *Sentences* and the *Institutes* in this regard. Both contain statements of theological truths, consideration of past thought, objections, and replies to the objections.[11] There are parallels in method and intention between Calvin and Lombard, also when it comes to the manner in which the truths of the faith are systematized.[12] Various topics are dealt with under a series of headings and in the final edition of the *Institutes*, one finds a division of four books, just as in Lombard. Of course, Calvin was not alone among the Reformers in following the *locus* method, nor was

---

9. David Steinmetz, "The Scholastic Calvin," in *Protestant Scholasticism: Essays in Reassessment*, ed. Carl Trueman and R. Scott Clark (Carlisle: Paternoster Press, 1999), 24.
10. Muller, *The Unaccommodated Calvin*, 23.
11. Muller, *The Unaccommodated Calvin*, 45.
12. Muller, *The Unaccommodated Calvin*, 57.

he the first. Muller identifies Philip Melanchthon as the one who established the locus method as the standard for sixteenth-century Protestant theology with his *Loci Communes Theologici*.[13]

The *locus* method became more pronounced in the *Institutes* with the publication of each new edition. This may be related to the observation that Calvin's deeper knowledge of medieval theology was a late development.[14] Nevertheless, when the first edition was published in 1536, the structure was clearly a standard approach to theology, one which dated before Luther.[15]

Like the Belgic Confession, the *Institutes* were written to serve the church and not the academy. They were intended as an expression of the faith of the Reformed churches and Muller warns against regarding the *Institutes* as a complete systematic theology in the modern sense.[16] When first published in 1536, the *Institutes* were intended primarily as a catechetical manual for those "hungering and thirsting for Christ." There was an apologetical thrust as well, but it was secondary.[17] The structure reflected this catechetical emphasis, taking over the medieval catechetical order giving attention to the Creed, the Ten Commandments, and the Lord's Prayer. However, as Calvin matured in his theology, adjustments were made to this catechetical order. Some of these adjustments led contemporaries such as Caspar Olevianus to see a more expressively creedal order (Father, Son, Spirit, Church), while others have noted Calvin's movement towards a redemptive-historical or Pauline structure.[18] According to Muller, by 1559 Calvin had realized his quest for a correct order of teaching (*ordo recte docendi*), and the *Institutes* featured "a finely tooled organization," using the *locus* method and successfully integrating creedal, catechetical, and redemptive-historical models from preceding generations of theologians.[19]

---

13. Muller, *The Unaccommodated Calvin*, 129. See also Lowell C. Green, "Melanchthon's Relation to Scholasticism," in Trueman and Clark, *Protestant Scholasticism*, 282-283.

14. Muller, *The Unaccommodated Calvin*, 12.

15. Muller, *The Unaccommodated Calvin*, 120.

16. Muller, *The Unaccommodated Calvin*, 7, 115. However, Clark notes that later in the sixteenth century the *Institutes* "functioned at Herborn as Lombard's *Sententiae* did in the Middle Ages . . . It became a primary text on which Calvin's students commented." See R. Scott Clark, *Caspar Olevian and the Substance of the Covenant* (Grand Rapids: Reformation Heritage Books, 2008), 85.

17. Muller, *The Unaccommodated Calvin*, 26.

18. Muller, *The Unaccommodated Calvin*, 73.

19. Muller, *The Unaccommodated Calvin*, 130, 137, 178.

Therefore, while Calvin sought Reformation in the content of the Christian faith, as far as method is concerned, there was continuity with the older scholastic tradition, especially as it reached its peak at the end of the twelfth century. This continuity in method extends not only to organization, but also to internal style. Here too, Muller asserts that Calvin followed the medieval/Renaissance tradition, particularly in regards to the use of syllogisms and other logical and rhetorical devices.[20] Consequently, a sixteenth-century ecclesiastic trained in the scholastic theology of the Middle Ages would have had no difficulty with the organization, style, and language of the *Institutes*. The communication channels would have been open, so to speak. The obstacles would have only existed in the content.

As we have seen above, the Belgic Confession followed Calvin's lead so far as organization is concerned. Therefore, we may also see continuity between the Belgic Confession and the locus method of the medieval church.[21] This is particularly suggested by a careful examination of the structure of de Brès' *Le baston*, essentially a Reformed *loci communes* in the tradition of Lombard and others, albeit polemically oriented. The same may be said for the Confession. Like the *Institutes*, it is organized according to the medieval locus method and integrates creedal, catechetical and redemptive-historical structural principles. It would be fair to describe the Belgic Confession as employing a synthetic model which tends to be deductive and teleologically oriented.[22]

While one cannot properly characterize it as a scholastic document, the Confession does follow the scholastic approach of presenting a number of loci. While these loci are not explicitly divided into books, they easily lend themselves to such a division. Furthermore, one finds the locus method followed in many of the articles. The positive statement of faith is given, supported by scriptural evidence. Syllogisms are occasionally employed. A substantial number of the articles conclude with rejections of false teachers.

The creedal structure is easily recognized. The initial articles deal with God in general, followed by a discussion of Scripture. This was a

---

20. Muller, *The Unaccommodated Calvin*, 110.
21. See Richard Muller, *Post-Reformation Reformed Dogmatics* (Volume Two: Holy Scripture, the Cognitive Foundation of Theology — Second Edition) (Grand Rapids: Baker, 2003), 81.
22. Richard Muller, *Post-Reformation Reformed Dogmatics* (Volume One: Prolegomena to Theology — Second Edition) (Grand Rapids: Baker, 2003), 62.

common pattern in sixteenth-century confessions and provides a set of quasi prolegomena — we will deal more with this momentarily.[23] After moving into the doctrine of creation, the creedal structure becomes more readily apparent: Father, Son, Holy Spirit, church, etc.

The catechetical structure is less apparent. The creed is readily visible in the background, but unlike in the *Institutes* there is no explicit mention of the Ten Commandments or the Lord's Prayer. However, there are allusions to the Decalogue in articles 24 and 25. The Lord's Prayer is explicitly mentioned in article 26, though it is not exposited. Being a summary document, this is understandable.

The redemptive-historical structure is evident in the movement of the Confession from God to creation to consummation. Naturally this is related to the redemptive-historical movement of the Creed. Like Calvin and the other Reformers, de Brès and the Belgic Confession realized that the doctrine of our salvation is a dramatic story.

Finally, we can take note of the way that the *Institutes* and the Confession begin. We have already noted that the first articles of the Belgic Confession (1-7) give a set of quasi prolegomena. There is a disjunction here with the 1559 *Institutes*. Whereas Calvin begins with the knowledge of God and then proceeds to his revelation, the Belgic Confession begins with God himself, and then proceeds to how we may know him and his revelation. It is a subtle difference — but one nonetheless. Richard Muller has drawn attention to the fact that several Reformation-era confessions, including the Belgic, begin with a juxtaposition between the doctrines of God and Scripture.[24] This reflects an incipient concern for the expression of an ontological or essential foundation (*principium essendi*) and an epistemological or cognitive foundation (*principium cognoscendi*). While the latter is a more recognizably Protestant development, the former was often the starting place for many medieval theologians, including Lombard (*Sentences*) and Aquinas (*Summa Theologiae*). Here too, the Belgic Confession reflects some continuity with medieval theology, perhaps even more so than the *Institutes*.

---

23. Muller, *Post-Reformation Reformed Dogmatics* (Volume Two), 81.
24. Muller, *Post-Reformation Reformed Dogmatics* (Volume 1), 439.

4.2 Structure of the Belgic Confession: Sixteenth-Century Contextualization?

Does this particular organization have anything to say about the missionary/missiological relevance of the Confession for its own age and for ours? We want to consider this question in connection with a subject of endless debate in missiological circles: contextualization. Can we say that the structure of the Belgic Confession represents a form of sixteenth-century contextualization? To answer that question responsibly, we first have to give some attention to the subject of contextualization.

4.2.1 Contextualization

There is no single or broadly-accepted definition of contextualization. Nevertheless, we can approximate a definition by describing its goal in a general way. So, we find the following in *EDWM*: "The core idea is that of taking the gospel to a new context and finding appropriate ways to communicate it so that it is understandable to the people in that context...it also includes developing church life and ministry that are biblically faithful and culturally appropriate."[25] The key word is *context*. Contextualization refers to communication that takes *context* into account. The development of Christian identity is also a component. At least, this is the way that contextualization has been generally understood in circles that take the authority and inspiration of the Bible seriously.

The concept of contextualization has appeared under different names in different periods. It has been called accommodation, inculturation, indigenization, and a term introduced by J. H. Bavinck, *possessio*.[26] Whatever the term used for the proposed solution, there has always been a recognition that missionaries face challenges with respect to communication and identity.

The term "contextualization" first appeared via ecumenical/conciliar circles in 1972, but the concept is actually far older. In fact, there are at least two examples in the New Testament. David Hesselgrave and Edward Rommen mention Acts 14:8-20 as an example of a contextualized communication of the gospel.[27] When Paul and Barnabas arrived in Lystra and began preaching, they quickly encountered two problems.

---

25. *EDWM*, s.v. "contextualization."
26. See *An Introduction to the Science of Missions*, 179-190.
27. David J. Hesselgrave and Edward Rommen, *Contextualization: Meanings, Methods, and Models* (Grand Rapids: Baker, 1989), 9.

First, there was the matter of language. The Lystrans likely understood Greek to some extent, but Lycaonian was their native tongue. Greek was therefore probably not the best language to use in communicating with them. The second and bigger issue was one of culture. An ancient myth alleged that Zeus and Hermes had once disguised themselves as men and had come to the hill country looking for hospitality. One couple welcomed them and were richly blessed by the gods with the transformation of their cottage into a golden temple. All the other citizens were punished with the destruction of their homes. So when Paul and Barnabas came and healed the cripple in Lystra, the townspeople believed that Zeus and Hermes had returned and they were not about to repeat their mistake. The apostolic missionaries may not have been aware of this myth, but when the Lystrans began worshipping them and calling them Zeus and Hermes, they soon deduced what was taking place. Paul and Barnabas then adapted their message to fit the situation. The content (the gospel) was not changed; however, the format in which the message came was. For instance, the missionaries began with the Lystrans' frame of reference in polytheism. They urged the Lystrans to turn from useless idols to the living God, from the old to the new. This "packaging" was quite different from the manner in which the gospel was communicated to Jews familiar with the divine revelation in the Old Testament. The issue here was: how to communicate the gospel in a culturally appropriate (and therefore optimally effective) way.

An example of contextualization with respect to identity can be found in Acts 15.[28] A council was called at Jerusalem to decide the question of whether or not Gentile believers were required to be circumcised, and whether they had to follow the Jewish ceremonial laws. The council decided that, in order to guard the unity of the church, there had to be a minimum of ritual cleanness, but there could be no insistence on circumcision. The apostolic church thus recognized that there are some things that transcend culture. There are other things (cultural forms) that can exist in one church, but do not have to in another.[29]

Further examples can be drawn from the history of the church through the ages. For instance, in the first centuries of the church's exis-

---

28. Hesselgrave and Rommen, *Contextualization*, 10-11.
29. For instance, with respect to worship we can think of the classical Reformed distinction between elements and circumstances. Elements transcend culture. Circumstances will and may differ according to culture.

tence, some of the early church fathers adopted Greek philosophical language in an attempt to make the gospel more meaningful. Through this means, not only the language but also frequently the concepts of Greek philosophers such as Plato and especially Aristotle entered into medieval Christian theology. However, this sort of adaptation was not limited to the ivory tower. It also found expression in mission.

Raymond Lull (1235-1315) was a Franciscan missionary to the Muslims. In an age where crusades were regarded as the only tool for converting the Muslim world, Lull advocated inter-religious dialogue. Lull also advocated for the introduction of Arabic into European universities for the very purpose of reaching the Muslim world.

While Lull exemplifies contextualization in a limited way, the Jesuit Matteo Ricci (1552-1610) does so maximally and consequently, controversially. While working in China he was faced with the issue of language (communication). After studying the matter, Ricci decided to adopt traditional Chinese religious terminology. With respect to identity, Ricci believed that ancestor reverence was not contrary to Roman Catholic faith.[30] The term "accommodation" is usually associated with Ricci's perspective on the interface between Roman Catholic faith and culture. Ricci's perspective was immensely controversial in the Roman Catholic Church. In 1704, the Vatican placed restrictions on the things that Ricci allowed in China, later followed by some permissions in 1720, and then again in 1742, a papal bull required strict adherence to everything Roman Catholic with no room for Chinese culture. This was in place until 1938.[31] This waffling is evidence of the controversial nature of what Ricci was doing, and indeed, of many attempts at contextualization.

The issues have always been there. However, it has only been in the last three or four decades that the issues have been defined and discussed more explicitly and clearly. In the 1950s, the World Council of Churches (WCC) developed an initiative called the Theological Education Fund (TEF). The TEF was geared towards enhancing theological education in the developing world. The TEF went through several mandates, resulting in the development of further thought on this issue. An increasing dissatisfaction grew with traditional models of theological education. This led to the publication of a document in 1972 entitled *Ministry in Context:*

---

30. For more on Ricci, see Stephen Neill, *A History of Christian Missions* (New York: Penguin, 1964), 162-165.
31. *EDWM*, s.v. "accommodation."

The Third Mandate Programme of the Theological Education Fund (1970-77). The term 'contextualization' first appeared in this document.

The TEF and WCC did not frame contextualization in a biblically faithful way. This is connected with the fact that respect for the authority and inspiration of Scripture was and is often lacking in these organizations. The neo-orthodox perspectives of Karl Barth and others were influential and reflected in statements such as the following: "The distance between the biblical text and the modern interpreter is to be overcome dynamically by allowing the Bible to pose questions which the interpreter must answer in accordance with his understanding of the biblical witness and of the ways in which God is working today."[32] This is something quite different than what the apostles were doing in Acts 14 and 15. The originators of the term 'contextualization' realized that as well. They were not starting with the biblical text to see what it says about the issues of communication and identity. Rather, their starting point was in the context in which people lived.

This was recognized very early on by some evangelical missiologists. Because of the WCC/TEF baggage and connotations, some argued against adopting the word 'contextualization,' insisting instead on the previously well-accepted term 'indigenization.' Yet, by the 1990s, the term 'contextualization' became almost universally accepted in every corner of Christianity, including evangelical circles. The term was redefined, and although meanings and methods were not taken over from the WCC/TEF, the term still found a home. However, surveying the journals and other literature reveals that there remains much disagreement on the exact definition of contextualization and, more importantly, how it should be done in the field.

In confessionally Reformed circles, there has been some discussion about it, but not much has been written, particularly not much in English. In 1989, the late Dr. K. Deddens presented a paper on the subject to the International Conference of Reformed Churches.[33] He was deeply critical of various models of contextualization, but also gave some positive direction. A more significant contribution to the Reformed discussion has been from C. J. Haak. His 2002 *Metamorfose* offered not only helpful

---

32. Hesselgrave and Rommen, *Contextualization*, 31.
33. Dr. K. Deddens, "Contextualization," in *Proceedings of the International Conference of Reformed Churches, June 19-28, 1989, Langley, BC, Canada* (Winnipeg: Premier, 1989), 240-258.

theoretical perspectives, but also concrete practical assistance.[34] Unfortunately, it has not been translated from the Dutch. Finally, the late Presbyterian missiologist Harvie Conn has also offered some contributions on the subject.[35]

On the side of those who claim to take the authority and inspiration of the Bible seriously, one of the most helpful writers on the subject of contextualization is David Hesselgrave. Along with Edward Rommen, he has analyzed the various models of contextualization and summarizes these with what he calls the contextualization continuum (see figure 1 below).

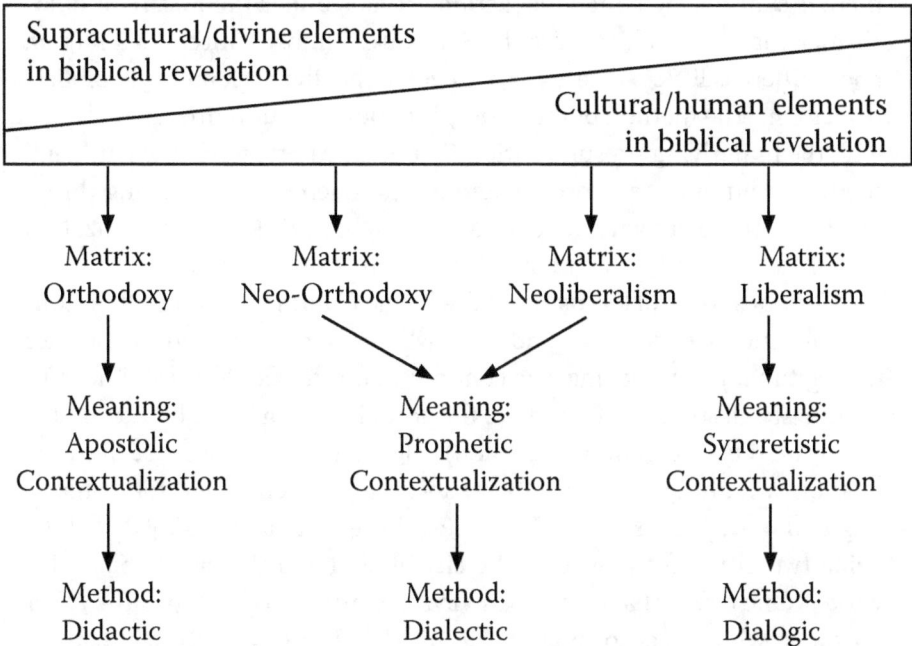

Figure 1: The Contextualization Continuum.[36]

---

34. C. J. Haak, *Metamorfose: Intercultureel begeleiden van kerken in een niet-christelijke omgeving* (Zoetermeer: Uitgeverij Boekencentrum, 2002).

35. Harvie Conn, *Eternal Word and Changing Worlds: Theology, Anthropology and Mission in Trialogue* (Grand Rapids: Academie, 1984); "Contextualization: Where Do We Begin?" in *Evangelicals & Liberation*, ed. Carl E. Armerding (Phillipsburg: Presbyterian and Reformed, 1977), 90-119; "Mission, Missions, Theology and Theological Education," in *The Urban Face of Mission: Ministering the Gospel in a Diverse and Changing World*, ed. Manuel Ortiz and Susan S. Baker (Phillipsburg: P&R, 2002), 11-26.

36. Hesselgrave and Rommen, *Contextualization*, 157.

Hesselgrave and Rommen categorize the various forms of contextualization under four headings or matrices. Apostolic contextualization falls under the matrix of orthodoxy and gives the most weight to the divine elements in biblical revelation that transcend every culture. The focus and intent in this approach to contextualization is didactic. Prophetic contextualization falls under the matrices of neo-orthodoxy and neo-liberalism. Less weight is given to the divine elements of biblical revelation and more to the cultural/human elements. Its method is to journey towards truth through dialectic, on a perpetual quest for the elusive synthesis. Finally, there is syncretistic contextualization. It falls under the matrix of liberalism, a matrix which regards the Scriptures almost entirely as a human book. There is little concern for or belief in the divine elements in biblical revelation. The method of this model is to pursue truth through dialogue, with the underlying presupposition that no one person has the truth and the truth can only be approximated or approached by discussing things together. These are very general categories, but this kind of organization of various forms of contextualization is fairly well accepted.[37]

The question still looms: does the Belgic Confession fit into "the Contextualization Continuum," and if so, where? First, we need to consider the legitimacy of imposing this continuum on the Confession. The continuum speaks to situations where the gospel is being brought into another culture (i.e. cross-cultural mission). However, there is a sense in which mission will always be radically cross-cultural, even when done among those who are ostensibly of the same culture. Augustine spoke of there being two cities in the world: the city of God and the city of man. He wrote, "One city is that of men who live according to the flesh. The other is of men who live according to the spirit."[38] These two cities, at least in principle (though not always in practice), are radically distinct from each other. In various ways, they manifest two different cultures. The cultural distance between citizens of these two cities can only be bridged by the Spirit and the Word. Consequently, the contextualization continuum applies to all mission, not just to those which are obviously cross-cultur-

---

37. Even if the names are different, a tripolar taxonomy is very common. Others define the three categories as translation, adaptation, contextual (Schreiner); conservative, modern, and progressive (Pinnock); anti-modern, modern, and postmodern (Tracy). See Marc Cortez, "Context and Concept: Contextual Theology and the Nature of Theological Discourse," *Westminster Theological Journal* 67 (2005): 87.

38. St. Augustine, *City of God* (New York: Image Books, 1958), 295 (14.1).

al. Combined with the missionary perspective of the Reformers (and de Brès/the Belgic Confession) that means we may legitimately investigate where the Belgic Confession belongs on this continuum.

To do so, we recall that the Confession, following Calvin, employed an integrative structure which owed a debt to the catechetical models of the medieval period. Departing slightly from the *Institutes* and instead following (whether intentionally or not) medieval theologians such as Lombard and Aquinas, the Confession prioritized the ontological or essential foundation (*principium essendi*) by beginning with God. Rather than being dialogical, the Belgic Confession is explicitly didactic, not only in terms of content and structure, but also in tone. The supracultural elements of divine revelation are emphasized. The structure, the language, and the format are at home in sixteenth-century ecclesiastical circles in Western Europe. The content, however, is explicitly biblical and the understanding is that this content transcends all cultures — consider again the original title before the text: "True Christian Confession Containing the Summary of the Doctrine of God and of the Eternal Salvation of the Soul." We may conclude that the Belgic Confession sets forth a sixteenth-century example of apostolic contextualization. This is especially true with regard to communication with those whom its framers and first confessors regarded as "the world."

Hesselgrave offers a helpful overview of the challenges faced in missionary communication of the gospel. There are several dimensions involved in bringing the message from the source to the respondent: worldviews, cognitive processes, linguistic forms, behavioural patterns, social structures, media influence, and motivational resources.[39] For our purposes, the dimensions that are most relevant are the linguistic forms, media influence, and cognitive processes.

Beginning with cognitive processes, Hesselgrave notes that the West (and he would extend this back to sixteenth-century Europe) enumerates its priorities as follows: conceptual, concrete relational, psychical.[40] In its organization and formulations, the Belgic Confession gives exclusive priority to conceptual cognitive processes and in doing so, was adapted to the world to which it was giving witness. However, it does have to be said that there is also a redemptive-historical movement in the Confession. Hesselgrave notes that drama and ritual have special appeal in settings

---

39. Hesselgrave, *Communicating Christ Cross-culturally*, 164.
40. Hesselgrave, *Communicating Christ Cross-culturally*, 304.

that privilege the concrete relational and we have noted the Chambers of Rhetoric in the sixteenth-century Lowlands (see 3.2.2).[41] The concrete relational may not have been central in the culture of the sixteenth-century Low Countries, but it was present to a substantial enough degree to remain evident nearly five centuries later. Furthermore, as already intimated, the Belgic Confession itself gives evidence of what has been called the "drama of dogma." So while the conceptual may take priority, there is also evidence for the place of the concrete relational.

Media forms and influence have little, if anything, to do with structure, but a brief consideration of this point will prove helpful for our broader purposes. Hesselgrave works with Marshall McLuhan's insights into the relationship between media and message. According to McLuhan, the medium is the message, and he distinguishes between hot media and cool media. Hot media have high definition, being amply supplied with information. Examples include the phonetic alphabet, photographs, and radio. Cool media are low definition, having gaps and require respondent participation. Examples include ideographs, cartoons, and television.[42] The Belgic Confession would be categorized as embodying a hot medium since it is high definition. Furthermore, its expansive dissemination depended on the invention of the printing press and moveable type — inventions which embodied the spirit of hot media according to McLuhan. Hesselgrave elaborates: "The printing press is the archetype of all mechanization. It introduced a galaxy of changes in the consciousness of Western man. It put an end, once and for all, to parochialism in both space and time. It brought the ancient and medieval worlds into fusion and was the harbinger of the modern world. It issued in nationalism, industrialism, mass markets, education, and a much higher level of literacy. It heightened the ability of people to collect information and cogitate while detached from one another and from events by both space and time."[43] Had de Brès and his Reformed contemporaries been the sixteenth-century equivalent of the Luddites, it is doubtful that the Confession would have had the impact that it did. So, also in its adoption of this media form, the Confession may be regarded as a contextualized witness.

---

41. Hesselgrave, *Communicating Christ Cross-culturally*, 338.
42. Hesselgrave, *Communicating Christ Cross-culturally*, 532.
43. Hesselgrave, *Communicating Christ Cross-culturally*, 531.

Little needs to be said about the linguistic dimension. Hesselgrave rightly insists that it is imperative for missionaries to learn the language of the culture in which they are working.[44] In the case of the Belgic Confession, Guido de Brès was a native French speaker and appears to have also been fluent in Dutch. From our perspective, it was a natural choice for him to write the Confession in French. However, some Reformation-era confessions were not initially written in the vernacular. The choice to write in French, rather than Latin, indicates that this Confession was prepared for a wide audience, rather than a select few.

Especially as it pertains to the structure, the Belgic Confession was a contextualized communication of the gospel to the world. But what about the other aspect of contextualization, namely identity? Here we can look back to the rationale for the development of the Confession. The Reformed Churches in the Lowlands could have conceivably adopted the French Confession. It was in their language and it expressed essentially the same content. However, they chose to formulate their own confession, departing from the French at certain points (especially in the emphasis on martyrdom, suffering, and persecution) and following it at others. In this respect, we can regard the Belgic Confession as a contextualized expression of the identity of the Reformed churches in the Low Countries in this era, perhaps even as a form of self-theologizing.

Concluding this part of our investigation, we can state that the Belgic Confession was a contextualized missionary communication of the gospel. Particularly as regards its organization, the Confession would have been familiar to many sixteenth-century people, particularly to those ecclesiastics with a scholastic education. This would have underscored the insistence of the Reformed that they were not revolutionaries, but simply expressing the apostolic Christian faith. It may have also had the effect of drawing in an increasing number of priests in parishes of the Lowlands. In fact, Crew has demonstrated that a substantial number of the Reformed ministers and lay preachers in the Lowlands were formerly priests or other ecclesiastics in the Roman church.[45] The impact that the Belgic Confession may have had on this phenomenon is something that requires further research.

---

44. Hesselgrave, *Communicating Christ Cross-culturally*, 355.
45. Crew, *Calvinist Preaching*, 185-196.

4.2.2 Options for Confessional Structures in Sixteenth-Century Europe

The conclusion above assumes that de Brès and the Reformed churches had options when it came to drafting a confession of faith in their context. But is this a legitimate assumption? What sorts of confessional structures/forms do we find among the Reformed churches in sixteenth-century Europe?

First of all, there were the catechisms. A question and answer format covering the essential teachings of the Christian faith (typically under the headings of the Creed, the Commandments, and the Lord's Prayer) was a very common pedagogical tool among the Reformed churches of the sixteenth century. In due time, many of these catechisms were also officially adopted as confessions.[46] Nevertheless, seldom were catechisms written and published with *the intention* that they would also be confessions of faith. A catechism does not appear to have been a real option for de Brès and the Reformed churches of the Low Countries.

A more rare form of confession was the thetical format. This would consist of a series of short statements or theses. No scriptural proofs would be given, and each "article" would consist of one or maybe two sentences. The Sixty-seven Articles of Zwingli (1523) provide an example of a personal confession of this nature, whereas the Ten Conclusions of Berne (1528) provide us with an ecclesiastical document. The Lausanne Articles (1536) also fall into this genre. This was an option for de Brès and his Reformed churches. The Belgic Confession could have been formulated as a document providing a few short theses or statements regarding where the Reformed churches differ or agree with the Roman church and the Anabaptists.

A third possibility is the chapter and article format. Some Reformation-era confessions are divided into chapters *instead of* articles — the Tetrapolitan Confession (1530) is one such document. Others, such as the Lutheran Smalcald Articles (1537) and the Hussite Bohemian Confession (1535) go further and break the chapters down into articles. Al-

---

46. Sinnema relates that the Convent of Wesel (1568) expected ministers to state their agreement with the Heidelberg Catechism, but formal subscription of the Catechism is not found until 1593. Subscription of the Belgic Confession took place as early as 1563, and its role as an adopted standard of orthodoxy dates to before its publication (cf. Gootjes, *The Belgic Confession*, 112-115). Donald Sinnema, "The Origin of the Form of Subscription in the Dutch Reformed Tradition," *Calvin Theological Journal* 42.2 (November 2007): 258, 262.

though it dates shortly after the Belgic, the Second Helvetic Confession (1566) adopts the same structure. This was also an option for the format of the Belgic Confession. It could have been formulated as a document with more of the feel of a book and in this way could even have been expanded into a more comprehensive statement of faith.

Other options such as poetry, drama, narrative or song were unknown in this period and would have been considered as too revolutionary as structures for a confession. Given the available options, the Reformed churches and de Brès chose to express their faith in a familiar genre: a Confession organized according to the locus method, following Calvin by integrating creedal, catechetical, and historical structures. The result was that, in terms of its organization, the Confession was a contextualized witness to the world, and therefore missionally relevant for its time.

4.2.3 INTENTION AND EFFECT: RATIONALE FOR LOCUS METHOD IN BELGIC CONFESSION

The question remains, however, as to whether de Brès and his fellow confessors deliberately chose this organization and structure, or whether it was simply assumed that they would go this direction, given the choices already made by Calvin and the Reformed churches in France. This is a question that is impossible to answer with any absolute certainty for there is no direct evidence one way or another. Nevertheless, there is some indirect evidence which supports the view that this was intentional.

The evidence comes from de Brès' 1555 work, *Le baston*. The French Confession dates from 1559, so this book of de Brès is independent, at least so far as that confession goes. As mentioned above, *Le baston* is also structured according to the locus method, although there is some variation in the order and number of topics according to the different editions. The 1558 edition used for this study has eighteen loci, whereas the 1562 edition used by L. A. Van Langeraad has twenty-three.[47] The later edition more closely follows the order of the Belgic Confession and suggests that it was revised for that purpose. The text history of *Le baston* is another area that requires further investigation, but for our purposes it is worth

---

47. Lambregt Abraham Van Langeraad, *Guido de Bray: zijn leven en werken* (Zierikzee: S. Ochtman & Zoon, 1884), 91. Van Langeraad was using the 1562 edition of *Le baston* published in Lyon. For some discussion on the text history of *Le baston*, see Braekman, *Guy de Brès*, 84-94.

noting that de Brès was familiar with and deliberately followed the locus method. This was true not only in terms of the structure of *Le baston*, but also in terms of content — citing the church fathers and Scripture almost exclusively, with very little editorial comment.

While we cannot decisively conclude that the structure of the Confession was intentional, we can observe what the result was. Whatever the intent, the effect of the Confession's organization was a contextualized witness to the world. The Confession was immediately recognized as a powerful statement of the main teachings of the Scriptures and this accounts for its rapid dissemination, not only in French, but also in Dutch, German, Latin, and many other languages.

4.3 Conclusion

There is a relationship between the structure of the Belgic Confession and its original missionary nature and intent. Except where Scripture required it, de Brès was deliberately not a revolutionary — and the Reformed churches followed in his path by adopting his Confession. In this chapter, we have seen that it may be interpreted as a contextualized witness to the non-Reformed world of the sixteenth century.

But can a sixteenth-century confession organized according to the locus method of the medieval church and integrating creedal, catechetical and redemptive-historical structures speak to the unbelieving world of the twenty-first century? Such an organization might prima facie be regarded as irrelevant. Most of the unbelieving world in our contemporary mission fields (home or foreign) knows nothing of creedal and catechetical elements, much less is the locus method remotely familiar even to the highly educated. There is a weakness here, and we will explore this further in the next chapter.

However, this weakness is mitigated somewhat by two counterpoints. According to Barrett et al., in mid-2000 there were over 1 billion Roman Catholics in the world, comprising 17.5% of the world's population and making up the majority of those who profess to be Christians. It is projected that by 2025, the number of Roman Catholics will increase to 1.36 billion, but will make up slightly less of the world's population at 17.4%.[48] These are significant numbers, and for our purposes they become more

---

48. David B. Barrett, George T. Kurian, and Todd M. Johnson, *World Christian Encyclopedia: A Comparative Study of Churches and Religions in the Modern World*, Second Edition (Vol. 1) (Oxford: Oxford UP, 2001), 4.

significant when we reckon with the ongoing Roman practice of catechesis as preparation for confirmation.[49] In principle, all confirmed Roman Catholics will have been catechized and will be familiar with the Creed, the Commandments, and the Lord's Prayer. Thus, in one of the world's largest mission fields, there is *in principle* a familiarity with the creedal and catechetical structures integrated in the Belgic Confession.

The second counterpoint pertains to the redemptive-historical structure of the Confession. The historical development, moving in general terms from creation to consummation, remains relevant. Though postmodernism sought to undermine or eradicate all sense of narrative and metanarrative, this venture was manifestly a failure. While vestiges of the postmodern eschewing of narrative remain in certain literary and academic circles, narrative is alive and well in various media in popular culture throughout the world. Because this is so, the structure of the Belgic Confession retains its relevance. It is an expression of what Dorothy Sayers called "the drama of dogma":

> Official Christianity, of late years, has been having what is known as a bad press. We are constantly assured that the churches are empty because preachers insist too much upon doctrine — dull dogma as people call it. The fact is the precise opposite. It is the neglect of dogma that makes for dullness. The Christian faith is the most exciting drama that ever staggered the imagination of man — and the dogma is the drama.
>
> That drama is summarized quite clearly in the creeds of the Church, and if we think it dull it is because we either have never really read those amazing documents or have recited them so often and so mechanically as to have lost all sense of their meaning.[50]

The development of redemptive-history is intimately tied to the doctrines of the Christian faith expressed in the Belgic Confession. Recognizing this truth leads one to a fresh appreciation for the structure and its missiological relevance. At the end of this chapter, we can let the British novelist with an appreciation for drama have the last word:

---

49. *Catechism of the Catholic Church,* Second Edition (New York: Doubleday, 1997), 365 (Art. 1309).

50. Dorothy L. Sayers, *Letters to a Diminished Church: Passionate Arguments for the Relevance of Christian Doctrine* (W Publishing Group, 2004), 1.

Now, we may call that doctrine exhilarating, or we may call it devastating; we may call it revelation, or we may call it rubbish; but if we call it dull, then words have no meaning at all. That God should play the tyrant over man is a dismal story of unrelieved oppression; that man should play the tyrant over man is the usual dreary record of human futility; but that man should play the tyrant over God and find him a better man than himself is an astonishing drama indeed. Any journalist, hearing of it for the first time, would recognize it as news; those who did hear it for the first time actually called it news, and good news at that; though we are likely to forget that the word Gospel ever meant anything so sensational.

Perhaps the drama is played out now and Jesus is safely dead and buried. Perhaps. It is ironical and entertaining to consider that at least once in the world's history those words might have been spoken with complete conviction, and that was upon the eve of the Resurrection.[51]

---

51. Sayers, *Letters*, 6-7.

CHAPTER FIVE

MISSIOLOGICAL STRENGTHS AND WEAKNESSES

5.0 INTRODUCTION

In the preceding four chapters, some of the potential missiological strengths and weaknesses of the Belgic Confession have been touched upon. In this chapter, we are going to give more detailed consideration of those points and others. In the balance of things, we will see that the strengths outweigh the weaknesses and the Confession continues to be a valuable statement of faith that also directs the church to its missionary task and meaningful reflection thereupon.

Before we can enter the substance of the discussion, however, we need to briefly attend to some preliminary items. One of those is the definition of "missiological." In chapter 2 (2.5), we concluded that when we speak about the missiological relevance of the Belgic Confession, we are inquiring about the precise relevance of the Confession for the study of mission in all its various aspects. What does the Belgic Confession say to the study of "the official sending of the church to go and make disciples by preaching and witnessing to the good news of Jesus Christ in all nations through the power of the Holy Spirit"? When we say "study," we mean to include not only the more academic or theoretical aspects of this field, but also the practical and concrete. So, in this chapter, we are considering the strengths and weaknesses that the Confession brings to the table as we reflect upon the mission of the church in all its various aspects.

Wanting to help us in this task is Donald McGavran. In 1972, he shared his vision for the contours of "a missionary confession of faith."[1] As the Christian Reformed Church wrestled with the question of whether it was in need of making a fresh confession (*in statu confessionis*), Mc-

---

1. Donald McGavran, "A Missionary Confession of Faith," *Calvin Theological Journal* 7.2 (November 1972): 133-145.

Gavran outlined his criticisms of the Confession of 1967, the product of another church (the United Presbyterian Church) which believed that it was in that situation. In this context, McGavran indicated what he believed to be the desiderata for a confession that takes the mission of the church seriously.

McGavran believed that while the Confession of 1967 dealt adequately with social justice, it was "tragically truncated on mission."[2] He asked why this Confession did not speak out against "unbelief, wrong belief and idolatry."[3] The implication was that a missionary-oriented confession must do this. According to McGavran, there are two billion people (this was in 1972) who do not believe, who are "grievously starved and unjustly deprived by their lack of faith in Christ." A truly missionary confession will call attention to this "spiritual thirst and agony."[4]

A second lacuna, according to McGavran, is that there is a "lack of missionary passion," not only in the Confession of 1967, but also in the creeds of many other churches. He connects this with the Holy Spirit. He provides an article from the statement of faith of some conservative church (he does not identify it). He notes that it is a garden-variety orthodox confession about the Holy Spirit. Then he adds: "But the article we are considering is entirely silent about the missionary function of the Holy Spirit, concerning which the New Testament speaks so often, namely that he thrusts the church out to proclaim the gospel, prepares men of other religions to believe on Christ, directs missionaries to some populations and away from others and, in general, commands and coordinates the discipling of the nations."[5] McGavran insists that a missionary confession will give considerable attention to the function of the Holy Spirit in the mission of the church, and this will, in turn, inspire missionary passion in churches.

He argues further that a "missionarily adequate" confession will directly address the question of non-Christian religions. Theologians and missiologists have a responsibility to ensure that there is no vagueness on this point: "They must not take refuge in omissions, implications and ambiguities."[6] Rather than brevity, we must strive for effectiveness in battle.

---

2. McGavran, "A Missionary Confession," 135.
3. McGavran, "A Missionary Confession," 138.
4. McGavran, "A Missionary Confession," 138-139.
5. McGavran, "A Missionary Confession," 141.
6. McGavran, "A Missionary Confession," 142.

His conclusion is that a missionary confession of faith must speak clearly and fully to the missionary task of the church: "A *missionary* confession of faith for today will *in every doctrine* similarly *spell out at great length* the will of God as revealed in the Scriptures that all men of every economic stratum, every tongue, every tribe, every religion, and every ideology be given the opportunity to say 'yes' to Jesus Christ."[7] McGavran sets extremely high standards for a missionary confession. For our purposes, we should note the difference between a missionary confession of faith (an ideal apparently never yet realized) and a missiologically *relevant* confession. A missionary confession of faith may and should attain to all the high standards outlined by McGavran, but a missiologically relevant confession need not be held to such high standards. The latter can approximate these standards or meet them to varying degrees. Consequently, in what follows, we will keep McGavran's high standards for a missionary confession of faith in mind as we consider the missiological strengths and weaknesses of the Belgic Confession.

5.1 MISSIOLOGICAL STRENGTHS

The Belgic Confession is regarded by its adherents as a faithful summary of the teachings of Holy Scripture. This is something which cannot be taken for granted and which is to be regarded as the foremost strength of this Confession, also when we consider its missiological relevance. From the perspective of its adherents, a confession cannot be relevant to the mission of the church if it does not take the Bible as its infallible basis. However, it falls outside the purview of this study to detail the biblical basis of each article in the Confession. Someone wanting to do that could refer to the commentaries or to Lepusculus Vallensis' helpful reference manual, *The Belgic Confession and Its Biblical Basis*.[8] In this section, we want to explore the missiological strengths of the confession on a broader level.

5.1.1 CONFESSION OF A CHURCH UNDER THE CROSS

In chapter 3 (3.1.4), we considered the Confession under the rubric of the metanarrative of martyrdom and concluded that, in this regard, the Confession is missiologically relevant. It was formulated on the foundation of martyrdom and suffering, a theology of the cross. It communi-

---

7. McGavran, "A Missionary Confession," 144. Italics are original.
8. Lepusculus Vallensis, *The Belgic Confession and Its Biblical Basis* (Neerlandia: Inheritance, 1993).

cates the missionary message of martyrdom and suffering. We saw that a rich missionary harvest resulted from the martyrdom and suffering directly associated with this confession. Among our conclusions (3.3) was that any church which gives up this Confession is impoverishing itself. We will now build further on that conclusion.

The precise extent of persecution and martyrdom today is notoriously difficult to measure. According to the most recent statistics of Barrett et al., 160,000 people were martyred for the Christian faith in 2000.[9] However, a number of things need to be considered. First, these numbers are rather elastic on several levels. Barrett's figures include 100,000 Roman Catholics, 14,000 Orthodox, 5,000 Marginal Protestants, and 1,000 Anglicans and Old Catholics. Also, as Schirrmacher notes, there are serious questions about the reliability of this data. Barrett is unwilling to discuss the data and "fails to give sufficient information on his statistic [sic] methods." There is no validity to Barrett's claims to offer only facts without interpretation. For instance, included in the figure are countless thousands who have died in civil wars such as those in recent times in African countries like Sudan.[10] Finally, if these numbers are close to being correct, Schirrmacher observes that, in proportion to the world's population, the overall number of martyrs has actually decreased since 1970.[11]

Nevertheless, both statistical and anecdotal evidence portrays a world in which many Christians continue to live under the specter of persecution.[12] While communism has fallen in eastern Europe, it continues to be a political reality in North Korea, Cuba, Laos, Vietnam, and the most populous nation on earth, China. Even as some of these countries just mentioned adapt themselves to a free(r) market economy, active repression of Christians continues, especially in more remote regions, away from Western eyes and ears. In other countries such as Burma/Myanmar, oppressive dictatorships or military juntas persecute believers. In many nations in the Middle East, Islam is the official national religion, and Christianity is barely tolerated, if at all. In those countries where *Shari'a* law is in place, it is a capital offence for a Mus-

---

9. Barrett et al., *World Christian Encyclopedia* (Vol. 1), 11.
10. Schirrmacher, *The Persecution of Christians*, 12.
11. Schirrmacher, *The Persecution of Christians*, 11.
12. For some of the anecdotal evidence, see Paul Marshall, *Their Blood Cries Out: The Worldwide Tragedy of Modern Christians Who Are Dying for Their Faith* (Dallas: Word Publishing, 1997).

lim to convert to Christianity. In India and other south Asian countries, militant Hinduism and Buddhism has accounted for a significant proportion of martyrdoms of Christian believers. In some regions of Mexico and elsewhere in Latin America, Roman Catholic persecution of Christians continues to be a reality, though martyrdom appears to be comparatively rare. Of course, all of that is just scratching the surface. No one who has given it any serious consideration will deny that suffering for the faith is an ongoing reality — and we expect it to continue this way until the return of the Lord Jesus.

When the gospel goes out into the world, there will inevitably be opposition. When the Lord Jesus sent out the disciples in Matthew 10, he sent them out "as sheep in the midst of wolves" (10:16). He warned them that they would be delivered up to councils and scourged in synagogues. They would be brought before governors and kings. They could expect opposition from family, even to the point of death. The disciples were to expect to be hated by all for the sake of Christ's name and being persecuted, to flee from one city to another. In John 16, the Lord Jesus spoke in a similar vein, though he added that "the time is coming that whoever kills you will think that he offers God service" (16:2). Those who do those things, according to Christ, do them because they know neither the Father nor him.

The metanarrative of martyrdom embedded in the Belgic Confession awakens the church to these realities, and this is one of its greatest strengths. This happens in at least four distinct ways.

First, the Belgic Confession awakens sending churches to the reality that when they send out missionaries, those missionaries may not return alive or in the same condition as they left. Missionary work can be dangerous, even life-threatening. The Confession reminds churches to count the cost. At the same time, it also encourages churches to know that if the highest price is paid by its missionaries, this too is in God's hands and he often uses it to build his church.

Second, the Belgic Confession speaks to individual missionaries and other mission personnel. Missionaries can be encouraged to know that, while their work may be dangerous and even frightening, it will never be in vain. The Confession continues to witness that even in the darkest hours, God is present and guiding the "cause of the Son of God." He did so during the troubles in the Lowlands in the sixteenth century and he will still do so today.

Next, this Confession testifies to the newer believers and younger churches on the mission fields themselves. They can read this Confession and take heart that the church has often appeared to be in dire straits, but that this was only the appearance of things. They can know that, because of their union with Christ, they are part of a greater story or metanarrative, and they are not alone in their experiences of suffering, persecution, and even martyrdom. Confessing the Belgic gives a depth of perspective to younger churches, and this encourages growth in grace and knowledge.

Finally, the Confession engages all its confessors on the reality of persecution, both historically and in the present. Of course, it is possible to superficially hold the Belgic and never have any conscious awareness of persecution and martyrdom at any point in history. It may even be possible to thoughtfully subscribe and confess the Belgic without that awareness — the lack of serious attention to this aspect in the commentaries certainly suggests that! However, this is an essential element of the Confession's (biblical) message and it deserves more attention. This is especially so for Reformed believers in the West, who tend to live very comfortably and who may have little awareness of persecution elsewhere in the world, let alone any sense of a theology of the cross. We need the Belgic Confession to remind us that our brothers and sisters elsewhere suffer for the faith, so that we may pray for them — and in so praying, we are in fact praying "for the cause of the Son of God."

5.1.2 An Elenctic Confession — a Confession of the Antithesis

Building further on chapter 3, we want to consider how the antithetical character of the Confession is a missiological strength. A better way of describing this antithetical character would be to use a word first introduced to contemporary missiology by J. H. Bavinck: "elenctic."[13] The term was first used by Gisbertus Voetius in the seventeenth century to describe the need for refuting and deconstructing non-Christian beliefs, something which had to be done before the Christian faith could be proclaimed and churches could be planted. He derived the term from Titus 1:13, "Therefore rebuke (e)legxe them sharply, that they may be sound in the faith." Abraham Kuyper revived the term in his day putting it forward "as the antithesis to pseudo-reli-

---

13. For a more recent treatment of the subject, see Cornelis J. Haak, "The Missional Approach: Reconsidering Elenctics," *Calvin Theological Journal* 44.1 (April 2009): 37-48 and 44.2 (November 2009): 288-305.

gion, alongside polemics as the antithesis to heresy and apologetics as the antithesis to pseudo-philosophy."[14]

Bavinck adopted the term to describe "the science concerned with a very special aspect of the [missionary] approach: our direct attack upon non-Christian religiosity in order to call a man to repentance."[15] He does not see it in reactive, defensive terms, as was the tendency of Kuyper. Bavinck writes: "Elenctics is strongly controlled by the missionary motive. It is not primarily a defense against the dangerous power of non-Christian religions, but it is rather itself a direct attack upon them. . . . Elenctics calls the non-Christian religions to a position of responsibility, and attempts to convince their adherents of sin and to move them to repentance and conversion."[16] At its heart, for Bavinck, elenctics is concerned with the conviction of sin and a key text for him in that regard is John 16:8, "And when he [the Paraclete] has come, he will convict (e)legcei) the world of sin, and of righteousness, and of judgment." Only the Holy Spirit can do this, says Bavinck, although he can and will use human beings as his agents.

From the perspective of de Brès and the Reformed churches in the Lowlands, Roman Catholicism and Anabaptism constituted non-Christian religion. The Belgic Confession reflects this stance and directly confronts Roman Catholics and Anabaptists with their responsibility. In the words of Bavinck quoted above, the Confession attempts to convict the adherents of Romanism and Anabaptism "of sin and to move them to repentance and conversion." Therefore, speaking historically, the Confession can be regarded as a form of elenctics.

When we look to our contemporary situation, there are a number of questions that need to be addressed. First of all, has the concept of the antithesis been eclipsed? Here we need to think not only of the antithesis between the church and the world (as broadly understood), but also of the antithesis between the church and non-Reformation religion. This is not an easy question to answer — anecdotal evidence is difficult to assess and hard statistical evidence is impossible to obtain. Consequently, it is best to leave the question as an unremitting challenge to Reformed believers. Reformed believers in every era have to be challenged to retain this notion.

Or do they? The next question that needs to be considered is whether the elenctic/antithetical position of de Brès, the Reformed churches and

---

14. Visser, *Heart for the Gospel*, 257.
15. Bavinck, *Introduction to the Science of Missions*, 233.
16. Bavinck, *Introduction to the Science of Missions*, 232.

the Belgic Confession can be sustained. Is it possible that the position of the Belgic Confession vis-à-vis Roman Catholicism and Anabaptism is overstated? If that is the case, then the elenctic character would be a liability rather than a strength. We must therefore briefly reflect on the nature of the historical and contemporary differences between the Reformed faith and Romanism and Anabaptism.

At the heart of the Reformed faith is the doctrine of justification by faith alone. This doctrine teaches that sinners are graciously declared right with God on the basis of the merits (his obedience, suffering, death, and resurrection) of Jesus Christ alone and this is appropriated only by the means of trusting and resting in Christ (faith). This doctrine is found in the Belgic Confession in article 22. This is not the place to lay out the exegetical support for this doctrine, but we must note that this doctrine has historically been regarded by the churches of the Reformation as of central importance.[17] The aphorism, "Justification is the article by which the church stands or falls" ("*Iustificatio — articulus stantis vel cadentis ecclesiae*") is often attributed to Luther, however, Reformed theologians such as J. H. Alsted (1588-1638) have also appropriated it and may be the source of the exact wording.[18] Contemporary theologians continue to maintain its crucial place in the Reformed faith.[19]

The central significance of the doctrine of justification for Reformation Protestants was also recognized historically by the Roman Catholic Church. During the sixth session of the Council of Trent (January 13,

---

17. For some exegetical developments of this doctrine, see S. J. Gathercole "Justified by Faith, Justified by his Blood: The Evidence of Romans 3:21-4:25," in *Justification and Variegated Nomism* (Vol. 2), ed. D. A. Carson, Peter T. O'Brien, and Mark A. Seifrid (Grand Rapids: Baker Academic, 2001), 147-184; D. A. Carson ed., *Right with God: Justification in the Bible and the World*, (Grand Rapids: Baker, 1992); Mark A. Seifrid, *Justification by Faith: The Origin and Development of a Central Pauline Theme*, (Leiden: E. J. Brill, 1992); J. V. Fesko, *Justification: Understanding the Classic Reformed Doctrine* (Phillipsburg: P&R, 2008).

18. For Luther, see *What Luther Says*, Vol. 2, 704. For Alsted, see his *Theologia Scholastica Didacta* (Hanover, 1618), 711.

19. For two recent examples, see the Faculty of Westminster Seminary California, "Our Testimony on Justification," in *Covenant, Justification and Pastoral Ministry: Essays by the Faculty of Westminster Seminary California*, ed. R. Scott Clark (Phillipsburg: P&R, 2007); Michael S. Horton, *Covenant and Salvation: Union with Christ* (Louisville: Westminster John Knox Press, 2007), 129. Horton describes justification as the "forensic basis of union with Christ and therefore the source of our calling, sanctification, and glorification."

1547), the Reformation doctrine of justification by faith alone was anathematized. In other words, according to Rome, those who hold to such a doctrine are accursed by God and outside of salvation. Historically, the Roman Catholic Church has regarded Reformed believers as belonging to another religion. In more recent times, Vatican II has softened the strident tones of Trent by referring to Protestants as "departed brethren." Discussions between Roman Catholics and Evangelicals in the 1990s reflected a spirit of détente, if only in certain American circles. Nevertheless, the official Roman Catholic doctrine of justification remains unchanged, and the canons of Trent continue to carry authority among Roman Catholics, at least in principle, if not in practice.

With regard to Rome, our conclusion must be that the elenctic position of the Belgic Confession was not overstated — neither in its original context nor in our context today. The Confession reminds us that the millions of Roman Catholic believers continue to constitute one of the largest mission fields in the world today. In this document, we have a voice telling us that (consistent) Roman Catholics are not our brothers and sisters in Jesus Christ, but are rather the lost who need our prayers and our witness.

When it comes to Anabaptism, the situation is more complicated. Already in the days of de Brès, Anabaptism was a theologically diverse movement and today it remains no less so. The Confession, however, distinguishes between the errors of the Anabaptists and their heresies. As noted previously (3.2.4), heresy was the more dangerous mode of erring from the Christian faith. The Belgic Confession regards the denial of infant baptism as an error, whereas defecting from the orthodox doctrine of the incarnation was regarded as heresy. Holding to the celestial flesh doctrine of Melchior Hoffmann and Menno Simons was considered to jeopardize one's salvation.

Here the Belgic Confession was simply echoing the ecumenical anathemas of the Athanasian Creed. In article 31, the Creed states, "He is God from the Father's substance, begotten before time; and He is man from His mother's substance, born in time." Article 42 concludes, "This is the catholic faith. Unless a man believes it faithfully and steadfastly, he cannot be saved. Amen." In article 9 of the Belgic Confession, the Athanasian Creed is willingly received as being in accordance with Scripture. As with justification by faith alone, a case can be made that belief in the orthodox doctrine of the incarnation of Jesus Christ is crucial for saving faith.[20] According to passages like 1 John 4:2, the Saviour we must believe in is the one revealed to us in Holy Scripture, and if he is revealed as having taken his human nature from his mother, we must believe in him as such if we are to be saved.

As we survey the contemporary scene, large numbers of Mennonites no longer adhere to the doctrine of Menno Simons. However, there are still some who do. Moreover, there continue to be countless other sects which hold to heretical Christologies or denials of the orthodox doctrine of the Trinity. In fact, much of the global growth of "Christianity" (very broadly defined) is among such sects. Thus, also with regard to the Anabaptists, the elenctic stance of the Belgic Confession continues to be justified. With this stance, the Confession guides us to see an expanded mission field around us at home and in foreign countries.

Donald McGavran indicated that a true missionary confession of faith would take a stand against "unbelief, wrong belief and idolatry." The Belgic Confession, though over 400 years old, continues to take that very stand and this is another one of its missiological strengths. No one can meaningfully confess these 37 articles without taking into account the antithesis between true faith and "unbelief, wrong belief and idolatry." No one can truly subscribe this confession without recognizing a mission field among Roman Catholics and among at least some of the heirs of the Anabaptists.

5.1.3 A Catholic Confession

When he defined the desired features of a missionary confession, McGavran did not mention catholicity. Whatever the reasons for that might be, it is worth considering whether this was an oversight on his part. Should a missiologically relevant confession (which we recognize as something different than what McGavran was calling for) have a catholic character? Why or why not? Furthermore, if catholicity is something missiologically helpful, does the Belgic Confession have that character?

We must begin with our definitions. What does it mean for a confession to have a catholic character? Jelle Faber rightly noted that there are three general modes of catholicity: the social, the geographical, and the

---

20. Daniel R. Hyde, *God With Us: Knowing the Mystery of Who Jesus Is* (Grand Rapids: Reformation Heritage Books, 2007), 59-75.

temporal.[21] The temporal is expressed in the belief that the church has existed from the beginning. The social is expressed in the belief that God calls his church out of every tribe, nation and tongue. The geographical comes to expression in particular local churches around the globe. Taken together, these three modes comprise catholicity. When discussing the character of this catholicity, Faber recognized a distinction between the quantitative and qualitative aspects.[22] While the Roman Catholic Church, and the Counter-Reformation in particular, has stressed the quantitative side of catholicity, the Reformation placed the emphasis on the qualitative or normative aspect. The aim of the Reformation was to bring the church back into line with the infallible Word of God. Faber concluded that the Reformation was correct in this emphasis and that catholicity is therefore closely associated with holiness and apostolicity.[23] In other words, a truly catholic confession will faithfully summarize the holy and apostolic faith received in the Scriptures.

Faber goes on to argue that the Belgic Confession embodies geographical and cultural catholicity. He begins with this:

> First of all, it should be noted the original title of this confession was, "True Christian Confession, Containing the Summary of the Doctrine of God and of the Eternal Salvation of Man." The Synod of Dort added a few words: True Christian Confession *of the Reformed Churches of the Netherlands*. It did this for political reasons. Guido de Brès, the author of the Confession had simply called it: True Christian Confession. It is quite obvious that he did not consider the Confession of the Reformed people in the Netherlands a sectarian specialty, or a confession for one land, one nation, one language only. Certainly not! "True Christian Confession" indicates a presentation of the catholic, undoubted Christian faith.[24]

There are several problems here. First, as indicated in chapter 3, the words referred to as a title by Faber are actually a sort of sub-title that appears before the text of the Confession. Second, that sub-title in 1561 did not read as Faber cited it. Instead, the actual sub-title is, "Truly Christian

---

21. J. Faber, *Essays in Reformed Doctrine* (Neerlandia: Inheritance, 1990), 77.
22. Faber, *Essays*, 74, 78.
23. Faber, *Essays*, 74, 78.
24. Faber, *Essays*, 79. Faber added the italics here.

Confession, Containing the Eternal Salvation of the Soul."[25] Finally, and most problematic for Faber's case, is the fact that the actual head title of the Confession reads, "Confession of faith, made with one common accord by the faithful *who live in the Lowlands*, who desire to live according to the purity of the Gospel of our Lord Jesus Christ."[26] Contrary to what Faber wrote, the Belgic Confession was intended only to be the confession of a group of churches in one specific region.

Faber continues by arguing that the catholicity of the Church is confessed by the Belgic Confession in article 27.[27] Faber is correct in this observation; however, he fails to make a case for a connection between the confession of the catholicity of the church and the catholicity of the Confession itself. Simply because the Confession indicates a belief in the catholicity of the church in one article does not mean that the Confession is the product of geographical and cultural catholicity. As far as that point of catholicity is concerned, we must conclude that the Belgic Confession is limited in its scope. Even the fact that the Confession in subsequent years was translated into many other languages and adopted in many countries does not automatically qualify it as a catholic confession, especially when one considers that this "catholicity" has often been generated by immigration and in its initial stages at least, must be regarded as artificial. There is no geographical or cultural catholicity intrinsic to the Belgic Confession.

The case is stronger for the temporal catholicity of the Confession. Faber connects this with the indefectibility of the church. He notes the many examples in the Confession that witness to its self-conscious effort to continue in the ways of the ancient fathers. The temporal catholicity becomes evident both negatively and positively: "The catholicity of the Belgic Confession becomes first of all evident negatively in the rejection of heresies, condemned by the Christian church of all ages on the basis of the Word of God.... Positively the catholicity of the church becomes manifest in that the Belgic Confession consciously seeks continuity with the decisions and decrees of the early church."[28] Faber notes the fact that the Confession has innumerable quotations and allusions

---

25. Faber here may be the *vorlage* for the Canadian Reformed rendition of the subtitle, a rendition which, strangely, was adopted contrary to the direction of General Synod Cloverdale 1983.
26. Italics added.
27. Faber, *Essays*, 79-80.
28. Faber, *Essays*, 81.

from many church fathers, including Gregory of Nyssa, Cyril of Alexandria, Chrysostom, Cyprian, Jerome, Bernard of Clairvaux, and most prominently of all, Augustine.[29]

It is in this temporal aspect that we see most clearly the catholicity of the Belgic Confession in its normative character. When de Brès drafted the Confession, the intent was to faithfully summarize the truths of Scripture, just as they had been believed and confessed by generations previous. Faber correctly assesses these efforts as a success.

However, we have still not addressed the question of how or whether catholicity is associated with mission. Going back to the definition of mission, we can note that it is the church which is sent out with the missionary task. Catholicity is one of the attributes of the church that is sent out by Jesus Christ. Being aware of the temporal, geographical, and especially social-cultural aspects of catholicity is essential for a missionary-minded church.

The Belgic Confession does call the church's attention to all these aspects of catholicity, even though it emerges from and is conditioned by a very particular cultural milieu. The Dutch/Belgian origins of this Confession may be considered a hindrance in regards to catholicity; however, the temporal aspect does mitigate that considerably. For churches sending missionaries today, the Belgic reminds them that they are part of a larger program of mission that extends to the time of the apostles. When used by missionaries as a teaching tool and the doctrinal basis of younger churches, the Confession testifies that the Reformed faith is not of recent pedigree, nor is it really a Dutch/Belgian peculiarity, even if it comes packaged in those colours. For Reformed missiologists who subscribe it, the Belgic Confession witnesses that there are public, objective truths confessed by God's people through the ages regardless of cultural attachments — in other words, despite the claims made by some missiologists today, the substance of Christian doctrine is not founded on subjective and fleeting socio-cultural allegiances.[30] While it is not ideal in this respect (and one wonders whether an ideal catholic confession is even possible), one can consider what is catholic about the Belgic Confession to be one of its missiological strengths.

---

29. Faber, *Essays*, 82-83.
30. Contra Charles H. Kraft, *Anthropology for Christian Witness* (Maryknoll: Orbis Books, 1996), 70.

5.1.4 Redemptive-Historical Framework

In chapter 4, it was noted that the Belgic Confession, because of its medieval roots, evidences a redemptive-historical framework. In broad outline, it reflects the dramatic movement of the Apostles' Creed. Now we will build on those insights and consider further how this trait may be considered a strength.

In the last decades, increasing attention has been given to the dramatic character of theology, and this has also had an effect on Reformed academia. Michael Horton has been at the forefront of an effort to emphasize the drama of redemption in systematic theology. He constructs a systematic theology which uses a redemptive-historical/eschatological method, an analogical mode, a dramatic model, and a covenantal context.[31] At the heart of this, however, is his understanding of drama as a metaphor for theology, a metaphor whose roots he traces back to Irenaeus and Athanasius. He also draws attention to the use of this analogy in Dante and Calvin.[32] Horton's own appropriation of this model is traced back to Geerhardus Vos and philosopher Alasdair MacIntyre.[33] According to Horton, a different analogy has dominated Western theology since Augustine, that of the picture. Richard Rorty defined this analogy in reference to philosophy: "The picture which holds traditional philosophy captive is that of the mind as a great mirror, containing various representations — some accurate, some not — and capable of being studied by pure, non-empirical methods."[34] Horton argues that the dramatic analogy is superior because, being holistic, it provides the conceptual space for encompassing both text-centered and history-centered theologies. "Drama," he says, "captures both individual and public aspects of theological discovery and its subject matter."[35]

Charles Van Engen has applied similar insights to mission theology. Instead of speaking of a dramatic analogy or model, he argued for the need to integrate the perspective of narrative theology into missiology. His thesis is "that narrative theology as viewed from an evangelical per-

---

31. Michael S. Horton, *Covenant and Eschatology: The Divine Drama* (Louisville: Westminster John Knox Press, 2002), 5-19.
32. Horton, *Covenant and Eschatology*, 11.
33. Horton, *Covenant and Eschatology*, 12.
34. Richard Rorty, *Philosophy and the Mirror of Nature* (Princeton: Princeton UP, 1979), 12. Cited by Horton, *Covenant and Eschatology*, 10.
35. Horton, *Covenant and Eschatology,*, 10.

spective offers a creative and fruitful way to integrate the Bible's affirmations about the mission of God with our understanding of mission theology and its multiple, dynamically interacting horizons of text, community and context."[36] Drawing on many of the same sources as Horton, Van Engen argues that an evangelical appropriation and reshaping of narrative theology would bear rich dividends for missiology, allowing it to draw "richly from both the warp of the contextual particularity of God's revelation at specific times and places, and the woof of the temporal universality of the mission of God."[37] He notes that narrative theology has dimensions that stretch beyond the story, including concrete historical rootedness.[38] Narrative theology is also *theology*, but it is more than propositional dogmatics because it is based on the community of faith, it is intertwined with human history, it involves a faith-pilgrimage over time, and it integrates word and deed.[39] He recognizes both positive elements and serious concerns in various evangelical assessments of narrative theology, but in the end, he is convinced that it has important contributions to make to mission theology.

Van Engen suggests five ways in which narrative theology can contribute to missiology. First, "it helps us understand that the narrative of Scripture is the story of God's Trinitarian mission."[40] Second, it provides us with ways of speaking about God and his work that integrate both objective (propositional) and subjective (experiential) language so that "being, knowing and doing come together in real life."[41] Third, he argues that narrative theology resolves the tension between the particularity of churches in cultural contexts and "the universality of Christ's lordship over all times, peoples, and cultures." Writes Van Engen, "In narrative theology, we do not stress so much the cultural distance as to affirm that despite cultural distance and multiple horizons there is a profound proximity of all cultures in Jesus Christ."[42] Fourth, he suggests that narrative theology may help Christians discover a way to assimilate text, context,

---

36. Charles Van Engen, *Mission on the Way: Issues in Mission Theology* (Grand Rapids: Baker, 1996), 44.
37. Van Engen, *Mission on the Way*, 46.
38. Van Engen, *Mission on the Way*, 52-53.
39. Van Engen, *Mission on the Way*, 55-57.
40. Van Engen, *Mission on the Way*, 65.
41. Van Engen, *Mission on the Way*, 65.
42. Van Engen, *Mission on the Way*, 67.

and the faith community. Lastly, Van Engen proposes that "narrative theology may provide us the images, pictures and metaphors, and stories that are necessary for rounding out the propositional, textual and historical aspects of today's global theological conversations in missiology."[43]

Both Horton and Van Engen are suggestive for how we might best understand the contribution of the Belgic Confession. Compared to Horton, Van Engen is more attached to a particular movement in theology (a movement with a questionable pedigree), and while his use of the concept of *Missio Dei* is debatable (see the discussion of Bosch in 2.4), he is correct in drawing our attention to the ways in which drama and narrative might be profitably employed in missiology. A dramatic, narrative framework lends itself to addressing some of the most difficult issues in the study of mission.

As noted in chapter 4, the Belgic Confession provides the general outlines of this framework and could conceivably contribute this framework to a narrative missiology. Employing this understanding, one could fruitfully write a missiology text self-consciously using the redemptive-historical framework of the Confession, applying the dramatic model of Horton to mission theology. As suggested by Van Engen, this approach would allow for treatment of the Trinitarian involvement in mission, an integration of the propositional and experiential, a resolution of particularity and catholicity (the one and the many), an assimilation of the various horizons of missiology, and the provision of tools to facilitate the global missiological conversation. It must be recognized that the while the Confession provides the skeletal framework for this approach, it would be up to Reformed missiologists to place most of the flesh on this skeleton.

5.1.5 Confession Providing a Doctrinal Foundation for the Further Development of Reformed Missiology

The Confession not only provides a helpful framework that is yet to be exploited in missiology, it also provides a doctrinal foundation. While Robert Recker has made some suggestions in evaluating this foundation (and we will explore his insights further in 7.1), this also generally constitutes an area that has been little explored.[44] Building on what was said in the last section, a missiological commentary on the Belgic Confession would be a profitable means of advancing Reformed thought in this field. As Klaas Schilder and others have written theological commentaries on

---

43. Van Engen, *Mission on the Way*, 67.
44. Recker, "An Analysis...," passim.

the Heidelberg Catechism, so also Reformed missiology would be well-served by a commentary on the Belgic Confession written with an eye to the mission of the church. In this section, we will explore how this might be done with a look at several articles.

ARTICLE 2 — HOW GOD MAKES HIMSELF KNOWN TO US

> We know him by two means: First, by the creation, preservation, and government of the universe; which is before our eyes as a most beautiful book, wherein all creatures, great and small, are as so many letters leading us to *perceive clearly the invisible qualities of God*, namely, *his eternal power and deity*, as the apostle Paul says in Rom. 1:20. All these things are sufficient to convict men and leave them without excuse. Second, he makes himself more clearly and fully known to us by his holy and divine Word as far as is necessary for us in this life, to his glory and our salvation.[45]

The doctrine expressed in this article is nothing novel among churches of the Reformation. In fact, article 2 of the Belgic is an expansion on article 2 of the French Confession. The Belgic Confession indicates that there are two "books" by which God is known: the universe (in its creation, preservation and government) and the written Word of God. There are important functional differences between these books.

The book of the universe operates in two ways, depending on the spiritual status of the "reader." For the believer, the universe is a most beautiful book (*un beau livre*) that leads our thoughts upward in contemplation of God's imperceptible attributes, particularly his eternal power and divinity. In other words, for Christians, the universe functions in a doxological manner. However, for unbelievers this revelation has an elenctic function; it works as a curse, convicting and leaving them without excuse. According to the Confession, building on Paul's treatment of this subject in Romans 1 and 2, nothing else is needed to achieve a conviction of people under sin. According to John Platt, at this point the Belgic Confession even outdoes Calvin in its insistence on the negative effects of the fall in relation to the first means of revelation.[46] For our purposes, the important thing to note is that God is never without a witness in the

---

45. BoP, 441. The italics in this quotation (and all subsequent ones of the Belgic Confession) are from the *Book of Praise* and indicate direct quotations of Scripture.

46. John Platt, *Reformed Thought and Scholasticism: The Arguments for the Existence of God in Dutch Theology, 1575-1650* (Leiden: Brill, 1982), 110.

world, even when the Bible is absent. This witness cannot save, but it does testify that there is a problem in the relationship between God and man, and man is responsible for this problem.

The answer to this problem is only found in the other book, God's holy and divine Word. Through a Scripture-engendered faith, we come to know God better, not only as judge (which we already knew from the first book), but also as our Father through Jesus Christ. The Bible exists to clearly and fully reveal God himself to us in all his attributes, so that we may exalt his worth and so that we may be saved. According to the Belgic Confession, the Holy Scriptures are indispensable for salvation.

Here the Confession provides a foundation and normative direction for reflection on the relationship between Christianity and other religions. There are some contemporary theological and missiological developments that make this reflection necessary. Radical religious pluralism (or normative pluralism) asserts that no one religion is superior over any other. Inclusivism affirms the objective truth of some basic Christian claims, yet insists that God has revealed himself salvifically in other religions. Both radical religious pluralism and inclusivism insist that salvation is available in other religions. Both are products of modernity or perhaps postmodernity.[47] Both are enormously influential, also in missiological circles. It would be helpful to survey a few examples.

Carl Braaten appears to adopt an exclusivist stance when he arraigns Raimundo Panikkar on the charge of identifying Christ with various Hindu deities.[48] However, he goes on to propose a model which "pictures Jesus Christ as the eschatological fulfillment" of all non-Christian religions. According to Braaten, "The gospel of Jesus Christ does not destroy but fulfills the religions."[49] While discussing the implications of these views for mission, he again seems to take the exclusivist position, warning that if religious pluralism triumphs, "the death of both the ecumenical and the missionary movements will ensue."[50] With his soft inclusivism, Braaten may be seeking for middle ground, but in the end his position is just as vulnerable as the one against which he warns. Carson notes that there are several lapses in Braaten's argument. Braaten equivocates on the two

---

47. Carson, *The Gagging of God*, 26-27.
48. Carl E. Braaten, *No Other Gospel! Christianity Among the World's Religions* (Minneapolis: Fortress Press, 1992), 78.
49. Braaten, *No Other Gospel*, 80.
50. Braaten, *No Other Gospel*, 109.

modes ("books") of revelation, at this point, essentially collapsing them into one. Carson writes:

> That there is "revelation" in some sense in all religions few Christian thinkers (except some in the Barthian tradition) would want to deny. Some would speak of the revelation implicit in the imago Dei; others would speak, quite dogmatically at that, of the general revelation that can be found in non-Christian religions; still others of the residual revelation not destroyed by the overlay of false religion. But Braaten moves from this weak sense of revelation to a much stronger sense, in which these revelations are "fulfilled" in Jesus Christ much as the old covenant is "fulfilled" in Jesus Christ. But in the Bible, the fulfillment of the old covenant in Jesus Christ (e.g. Matt. 5:17-20) is the fulfillment of what systematicians have called special revelation, and "fulfillment" itself means not the satisfaction of religious and personal aspirations, but the arrival of the eschatological event to which the old covenant Scriptures pointed in promise and type. Although the Bible as a whole can sometimes speak of the gospel and of Jesus as bringing to fruition the aspirations of the pagans who surround the covenant community, it does not speak of the gospel or of Christ as fulfilling their religion.[51]

Admittedly, Guido de Brès knew nothing of Braaten's soft inclusivism when he wrote the Belgic Confession — there was nothing like it in his day. Nevertheless, the Belgic Confession speaks to this issue. When Braaten describes Bhakti Hinduism and Mahayana Buddhism as religions of grace, or when he refers to Francis Xavier's identification of Jodo Shinsu as "the Lutheran form of Buddhism" (because of its supposed reliance on grace), or when he refers to Paul Althaus and Paul Tillich's recognition of a "real knowledge of God" apart from Christian revelation, he is in danger of drifting from the absolute necessity of the gospel revealed in the written Word of God.[52] He arrives there when he asserts that when it comes to adherents of non-Christian religions, "we are free to waffle somewhere between reverent speculation and silent agnosticism." He states that the salvation of those who do not believe in Christ "is ultimately a mystery which we cannot unveil by speculation."[53]

---

51. Carson, *The Gagging of God*, 31.
52. Braaten, *No Other Gospel*, 72-73.
53. Braaten, *No Other Gospel*, 80-81.

The Belgic Confession brings us back to the Word of God and witnesses that speculation or agnosticism are unwarranted. The unbelieving world needs the gospel of Jesus Christ that has been revealed in the inscripturated Word.

If the Confession rebukes the soft inclusivism of a Carl Braaten, it does so even more forcefully to the radical religious pluralism of a John Hick. Hick's starting point is in his view of the Bible as an exclusively human book. He maintains the position that the Bible is an account of the religious experiences and histories of individuals, a nation (Israel), and a group of religiously like-minded people (the church). As far as Jesus Christ is concerned, he is convinced that the literal, historic incarnation and virgin birth are problematic. Regarding the gospels he writes, "We should not think of the four Gospels as if they were eyewitness accounts by reporters on the spot. They were written between forty and seventy years after Jesus' death by people who were not personally present at the events they describe."[54] Already here there is a significant dissonance between the stance of the Belgic Confession and its confessors and Hick. One regards the Scriptures as God's "holy and divine Word," and the other sees them as exclusively human documents.

The gap widens as Hick relates how he adopted his pluralistic perspective on the relationship between Christianity and other religions. Though he was once a self-described "fundamentalist" who took the Bible seriously, he began questioning the literal historicity of the virgin birth while teaching at Princeton Theological Seminary in 1961.[55] After his departure from belief in the inspiration of Scripture, he began frequently attending Muslim mosques, Sikh gurdwaras, Hindu temples, and Jewish synagogues in connection with inter-faith activism in the British city of Birmingham.[56] This led him to realize that "the God-figures of the great theistic religions are different human awarenesses of the Ultimate."[57] From there, it was no great step for Hick to assert that salvation exists outside of Christianity, for freedom from the Bible allows one to develop one's own understanding of what salvation actually is:

---

54. John Hick, "A Pluralist View," in *Four Views on Salvation in a Pluralistic World*, John Hick, Clark H. Pinnock, Alister E. McGrath, R. Douglas Geivett, and W. Gary Phillips (Grand Rapids: Zondervan, 1995), 34-35.
55. Hick, "A Pluralist View," 32.
56. Hick, "A Pluralist View," 38.
57. Hick, "A Pluralist View," 39.

> If we define salvation as being forgiven and accepted by God because of Jesus' death on the cross, then it becomes a tautology that Christianity alone knows and is able to preach the source of salvation. But if we define salvation as an actual human change, a gradual transformation from natural self-centeredness (with all the human evils that flow from this) to a radically new orientation centered in God and manifested in the "fruit of the Spirit," then it seems clear that salvation is taking place within all of the world religions — and taking place, so far as we can tell, to more or less the same extent.[58]

Hick is saying that if only we autonomously and unilaterally redefine salvation to mean "moral transformation," then salvation is a reality found in all religions, not just Christianity.

A Reformed missiologist will recognize the deadly flaws inherent in Hick's method. The Belgic Confession informs his understanding that "salvation" is not to be defined apart from God's "holy and divine Word." The Confession keeps Reformed missiology grounded in truly objective truths, rather than fertilizing views that are based on supposedly objective "observable realities of human life."[59] Radical religious pluralism is not an option for anyone who subscribes the Belgic Confession meaningfully. In fact, the Confession's biblical stance strongly militates against anything short of the exclusivist position.

It is also worthwhile to briefly compare the position of the Belgic Confession with that of the Roman Catholic theologian Karl Rahner. Rahner argued that Christianity is indeed the only way for salvation. Unlike other religions, including Islam, Christianity maintains that it is the "one and only valid revelation of the one living God."[60] Christianity is the absolute religion, intended for all people.[61] Up till this point, the Belgic Confession agrees. Rahner went on, however, to argue that non-Christian religions contain not only elements of a natural knowledge of God, elements that have been vandalized by original sin and other ill effects. They also contain "supernatural elements arising out of the grace which is given to men

---

58. Hick, "A Pluralist View," 43.
59. Hick, "A Pluralist View," 43.
60. Karl Rahner, *Theological Investigations* (Vol. 5) (New York: Crossroad, 1983), 116.
61. Rahner, *Theological Investigations*, 118.

as a gratuitous gift on account of Christ."[62] To varying degrees, then, non-Christian religions can be recognized as lawful, and they can even have positive salvific significance. Just as there was salvation in non-Christian Judaism before the coming of Christ, one may also consider non-Christian religions to offer real salvation to their adherents. Essentially, under their guidance of their religions (natural law), non-Christians can equally attain to the moral transformation which enables them to attain to God's grace.[63] From here, Rahner concluded that Christians must regard adherents of non-Christian religions as "anonymous Christians," for they too, are working towards salvation.[64] But then why should anyone be called to the Christian faith? Does not Rahner's position undermine the missionary enterprise? Rahner anticipated that objection and responded that it is necessary "because the individual who grasps Christianity in a clearer, purer and more reflective way has, other things being equal, a still greater chance of salvation than someone who is merely an anonymous Christian."[65] The missionary's task, then, is merely to bring anonymous Christians to an explicit consciousness of what already belongs to them.

While there are differences, Rahner's position is on the same trajectory as the soft inclusivism of Braaten. The objections we raised with Braaten apply equally to Rahner. Yet we can and must go further. Like Hick, Rahner's conception of salvation includes moral transformation, not as the goal perhaps, but certainly as an efficient cause. While this subject is not addressed in article 2, the Belgic Confession has a radically different view. Apart from faith in Jesus Christ (faith being instrumental), there is no salvation. The revelation given in creation only functions *elenctically* for adherents of non-Christian religions.

The Belgic Confession not only speaks to the problem of non-Christian religions, it also speaks to the contemporary "resurgence" of atheism in the West. Leading the charge are Richard Dawkins and Christopher Hitchens, whose books were on North American best-seller lists for a period of time, which may suggest a revitalized (if it ever was all that vital) atheist movement.[66] This is not the place to rehearse their arguments;

---

62. Rahner, *Theological Investigations*, 121.
63. Rahner, *Theological Investigations*, 130.
64. Rahner, *Theological Investigations*, 131-132.
65. Rahner, *Theological Investigations*, 132.
66. Richard Dawkins, *The God Delusion* (Boston: Houghton Mifflin Company, 2006); Christopher Hitchens, *God is Not Great: How Religion Poisons Everything*

rather, what we want to consider is how the Confession leads us to reflect on these developments and what, if any, suggestions may be given by the Confession to address these developments.

Perhaps the best line of approach is to consider whether, according to the Confession, atheism actually exists, or better, whether it is possible for people to be atheists. In principle, the Confession allows for the existence of atheism as a school of thought. In practice, however, the Confession follows the Pauline position that all men are aware of God's existence but suppress this truth in unrighteousness, leaving them without excuse. Individual men can suppress the truth in unrighteousness, and likewise, a conglomerate of men forming a school of thought.

Cornelius Van Til adds some nuance to this position:

> As made in the image of God no man can escape becoming the interpretative medium of God's general revelation both in his intellectual (Romans 1:20) and in his moral consciousness (Romans 2:14,15). No matter which button of the radio he presses, he always hears the voice of God. Even when he presses the button of his own psychological self-conscious activity, through which as a last resort the sinner might hope to hear another voice, he still hears the voice of God. "If I make my bed in hell, behold, Thou art there." It is in this sense that we must, at least to begin with, understand the matter when we are told that there are no atheistic peoples and no atheistic men. Psychologically there are no atheistic men; epistemologically every sinner is atheistic.[67]

In his Van Til reader, Greg Bahnsen elaborates, "Van Til distinguishes here between the way men actually think ('psychologically') and their proposed pictures of themselves as thinkers ('epistemologically')."[68]

This is suggestive for the incorporation of general revelation (the first book) into our missiology. When we consider the unbelieving world, whether other religions or the self-identified non-religious, we can build on the formulation of the Belgic Confession. God is not without a witness in the world; the question is: what have people done with that witness?

(Toronto: McClelland & Steward Ltd., 2007).
67. Cornelius Van Til, *Common Grace and the Gospel* (Phillipsburg: Presbyterian and Reformed, 1972), 53-54.
68. Greg L. Bahnsen, *Van Til's Apologetic: Readings & Analysis* (Phillipsburg: P&R, 1998), 191.

This is not an issue of cognition, but of ethics. As Paul says, they have "suppressed the truth in unrighteousness." The Belgic Confession captures that biblical truth and informs Reformed missiology that, like Paul in Acts 17, general revelation can and must function as a point of contact for missionaries in any situation. In other words, the Confession supports and provides a foundation for the development of missionary elenctics.

Article 7 — the Sufficiency of Holy Scripture

> We believe that this Holy Scripture fully contains the will of God and that all that man must believe in order to be saved is sufficiently taught therein. The whole manner of worship which God requires of us is written in it at length. It is therefore unlawful for any one, even for an apostle, to teach otherwise than we are now taught in Holy Scripture: yes, *even if it be an angel from heaven*, as the apostle Paul says. Since it is forbidden to add to or take away anything from the Word of God, it is evident that the doctrine thereof is most perfect and complete in all respects.
>
> We may not consider any writings of men, however holy these men may have been, of equal value with the divine Scriptures; nor ought we to consider custom, or the great multitude, or antiquity, or succession of times and persons, or councils, decrees, or statutes, as of equal value with the truth of God, since the truth is above all; for all men are of themselves liars, and *lighter than a breath*. We therefore reject with all our heart whatever does not agree with this infallible rule, as the apostles have taught us: *Test the spirits to see whether they are of God*. Likewise: *If any one comes to you and does not bring this doctrine, do not receive him into your house or give him any greeting.*[69]

This article expresses a key component of the Reformed doctrine of Scripture. The Bible fully contains both the law (the will of God) and the gospel (what man must believe in order to be saved). This is, of course, the Reformation concept of *sola Scriptura*. The Bible alone is our foundation and guide for life before the face of God. The Bible alone is the source for the gospel. Nothing is of equal value or authority with Scripture and whatever does not agree with it is to be rejected. Here too, the Belgic Confession stands side by side with other expressions of the Reformed

---

69. BoP, 443-444.

faith in the sixteenth century, including and especially the French Confession of Faith of 1559.

The missionary message is articulated in the first sentence: "We believe that this Holy Scripture fully contains the will of God and that all that man must believe in order to be saved is sufficiently taught therein." As already indicated, the division here is between law and gospel, a distinction found elsewhere in the Reformed confessions. Missionaries are to preach the law of God which convicts men of their sin. Missionaries are also to preach the gospel of Jesus Christ which reconciles sinners to God. The Confession lays out this basic message (which is not only relevant for mission fields, but also for established churches), but it does not provide us with a Reformed missionary homiletics (or ethnohomiletics). This is something which appears to remain a lacuna in Reformed missiology.[70]

Missionary liturgics (ethnoliturgics) is another area which remains undeveloped in Reformed missiology. The Belgic Confession draws this to our attention by saying that "the whole manner of worship which God requires of us is written in it at length." This is a brief statement of the regulative principle of worship which appears again later in the Confession (article 32) and also in the other Reformed confessions.[71] The regulative principle states that we may not worship God in any other way than he has commanded in his Word — that means the Word is not only sufficient for our salvation, but also for our worship. In its maintenance of this principle, the Belgic Confession also speaks to the question of the shape and character of worship on the mission field. When the gospel comes into another culture and God gathers his people from that culture, what should their worship look like? Should it look like the worship of the missionaries? Or should it take on the pre-Christian worship of the receptor culture in any way, shape, or form? These are difficult questions to answer and the Belgic Confession provides an answer with its statement of the regulative principle.

---

70. Some of the papers presented at a Reformed mission conference held in Hamilton, ON in 2005 dealt with this subject; see Wes Bredenhof ed., *Papers Presented at the First Reformed Missions Conference* (Hamilton: Theological College of the Canadian Reformed Churches, 2005). See also the sources on missionary homiletics mentioned in Jan A. B. Jongeneel, *Philosophy, Science and Theology of Mission in the 19th and 20th Centuries: A Missiological Encyclopedia, Part II: Missionary Theology*, Frankfurt am Main: Peter Lang, 1997, 267-289.

71. Wes Bredenhof, *The Whole Manner of Worship: The Sufficiency of Scripture and Worship in Article 7 of the Belgic Confession* (Edmonton: Still Waters Revival Books, 1997).

The Confession states that God's Word lays out the "whole manner of worship." Context is necessary for interpretation. In the Reformed churches, a classical distinction exists between the *elements* and *circumstances* of worship. Elements are the divinely ordained parts of the worship service such as preaching, prayer, and singing. Elements are supracultural and, in principle, should be the same from culture to culture. A Reformed church in Brazil should have the same elements as a Reformed church in the Congo or in Canada. Circumstances are culturally determined and can vary from church to church, even within a given culture. Circumstances include things such as the architecture of a building, the furniture within, the times of the worship services, the music used to accompany the singing and so on. Circumstances are determined with wisdom informed by Scripture, and there is considerable freedom in this area. Recognizing this distinction helps to answer many questions in missionary liturgics.

The remainder of article 7 directs our attention to how Scripture must function as the infallible basis for the entire Christian life. We can extend that to include Scripture functioning as the infallible basis for the study and practice of Christian mission. This does not mean that it is the only source for missiological reflection, but that it is the touchstone or the standard by which all other sources are evaluated. Similarly, Alan Tippet wrote that for his development of missiology, the Bible was his "frame of reference." The Bible is a tool for testing missiology, for classifying and evaluating material coming from historical and archival sources, as well as anthropological research.[72] Tippet went on to explicitly reject any higher critical approach to the Scriptures; the Bible must be accepted as a package deal. "If you give it up, you give up Christian mission and missiology with it."[73]

Unfortunately, the high view of Scripture found in Tippet and the Belgic Confession is a rare commodity in much of contemporary missiology. While the Bible is often recognized as a source for missiology, there are many who fail to see it as a normative source, or as a standard by which other sources are to be evaluated. There are still others who do not even see this as an issue.[74]

---

72. Alan Tippet, *Introduction to Missiology* (Pasadena: William Carey Library, 1987), 14.

73. Tippet, *Introduction to Missiology*, 15.

74. For example, a recent dictionary does not even have an article on the place of the Bible in missiology. See John Corrie, ed., *Dictionary of Mission Theology* (Downers Grove: InterVarsity Press, 2007). This is more of a case of taking things for granted, because the introduction does say (xvi) that the dictionary endeav-

Donald Senior indicated that most contemporary theologies of mission begin with a biblical basis. Yet, there is diversity on the question of the normativity of this biblical basis. In fact, the more recent essays have adopted a dialectical approach which places contemporary experiences and observations on an equal footing with the major motifs or dynamics of the Bible. Additionally, there is a tendency to emphasize "the diversity of the biblical witness" in order to provide a foundation for "a pluralistic approach to mission."[75] All of this is to say that higher critical approaches to Scripture are in the ascendancy in much of missiology.

This is nowhere more evident than with the most influential voice in contemporary missiology, David Bosch. In his 1980 work, *Witness to the World*, Bosch noted that there is widespread agreement on the necessity of a biblical foundation for missiology. However, historically an emphasis on the Bible as the *only* foundation was little in evidence, both in Protestant and Roman Catholic circles.[76] He went on to distinguish between two ways in which one may construe the Bible as the foundation for missiology: inductive or deductive. The deductive construal is found in theologically conservative circles and works from the text of Scripture, developing normative principles for the contemporary situation. The inductive construal is favoured in ecumenical circles and involves taking the point of departure in the situation — the context becomes the hermeneutical key which makes a correct (or perhaps "useful") understanding of the Bible possible. For Bosch, each construal has its difficulties. The deductive method is impractical because "nineteen centuries separate us from the most recent biblical document. We have no immediate access to it."[77] The inductive method is practical, but not justifiable. "Historical events and personal or group experience are too ambivalent to serve as key for the interpretation of a biblical text."[78] Bosch resolved this bifurcation by proposing to make use of both approaches, recognizing the limitations and relativity of both.

---

ours to have "a respect for the priority of the biblical text as the authoritative source of theological and missiological thinking."

75. Donald Senior, "Bible," in *Dictionary of Mission: Theology, History, Perspectives*, ed. Karl Müller, Theo Sundermeir, Stephen B. Bevans, and Richard H. Bliese (Maryknoll: Orbis Books, 1997), 44-45.

76. David J. Bosch, *Witness to the World: The Christian Mission in Theological Perspective* (Atlanta: John Knox Press, 1980), 42-43.

77. Bosch, *Witness to the World*, 44.

78. Bosch, *Witness to the World*, 44

Bosch's treatment of this subject is problematic on a number of levels. His portrayal of the deductive construal is accurate as far it goes, and it seems to express what the Belgic Confession has to say to missiology on this point. However, when he portrays the inductive construal, he confuses foundations and constructions and in so doing reveals his higher critical prejudices. The inductive method does not have the Bible as its foundation. That much is clear from the fact that its starting point is in the human situation rather than in the text of Scripture. The Bible is only brought in at a later point in the process, and then it becomes part of a construction, rather than a foundation. Next, Bosch is evidently biased against the very possibility of the deductive construal when he alleges that an objective reading of Scripture is impossible because of historical distance and other factors. Finally, connected with the preceding, when he proposes to use *both* methods, he has tipped his hand. The deductive method *by its very nature* excludes the inductive, and vice-versa. One cannot say that the Bible is the only normative source (foundation) for missiology and then use the context as a hermeneutical key for understanding the Bible. The two are mutually exclusive.

What Bosch did in *Witness to the World* set the stage for his missiological adaptation of Thomas Kuhn's paradigmatic methodology in *Transforming Mission*. Of course, adapting Kuhn's work on this process had been done before in theology by Hans Küng. However, Bosch was apparently the first to apply it to missiology, and this development seems to be related to his view of missiological foundations. In *Transforming Mission*, the discussion of the foundations of missiology is threadbare. He noted that Warneck had argued for the Bible as the supernatural foundation of mission, while others had turned results into the foundation for mission.[79] As for Bosch's position, it was no easier to pin down than in 1980, though his prejudices are more apparent. He cited Kramm's assertion that a theological foundation for mission "is only possible if we continually refer back to the ground of our faith: God's self-communication in Jesus Christ." Then he articulated the following: "The Bible is not to be treated as a storehouse of truths on which we can draw at random. There are no immutable and objectively correct 'laws of mission' to which exegesis of Scripture gives us access and which provide us with blueprints we can apply in every situation. Our missionary practice is not performed in unbroken continuity with the biblical witness; it is an altogether ambiva-

---

79. Bosch, *Transforming Mission*, 4-6.

lent enterprise executed in the context of tension between divine providence and human confusion."[80] In what follows, Bosch examines "New Testament Models of Mission," but these are not normative in any sense. Bosch is simply making historical observations. The contours of mission and mission theology found in Scripture, while suggestive and perhaps helpful, do not carry any weight for coming generations which develop their own paradigms. The very notion of a "paradigm" is meant to be value-neutral and objective. However, this concept carries its own freight of epistemological presuppositions, and this is reflected in Bosch's insistence that one can no longer speak about "Christian theology," but that one must now speak about "Christian theologies."[81] While what he writes remains valuable, Bosch has undermined the very notion of an accessible, public, objective truth.

The Belgic Confession with its simple biblical statements challenges the missiological prejudices of Bosch and others when it comes to foundations and norms. The Bible alone is the infallible Word of God which gives God's people public, objective truth. While it is not a "storehouse of truths on which we can draw at random" (the very expression is prejudicial!), it is a steadfast and reliable foundation, also for missiology. In this era when the doctrine of Scripture continues to be embattled (think of the Emergent movement in North America), this article reminds Reformed missiologists (and believers in general) that nothing can be taken for granted.

ARTICLE 10 — JESUS CHRIST TRUE AND ETERNAL GOD

> We believe that Jesus Christ according to his divine nature is the only-begotten Son of God, begotten from eternity, not made, nor created — for then he would be a creature — but of the same essence with the Father, equally-eternal, *who reflects the glory of God and bears the very stamp of his nature*, and is equal to him in all things. He is the Son of God, not only from the time that he assumed our nature but from all eternity, as these testimonies, when compared with each other, teach us: Moses says that God created the world; the apostle John says that all things were made by the Word which he calls God. The letter to the Hebrews says that God made the world through his Son; like-

---

80. Bosch, *Transforming Mission*, 9.
81. Bosch, *Transforming Mission*, 182.

wise the apostle Paul says that God created all things through Jesus Christ. Therefore it must necessarily follow that he who is called God, the Word, the Son, and Jesus Christ, did exist at that time when all things were created by him. Therefore he could say, *Truly I say to you, before Abraham was, I am,* and he prayed, *Glorify thou me in thy own presence with the glory which I had with thee before the world was made.* And so he is true, eternal God, the Almighty, whom we invoke, worship, and serve.[82]

This article is concerned with the question: who is the Christ? In its original context, the Belgic Confession at this point was asserting the orthodoxy of the Reformed churches. There is nothing in this article that a Roman Catholic in the sixteenth century (or any era, for that matter) would find objectionable. It is a straightforward confession of Nicene and Chalcedonian/Athanasian orthodoxy.

The main emphasis in this article is on expressing the eternal sonship of Jesus Christ and the concomitant doctrine of his divinity. The Belgic Confession insists that Jesus Christ has always been the Son of God and always will be. Likewise, he is "of the same essence with the Father," and possesses a divine nature. The historical reason for this article (which does not have a correlative in the French Confession) is the doctrine of incarnational sonship found among some of the Anabaptists.[83] Some of the Anabaptists (such as Menno Simons) held that Jesus became the Son of God at his incarnation and is only the eternal Son of God in the forward looking sense of "eternal." However, with the ecumenical creeds, de Brès and the Reformed churches insisted that "eternal" is both backward- and forward-looking — he has always been the Son of God and always will be. Some of the Anabaptists also had problems with the humanity of Christ and those are dealt with in article 18 — which we will also deal with shortly.

For our purposes, we need to inquire whether this article has any contribution to make to the development of Reformed missiology. In the first place, it speaks out of the Scriptures to the question of the content of the missionary message. We noted above that article 7 indicates law and gospel as the broad categories of content for preaching (missionary and otherwise). But when we consider the nature and content of the gospel, we are also confronted with the question of the identity

---

82. BoP, 447.
83. See Vonk, *De Voorzeide Leer* (IIIa), 258.

of Jesus Christ. Who is this Saviour that missionaries must preach? In other words, Christology is at the heart of missionary proclamation. If we follow the biblical lines of the Belgic Confession, missional preaching must present him as the eternal Son of God, the one who presents us with the mystery of the incarnation: the eternal God who has come in human flesh and blood.

While this orthodox, biblical Christology is, in principle, an ecumenical truth, the reality is that there are endless varieties of erroneous and defective Christologies. This is a universal problem in Christian theology, but it is especially acute in missiology. Wilbur Shenk noted the range and variety of Christologies in the world today.[84] He reported on the observations of Saul Trinidad and Juan Stam regarding Protestant preaching in Latin America, noting that its Christology was Docetic, presenting a Christ who was removed from the concerns of the poor and oppressed. Shenk also discussed the efforts of C. Rene Padilla to present a missional Christology "that is historically situated and responds to the cries of the poor and disenfranchised of the world."[85] According to Padilla, the humanity of Jesus is the sine qua non for establishing a connection between his mission and that of his disciples. For Padilla, however, it becomes clear that as a liberation theologian, mission means addressing injustice, oppression, and poverty on the earth. It has nothing to do with reconciling sinners to a holy and just God. Consequently, liberation theology depends on a Christology from below.

The Belgic Confession presents a Christology that is not weighted towards "above" or "below," but presents both, as found in the Scriptures. Article 10 presents us with a biblical Christology from above, whereas article 18 presents us with the Christology from below. Both are important, and one ought not to stress one above the other. Rather than allowing cultural or socio-economic circumstances to determine our Christology (as Shenk suggests), we simply need to let Scripture speak. The Belgic Confession provides a balanced map or guide to what the Scriptures teach on this point and indicates that a Reformed missiology will do likewise.

Imbalance, however, is not the only concern when we reflect on the current status of Christology in global missions. The error of incarna-

---

84. Wilbur R. Shenk, "Recasting Theology of Mission: Impulses from the Non-Western World," in *International Bulletin of Missionary Research* 25.3 (July 2001): 102.
85. Shenk, "Recasting Theology," 104.

tional sonship still exists in — and is still propagated by — churches such as the anti-Trinitarian United Pentecostal Church (UPC). The UPC has a significant global presence with missionaries in numerous countries. Especially in the southern hemisphere, Pentecostalism and its charismatic effluents continue to be in ascendancy, and this presents a challenge for Reformed churches. The Belgic Confession continues to provide a biblical, elenctic witness against these sects, especially those who hold to erroneous Christologies and heretical views of the Trinity. Reformed missionaries report that, in many of these situations, especially in Latin America, the Belgic Confession speaks as if it was written yesterday.

Being clear on the identity of the Christ to be proclaimed is essential. The Confession speaks clearly and elenctically on this issue. It positively summarizes what the Bible teaches and negatively identifies where people have historically strayed from this biblical teaching. In so doing, the Confession continues to provide a biblical foundation for the restatement and development of Christology within the discipline of missiology.

ARTICLE 16 — DIVINE ELECTION

> We believe that, when the entire offspring of Adam plunged into perdition and ruin by the transgression of the first man, God manifested himself to be as he is: merciful and just. *Merciful*, in rescuing and saving from this perdition those whom in his eternal and unchangeable counsel he has elected in Jesus Christ our Lord by his pure goodness, without any consideration of their works. *Just*, in leaving the others in the fall and perdition into which they have plunged themselves.[86]

It is not surprising to find this article in a Calvinistic confession. John Calvin is well-known for his teaching of predestination, and the French Confession (in which he had a hand and on which the Belgic is based) reflects this teaching as well in article 12. Of course, this doctrine did not originate with Calvin but can be traced back to Augustine and earlier church fathers, and from them, back to the divine source in Scripture. In closer proximity to the sixteenth century, medieval theologians such as Duns Scotus had also anticipated and approximated the Calvinistic formulation.[87]

---

86. BoP, 452.
87. Ozment, *Age of Reform*, 33-35. Cf. David C. Steinmetz, *Calvin in Context* (New York: Oxford UP, 1995), 40-52.

The doctrine expressed here lays the blame for the fall into sin at the feet of Adam ("the first man"), but the effects were not restricted to Adam. His transgression plunged his entire offspring into eternal and temporal damnation and destruction. When this happened, God showed his attributes of mercy and justice. On the positive side, his mercy is revealed in his "eternal and unchangeable counsel," whereby he has saved those whom he has chosen in Jesus Christ. This choice was entirely out of his pure goodness and had nothing to do with what the elect would do — in other words, predestination on the basis of foreseen faith or works is ruled out by the Confession. God's justice is revealed in his leaving others in their fallen condition. The Confession emphasizes that this fallen condition is the reprobates' own responsibility — they have plunged themselves into this status.[88]

During the late sixteenth and early seventeenth centuries, the Belgic Confession came under fire from Jacobus Arminius and especially those associated with him. This article was one of the central points of contention of the Arminian party. In 1593, Arminius stated that while he was unable to explain article 16, he was willing to adhere to it. During the next ten years, there was no indication from Arminius that he had any troubles with the Confession on this or any other points.[89] In 1608, he was called before the Dutch States General to explain his views on election and he stated his belief that his views of election as being on the basis of foreseen faith was in agreement with article 16.[90] In subsequent years, following the death of Arminius in 1609, the Arminian party moved towards a recognition that the Confession contradicted its position. At the Synod of Dort 1618-19, the Arminians presented a submission in which they questioned the formulations of the Belgic Confession on a number of issues, including the doctrine of election as expressed in article 16.[91] At the instigation of the Arminians, several articles of the Confession were revised to better establish the Reformed position. However, interestingly, article 16 was not among those articles. Rather than revising the article to strengthen it, the Synod prepared the Canons as a further explanation of the doctrine of election together with its corollaries.

---

88. The 1561/62 versions of this article were quite a bit longer, giving further emphasis and explanation to this particular point.
89. Gootjes, *The Belgic Confession*, 135.
90. Gootjes, *The Belgic Confession*, 136.
91. Gootjes, *The Belgic Confession*, 145.

Historically speaking, this article has been no stranger to theological controversy. The same is true when we turn to missiology. While there has been little discussion about article 16 as such, the doctrine expressed in this article has been and is frequently maligned as a death-sentence for Christian mission. The infamous words of John Ryland to a young William Carey in 1786 are regularly marshaled as proof: "Young man, sit down; when God pleases to convert the heathen, he will do so without your aid or mine." David Cloud is one modern author who cites Ryland's alleged words as proof that "Calvinism tends to cool evangelistic fervour" and that evangelistically-minded Calvinists are the exception rather than the rule.[92] John Piper related hearing a former president of Intervarsity Christian Fellowship who stated that when he began his missionary career he was convinced that a belief in predestination was incompatible with Christian mission.[93] Terry McGovern, a Baptist missionary in Papua New Guinea, asserted that Calvinism is one of the biggest dangers to the gospel and mission.[94] Such sentiments are not uncommon.

Does the Reformed doctrine of election as expressed in article 16 destroy the missionary impulse? Of course, this is a question that has been asked and answered repeatedly.[95] Nevertheless, the fact that it is still frequently answered in the affirmative indicates that Reformed missiology must continually attend to it. Briefly, we may note that the Belgic Confession does not intimate that the election described here is immediate. Context again is critical, for, in the next article, the Confession states that God sought man and extended the evangelical promise of Genesis 3:15 to him. In article 22, we discover that, for believers in every age, the Holy Spirit is the one who kindles true faith in their hearts. Article 24 states the same thing and adds the "hear-

---

92. David Cloud, "Calvinism on the March among Evangelicals," *Friday Church News Notes* 7.38 (September 29, 2006), 1.

93. Piper, *Let the Nations Be Glad*, 55.

94. Http://missionary-insights.blogspot.com/2006/10/calvinism.html, accessed July 24, 2009.

95. For some efforts, see James Montgomery Boice and Philip Graham Ryken *The Doctrines of Grace: Recovering the Evangelical Gospel* (Wheaton: Crossway Books, 2002), 111-112; Michael Horton, *Putting Amazing Back into Grace: Embracing the Heart of the Gospel* (Second Edition) (Grand Rapids: Baker, 2002), 242-243; J. I. Packer, *Evangelism & the Sovereignty of God* (Downers Grove: IVP, 1961), passim. For a work that addresses one of election's corollaries (limited or particular atonement) and its connection to evangelistic zeal, see Robert A. Peterson and Michael D. Williams, *Why I Am Not An Arminian* (Downers Grove: IVP, 2004), 192-215.

ing of God's Word" as an instrument in man's salvation. Synthesizing this data, the preaching of the Word is the instrument of the Holy Spirit to gather in God's elect. That preaching is done by human beings, both in established churches and on mission fields around the world. Reformed churches have always recognized that God's ordained kerygmatic instrument entails a human responsibility, both inside churches and outside. Thus, it has been vehemently denied that Ryland's words to Carey emerge from a Calvinistic perspective — indeed, the veracity of the legendary account is even doubtful.[96]

Switching to a more constructive mode, we ought to consider how the doctrine of election expressed in article 16 might be profitably employed in Reformed missiology. In *Transforming Mission*, the doctrine of election was only discussed by Bosch as one of the relevant characteristics of Puritan mission theology.[97] Presumably because of its parochial pedigree, it does not feature as part of the "emerging ecumenical missionary paradigm." Bavinck comes close to discussing election when he says that the single foundation of the missionary enterprise is "the gracious good pleasure of God in Christ Jesus."[98] However, election did not function as an important element in Bavinck's missiological thinking, and the absence of this subject in Paul Visser's dissertation bears this out.[99] Jongeneel noted that Calvinists have often emphasized the link between mission and predestination and that this finds its origins in Voetius. He writes, "Voetius based mission, in a voluntaristic way, not only on the Great Commission of Matthew 28 and the messianic promises of the Old Testament, but also, and even primarily, on God's decrees: mission should be undertaken to convert the elect."[100] For

---

96. "The popular story is repudiated by Ryland's son, John Ryland, Junior, who was Carey's close friend and a fellow member of the Northampton Association, being assistant minister at his father's church at the time when the incident was supposed to have happened. 'I never heard of it till I saw it in print, and cannot give credit to it at all.' Among the reasons he gives for rejecting its authenticity it is interesting to note that he says, 'No man prayed and preached about the *latter-day glory* more than my father.'" Iain Murray, *The Puritan Hope: Revival and the Interpretation of Prophecy* (London: Banner of Truth Trust, 1971), 280. Murray cites as source John Ryland, *Life of Andrew Fuller* (1816), 175. For further confirmation, see W. A. Jarrel, *Baptist Church Perpetuity: Or the Continuous Existence of Baptist Churches* (Dallas, 1894), 417. Jarrel quotes Ryland's son as insisting that his father was not even present at the Northampton meeting.

97. Bosch, *Transforming Mission*, 258.

98. Bavinck, *An Introduction to the Science of Missions*, 62.

99. Visser, *Heart for the Gospel*.

100. Jongeneel, *Philosophy, Science and Theology* (Part II), 58.

Voetius, the primary theological basis of mission was both the hidden and the revealed will of God: predestination *and* the promises of God combined with the specific mandate of Christ before his ascension.[101] While Jongeneel in his encyclopedia states that Calvinist missiologists have followed in Voetius' footsteps, the evidence, especially in recent times, is slim. We already noted Bavinck, but one also searches in vain for a discussion on election in the much more recent introduction by Roger Greenway.[102]

However, one missiologist who thoughtfully integrated the decree of predestination into his missiology was Lesslie Newbigin. Paul Weston noted that the doctrine of election constituted an important theme in Newbigin's thought.[103] Newbigin emphasized that this doctrine not only spoke in terms of the individual, but also in terms of God's choice of a people at certain times and places in order to execute his reign over the earth. He echoed a Barthian theme when he asserted that this purpose finds its fulfillment in the election of Jesus Christ himself. According to Newbigin, this corporate election is unto mission:

> Not that the world exists for the sake of the chosen people; precisely the opposite: the chosen people are chosen for the sake of the world. The mission of the Church is the clue to the meaning and end of world history. But the Church does not exist for itself, it exists for the sake of fulfilling God's purpose for the world. Therefore we must state, and this is the point I am trying to make here, that the duty and authority of the Church to preach the gospel to all nations rests upon the fact that God has chosen it for this purpose, to be the witness, the first fruit and the instrument of his saving deeds.[104]

It is readily apparent that election functioned differently here for Newbigin than it did for Voetius. For the former, election was seen more as a motive or imperative for mission than as a foundation. In the missiological scheme of things, Voetius understood election primarily as an individual concept and located it in the prolegomena to missiology, whereas

---

101. Jan Jongeneel, "The Missiology of Gisbertus Voetius: The First Comprehensive Protestant Theology of Missions," *Calvin Theological Journal* 26.1 (April 1991): 56.
102. Greenway, *Go and Make Disciples*.
103. *Lesslie Newbigin: Missionary Theology, A Reader*, comp. Paul Weston (Grand Rapids: Eerdmans, 2006), 48.
104. *Lesslie Newbigin: Missionary Theology*, 51.

Newbigin, while recognizing the individual aspect of election, emphasized the corporate and explicitly located it in the body of his missiological thinking.

While Newbigin's approach is helpful in its own way, the approach of Voetius is more in line with the understanding of election found in article 16. The Belgic Confession understands election to be election of the individual person, rather than election of a collective body and this becomes evident from the elaboration on the Confession found in the Canons of Dort. For instance, when election is defined in article 7 of chapter 1, we read that it involves "a definite number of specific persons." Related to this is the fact that the Canons and the Belgic Confession speak of a "divine election to eternal life," whereas Newbigin's predestination is with reference to the execution of God's reign on earth.[105]

As outlined by Voetius, because of its logical and historical underpinnings, the decree of election to eternal life belongs with other items of prolegomena in missiology. It is a component of the theological basis and motivation of mission. God has chosen a certain number of individual people to eternal life, and the means through which this decree is executed in history is the mission of the Christian church. Furthermore, earlier (2.4) we discussed the notion of a *missio Dei*. Disregarding the etymology of *missio*, this could be a place in which that notion may be profitably employed in Reformed missiology. In his good pleasure, God rescues and saves some from perdition. "His eternal and unchangeable counsel" has a missionary character, for it ultimately determines the end result of the church going and making disciples by preaching and witnessing to the good news of Jesus Christ in all nations through the power of the Holy Spirit.

Because of its mysterious aspects, the doctrine of divine election to eternal life will likely never prove to be a missiological cornucopia. Conversely, there is no need to regard it as poisonous to the missionary enterprise. The doctrine portrays God, who could justifiably leave all mankind under his wrath. Instead in his grace, he indefatigably pursues some and invincibly brings them to eternal life. In so doing, he uses means, including not only those who confess this doctrine, but even (most wonderfully) those who reject it.

---

105. The phrase "divine election to eternal life" comes from the Canons of Dort, Rejection of Errors 2, *BoP*, 540.

ARTICLE 18 — THE INCARNATION OF THE SON OF GOD

> We confess, therefore, that God has fulfilled the promise he had made to the fathers by the mouth of his holy prophets when, at the time appointed by him, he sent his one and only eternal Son into the world. He took the form of a servant and was born in the likeness of men. He truly assumed a real human nature with all its infirmities, without sin, for he was conceived in the womb of the blessed virgin Mary by the power of the Holy Spirit and not by the act of a man. He not only assumed human nature as to the body, but also a true human soul, in order that he might be a real man. For since the soul was lost as well as the body, it was necessary that he should assume both to save both.
>
> Contrary to the heresy of the Anabaptists, who deny that Christ assumed human flesh of his mother, we therefore confess that Christ partook of the flesh and blood of the children. He is a fruit of the loins of David; born of the seed of David according to the flesh; a fruit of the womb of the virgin Mary; born of woman; a branch of David; a shoot from the stump of Jesse; sprung from the tribe of Judah; descended from the Jews according to the flesh; of the seed of Abraham, since the Son was concerned with the descendants of Abraham. Therefore he had to be made like his brethren in every respect, yet without sin.
>
> In this way he is in truth our Immanuel, that is, God with us.[106]

The doctrine of the incarnation serves as the basis for virtually all contemporary missiology. This is true not only in general, but also with regard to particular issues such as contextualization and liberation theology. In chapter 2, we dealt with John 20:21 and the use of this passage. In this section, we will look more closely at the way the doctrine of the incarnation functions in contemporary missiology. However, first we will explore whether the Belgic Confession has a contribution to make to the integration of the incarnation in Reformed missiology.

From the sixteenth-century Roman Catholic perspective, article 18 of the Belgic Confession did not present any theological novelties. The Confession presented a simple Chalcedonian Christology, straight from the Scriptures. The only-begotten and eternal Son was sent into the world by God, according to the promises made in the Old Testament. In the incar-

---

106. BoP, 452-453.

nation, he took on a real human nature along with all of its weaknesses, yet without sin. He was conceived in the womb of Mary by the power of the Holy Spirit apart from the involvement of any human male. Further, his incarnation included not only the body, but also the soul. He was a true human being in every respect, yet without sin.

In chapter 3 and in this chapter, we have already noted that some of the sixteenth-century Anabaptists departed from orthodoxy on the question of Christ's incarnation. During the Reformation, the position and role of Mary was being re-evaluated by many ex-Roman Catholics. To explain the sinlessness of the Lord Jesus, the Roman church had resorted to the doctrine of the immaculate conception. That doctrine states that not only was the Lord Jesus free from original sin, but also his mother. The conception of Mary *in her mother* was immaculate. Melchior Hoffmann, an early Anabaptist, believed that Jesus was born sinless, but he could not agree that this was because of the sinlessness of his mother. Consequently, Hoffmann taught instead that Jesus was born from Mary, but that Mary did not contribute anything to Jesus' being or substance. She was simply the vessel in which the heavenly Jesus came to earth in the form of a man.

Menno Simons shared Hoffmann's concern for an explanation of Jesus' sinlessness that would not resort to an immaculate conception of Mary. Like Hoffmann, Simons argued that Christ's person (divine and human) had been implanted in the virgin Mary, and she had made no material contribution to his being whatsoever. She was simply the field in which the seed had been sown. To support his position, Simons appealed to Scripture. However, even contemporary Anabaptist scholarship recognizes that Simons' view was also influenced by the Greek philosopher Aristotle who held that the woman is entirely passive in the normal reproductive process. According to Aristotle, the father has the seed of life and implants that seed in the woman, who then nourishes it to the time of birth. If Scripture taught the same thing, Simons reasoned, then Mary could not have contributed anything to the person of Jesus. He found support in passages like Hebrews 11:11, and this led him to conclude that Jesus did not assume human flesh from his mother, but from heaven.

It was this celestial flesh view of the incarnation to which the Belgic Confession was responding in the last half of article 18. This view was identified as being heretical.[107] De Brès then went on to provide a chain

---

107. For more on de Brès and the "heavenly flesh" Christology, see W. L. Bre-

of biblical passages proving the orthodox stance, namely that Christ received his human flesh from Mary, his mother.

But what does this contribute to Reformed missiology? Commenting on the Confession's position that Christ possessed a true human body *and* soul, Recker states, "Here we have laid a basis for the modern missiological emphasis on our call to involvement in the world and the need for a ministry to the whole man — a reaching out to and a seeking of man in his concrete situation."[108] Unfortunately, Recker does not develop this any further, but it would seem that Recker understands the incarnation to provide a theological basis for the concept of a holistic or comprehensive understanding of mission.

Under the comprehensive approach to mission, evangelism and social responsibility ostensibly receive equal weight. However, in practice, the latter tends to eclipse the former. In the part of article 18 that Recker builds on, it says, "For since the soul was lost as well as the body, it was necessary that he should assume both to save both." The key word in this sentence is *save*. Save from what? From article 17, we discover that it is physical and spiritual death; from article 20, we learn that it is God's justice and damnation; and from article 21, we confess that it is God's wrath. The incarnation, therefore, has in view the redemption of mankind from sin and its effects. The incarnation did not occur with a view to solving issues of social justice in this age (indeed, did not the Lord Jesus say that poor would always be with us?), but to reconciling God and man through the blood of the cross.

While the incarnation does not provide a theological basis for the comprehensive approach, it does remind us of the comprehensive character of Christ's salvation. It is not merely our souls which are saved by Christ, but also our bodies. The message proclaimed by Reformed missionaries will give attention to this comprehensive salvation, eschewing all forms of Gnostic or quasi-Gnostic dualism. This is where the doctrine of the incarnation confessed in article 18 has much to offer Reformed missiology. When Christ adopted a human body (as well as a human soul), he echoed God's recognition of the goodness of creation in Genesis 1. Material substances, while groaning under the curse of sin, are not inherently evil. Concomitantly, the human body is not in-

---

denhof, "De Brès vs. Simons: A Sixteenth Century Debate that Still Matters," *Clarion* 57.24 (Year-End Issue): 638-641.

108. Recker, "An Analysis," 163-164.

herently evil. This becomes important for the development of Reformed elenctics. The elevation of the spiritual over the physical is a common feature in many religions. The incarnation confronts this essentially Gnostic perspective and challenges it with the gospel. According to God's Word, matter is not evil.

Bosch noted that "Protestant churches, by and large, have an undeveloped theology of the incarnation. The churches of the East, Roman Catholics, and Anglicans have always taken the incarnation far more seriously."[109] This is an intriguing statement. While one can readily agree that many Protestants have been weak on the doctrine of the incarnation, the idea that the Eastern Orthodox, Roman Catholics, and Anglicans have given it more attention is disputable. Some have argued that an unbalanced emphasis on Christ's divinity among these groups is part of what accounts for the worship of Mary.[110] Bosch goes on to assert that it is liberation theology which has "viewed the Christian mission in terms of the incarnate Christ, the human Jesus of Nazareth who wearily trod the dusty roads of Palestine where he took compassion on those who were marginalized."[111] However, whereas the comprehensive approach, in principle, weighs evangelism and social justice equally, liberation theology usually, in principle, either identifies evangelism with social justice or explicitly allows social justice to eclipse evangelism. Neither approach is compatible with the doctrine of the incarnation elucidated in the Belgic Confession.

Along similar liberation theology lines, we find the call of Emefie Ikenga-Metuh for "a pursuit with greater vigor of the process of incarnating the Gospel in African culture."[112] According to Ikenga-Metuh, in former times, African culture was often regarded as the product of evil spiritual forces or perhaps neutral forces. However, in more recent times, it is being increasingly recognized that "God has always been incarnate in human cultures."[113] To defend that assertion, he appealed to Hebrews 1:1-2. He acknowledged that divine revelation climaxed in Jesus Christ, and

---

109. Bosch, *Transforming Mission*, 512.

110. Charles D. Drew, *The Ancient Love Song: Finding Christ in the Old Testament* (Phillipsburg: P&R, 1996, 2000), 91.

111. Bosch, *Transforming Mission*, 512-513.

112. Thomas, *Classic Texts*, 182.

113. Thomas, *Classic Texts*, 182. Thomas is excerpting from Ikenga-Metuh's article, "Contextualization: A Missiological Imperative for the Church in Africa in the Third Millennium," in *Mission Studies* 6.2 (1989): 5,7, 11-12.

with his incarnation, he "illuminated, judged, and elevated" Judeo-Hellenic culture. Similarly, "African incarnation theology seeks to incarnate the word of God into African culture."[114] When this incarnation is complete, the gospel would change African culture at every level. As to what is meant by "incarnation" in this context, Ikenga-Metuh quotes the Report of the African Bishops to the 1974 Synod on Evangelization: incarnation is "the movement by which what is considered essential in the message of Christ penetrates and takes flesh in a culture."[115]

There are several problems with this approach to integrating the doctrine of the incarnation in missiology. For instance, the statement, "God has always been incarnate in human cultures" seems to equivocate on the meaning of "incarnation." Hebrews 1:1-2 reads: "God, who at various times and in various ways spoke in time past to the fathers by the prophets, has in these last days spoken to us by his Son." These words were originally addressed to Jewish Christians and they refer to the patriarchs of the Old Testament, not the patriarchs of any African cultures. Finally, the notion of incarnating the Word of God into African cultures is so imprecise here as to be virtually useless. Even the Bishops' definition of incarnation suffers from imprecision. What exactly does it mean for the message of Christ to "take flesh in a culture"? Is "incarnation" really the best model for contextualization?

Nevertheless, Ikenga-Metuh does point us to some important questions that need due consideration in Reformed missiology. Article 18 of the Confession summarizes biblical teaching and tells us that Christ assumed a true human body and true human soul. Consequently, as we have seen, we confess that matter (including the human body) is not inherently evil. In the second half of the article, the Confession responds to the Anabaptist celestial flesh Christology with a string of twelve biblical references. From those references, it is clear that Christ assumed a true human body and soul in the context of a true human culture. This raises the question of whether or not human cultures are inherently evil. In the words of Ikenga-Metuh, did Christ's incarnation "illuminate, judge and elevate" a particular human culture, and if so, what are the implications for all human cultures? While we will not explore these questions here, these are the sorts of inquiries that could be profitably pursued in a full missiological commentary on the Belgic Confession.

---

114. Thomas, *Classic Texts*, 183.
115. Thomas, *Classic Texts*, 183.

It would not be unfair to say that the doctrine of the incarnation is one of the most misused and abused Christian doctrines in contemporary missiology. However, we must not allow its misuse or abuse to prevent us from integrating it into a Reformed missiology. The incarnation is critically important for us. Not only do we lack a gospel message apart from it (we need a Saviour who was true man), it also sharpens our perspectives on the comprehensive nature of the salvation worked by Christ, the nature of matter (including the human body), and the nature of human culture.

5.2 MISSIOLOGICAL WEAKNESSES

By now it will be readily evident that the Belgic Confession is indeed missiologically relevant. It brings several strengths to the development of Reformed missiology. However, in the interests of a balanced appraisal, we also need to give some attention to some potential areas of weakness. In the following sections, we will explore those areas.

5.2.1 A EUROPEAN CONFESSION OVER 400 YEARS OLD

Jaroslav Pelikan notes how transplanting creeds and confessions to other cultures is often a very complicated assignment in terms of theology and strategy.[116] Involved in the equation are historical factors, as well as cultural. A mere translation does not automatically make a creed or confession at home in a new setting.[117] These factors also have to be weighed as we consider the Belgic Confession.

In chapter 4 (4.2.1), we briefly discussed Hesselgrave's work on cultural differences and cognitive processes. Appropriating the work of F. H. Smith, Hesselgrave enumerated three cognitive approaches to reality: 1) the conceptual, 2) the concrete relational, and 3) the intuitive or psychical.[118] The conceptual approach emphasizes definition, analysis, categorization, and the use of systematic tools, including logic. As we noted in chapter 4, the Belgic Confession embodies this conceptual approach, but just as Western European cultures are not exclusively or consistently conceptual, so too the Confession also uses elements belonging to the concrete relational approach. In this approach to reality, "life and

---

116. Jaroslav Pelikan, *Credo: Historical and Theological Guide to Creeds and Confessions of Faith in the Christian Tradition* (New Haven: Yale UP, 2003), 317-318.
117. Pelikan, *Credo*, 325.
118. Hesselgrave, *Communicating Christ Cross-Culturally*, 302.

reality are seen pictorially in terms of the active emotional relationships present in a concrete situation." This approach emphasizes symbols, stories, events, objects, and often communicates through gesture, sign language, music, ritual, drama, and the like.[119] It tends to be found, not only among tribal peoples, but also among the Chinese. Finally, the intuitive or psychical approach emphasizes the mystical in contrast to the intellectual. Members of intuitional cultures stress the universal, prefer the negative, minimize individuality and particulars, emphasize the unity of all things, take an introspective stance, and often adopt a tolerant and conciliatory attitude.[120]

As noted previously, the Belgic Confession can be understood as a contextualization of the gospel in a particular Western European culture that privileges conceptual thinking. As such, it would also have abiding usefulness in other cultures, European or not, that also privilege this cognitive approach to reality. It may also work as a confession in cultures that privilege the concrete relational. As an aside, it should be made clear at this point that what we are envisioning here is a pedagogical missionary use of the Confession.

At first glance, such a pedagogical missionary use would appear to have limited or even non-existent application to intuitional contexts. In these contexts, Hesselgrave warns against overintellectualizing and oversimplifying, particularly by presenting the Christian faith as "the logical and inescapable conclusion of several simple premises."[121] Such an approach undermines the credibility of the Christian faith to intuitional peoples. The Belgic Confession takes this approach in a number of places — article 10 presents a logical argument to prove the eternal deity of Christ; article 27 employs a truncated syllogism to prove that the church has existed from the beginning of the world and will be to the end. If Hesselgrave is correct, the Confession's presentation of the Christian faith may have limited value in cultures that privilege the intuitional cognitive approach to reality.

On the other hand, Hesselgrave also insists that, in these intuitional contexts, "the missionary must communicate a sense of the mystery of

---

119. Hesselgrave, *Communicating Christ Cross-Culturally*, 325.
120. Hesselgrave, *Communicating Christ Cross-Culturally*, 314. Hesselgrave cites Philip P. Wiener, ed., *Ways of Thinking of Eastern Peoples* (Honolulu: East-West Center, 1964), passim.
121. Hesselgrave, *Communicating Christ Cross-Culturally*, 318.

knowing God and the awe of approaching him."[122] The concept of mystery is found in the Belgic Confession and could be emphasized in intuitional cultures. For instance, in article 13, we confess with regard to God's providence,

> And as to his actions surpassing human understanding, we will not curiously inquire further than our capacity allows us. But with the greatest humility and reverence we adore the just judgments of God, which are hidden from us, and we content ourselves that we are pupils of Christ, who have only to learn those things which he teaches us in his Word, without transgressing these limits.[123]

Article 22 speaks about "true knowledge of this great mystery" of salvation through Christ and in article 35, we confess that we do not understand the manner in which Christ works in us through the sacraments, "just as we do not comprehend the hidden activity of the Spirit of God."[124] Hence, it would not be accurate to say that the Confession has absolutely no potential for pedagogical missionary application in intuitional contexts. It may be limited and perhaps there are better confessions available (or, at least, there should be), but one cannot entirely exclude it.

Besides being a European confession, we also have to recognize that it is over four hundred years old. Four hundred years of church history have raised a variety of missional issues not directly — or even indirectly — addressed by the Confession. Here we are particularly thinking of the way in which the Confession might guide reflection on the church's missionary task.

When the Confession was written, the concept of short-term missions (STMs) was a distant future reality. The rise of STMs begins in the southern United States in the 1950s and 60s. Agencies such as Operation Mobilization and schools such as Wheaton College were looking for ministry opportunities for young people and others. At the time, because of easy accessibility, the focus was on First Nations in the American Southwest and Mexico. Through the 1950s and '60s, small groups of American Christians spent short periods of time doing evangelistic work either on reservations or south of the border.

Since the 1960s, the STM movement has grown exponentially. This can be accounted for in four ways. First of all, the development of vi-

---

122. Hesselgrave, *Communicating Christ Cross-Culturally*, 318.
123. BoP, 450.
124. Hesselgrave, *Communicating Christ Cross-Culturally*, 469.

able commercial air transport after the Second World War made the world dramatically more accessible to North Americans. The growth of the North American economy is another factor. North Americans have relatively large amounts of disposable income compared to people in many other areas of the world. The third factor is globalization. Because of television, the Internet, and advanced telecommunications, the world has shrunk. Our perception of the world as North Americans is entirely different today. Many North Americans are intrigued by other cultures, rather than intimidated. Finally, today churches and their members want to be more directly involved with missions. These factors combined (and possibly others) have led to the rise of the STM movement in the last four decades. One can easily understand why such a trend would have been unimaginable in the sixteenth century and why the Belgic Confession has little, if anything, to offer as we reflect on this phenomenon.

An associated issue is the relationship between word and deed in Christian mission. As we have seen, in the time of the Confession, mission was conceived of in purely evangelistic and kerygmatic terms. The pressures of the comprehensive or holistic approach and the liberation theology movement have called this conception into question in the last two centuries. Owing to its place in history, one cannot expect the Belgic Confession to offer much with regard to meaningful missiological reflection on the integration of word and deed ministry.

Finally, the "Age of Discovery" was just over a half-century old when the Belgic Confession was written. In the centuries to follow, the world would become not only a less mysterious place, but also a place of deeper connections and unity. Guido de Brès could never have envisioned the phenomenon of globalization and the challenges this presents to the Christian faith and to the missionary endeavour. For instance, what does the Confession say to the notion of partnerships between older and younger churches from radically different cultures? Aside from generalities about the catholicity of the church (article 27), we cannot expect the Confession to answer this kind of question in a meaningful way. There can be little question that on this and other issues, the age of the Confession may be considered a liability.

5.2.2 Limited Perspective on World Religions

Above (5.1.2) we noted that the Confession speaks out "against unbelief, wrong belief and idolatry." It gives the church an elenctic voice, and this is a strength. That point notwithstanding, we recognize that the Confession only gives a limited perspective on world religions.

Only two world religions are directly mentioned in the Belgic Confession. In article 9, Jews and Muslims are identified as being in error on the doctrine of the Trinity — in fact, they are deniers of the doctrine. This reference indicates that de Brès and the Reformed churches were aware of both Judaism and Islam, though it is likely they were less familiar with the latter. Because of the geopolitical situation, it is improbable that de Brès ever encountered any Muslims during his lifetime. With the Ottoman Empire threatening central Europe, we could expect that there was some awareness of Islam. Throughout Western Europe, small communities of Jews existed, and so it may have been possible for de Brès and the Reformed churches to have some familiarity with sixteenth-century Judaism.[125] Judging from some of the intricate discussions in *La racine*, de Brès appears to have been proficient in Hebrew, but the provenance of his Hebrew skills is not clear.

The fact that the Confession says so little about Judaism and Islam would indicate that de Brès did not regard these religions as threats to the Reformed churches of the Lowlands. Today, in many parts of the world, the situation is different. While Judaism historically experiences most of its growth from within, Islam is one of the most aggressively missionary non-Christian religions. While the doctrines of Scripture found in the Confession indirectly address Islam, it might be beneficial in many mission fields to have a confession which directly addresses the Islamic challenge, in much the same way as the Belgic directly addresses the Romanist and Anabaptist challenges. Here again, we are referring to a pedagogical missionary use of the Confession; however, the use of the Confession as a guide to missiological reflection is not outside our purview.

Obviously, Judaism and Islam are not the only world religions challenging the Christian faith today. Here again, the Belgic Confession indirectly addresses many, if not all, of these with its elenctic stance. But could it not be helpful for Chinese believers to have a confession that explicitly addresses the challenges of Buddhism, Confucianism, or Taoism? Could it not be profitable for Indian Christians to develop a

---

125. Steven Ozment, *The Bürgermeister's Daughter: Scandal in a Sixteenth-Century German Town* (New York: HarperPerennial, 1996), 76-77. Ozment relates the story of Hall's Jews, but notes that it is paradigmatic for Europe.

confession that overtly speaks to the challenges of Hinduism, Sikhism, or Jainism?

The Belgic Confession only provides a limited perspective on world religions and, in certain contexts, this can be a weakness. One cannot realistically expect a sixteenth-century Western European confession to directly address all the challenges faced by Christian believers in a variety of global contexts. Recognizing this does not denigrate the Confession in any way, as if there is something inherently wrong with it. Rather, we are simply recognizing that it emerges from an age very different from our own. Some of the challenges faced by that age are the same today (i.e. Romanism, Anabaptism) and others are quite different.

5.2.3 The Holy Spirit

The Holy Spirit is mentioned twenty-one times in the Belgic Confession. Article 11 deals with him directly as the third Person of the Trinity and other articles discuss his various works. However, there is precious little said about his role in mission and very little guidance given with respect to errors regarding the Holy Spirit.

What little there is with regard to mission can be gleaned from article 22 on justification through faith in Christ. There it is confessed that "the Holy Spirit kindles in our hearts a true faith."[126] When missionary preaching is met with faith, we recognize that the Holy Spirit is the one who has worked this faith. We recognize, therefore, our utter dependence on the Holy Spirit.

That is an important truth, but much more could be said. Roger Greenway pointed to five ways in which the Holy Spirit works a missionary zeal in believers. First, he stirs up an interest in mission in the hearts of Christian. Next, he gives Christians a heart-felt compassion for the lost. Third, he builds faith in the promise of God that the preaching of the evangel will bear fruit of one sort or another. Fourth, he gives believers the motivation to obey the Great Commission. Finally, he breaks down prejudices and transforms Christians so that they love those who are different and welcome them into the kingdom of Christ.[127]

Greenway also described the work of the Holy Spirit in mission. First of all, he pointed out that the Spirit creates a bond of spiritual fellowship between missionaries and believers on mission fields and with missionary supporters. Second, the Holy Spirit is the one who opens and closes

---

126. BoP, 456.
127. Greenway, *Go and Make Disciples*, 54-55.

doors for the gospel advance. Next, he prepares unbelievers "to desire what Christ offers, to inquire of the Christian faith, and to convict them of their sin and their need for salvation." This particular element is virtually the same as what we find in article 22 of the Confession. Finally, the Spirit protects and nurtures the results of missionary work.[128] From this, already it is evident that more can be said about the person and work of the Holy Spirit in regards to mission. Here we can think back to McGavran's insistence (5.0) that a missionary confession will speak about the function of the Spirit in mission. The Confession does not do this. It is definitely not a missionary confession on this point and, more to our purposes, it is also of limited missiological relevance.

In today's global context, Reformed believers also experience the challenge of the rise of the Pentecostal/Charismatic movement. The Belgic Confession addresses some of the distinctives of this movement indirectly with its insistence on Scripture alone as the source of divine revelation. Revelatory cessationism is implied. Yet, there are other distinctives which remain unanswered. During the sixteenth century, there were spiritualists who anticipated the modern Pentecostal/Charismatic movement. For some reason, these do not seem to find a place in the Belgic Confession. Perhaps it was because they were widely recognized as being on the fringes of anything remotely Christian, or perhaps because they were such a small minority. Whatever the reason may be, today the situation is quite different. The preachers of the so-called prosperity gospel are now recognized as being mainstream in global Christianity. Even the most extreme Pentecostal/Charismatic figures are often accepted as legitimate and worthy of a hearing. Meanwhile, the Pentecostal/Charismatic movement is reportedly expanding exponentially in size every year.

Most of this growth is taking place in the southern hemisphere. Reformed believers in Europe and North America will encounter the challenges of this movement as well, but not as dramatically as those in the global south. For those believers in young Reformed churches faced with this serious challenge, the Belgic Confession offers little pedagogical guidance. Again, this is not something one could expect from a sixteenth-century European Reformed confession. It is no surprise that a group of Reformed leaders from seven countries collaborated in 2004 on what they called the Candlestand Statement.[129] This statement was drafted to

---

128. Greenway, *Go and Make Disciples*, 56–57.
129. This can be found online at www.candlestand.nl in English and Dutch. It

address the challenges faced by Reformed churches from the Pentecostal/ Charismatic movement. It covers revelation and the Bible, God the Holy Spirit (his person, work, experience of, and gifts), and the Christian life. While it only claims to be a working document (*werkdokument*), the fact that it was drafted may indicate a weakness in the Three Forms of Unity (including the Belgic Confession) in this area.

5.2.4 Role of the Civil Government

Earlier (1.1.2) we noted that many in the sixteenth century had an understanding of the interplay between religion and politics that is no longer in vogue today. Article 36 of the Confession embodies this particular understanding and leads us to consider whether this perspective may be regarded as a weakness. According to the Belgic Confession, what is the role of the civil government with respect to the ministry of the church, including its mission to the world? Is this perspective a liability or an asset?

Most modern editions of the Confession have a footnote in article 36. The footnote is attached to this sentence and is referenced with the asterisk:

> Their task of restraining and sustaining is not limited to the public order but includes the protection of the church and its ministry in order that * the kingdom of Christ may come, the Word of the gospel may be preached everywhere, and God may be honoured and served by everyone, as he requires in his Word.[130]

The footnote in the Canadian Reformed edition reads: "The following words were deleted here by the General Synod 1905 of the Reformed Churches in the Netherlands (Gereformeerde Kerken in Nederland): all idolatry and false worship may be removed and prevented, the kingdom of antichrist may be destroyed."[131] The Christian Reformed Church took a different approach. The Synod of 1958 rewrote this section of the Confession to read as follows:

> And being called in this manner to contribute to the advancement of a society that is pleasing to God, the civil rulers have the task, subject to God's law, of removing every obstacle to the preaching of the gospel and to every aspect of divine worship. They should do this while completely refraining from every ten-

---

can also be found in Ukrainian at this website: http://www.reformed.org.ua/index.php?wl=1&id_mat=40

130. BoP, 470.
131. BoP, 471.

dency toward exercising absolute authority and while functioning in the sphere entrusted to them, with the means belonging to them. They should do it in order that the Word of God may have free course; the kingdom of Jesus Christ may make progress, and every anti-Christian power may be resisted.[132]

From this it is evident that article 36 has received much scrutiny from Reformed churches in the last century.[133]

It has also received its fair share of misunderstanding. For instance, John Coakley argued that, while adherents of the Belgic Confession believed that the gospel was to be spread in the world, they nonetheless held to a peculiar view (from a contemporary perspective) of how that mission was to be executed: "As for the activist work of establishing places for the gospel to be heard, what we would now call 'church extension,' the Belgic Confession assigned this not to the church per se, but rather to the civil government. It is the magistrates, not the ministers, elders, deacons, or assemblies of the church, who are charged 'to promote the kingdom of Jesus Christ and to take care that the word of the gospel be preached everywhere, that God may be honored and worshipped by everyone, as he commands in his word.'"[134] From Coakley's perspective, article 36 is a liability for the missiological relevance of the Confession since it takes mission out of the hands of the church.

It is possible to read the Confession in this way, particularly in its original French:

> Et non seulement leur office est de reprimer et veiller sur la politique, ains aussi sur les chose ecclesiastique, pour oster et ruiner

---

132. *Ecumenical Creeds and Confessions*, Christian Reformed Church (Grand Rapids: CRC Publications, 1988), 117.

133. For the text history of this article in the Netherlands, see J. G. Feenstra *Onze Geloofsbelijdenis* (Tweede druk) (Kampen: J. H. Kok N.V., 1947), 468-471. For the history in the CRC (up until the 1940s), see D. H. Kromminga, *Article XXXVI of the Belgic Confession and the Christian Reformed Church* (Grand Rapids: Baker, 1943). For reflection on the later history of this article in the CRC (up until 1979), see J. Faber, "The Civil Government in Article 36 B.C.," *Clarion* 28.24 (December 1, 1979): 510-512. Faber interacts with Report 33 to CRC Synod 1979 and its pitting the 1561 text of the Confession versus the 1566/1619 texts of article 36.

134. John Coakley, "The Reformed Church in America as a National Church," in *Church, Identity and Change: Theology and Denominational Structures in Unsettled Times*, ed. David A. Roozen and James Nieman (Grand Rapids: Eerdmans, 2005), 403.

toute Idolatrie et faux service de Dieu, pour destruire le royaume de l'Antichrist, et advancer le royaume de Iesus Christ, fair prescher la parole de l'Evangile par tout, afin que Dieu soit honnoré et servi d'un chacun, comme il le requiert par sa parole.[135]

The important words here are *'pour oster et ruiner'* and *'pour destruire.'* It is true that *'pour'* can sometimes indicate a direct result, as if de Brès envisioned that it would be the civil magistrate who would himself do these things. However, *'pour'* plus the infinitive indicates a calculated result, meaning that it was the intent of de Brès that the magistrate would protect the ministry of the Word with the consequence that, because of that protection, the church would see to it that idolatry and false worship were destroyed, the gospel would be preached, the kingdom of antichrist destroyed and the kingdom of Christ advanced. Thus, Coakley was incorrect in alleging that the Confession placed mission in the hands of the magistrate rather than the church. It is especially inconceivable that de Brès would have imagined that the state would be responsible for the preaching of the gospel to everyone. That is the most important clue to tip us off to a different reading of this article.

David Bosch noted that in the seventeenth century, the Reformed churches in the Netherlands were involved in mission within the context of Dutch colonialism. While he curiously calls this a "superficial missionary effort," he adds, "It does credit to many Dutch theologians and missionaries, however, that as a matter of principle, they did not regard mission as a responsibility of the state."[136] Since this church adhered to the Belgic Confession, we can conclude that the Belgic Confession was not understood to be saying that mission was the responsibility of the civil magistrate in its first century of use in the Reformed churches.

In his commentary, J. Van Bruggen argued that the deletion of the controversial words from article 36 was regrettable and based on a mis-

---

135. "And not only is their duty to rein in and watch over political matters, but also in ecclesiastical things, to remove and ruin all idolatry and false worship of God, to destroy the kingdom of the Antichrist, and to advance the kingdom of Jesus Christ, to preach the word of the Gospel to everyone, to the end that God may be honored and served by each one, as he requires it in his Word." Translation mine. The original French quoted above comes from: Guido de Brès, *Confession de foy, faicte d'un commun accord par les fideles qui conversent és pays bas* (Rouen: Abel Clemence, 1561), 32. Other editions published in 1561/62 have the same wording.

136. Bosch, *Witness to the World*, 127.

reading of the Confession. A careful reading, he maintained, proved that the Confession's original position conformed to the teaching of Scripture. Article 36 did not mean that the government was responsible to organize the church or perform its ministry, but simply that it was to protect the church, guard it from hindrances, and provide it with the room it needs to conduct its ministry. With regard to the removal and prevention of idolatry, Van Bruggen argued that in "the domain of public life, the practice of idolatry and false religion ought to be prevented and forbidden."[137]

Clarence Bouwman has argued in a similar manner: "De Brès' point with the removed words was that when the government gives the church space to preach the gospel, idolatry and false worship in fact are being removed from the community."[138] Seen from this perspective, there is no weakness at this point in the Belgic Confession, either in its redacted or original forms. The church has its responsibility to preach the gospel, and this is a missionary responsibility. The state has a responsibility to protect the church so that the church can faithfully and effectively carry out its gospel ministry. From passages like Psalm 2 and 1 Timothy 2:1-4, we can recognize this as a biblical position.

Much more could be said about the relationship of article 36 to the mission of the church, but that would be best left for a missiological commentary. It can be stated with confidence that the position taken is not a weakness, but should be regarded as a strength. The Confession equips Reformed missiologists with a timeless biblical position on the relationship between church and state. While this relationship is not currently in place, it is something for which to strive.

5.3 Conclusion & Evaluation

The Belgic Confession, coming from another era, brings a number of neglected emphases to our contemporary missiological reflection. A cross-oriented and elenctic approach are both desperately needed in our day. Its catholicity reminds us of the bigger picture. The value of the redemptive-historical perspective is being increasingly recognized, and incorporating this perspective as found in the Belgic Confession will prove to be a boon for Reformed missiology. We have also seen that a missiological commentary on the Confession is not only possible, but also desirable.

---

137. Van Bruggen, *The Church Says Amen*, 218-219.
138. Bouwman, *The Overflowing Riches*, 396.

While the above are all strengths, there are also weaknesses. The most acute of these is the age and cultural origins of the Confession. These limit its effectiveness in speaking to newer issues and in certain cultures. Theological development has not stopped since the Reformation, and much more attention is given today to the Holy Spirit. While he is mentioned in the Confession, not much can be gleaned for missiological reflection. This particular weakness might be mitigated by the Heidelberg Catechism and the Canons of Dort (among those holding to the Three Forms of Unity). This is something that would require further research. Finally, we reflected on a potential weakness in the area of civil government, and it turned out that this should actually be placed on the positive side of the ledger.

How do we weigh these strengths and weaknesses? The overall missiological strength of the Confession is that it is speaking where others are not. The overall weakness is that it fails to speak in some areas of contemporary mission discussion. We have plenty of voices speaking on the role of the Holy Spirit. We have much discussion about other global missiological issues. Most of the voices in those discussions are not Reformed, and so there is a need for a Reformed contribution in those areas. But the Confession speaks to areas that are not being discussed as avidly, areas that need more intense discussion, not only by Reformed missiologists, but also others. For this reason, we can conclude that its strengths do indeed outweigh its weaknesses.

CHAPTER SIX

SEVENTEENTH-CENTURY USES

6.0 INTRODUCTION

The seventeenth century provides us with an opportunity to test the missiological significance of the Belgic Confession. In 1609, Reformed churches in the Netherlands began to undertake overseas mission work in the East Indies (Indonesia). This work would soon extend to Formosa (Taiwan), Ceylon (Sri Lanka), Brazil, and New Netherland (mostly New York state in the USA). Additionally, this was a period when some Reformed theologians began to reflect in a systematic fashion on the missionary task of the church. Consequently, it is worth investigating whether or not the missionary relevance of the Belgic Confession was recognized in this era. Did Reformed believers turn to the Confession for guidance in scholarly reflection on the missionary task and in the practical execution of that task? This chapter explores that question by examining the missiology of Gisbertus Voetius and the missionary work done in New Netherland, especially by Johannes Megapolensis.

6.1 THE FIRST REFORMED MISSIOLOGIST: GISBERTUS VOETIUS

Gisbertus Voetius (1589-1676) was a prominent theologian of the so-called *Nadere Reformatie*, or Further Reformation. He was born March 3, 1589 in Heusden (North Brabant) to a Reformed family.[1] He was

---

1. The biographical information comes from *The Oxford Dictionary of the Christian Church* (Third Edition), ed. F. L. Cross and E. A. Livingstone (Oxford: Oxford UP, 1997), s.v. 'Voetius, Gisbertus,' 1706; Joel R. Beeke, "Gisbertus Voetius: Toward a Reformed Marriage of Knowledge and Piety," in *Protestant Scholasticism: Essays in Reassessment*, ed. Carl R. Trueman and R. Scott Clark (Carlisle: Paternoster Press, 1999), 225-232; Jan Jongeneel, "The Missiology of Gisbertus Voetius: The First Comprehensive Protestant Theology of Missions," *Calvin Theological Journal* 26.1 (April 1991): 47-48.

GISBERTUS VOETIUS
(1589-1676)

trained as a minister at the University of Leiden and there he studied under Franciscus Gomarus and Jacobus Arminius — the former being Voetius' greatest theological influence. While still a student, he lectured in logic and developed a reputation as a defender of Reformed orthodoxy. With the temporary triumph of the Remonstrant party in 1610, the university in Leiden became antagonistic towards Gomarus and his disciples, forcing Voetius to temporarily abandon his aspirations for an academic career. Instead, he accepted a call to pastor a church in Vlijmen in his home province of North Brabant. There he ministered from 1610 to 1617. In 1617, he took a call to his home town of Heusden and served as a pastor there until 1634.

Voetius was a mere 29 years old when he was delegated to the Synod of Dort 1618-1619. While at the Synod, his defence of the supralapsarian Johannes Maccovius was his most noteworthy activity. He also developed close friendships with a number of the English delegates.[2] However, for our purposes it is important to note that the subject of mission also caught his attention as a delegate at Dort.

The Walcheren classis and Amsterdam consistory had sent missionaries to the East Indies. In 1618, these missionaries had sent back a request for advice on what to do about the baptism of native children brought into Christian families. The scenario often involved the children born from adulterous relationships between Dutch nationals and native women. The Amsterdam consistory forwarded this matter to the Synod, asking for its advice on how to proceed. Voetius participated in the discussions, and he also wrote the text of the advice. Briefly, these children were only to be baptized after they had been catechized and made public profession of their faith.[3]

Having served the church at Heusden for seventeen years, Voetius was appointed in 1634 to teach Semitic languages (Hebrew, Arabic, and Syriac) and theology at the new Academy of Utrecht. He also returned to his former subject matter, giving lectures on logic and metaphysics.

---

2. Beeke, "Gisbertus Voetius," 229-230.
3. Jongeneel, "The Missiology of Gisbertus Voetius," 48.

Voetius lectured and wrote extensively, especially in the area of practical theology. His life's work was characterized by the Puritan impulse to wed serious piety with precise scholarship. He died on November 1, 1676, leaving behind disciples in every university in the Netherlands.

6.1.1 Brief Overview of Voetius' Missiology

As a direct consequence of his adoption of scholastic structures, the missiology of Voetius is relatively easy to break down into its component parts. His missiological thinking is mostly found in his *Politica Ecclesiastica* and *Selectae Disputationes*. In what follows here, we will mostly follow the outline of Voetius' missiology provided by Jongeneel.[4]

Foundation for Mission

For Voetius, mission work is grounded in God himself, particularly in the hidden and revealed will of God. The hidden will of God has to do with God's decree of election. The revealed will of God is expressed both in his promises and in the mandate for mission found in passages like Matthew 28:19 — a passage which Voetius regarded as having abiding application to the church of Jesus Christ in all ages.

Who are the Senders?

The church has been sent out into the world by Jesus Christ. Consequently, the true church has an obligation to send out missionaries. Voetius protested against papal missions because he denied the claims of the pope to be Christ's vicar on earth. He also registered his opposition to the idea of individual believers sending themselves out to do missionary work. While granting a supporting role to the civil magistrate, Voetius rejected the idea that it could be a sending agency. Finally, he also dealt with the question of whether commercial entities may send missionaries; here too, his answer was negative. Only the church may send missionaries.

To Whom and Where are They Sent?

As far as the object of Christian mission went, Voetius was very broad. He included unbelievers (*infideles*), heretics (*haeretici*), and schismatics (*schismatici*). In earlier writings, he was less nuanced and included all of the following as being the objects of mission: pagans, Jews, Muslims, Libertines, Socinians, and Roman Catholics. Voetius also came to distinguish between those living within and those outside the so-called Chris-

---

4. Jongeneel, "The Missiology of Gisbertus Voetius," 56-75.

tian world (*corpus Christianum*). In brief, Voetius saw the objects of mission as being all unbelievers everywhere.

The Variety of Missions

Voetius wrote of seven types of missions. This again reveals a broadness in his thought that seems more to come from our era than his:

- the conversion of unbelievers and the planting of churches
- the regathering of churches scattered because of either persecution or internal collapse
- the reformation of one or more of the following aspects of church life: doctrine, life, or discipline
- the reunification of divided or separated churches
- the financial support of oppressed, persecuted, plundered, scattered or impoverished churches
- persuasion of princes and magistrates to provide religious liberty and remove obstacles which hinder outreach and growth
- the writing of petitions, admonitions and apologies to princes and magistrates to persuade them regarding the last point[5]

We may observe that Voetius does not provide much explicit biblical basis for these types of missions. Further, the first type is that which receives the greatest emphasis in his missiology.

Who are Sent?

Generally speaking, Voetius argued that missionary candidates should possess "outstanding social skills, be eloquent in speech, prudent and discreet, cheerful and diligent."[6] They should also be well-grounded in the Christian faith and able to divide the Word rightly. When working among "the more cultured peoples," additional training in philosophy, science, and history is also necessary. When working with any people, skills in medicine will also open doors for the gospel. Missionaries need to be men who will carefully study the culture wherever they are sent. Because of these wide-ranging skills, Voetius advocated that missionaries not only receive the standard theological education of ministers, but also additional training. He also recognized the need for other, non-ordained

---

5. Jongeneel, "The Missiology of Gisbertus Voetius," 63-64.
6. Jongeneel, "The Missiology of Gisbertus Voetius," 68.

personnel to be sent to the mission fields as catechists, visitors of the sick, teachers, and doctors, but did not state whether or not such personnel should properly be regarded as missionaries.

The Means of Mission

As one might expect, Voetius saw the Scriptures as the foremost means by which unbelievers come to a saving knowledge of Jesus Christ. But he also itemized a number of other means by which the gospel may advance and in which the Scriptures would be proclaimed:

- civil governments who rule over unbelieving peoples and who provide protection for missionaries
- trading companies which often have their own preachers
- military expeditions to unbelieving nations, since they are typically accompanied by chaplains
- ambassadors who enjoy personal freedom of religion because of their diplomatic status
- travellers abroad
- banning and imprisonment, such as happened with the Apostle John on Patmos[7]

It is not clear whether this part of Voetius' missiological thinking is descriptive or prescriptive. Finally, it is also worth noting that he advocated for the establishment of schools on mission fields. At these schools, education would be provided for native inhabitants, albeit in the Dutch language. Such institutions might be instrumental in introducing young people to the gospel.

Summary

Voetius was remarkably thorough in all of his theological reflections, and what he writes about mission is no different. For his time, he gave careful thought to many different aspects of the church's task. Not all of his reflections were directly or obviously based on Scripture, but many of them were. To sum up Voetius' missiology, Jongeneel writes, "It is best not to consider Voetius's theology of mission as christocentric or basileiocentric (focusing on the kingdom), but rather as theocentric and ecclesiocentric missiology in context. Above all, Voetius's missiology must be

---

7. Jongeneel, "The Missiology of Gisbertus Voetius," 71.

characterized as a theocentric theology of mission. More precisely it is a predestinarian and doxological theocentric theology of mission."[8] Unfortunately, his missiological influence soon waned, and it is only in recent years that his value as a missiologist is being rediscovered.

6.1.2 USE OF BELGIC CONFESSION

Jongeneel's article does not mention anything about the Belgic Confession and its possible use by Voetius for missiological reflection. On this specific point, he only reiterates what Van Andel pointed out in his dissertation on Voetius and mission, viz., that Belgic Confession article 36 was functioning in the background of seventeenth-century thinking on the responsibilities of the magistrate with regard to true and false religion.[9] While he definitely endorsed and embraced the cooperative model found in article 36, there is no indication that Voetius himself actually referred to this article or commented on it in any substantial way.[10] Similarly, we noted earlier (5.1.5) that the doctrine of election was important in Voetius' missiology. Here too, it appears that article 16 of the Confession is only functioning in the background. The background roles of articles 16 and 36 have been confirmed with a survey of the relevant portions of *Politica Ecclesiastica* and *Selectae Disputationes*. Nevertheless, it is true that these confessional perspectives were functioning in the missiological thinking of Voetius.

We may say the same for his missionary ecclesiology and elenctics. In *Selectae Disputationes*, Voetius distinguished several species of apostasy from the true worship of God: atheism, epicureanism, ethnicism, libertinism (and semi-libertinism), Judaism (and semi-Judaism), Islam, neo-Arianism (also Socinianism, Anabaptism, and Arminianism), and Roman Catholicism.[11] While he does not identify them at this point as objects of mission, he does come to do this in later writings. Furthermore, speaking practically, in his first pastorate, Voetius was instrumental in bringing many Roman Catholics into the Reformed church in Vlijmen.[12] Similarly,

---

8. Jongeneel, "The Missiology of Gisbertus Voetius," 76.
9. Jongeneel, "The Missiology of Gisbertus Voetius," 49. H. A. Van Andel, *De Zendingsleer van Gisbertus Voetius* (Kampen: J. H. Kok, 1912), 158.
10. For more on this "cooperation model," see Joosse, *Geloof in de Nieuwe Wereld*, 52-64.
11. Gisbertus Voetius, *Selectarum Disputationum Theologicarum* (Vol. 2) (Utrecht: Joannes à Waesberge, 1655), 77.
12. "Voetius, Gysbertus," in *Cyclopedia of Biblical, Theological and Ecclesiasti-*

in 1630 when Bois-le-Duc (also known as 's-Hertogenbosch) was retaken from the Spanish, he eagerly gave himself to propagating the Reformed gospel in this Brabant town.[13] He was apparently not satisfied to leave people in the Roman Catholic Church.[14] This ecclesiology is exactly modelled on that of the Belgic Confession in article 29. Those not in the true church of Christ are essentially of the world and therefore objects of mission. Again, Voetius does not explicitly appeal to article 29, but it is impossible to see the correspondence as coincidental, especially given his subscription of this confession and his reputation for being strictly Reformed.

We know for certain that Voetius regularly gave attention to the Belgic Confession in his work at the university. This was not necessarily because of any special interest in the Confession as such, but more likely the result of his having subscribed it. He wrote, "We ourselves at our first arrival in this university introduced, along with the lectures on the loci communi and the weekly disputations, a regular discussion of the Belgic Confession, the third section of the catechism, the liturgy and the ecclesiastical regulations."[15] Elsewhere in his theological writings, we do find the Belgic Confession mentioned on occasion.[16] So, he is not only aware of the Confession, he also uses it in his teaching and in his theology, although it does not figure prominently. That fact should not surprise us given that attention to Scripture was generally considered a higher priority among Reformed scholastics of this era.

There is one place in his missiological discussions where the Confession is explicitly mentioned. In *Politica Ecclesiastica*, when he discussed

---

cal Literature (Vol. 10), John M'Clintock and James Strong (Grand Rapids: Baker Book House, 1970 reprint), 808.

13. S. D. van Veen, "Voetius, Gisbertus," in *The New Schaff-Herzog Encyclopedia of Religious Knowledge*, ed. Samuel Macauley Jackson (Grand Rapids: Baker Book House, 1969 reprint), 220.

14. Nevertheless, we must acknowledge that Voetius was much indebted to Roman Catholic theologians also in the area of missions: "...Voetius's theology of mission to a large degree developed out of and in dialogue with, not to mention in disagreement with, the Roman Catholic missiology contemporaneous to him." Jongeneel, "The Missiology of Gisbertus Voetius," 54.

15. Gisbert Voetius, "Selectae Disputationes Theologicae," in *Reformed Dogmatics: J. Wollebius, G. Voetius, F. Turretin*, ed. and trans. John W. Beardslee III (New York: Oxford UP, 1965), 267.

16. See, for example, Gisbertus Voetius, *Tractatus Selecti de Politica Ecclesiastica* (Vol. 2), ed. F. L. Rutgers (Amsterdam: J. H. Kruyt, 1885), 42.

the variety of missions, he indicated that mission can be envisioned as including the writing of petitions, admonitions, and apologies. Then he writes the following:

> In the name of the underground churches of the Netherlands, a letter was written to Phillip II, the king of Spain and ruler of the Netherlands, which was to be sent with a copy of the recently written confession of the churches of the Netherlands; however it was not sent because the circumstances did not allow it. Nevertheless, it was protected among the ecclesiastical documents and a copy was published with the first edition of the Confession. It was published anew in the year 1615 in quarto with the confession and Heidelberg Catechism, along with an exhortation or petition of the Reformed in the Netherlands to the Nobles and Magistrates of the Dutch provinces, written by Anthony Thysius, then a professor at Harderwijk, later at Leyden.[17]

As an example of this type of mission, Voetius mentions the Belgic Confession and specifically the Dedicatory Epistle to Philip II. He states that the epistle was not initially sent because of the circumstances in which the churches found themselves; yet it was included in the first and subsequent printed editions of the Confession. Voetius does not seem to be aware that the Confession (including the epistle) was thrown over the castle wall at Tournai with the intention that it would be passed on to Philip II. That notwithstanding, Voetius does see some missionary relevance here for the Belgic Confession, and this is worthy of some further reflection.

We noted earlier that when it comes to the types or varieties of missions, Voetius does not provide much in the way of biblical basis. That could be because he thought some of them should be immediately obvious. With regard to the fifth point, mission as the financial support of oppressed, persecuted, plundered, scattered, or impoverished churches, he

---

17. "Nomine clandestinarum ecclesiarum Belgicarum scripta erat epistola ad Phillipum II. Regem Hispaniarum, & principem Belgarum, quae cum exemplari confessionis ecclesiarum Belgicarum typis tunc descriptae mittenda erat; missa tamen non est, quod occasio defuerit. Nihilominus inter chartas ecclesiasticas ea custodia, & typis edita fuit una cum primis editionibus Confessionis. Denuo edita est anno 1615 in 4. cum confessione & catechisi Belgica, & alloquio seu petitione reformatorum in Belgio ad Ordines & Magistratus provinciarum Belgicarum ab Antonio Thysio tunc theologiae professore Harderoviceno, postea Leydensi." Gijsbert Voetius, *Politica Ecclesiastica* (Vol. 3) (Amsterdam: Johannes Janson à Waesberge, 1676), 334.

appealed to 2 Corinthians 8 and 9 and the collections for the poor believers in Jerusalem. However, the seventh point of making petitions, admonitions, and apologies did not include any explicit reference to Scripture. Given the other points and his appeal to 2 Corinthians 8 and 9, we might surmise that he based this on what the Lord Jesus said to Ananias about Paul's commission in Acts 9:15 and on the example of the apostle Paul in Acts 24-26. Based on such passages, it would be legitimate to conclude that the church has been sent into the world also to witness to magistrates and governments. Ideally, that would be done in person, as Paul did, but Voetius recognized that circumstances do not always allow that.

By the time Voetius wrote the words quoted above, the situation had drastically changed for Reformed believers in the Netherlands. Nevertheless, the history of Spanish persecution was still quite fresh in Reformed minds in the seventeenth century. As a result, when reflecting on the types of mission, Voetius could easily think back to the situation that prevailed during the days of Guido de Brès. He could identify the dedicatory epistle of the Belgic Confession as one model of what mission could look like in that situation. In doing this, he allowed for the possibility that such a situation could present itself again, whether in the Netherlands or elsewhere.

The objection might be made that Voetius spoke only of the epistle and not the Confession itself. It is true that he himself makes a distinction when he speaks of the edition published by Thysius in 1615. Still, it is equally true that the first French editions of 1561-62 all included the epistle as an integral part of the Confession. It was published with the thirty-seven articles and belongs with them. Historically speaking, the epistle cannot stand on its own apart from the formal Confession that follows it. So, while Voetius himself may have made the distinction, it is technically artificial and for our purposes may be disregarded.

It is also important to recognize the "ecclesiocentric missiology" of Voetius at work here. He recognized that the Belgic Confession was not the personal testimony of Guido de Brès, but rather a witness of the churches in the Low Countries. So also the epistle to Philip was not a personal effort, but something written in the name of the underground churches of the Low Countries.[18] Therefore it is evident here too that, in principle, if not always in practice, the missiology of Voetius gives weight to the fact that the Lord Jesus sent out *his church* into the unbelieving world.

---

18. "Nomine clandestinarum ecclesiarum Belgicarum..."

Aside from the above quoted passage, we do not seem to encounter the Belgic Confession again in the missiology of Voetius. When he discusses the means of mission, there is a place at which one might expect the Confession to be mentioned. This occurs in the context of the consideration of how schools might serve the cause of the gospel on a mission field. He reports the advice of an esteemed minister (Justus Heurnius) who had served 18 years in the East Indies. He speaks of the pedagogical use of Dutch books on the mission field, and he mentions the Heidelberg Catechism and books outlining some of the important historical passages in Scripture.[19] But the Belgic Confession is not mentioned here. Of course, Voetius is reporting here the advice of another, and not necessarily putting forward his own opinion. Nevertheless, when a confession is mentioned again in Voetius' missiology, it is the Heidelberg Catechism and not the Belgic Confession which receives attention. This is entirely understandable in this context. Still today, established churches typically use the Catechism to train their youth initially and only later introduce them to the Belgic Confession. The Catechism was written for the express purpose of training youth, whereas the Confession was written primarily as a witness to the world of where the church stands with regard to the Christian faith.

6.1.3 Evaluation

Surveying the efforts of Voetius to develop the first Protestant theology of mission, one encounters a limited use of the Belgic Confession. The Confession was functioning in the background of his theological thinking here and elsewhere. It set the boundaries of his theology, and he sought to do his work in continuity with it. He certainly knew the Confession and explicitly said that he taught it. When it came to his missiology, we find article 36 implicit in his understanding of the cooperative relationship between the magistrate and the church when it came to mission. We only see it directly functioning as an example of how mission might be conducted in a situation of persecution.

---

19. "Tantum commendo consilium Reverendi ministri, qui in partibus Indiae Orientalis per 18 annos Christum praedicaverat, de introducendo usu linguae Belgicae & aperiendis in quavis civitate aut pago scholis alphabetariis, ubi Indorum liberi a ludimagistris Belgicis instituantur in lectione & intelligentia librorum Belgicorum, imprimis in lectione & intelligentia catechesios & selectarum ac capitalium historiarum V. & N. Testamenti, quales sunt Genes. Cap. 1.2.3. & Genes. 6.7.8.9 & Genes. 11. Luc. 2. Math. 26.27.Math. 28. Act.1.1. Actor.2." Voetius, *Politica Ecclesiastica*, 341.

This ties into what we concluded at the end of the last chapter regarding the missiological strengths of the Confession. Voetius rightly recognized that persecution, even though not a concern in his day in the Netherlands, could very well happen elsewhere, and then the Belgic Confession might function as a model of how to carry the gospel forward in that context. Voetius' insights at this point remain substantially undeveloped, but yet he understood the value of the Confession here. This is something that later generations of missiologists (Reformed and otherwise) would lose sight of — something that is in need of recovery.

But the question may also be asked: were there any places in Voetius' missiology where the Confession might have been helpful? Here we are not interested in imposing later developments in missiology on the Utrecht professor. Rather, given what he himself proposed as a theology of mission, are there places where he might have benefited from explicit and direct reflection on the Belgic Confession?

As we noted in the last chapter (5.1.2), Voetius was the first to use the term 'elenctics' and to develop any kind of systematic thought on this area. The elenctic perspective pervades his missiological reflections. On numerous occasions, he sets the orthodox Christian faith off against not only pagan rivals, but also against counterfeits bearing the name "Christian." Here indeed is a place where Voetius might have found profit in introducing the antithetical perspective of the Belgic Confession and fully exploiting it. For instance, while it is clear both from his writings and his actions that he regarded consistent Roman Catholics as lost, he might have appealed to the history of the Confession, and particularly the original rationale for the confession. He makes a strong case as it is, but his case could be even stronger if he would have demonstrated from the Confession and its history that the intense hatred of the Roman Catholic Church for the Reformed churches rests in the age-old struggle between the seed of the serpent and the seed of the woman. The Confession testifies that this places a responsibility on Reformed believers to bring the gospel to those who are still in the Roman Catholic Church.

Since he did give attention to the subject, Voetius might also have used the Confession to explore further the relationship between the doctrine of election (article 16) and mission. As noted in chapter 5 (5.1.2), the location of his discussion of this doctrine is in what we would call the prolegomena to the theology of mission. Using article 16, Voetius might have gone further to explore the intrinsically missionary character of God's election; that is to say, from the beginning, God has revealed his mercy by calling to himself those whom he has elected in Christ Jesus. More particularly, he might have developed from article 16 how God's decree of election is not a static word or revelation of a word, but a dynamic activity oriented towards mission.

In the foregoing, we have by no means exhausted the relationship between Voetius and the Belgic Confession on the subject of mission. There are likely more connections, perhaps even more explicit ones. Nevertheless, it is evident that the first Protestant missiologist did in fact give us confirmation, if only in a limited way, that the Confession does have relevance for the study of mission.

6.2 The Belgic Confession in New Netherland & Johannes Megapolensis

Although he also served as a pastor and was involved in evangelistic efforts among Roman Catholics, Gisbertus Voetius was primarily an academic. On the other hand, Johannes Megapolensis was a practitioner of Reformed mission. While Voetius serves as a test case for the use of the Belgic Confession in the academy, Johannes Megapolensis serves as our test case for its use on the mission field by Reformed missionaries in the seventeenth century.

6.2.1 Overview of Dutch Reformed Mission Work in New Netherland

If one reads the histories of mission, one might be left with the impression that any missionary zeal that existed in the days of the Reformation disappeared with the deaths of the first or second generation of Reformers. For example, Stephen Neill makes no mention of the fact that the Dutch Reformed were involved with mission work in North America in the seventeenth and eighteenth centuries.[20] From Neill it would appear that no Protestant mission work was done among native peoples in the early days of settlement apart from that of John Eliot and David Brainerd. However, this is simply not the case. The Reformed churches in the Netherlands sent out ministers with the dual task of pastoring colonialists and discipling native peoples. This task took place in the context of a cooperative arrangement between the Reformed church and the Dutch West India Company.

---

20. Stephen Neill, *A History of Christian Missions*. The same has to be said for Ruth A. Tucker's *From Jerusalem to Irian Jaya: A Biographical History of Christian Missions* (Second Edition) (Grand Rapids: Zondervan, 2004).

The West India Company had been founded in 1621 partly with the intent of establishing colonies in North America and so providing a base from which to engage in fur trade with the indigenous peoples. During this time, the state exerted a significant amount of control over the Reformed Church. In the North American context, the West India Company effectively took the place of the state, and so it was assumed that the Company would take care of certain religious matters as well.[21]

Thus it happened that the churches would select ministers and teachers for the colonies, but the financial support for these would come from the Company. It was on these terms that on March 28, 1624, the Directors of the Company passed some legislation regarding the governance of the new settlement in New Netherland (an area which today includes much of New York state and parts of neighbouring states). The second item in this legislation is particularly interesting. It reads: "Within their territory they shall only worship according to the true Reformed religion, as it is done within this country at present, and by a good Christian life they shall try to attract the Indians and other blind persons to the knowledge of God and his Word, without, however, committing any religious persecution, but freedom of conscience shall be left to every one."[22] From this it is clear that the colonists as a collective entity had a missionary or evangelistic calling and intent, even if this was only in terms of lifestyle. Further, it should be noted that while the Company's many devoutly Reformed backers insisted on facilitating the spread of the gospel, this principle on the home front often met with passive resistance from the front line merchants and traders overseas. For those on the ground, everything was subordinate to business and financial interests.[23]

The head office of the West India Company was within the region of Classis Amsterdam. It therefore naturally developed that this Classis managed the pastoral work in New Netherland, including whatever mission work was being done. This was done through a committee, *Deputati ad Res Externas*. So, in a real sense, this committee became the foreign mission board of the Netherlands Reformed Church, at least insofar as it pertained to North America.[24]

---

21. Charles E. Corwin, "Efforts of the Dutch-American Colonial Pastors for the Conversion of the Indians," *Journal of the Presbyterian Historical Society* 12.4 (October 1925): 228.
22. Corwin, "Efforts of the Dutch-American Colonial Pastors," 228-229.
23. Donna Merwick, *The Shame and Sorrow: Dutch-Amerindian Encounters in New Netherland* (Philadelphia: University of Pennsylvania Press, 2006), 117.
24. Corwin, "Efforts of the Dutch-American Colonial Pastors," 229.

The first minister to arrive in New Netherland was Jonas Michaelius (born 1584; date of death unknown), a cousin of the better-known professor at Dordrecht, Johannes Michaelius. Michaelius arrived in New Netherland in 1628 with a mandate to minister both among the colonists and among the local native peoples. This latter work was done with zeal and interest, but also with much frustration. Michaelius was in New Netherland for only four years and his missionary efforts bore little visible fruit in that time.[25] Johannes Backerus succeeded Michaelius from 1647-1649, but he does not appear to have done any work among the native population.[26] Several years before this, however, we find the man would be called "the chief apostle to the Indians under the Dutch regime."[27] That man was Johannes Megapolensis.

6.2.2 Johannes Megapolensis: Pioneer Reformed Missionary to the Mohawks[28]

Megapolensis was born to Roman Catholic parents in 1603 in Koedijk, a town in the Dutch province of North Holland.[29] It appears likely the original form of his surname was Van Meckelenburg, although Grootstadt is also a possibility (depending on whether his family originates from Germany or the Low Countries). At some point, he hellenized the surname to Megapolensis, following the example of an uncle who was also a Reformed minister. It was this same uncle, also named Johannes Megapolensis, who appears to have been instrumental in his conversion from Roman Catholicism to the Reformed faith. This took place when he was 23 years old, and it resulted in his parents literally disowning him.[30]

---

25. Charles E. Corwin, "The First Dutch Minister in America," in *Journal of the Presbyterian Historical Society* 12.3 (April 1925): 144ff.

26. Corwin, "Efforts of the Dutch-American Colonial Pastors," 233.

27. Corwin, "Efforts of the Dutch-American Colonial Pastors," 233.

28. Much of this section is a summary of my article "Johannes Megapolensis: Pioneer Reformed Missionary to the Mohawks," *The Confessional Presbyterian* 5 (2009): 161-169.

29. Unless otherwise noted, most of the biographical information here was gleaned from Gerald Francis De Jong, "Dominie Johannes Megapolensis: Minister to New Netherland," in *The New York Historical Society Quarterly* 52.1 (January 1968): 7-47.

30. State of New York, *Ecclesiastical Records of the State of New York* (Vol. 1) (Albany: James B. Lyon, 1901), 152-153. See also Joosse, *Geloof in de Nieuwe Wereld*, 255.

We know little about the years preceding or immediately following this event. We know that at some point as a young man he studied at Cologne.[31] Further, we know that he decided to become a Reformed minister, and thus in 1634, we find him accepting a call to the church at Wieringerwaard, just north of Alkmaar. He was more oriented to the classic orthodoxy of the Reformed church than to the pietistic (*Nadere Reformatie*) side.[32] He remained in Wieringerwaard for four years and then also served churches at Schoorl and Bergen, both also near Alkmaar. At some point during this same time period, he married Machtelt Steengen, the stepdaughter of his uncle, Johannes Megapolensis, Sr. Together with his wife, the younger Megapolensis raised four children — three sons and a daughter.

In 1642, Megapolensis was called to serve in the colony of New Netherland. Having been honourably discharged by Classis Alkmaar, he and his family set sail on June 3, 1642 and finally arrived on August 4. Megapolensis had agreed to serve as a pastor in a settlement being developed by a diamond merchant and landowner from Amsterdam, Kiliaen Van Rensselaer. Under the patroon system, Van Rensselaer had received a large grant of land in the area of present-day Albany, New York. This patroonship consisted of over 700,000 acres and was known as Rensselaerswyck. Under the patroon system, Van Rensselaer was given certain quasi-feudal rights and privileges with respect to the colonists, and he was also responsible for their spiritual well being. This resulted in a contractual arrangement between Megapolensis (who had been looking to go overseas) and Van Rensselaer. Under this contract, Megapolensis agreed to serve at the settlement for a six year period, receiving his salary from the patroon. The contract provided a pension for his wife and family in case of death and was otherwise fairly generous.

This contract also stipulated that Megapolensis was to work "for the edifying improvement of the inhabitants and the Indians."[33] He received a similar charge from Classis Amsterdam. In a letter to the Consistory of New Amsterdam (which resembles in many ways an attestation), we read this regarding Megapolensis:

> [With Johannes Megapolensis] Rev. Bogardus and his entire Consistory are admonished and exhorted to hold correspon-

---

31. *Reply of Rev. Johannes Megapolensis to a Letter of Father Simon Le Moyne* (New York: The Collegiate Church, 1907), 16.
32. Joosse, *Geloof in de Nieuwe Wereld*, 252.
33. *Ecclesiastical Records*, 144.

dence and communion, so far at least as the circumstances permit; and thus with united hands to proclaim the Word of the Lord, not only among our own nationality, but also among the blind heathen in America. Thus we will all heartily rejoice that the Kingdom of Christ Jesus is more widely extended there. May the Lord bless the labours of both these ministers abundantly, strengthen them by the power of the Holy Ghost, and grant that they may faithfully use their talents to the magnifying of His Holy Name, to the extension of the kingdom of our Saviour Christ, and to the conversion and salvation of men.[34]

Thus, as Michaelius before him, Megapolensis was sent out with a dual task: pastor and missionary.

Megapolensis and his family wasted no time in making the journey northward up the Hudson River, and he preached his first sermon to his new flock on August 17. Besides preaching and pastoring, he also served as a special advisor to various government officials and as a mediator in various disputes. In addition, Megapolensis worked zealously among the Mohawk people of that area. There is much more to be said about Megapolensis and his years in New Netherland, but it is especially his missionary efforts that are relevant for our topic.

From the very beginning of his time in Rensselaerswyck, Megapolensis worked at learning the Mohawk language. It is evident that he managed to attain some level of fluency and was able to communicate somewhat with these native people. Still, it is not certain whether or not he was so fluent as to be able to preach in Mohawk.[35]

With regard to the methods used, it appears that there were three particular ways. This becomes evident in a letter written to a friend in 1644. This letter, published during his lifetime without his consent, is the most important primary source for our knowledge of Megapolensis and his missionary efforts. In this letter, he describes his work among the Mohawks: "We go with them into the woods, we meet with each other, sometimes at an hour or two's walk from any houses, and think no more about it than as if we met with a Christian. They sleep by us too, in our chambers before our beds. I have had eight at once lying and sleeping upon the floor near my bed, for it is their custom to sleep simply on the bare ground, and to have only

---

34. *Ecclesiastical Records*, 151.
35. De Jong, "Dominie Johannes Megapolensis," 45.

a stone or a bit of wood under their heads."[36] The missionary would go out with them into the forest, but he would also welcome them into his home. It appears that it was primarily through these two means that he became better acquainted with the Mohawks and also began to bring them the gospel. However, there was also the regular preaching of the Word in a worship service. Some of the Mohawks would occasionally attend the regular worship services in Rensselaerswyck: "When we deliver a sermon, sometimes ten or twelve of them, more or less, will attend, each having a long tobacco pipe, made by himself, in his mouth, and will stand awhile and look, and afterwards ask me what I am doing and what I want, that I stand there alone and make so many words, while none of the rest may speak."[37] Obviously these sermons were preached primarily for the benefit of the settlers and therefore in Dutch. However, it is worth noting that Megapolensis goes on to say that he would explain the sermon afterwards to them in their own language. The Dutch preacher/missionary at this point indicated that he was preaching the law of God to his parishioners and that he would in due time "preach the same to them and come to them in their own country and castles when I am acquainted with their language."[38] The fact that he was allegedly able to communicate this much at this point is quite a feat, considering that he had only been in the area for two years. There is no information available as to whether Megapolensis was able to attain his goal of travelling deeper into Mohawk country to bring the gospel in their own language.

Megapolensis was able to establish relatively good relationships with the Mohawks of his area, and he was also able to establish relatively effective communication with them. Nevertheless, because of perceived hypocrisy among the settlers who claimed to be Christians, there was a hesitancy among the Mohawks to accept the gospel. Additionally, many Mohawks were not prepared to appreciate the Reformed (and we would say "biblical") insistence on a religion primarily oriented towards the auditory rather than the visual.[39] Furthermore, we can note that Megapolensis

---

36. *Narratives of New Netherland, 1609-1664*, ed. J. Franklin Jameson (New York: Charles Scribner's Sons, 1909), 175.

37. *Narratives of New Netherland*, 177-178.

38. *Narratives of New Netherland*, 178.

39. Allen W. Trelease, *Indian Affairs in Colonial New York: The Seventeenth Century* (Ithaca: Cornell UP, 1960), 171. Trelease says that the Mohawks were not ready "to appreciate the introspective and unadorned Calvinism offered by the Dutch Reformed Church." Roman Catholic liturgical and spiritual practice was generally found to be much more appealing by the Mohawks.

and other colonial Reformed pastors were only part-time missionaries; most of their efforts were directed towards establishing a regular church life for the Dutch colonists.[40] An additional challenge came by way of the general lack of concern of the West India Company traders and other officials in New Netherland for the spiritual welfare of the native people. This lack of concern invariably translated into a lack of support for the missionary. Faced with all of these challenges, the numerical results of Megapolensis' missionary efforts are not clear. Although Corwin claims that thirty Mohawks were admitted to church membership after being carefully examined, he cites no primary source for this information, nor does he indicate whether these members remained until death.[41]

Later in his career, Megapolensis would move to New Amsterdam (present-day New York City), and his efforts there among native peoples continued. However, the native peoples around Manhattan Island were more hostile than the Mohawks and these efforts apparently bore no lasting fruit. It was not until later, after Megapolensis' death, that more fruit was seen. Godfreidus Dellius pastored at Albany and Schenectady in the period from 1683-1699. Within ten years, Dellius had established a native church in the Albany area, a church which was reported to consist of some 200 attendees, of whom sixteen were full communicant members. By the end of his ministry in 1699, he had baptized at least 131 aboriginals, mostly Mohawk.[42] Likewise, Peter Tesschenmaeker was able to establish a smaller church of approximately 40 converts in the Schenectady area.[43] Thus, it was only after nearly 80 years that it was possible for Reformed churches to be established among the Mohawks of upstate New York. Megapolensis was among the pioneers, and it is only regrettable that he was not able to see some of the blessing that later came upon this work.

6.2.3 Use of the Belgic Confession

In the sources that come directly from the hand of Johannes Megapolensis, there does not appear to be even one explicit mention of the Belgic

---

40. Gerald F. De Jong, *The Dutch Reformed Church in the American Colonies* (Grand Rapids: Eerdmans, 1978), 153.
41. Corwin, "Efforts of the Dutch-American Colonial Pastors," 234. Trelease (170) is one of those who dispute Corwin's claim.
42. Corwin, "Efforts of the Dutch-American Colonial Pastors," 240; Daniel K. Richter, "Some of Them...Would Always Have a Minister with Them: Mohawk Protestantism, 1683-1719,"*American Indian Quarterly* 16.4 (Autumn 1992): 471.
43. Corwin, "Efforts of the Dutch-American Colonial Pastors," 244.

Confession. We do not find him teaching the Belgic Confession either to his congregants or to the native inhabitants of New Netherland — this is not to say that he never did this, only that we have no record. Similarly, we have no indication that Megapolensis turned to the Belgic Confession as a guide for missionary reflection or praxis. It would seem, prima facie, that the Belgic Confession held no missiological relevance for this seventeenth-century Reformed pastor and missionary.

Earlier (6.1.2), we noted Voetius' cooperative model for the relationship between the magistrate and the church and the bearing this had on mission. This cooperative model had its roots in article 36 of the Belgic Confession and had been in the ascendancy since Walaeus in 1615. According to Joosse, this model was also evident in discussions between Van Rensselaer and Megapolensis. Under this conception, the church and magistrate would be mutually subordinate.[44] Yet, as with Voetius, article 36 lies in the background of this concept and does not appear to have been explicitly referenced.

There are at least two places where the Confession can be more clearly discerned to have held some importance to Megapolensis and his missionary efforts. In 1636, Classis Amsterdam adopted a standard form for letters of call to preachers being sent out to the East or West Indies. This letter of call included the responsibility to lead to religion those who were alienated from it and "to proclaim to men, in God's name, repentance towards God, and reconciliation with him through faith in Jesus Christ." Those who were sent out would be expected to carry out their work "in accordance with God's Word and in conformity with the Confession of the Netherland Churches and the Christian Catechism."[45] The "Confession of the Netherland Churches" is, of course, the Belgic Confession and it is held up as being of importance as a doctrinal standard, not only for regular ministers, but also for colonist ministers/missionaries.

Two years later, Classis Amsterdam adopted a set of "Proposed Articles for Colonization and Trade of New Netherland." The Classis decided that "religion shall be taught and preached there according to the Confession and formularies of union here publicly accepted in the respective churches, with which every one shall be satisfied and content."[46] It is interesting here that the Confession is mentioned by

---

44. Joosse, *Geloof in de Nieuwe Wereld*, 56.
45. *Ecclesiastical Records*, 93.
46. *Ecclesiastical Records*, 120.

name, while the Catechism and Canons of Dort are described as the "formularies of union."

All of this comes together when, on March 22, 1642, the Classis prepared the letter of call to Johannes Megapolensis. The letter begins by noting that God has opened a door in New Netherland "for the preaching of the Gospel of Jesus Christ for the salvation of men." It continues and notes that good fruits "have been already witnessed there through God's mercy."[47] That is an intriguing statement, and it is regrettable that it is impossible to know what this is referring to, whether work among the colonists or among the native inhabitants. The letter outlines Megapolensis' duties. Among other things, he was expected "to preach God's Word in the said colony," "perform the duty of the Gospel to the advancement of God's Holy Name and the conversion of many poor blind men," and "to proclaim Christ to Christians and heathens in such distant lands." The missionary calling could not have been more clear. Equally clear, however, was the standard by which Megapolensis was to do this work. His work was to be done "in conformity with the government, confession and catechism of the Netherland Churches and the Synodal Acts of Dordrecht, subscribed by him, to this end, with his own hand, and promised in the presence of God at his ordination..."[48] The Belgic Confession had been subscribed in its entirety by Megapolensis without any reservations. Along with the other Forms of Unity, it was to form the doctrinal basis for his pastoral and missionary efforts in New Netherland. There is no indication whatsoever that he ever departed from this whole-hearted commitment to the Confession.

Our second indication of some limited significance for the Belgic Confession in the missionary work of Megapolensis comes from his interactions with a French Jesuit missionary. We first find mention of Simon Le Moyne in a letter from Megapolensis and Samuel Drisius (another Reformed minister) to Classis Amsterdam on September 24, 1658. In this letter, these two ministers of New Amsterdam appeal to the Classis for

---

47. *Ecclesiastical Records*, 146.
48. *Ecclesiastical Records*, 147. See also De Jong, *The Dutch Reformed Church in the American Colonies*, 7. De Jong writes: "The Belgic Confession, the Heidelberg Catechism and the Canons of Dort became the cornerstones of the Reformed Church in the Netherlands. As such, they were transplanted to the New World, so that the churches established by Netherlanders in the American colonies became virtually as Dutch Reformed in doctrine as if they had been organized in the Netherlands itself."

more ministers in New Netherland on account of the growing presence of Jesuits coming south from Canada/New France. As an example, the visits of Simon Le Moyne to Fort Orange and Manhattan are briefly mentioned, but not elaborated upon.[49]

Further elaboration came in another letter just four days later.[50] While this letter indicates at the beginning that it is from Megapolensis and Drisius, it quickly becomes evident that the former is the author and in fact the letter is signed only in his name. Megapolensis begins by going back to some events in 1642, when he was a minister in Rensselaerswyck. He describes the capture and rescue of Isaac Jogues, another French Jesuit. The Mohawks had captured Jogues and were intent on putting him to death, but Megapolensis helped him escape. In 1644, yet another French Jesuit (Bressani) had been captured by the Mohawks and ended up at the Megapolensis household where his injuries were treated and eventually he was sent on his way back to France. Megapolensis had developed a reputation as being very kind and helpful, and so some years later, as Simon Le Moyne was in Manhattan, he stopped to pay his respects to the Reformed minister.

Both Jogues and Bressani had written letters to Megapolensis thanking him for this kindness and urging him to return to the Roman Catholic Church. Regarding Bressani, Megapolensis wrote: "He wrote me a letter, as the previously mentioned one had done, thanking me for the benefits I had conferred on him. He stated also that he had not argued, when with me, on the subject of religion, yet he had felt deeply interested in me on account of my favours to him; that he was anxious for the life of my soul, and admonished me to come again into the Papal Church from which I had separated myself. In each case I returned such a reply that a second letter was never sent me."[51] At his third encounter with a Jesuit priest, Megapolensis began debating immediately in person about the subject of religion. However, Le Moyne was not interested in arguing at this point: "He told me that he had lived about twenty years among the Indians. When he was asked what fruit had resulted from his labors, and whether he had taught the Indians anything more than to make the signs of the cross, and such like superstitions, he answered that he was not inclined to

---

49. *Ecclesiastical Records*, 434.
50. *Ecclesiastical Records*, 436-439.
51. *Ecclesiastical Records*, 437.

debate with me, but wanted only to chat."[52] At this point, it is worthwhile to observe that Megapolensis was concerned about whether this Roman Catholic priest was bringing a true gospel message to the Mohawks.

This was not the end of Megapolensis' interaction with Le Moyne. In the spring, Le Moyne travelled to Fort Orange and from there prepared and sent three documents to Megapolensis in New Amsterdam. Megapolensis explains the contents: "On his journey, when at Fort Orange, he did not forget me, but sent me three Catalogues: The first, on the succession of the Popes; the second, on the Councils; and the third was about heresies, all written out by himself. He sent with them also, a letter to me, in which he exhorted me to peruse carefully these Catalogues, and meditate on them, and that Christ hanging on the cross, was still ready to receive me, if penitent."[53] Unfortunately, the letter mentioned here is no longer extant.

The reply of Megapolensis to Le Moyne *is* extant, but only because he took care to send a copy to the Netherlands. The original was never received by Le Moyne since the ship that was carrying it to New France was lost at sea. In his reply, Megapolensis echoes the Belgic Confession at several points.

Le Moyne's letter had attempted to entice Megapolensis back to Rome with the authority of popes and councils. In reply, Megapolensis wrote: "Indeed, the Orthodox Faith and true religion come not from local or personal succession, as you falsely pretend; nor from human decrees and traditions, in which you abound; but we hold firmly that it must be drawn out and established from the immutable and infallible Word of God, as contained in the Old and New Testaments."[54] There are definite echoes here of what the Reformed churches confess in article 7 of the Belgic Confession.

The letter is also as deeply engaged in polemics against Rome as anything from the Reformed churches in the mid-sixteenth century. In his letter, Le Moyne put Jesus Christ as the first pope of the Church. This caused Megapolensis to write: "I am even in doubt, whether, on account of your dreadful blasphemy, you are more worthy of anger or of pity; because you have attempted to attach such hideous and impure members to Jesus Christ, who was not the head of the Roman Pontifical Church, but of the Holy Catholic Church....Why, therefore, do you desire to set up such

---

52. *Ecclesiastical Records*, 438.
53. *Ecclesiastical Records*, 439.
54. *Reply of Rev. Johannes Megapolensis to a Letter of Father Simon Le Moyne*, 6.

Dagons in the same place as the Ark of the Lord? Why do you not blush to assert that such Belials have had fellowship with Christ?"[55] As we have seen, the language of idolatry was regularly applied to the Roman Catholic Church in the days of the Belgic Confession. Furthermore, according to the Confession, the Roman Catholic Church is not just one brand of the Christian church; rather, it is the false church, and its members, if they consistently believe and embrace Roman Catholic dogma, are not Christians. Megapolensis was of the same mind:

> And, consequently, we confess that Christ had his church even at Rome, just as he had it at Corinth, at Athens, and Antioch, etc., but even as God, on account of their sins, ingratitude, contempt of the Divine Word, etc., according to his threats, removed his candlestick from these places, taking his vineyard from them, and giving it out to others: in like manner is it now with the Roman Church; so that we do not recognize the modern papal herd as the Church of Christ, nor even as a member of him; but as the dregs of Antichrist. For after that the devil, through the man of sin, fixed his throne at Rome, your Rome became the Babylonish harlot, who, drunk with the blood of the holy martyrs, has made the kings of the earth drunk and poisoned them with the wine of her harlotry.[56]

It is clear that Megapolensis shared the ecclesiological perspective of article 29 of the Belgic Confession. Le Moyne and others of like faith are those who "wander from the true Church of Christ and from the way of salvation."[57] Indeed, Megapolensis confessed that he himself was also lost when he was a Roman Catholic (in "that way of perdition"), but he was, by God's grace, converted to Christ at 23 years of age.[58]

This leads us to also reflect on Megapolensis' evangelistic appeal to Le Moyne. As he drew to the end of his letter, he alluded to the fact that both of them were getting on in years, and therefore it was even more important than ever that Le Moyne hear the call of the true gospel and believe it. Megapolensis did not hold back: "Therefore I beg of you, even now in your declining years to which you have already come, as well as myself, that you would ponder what you will respond to Christ, the Universal Judge, when

---

55. *Reply*, 9.
56. *Reply*, 11.
57. *Reply*, 18.
58. *Reply*, 20.

he comes for judgment; and what account of your stewardship you will render him."[59] In a moment we will come back to the "stewardship" mentioned here. At the end of the letter, Megapolensis expressed his prayer that God would lead Le Moyne "to the true knowledge of Christ and of his merits."[60] It is self-evident that Megapolensis' appropriation of the ecclesiology of the Reformed faith as expressed in the Belgic Confession led him to make an evangelistic appeal to this Jesuit priest.

It also led him to be concerned for all those whom the Jesuit had falsely taught. This ties back into the "stewardship" mentioned above. For over twenty years, Le Moyne had travelled through the wilds of North America bringing a message to the native inhabitants. Nevertheless, says Megapolensis, it was all for nothing because the message that was brought was nothing that saves. Megapolensis chided Le Moyne, "For you do not lead men from Gentilism to Christianity, but only from paganism to popery."[61] When Megapolensis would speak with the "converts" of Le Moyne, he would find that they did not have any proper knowledge of God or of the gospel. Roman Catholic missionaries, according to Megapolensis, left unbelievers in the dark — it was a classic case of the blind leading the blind.

6.2.4 Evaluation

We may say that Megapolensis knew the Belgic Confession, having subscribed it. Its formulation of the relationship between church and magistrate seems to have informed his preparatory discussions with Van Rensselaer. He was sent out with the understanding that he would perform his duties according to it. From his approach to a French Jesuit priest, we know that he did embrace the ecclesiological and soteriological perspectives of the Confession. However, at the same time we must admit that there is no place where he explicitly gives credit to the Confession or explicitly acknowledges that the Confession was guiding his missionary thought or practice.

As with Voetius, we might also ask whether there were any areas where Megapolensis might have benefitted from a more conscientious use of the Confession. To further delineate our investigation, we will limit this to the pedagogical use of the Confession on the mission field. Could missionary Megapolensis have used the Confession, and if so, how?

---

59. *Reply*, 20-21.
60. *Reply*, 22.
61. *Reply*, 22.

First of all, we need to consider whether the Confession might have functioned well in this missionary context. In 5.2.1 we noted that the Belgic Confession embodies a conceptual cognitive approach to reality. However, native North American cultures are typically examples of the concrete relational approach. In the concrete relational approach to reality, "life and reality are seen pictorially in terms of the active emotional relationships present in a concrete situation."[62] This approach emphasizes symbols, stories, events, and objects, and often communicates through gesture, sign language, music, ritual, drama, and the like. Still, we did note that there are elements of the concrete relational approach in the Belgic Confession, and it could work in those cultures which privilege that approach. So, the Belgic Confession might have been able to effectively function as a pedagogical tool among the Mohawks of New Netherland. It may have been a worthwhile endeavour to translate the Confession and disseminate it as a helpful guide to the key teachings of Scripture.

In the nature of the case, Megapolensis seems to have had other ideas about teaching the Christian faith to the Mohawks. During his years in New Amsterdam, he wrote a catechetical book entitled, "Examination and Confession for the Benefit of Those Who Are Inclined to Approach the Table of the Lord." According to Frans Schalkwijk, this catechism was intended for use among the Mohawks — though from the ensuing minor controversy it would seem that it was also meant for use among the colonists.[63] Megapolensis submitted a copy of this catechism to Classis Amsterdam in 1651 with the suggestion that it receive widespread use in the colonies of New Netherland and Brazil. The Classis did not accede to this request, insisting instead that the Heidelberg Catechism and the Compendium of Herman Faukelius be used.[64] In 1656, Megapolensis tried again, but once again the Classis refused him.[65] Nevertheless, the catechism *was* published, and it was quite likely used in New Amsterdam and elsewhere in the colony. We have no record of whether it was used among the Mohawks. But it would seem that Megapolensis was not satisfied with the existing confessions and felt that there was a need to improve on them specifically for use among the colonists and also possibly among the Mohawks.

---

62. Hesselgrave, *Communicating Christ Cross-Culturally*, 325.
63. F. L. Schalkwijk, *The Reformed Church in Dutch Brazil (1630-1654)* (Zoetermeer: Uitgeverij Boekencentrum, 1986), 227.
64. *Ecclesiastical Records*, 287.
65. *Ecclesiastical Records*, 349.

For the sake of argument, let us imagine that Megapolensis had translated the Belgic Confession into good, idiomatic Mohawk and was eager to use it among them. Working with what Megapolensis himself relates about Mohawk spiritual beliefs, there is one place where he might have used the Belgic Confession to good effect. He related the Mohawk creation narrative as it was told him by an old native woman. Contemporary retellings of the narrative illustrate that Megapolensis correctly reported the basic elements of the story.[66] It involves a pregnant woman falling down from heaven and having a tortoise take her on its back. As the woman sat on the tortoise, she "groped with her hands in the water and scraped together some of the earth, whence it finally happened that the earth was raised above the water."[67] Megapolensis notes this creation narrative, but he does not give any indication whether he used this potential point of contact in his discussions with the Mohawks.[68] Having a translation of the Belgic Confession in the Mohawk language, Megapolensis might have been able to put article 12 to good elenctic use comparing and especially contrasting the Mohawk narrative with the biblical one. This would have been especially helpful if literacy had been established among the Mohawks and they could read it for themselves, but even otherwise he might have been able to read to them what the Reformed churches confess from the Bible. Naturally, he might have been able to do that without the Confession and in his own words (informed by the Confession which he subscribed), but an official Confession might have established more solidly the fact that the views expressed were not simply those of one man, but of a great body of believers.

As with Voetius, it is unlikely that this investigation has exhaustively probed Megapolensis' use of the Confession. For example, we have not examined his catechism to determine what use (if any) he made of the Belgic Confession in its preparation. Megapolensis' sermons would also be an important primary source to consider. Unfortunately, at this time, neither his catechism nor his sermons appear to be extant. Perhaps future research will uncover them and reveal more about his use of the Belgic Confession in New Netherland, especially among the Mohawks.

---

66. See, for example, Clara Sue Kidwell, Homer Noley, and George E. "Tink" Tinker, *A Native American Theology* (Maryknoll: Orbis Books, 2001), 37-38.
67. *Narratives of New Netherland*, 178.
68. Joosse, *Geloof in de Nieuwe Wereld*, 315.

6.3 Conclusion

In both mission praxis (as by Megapolensis) and theory (as by Voetius), the Belgic Confession played a limited role in the seventeenth-century Reformed churches in the Netherlands. The missiological relevance of the Confession was not fully recognized or exploited in either the academy or the mission field. There were places where, especially in the work of Voetius, the significance of the Confession was realized in a partial fashion. This does confirm our previous conclusion that the Confession does have relevance for the study of mission. However, for the most part, we admit that the Belgic Confession functioned in the background as a confession to be subscribed, but not deeply explored from a missiological perspective. This limited recognition of its missionary value in this era would lead to more discussions in another era. That will be the subject of the next chapter.

ROBERT RECKER (1923-2007)

HARRY BOER (1913-1999)

Photo credits: Archives, Calvin College, Grand Rapids, MI, by permission

Chapter Seven
Late Twentieth-Century Judgements

7.0 Introduction

We have established that, in light of its strengths and weaknesses, the Belgic Confession has missiological relevance. It provides material for missiological reflection, it guides the mission of the church in key areas, and it could also be used with profit on many mission fields. As we saw in the last chapter, there was a limited recognition of this in the seventeenth century. In this chapter, we explore and evaluate some of the developments closer to our own era, particularly in the Christian Reformed Church in North America (CRC).

7.1 Robert Recker

Robert Richard Recker was a Christian Reformed missiologist. He was born November 28, 1923, in Highland, Indiana. He received his primary theological training at Calvin Theological Seminary, graduating in 1947. In 1973, he received a Th.M. from the Vrije Universiteit in Amsterdam. He was ordained as a CRC pastor in 1947 and he served as a CRC missionary to Nigeria from 1949 to 1965. He was on the Board of Foreign Missions from 1967 to 1969. In 1969, he was appointed as a professor of missions at Calvin Theological Seminary and he served there until 1988. Robert Recker passed away in late 2007.[1]

7.1.1 "An Analysis of the Belgic Confession as to its Mission Focus"

Recker's 1972 article was published in a special issue of *Calvin Theological Journal* devoted to the subject of mission and the Three Forms of

---

[1] This biographical information comes from the Christian Reformed Church Ministers Database (http://www.calvin.edu/library/database/crcmd/). Accessed October 24, 2009.

Unity. As we shall see later in this chapter, this was a topic of discussion in the Christian Reformed Church for some years before, during, and after this time. Unlike with the contributions by Fred Klooster (Heidelberg Catechism) and Anthony Hoekema (Canons of Dort), it is not readily apparent why the Belgic Confession was assigned specifically to Recker. Klooster and Hoekema have written extensively elsewhere on the Catechism and the Canons, but there is no record of such writings by Recker on the Belgic Confession.

Recker begins by acknowledging that one has to take into account the fact that the Belgic Confession was written in 1561. It is anachronistic to a degree to evaluate the missionary consciousness of the Confession by the standards of 1972. Nevertheless, he decides to proceed and do so.[2]

He notes that the Confession has a limited purpose as an apology for persecuted Christians. As such, "it is primarily concerned with an in-group in its historical context."[3] Moreover, it comes from an era in which Protestant Christians were still trying to carve out a niche for themselves in a Roman Catholic environment. These Protestant believers were "unimpressed" with the discoveries of the non-European world across oceans and continents.[4]

Looking at the structure of the Confession, Recker notes that it is not a comprehensive exposition of the Christian faith. Rather, it is partial, reflecting apologetic and polemical purposes. The Confession is not outward-looking. Only if one conceives of a "speaking to the various sections of the household of faith as a missionary function" can one be in admiration of the Confession's power and effect. Yet, from the "broader, biblical missionary point of view," the Confession is "really an *inter nos* [among us] document." Recker also draws attention to the historical distance between himself and the Confession. Not only are the language, sentence structure and argumentation in need of a modern revision, but also the "yawning gaps" need to be filled in with "simple, clear, biblically-based statements."[5]

Recker then proceeds to follow the division of the Confession suggested by A. D. R. Polman:

---

2. Recker, "Analysis," 158.
3. Recker, "Analysis," 159.
4. Recker, "Analysis," 159.
5. Recker, "Analysis," 159-160.

Articles 1-11: God and the Means Whereby He Makes Himself Known

While acknowledging that the first three articles are simple and beautiful, Recker finds that the Confession is missing the picture of the biblical God on a mission. He states that the Confession gives "a picture of a static God," rather than one who is accomplishing his purposes in human history.[6] In the background of this criticism seems to be an appropriation of the concept of *missio Dei* — and in fact, this concept explicitly comes out as he deals with the next group of articles.

Towards the end of his article, Recker briefly elaborates on his critique of each section. Concerning articles 1-11, he asserts that the image of the Godhead found here does nothing to stir up missionary passion in the true believer. He compares the Confession with 2 Cor. 5:11-21. The Confession lacks a picture of God the Father who asserts his ownership over the world and who will indefatigably redeem and remake it. The Confession lacks a picture of God the Son who is victorious, going on to greater and greater victories. The Confession lacks a picture of God the Holy Spirit who "bursts with Pentecostal power, able to renew the face of the ground not only, but also the sin-ravaged heart of man."[7]

Articles 12-15: Creation, Providence, the Fall and Its Effects

In article 13, Recker finds the assertion of God's governance over all things to be basic for the concept of *missio Dei*, giving motivation to human missionary activity. Article 14 is also basic, asserting man's incapability. However, the article is negatively focussed on guarding the justice and holiness of God and placing emphasis on the divine initiative and sovereignty. Article 15 goes further and states the church's position on original sin. Recker concludes, "the conviction that man is a sinner by nature is basic to the missionary crusade, both as to its necessity and its motivation and appeal."[8]

Coming back to this section at the conclusion of his essay, Recker appreciates the strong statement of man's problem. But he does not believe the Confession goes far enough. He would like to see a reflection of the apostle Paul's passion and agony for unbelievers, as reflected, for instance, in Romans 10:1-4.[9]

---

6. Recker, "Analysis," 161.
7. Recker, "Analysis," 175.
8. Recker, "Analysis," 162-163.
9. Recker, "Analysis," 176.

Articles 16-17: Election unto salvation

Recker finds confirmation of the *inter nos* character of the Confession in these articles. He notes a good basis here again for the concept of *missio Dei*, "but the Confession is content only to underscore the divine initiative." It does not go further to elaborate on what Recker sees as the biblical motif of "election-unto-service," or being elect unto good works.[10] Later, Recker comes back to these articles and argues that even the concept of *missio Dei* needs to be strengthened here. There needs to be a more biblically precise delineation of this truth.[11]

Articles 18-21: The Christ

When the Confession speaks of the incarnation of the Son of God, there one can find "a basis for the modern missiological emphasis on our call to involvement in the world and the need for a ministry to the whole man — a reaching out to and a seeking of man in his concrete situation." Article 20 speaks of Christ as being a high priest in the order of Melchizedek, and this gives missiology the chance to explore the connection between the creation and recreational work of God. This article also sets forth Christ as the only Saviour. Nevertheless, the Belgic Confession missed "a good opportunity to issue a rallying call for the proclamation of the gospel." Instead, it focussed only on the anti-Roman Catholic apologetic.[12]

Recker also asserts that these articles fall short in their portrayal of Christ. His resurrection and glorious Lordship are missing, as is "the concept of Christ the Word of God who is the effulgent revelation of the Father's splendour." Recker does not see Christ portrayed as he is in the gospels, as one who is a powerful prophet, healer and Lord, nor as the one who sends out believers as he was sent out by the Father. Finally, the Confession lacks a picture of the Christ who wept over Jerusalem and who asked the Father to forgive those who crucified him.[13]

Articles 22-26: The benefits of salvation

According to Recker, the role of the Holy Spirit in mission was a burning issue in his day. The Confession speaks in article 22 about the fact that the Spirit kindles faith in the hearts of human beings. Here the Bel-

---

10. Recker, "Analysis," 163.
11. Recker, "Analysis," 176.
12. Recker, "Analysis," 165.
13. Recker, "Analysis," 176-177.

gic Confession, distracted by its polemical/apologetic purposes, failed to exposit the role of the Spirit in mission and provide the direction that the church needs.[14]

Article 24 treats man's sanctification and good works. Here the confession, especially its opening sentence, could be foundational "for the missiological development of the role of the Christian man and of the church in human society." However, the Confession is again overtaken by apologetic concerns "and we are left unsatisfied."[15]

Christ's intercession and mediatorial work receives attention in article 26. As with the other articles, Recker approves of this as far it goes — but it does not go far enough. Recker writes, "Now that is fine for the in-group in a Roman Catholic context, but what about the animists, the Muslims, and other millions on the face of the earth? *Certainly the fact that Christ is the only high priest and advocate has a message for them too.* Does he pray also for those not yet gathered in? Does his love, his power, and his majesty have anything to say to them? Does he sit at the right hand of God receiving the nations as his messianic inheritance or not? We do not hear about this!"[16] Recker's concern is that the mediatorial work of Christ be seen and confessed as extending beyond those already in the church to include those who will someday become Christians.

He adds later in the essay that the Belgic Confession would have a greater mission focus if it would draw out more of the benefits that flow from Christ. Specifically, Recker has in mind the breaking down of barriers between "nations and peoples, between master and slave, between rich and poor, between white and black!" He also has in mind the meaning of Christ for community, the significance of Christ's present rule over the nations, and religious freedom. As it is, the Confession is limited by its historical context and the interests of the Reformed churches in the Netherlands in the mid-sixteenth century.[17]

ARTICLES 27-35: THE CHURCH AND THE MEANS OF GRACE

In these articles, Recker laments the fact that the kingship of Christ is restricted to the church: "The yoke of Christ is *conceived of ecclesiastically* as being in submission to the church's doctrine and discipline, and

---

14. Recker, "Analysis," 165.
15. Recker, "Analysis," 166.
16. Recker, "Analysis," 168. Italics are Recker's.
17. Recker, "Analysis," 177.

not as being under (*sub*) or as being caught up in the mission of God."[18] Again, Recker's emphasis on *missio Dei* comes to the fore in this part of the discussion.

When he comes to article 29 and the marks of the church, Recker bemoans the fact that the Belgic Confession speaks of church discipline being "exercised in punishing of sin." He recognizes the fact that this is more of an issue with the CRC edition than with the original Belgic Confession, yet he still wants to draw out that this is a deficient understanding of church discipline that has implications for the missionary task of the church. This is because church discipline is also a "missionary vehicle" that expresses the love of Christ calling men to repentance.

Recker also takes issue with article 29 when it speaks about the marks of Christians. While affirming what article 29 does say, he believes that Psalm 51:12-13 would indicate a great gap in the Confession at this point. There is a general duty of loving God and loving one's neighbour, but this should be borne out also in proclaiming the gospel beyond the walls of the church. According to Recker, the same article fails to say anything "about the falseness of the church which dispenses no life-giving water to others, a church which is not a light to the world."[19]

Article 30 treats the government of the church and states that part of the task of office-bearers is to see to the spread of the true doctrine. Recker sees the horizons of the church being broadened here. There is also mention of the ministry of mercy, and he finds that to be especially encouraging.[20]

The articles dealing with the sacraments are stated by the Confession to be the gospel dramatized. That being the case, Recker argues that their missionary dimension must be expounded upon. This is done in Scripture in Acts and some of Paul's epistles, but not in the Belgic Confession. Unfortunately, Recker himself does not elaborate on what he means by the "missionary dimension of the sacraments."[21]

Other missionary elements that Recker identifies as missing from the Confession's ecclesiological articles include: the need to hear about how ecumenics and ecumenical efforts can serve mission; the lifestyle of office

---

18. Recker, "Analysis," 168. Italics are Recker's.
19. Recker, "Analysis," 170-171.
20. Recker, "Analysis," 171.
21. Recker, "Analysis," 173.

bearers as a key element of mission; and the need for the church to pray in the spirit of 1 Timothy 2:1-7.[22]

ARTICLES 36-37: THE CIVIL GOVERNMENT AND THE LAST THINGS

In this last section, Recker notes the "very interesting" fact that the "explanation of the divine purpose for the existence of human society, as well as the missionary focus of the church, comes out in this article which deals with the role of civil government."[23] He asks whether this might be a carry-over from the sixteenth-century view of the relationship between the State and the Christian faith. But he does not evaluate or critique this relationship or what the Confession says at this point. He does come back to it later, and raises a number of questions, but gives no answers.[24]

With regard to article 37, he notes the same thing. There are all manner of eschatological questions that the Belgic Confession simply does not address. Among these is how the church should regard the nation state of Israel or the Jewish people, and how one should interpret the Revelation to John. These are sensitive and important issues for today, and the Confession gets a failing grade at this point.[25] Still, in the foregoing discussion, Recker acknowledges that the Confession does give a proper biblical and historical perspective for life before God: "It has a grandness about its vision and expectation; the good and evil of history do have meaning, and there will be a grand finale in which accounts are righted by the divine Judge." This perspective is basic for a scriptural approach to the science of mission.[26]

CONCLUSION

In his concluding remarks, Recker repeats his assertion that the Belgic Confession portrays not a witnessing church, but a protesting church. As a result, the document is ultimately unsatisfying for a missiologist. It portrays the church speaking with itself, rather than the church witnessing to the world. While its place in history rescues it from excessive inculpation, Recker cannot fail to judge the Confession as being at best partial and inadequate with regard to mission.[27]

---

22. Recker, "Analysis," 177-178.
23. Recker, "Analysis," 174.
24. Recker, "Analysis," 179.
25. Recker, "Analysis," 179.
26. Recker, "Analysis," 179.
27. Recker, "Analysis," 179-180.

7.1.2 Evaluation

In chapter 5, we noted that the Belgic Confession does have certain weaknesses when it comes to the study and practice of mission. Chief among these are the age and cultural origins of the Confession. Recker would agree with this assessment. However, we also noted that there are several strengths and these actually outweigh the weaknesses. Here Recker parts ways with the main thrust of this book. This parting of ways happens for a number of reasons.

First of all, there is a methodological difference. While Recker does acknowledge certain points in the Confession as basic for missiological reflection, his main approach is to highlight its numerous missiological lacunae. For instance, the Confession lacks the *missio Dei*, or a conception of Christ as high priest and mediator that would speak to Muslims and animists, or an exposition of how Christ's redemptive work tears down the barriers between the races. Recker is quite right on all these points — they are missing in the Belgic Confession. Perhaps many more points could be added. Nevertheless, is it reasonable to expect the Confession to speak to any of these things? First of all, we have the problem of age and cultural origins. But second, and more importantly, if Recker's expectations were to be satisfied, the Belgic Confession would no longer be a booklet of some 10,000 words, but a much longer book. A better, more responsible, and more sympathetic method would be to take the Confession on its own terms and work with what the Confession gives. If the Confession is seen to give nothing of missiological value, then we have nothing to say. However, even Recker recognizes that the Confession does have a contribution to make, even if it is far more circumscribed than what we have offered in the preceding chapters.

A second significant issue is Recker's definition of mission(s). We have seen in chapter 2 that the definition of mission is crucially important for this topic. We need to give careful consideration not only to the sixteenth-century understanding of mission, but more importantly what the Bible teaches about the definition of mission. There is no discussion on this topic in Recker's essay nor any material cited which might provide an explicit frame of reference for his understanding of mission(s). His definition is unstated. Yet, it would seem from his essay that his operative understanding is considerably broader than what was concluded from our biblical exploration in chapter 2, as well as the sixteenth-century Reformed understanding.

Related to the foregoing is Recker's appropriation and presupposition of the concept of *missio Dei*. Here again, there is no explicit discussion of this concept, nor are any references provided that might help us understand Recker's position on this. He appears to assume it as a given that the concept of *missio Dei* is well-accepted in missiology. Of course, in broader ecumenical circles in 1972 that would probably have been the case. However, Recker was writing in the journal of the Christian Reformed seminary, presumably mostly for a confessionally Reformed audience. Considering the weight that Recker gives this concept in his analysis of the Belgic Confession, we could expect him to be more direct and clear as to what exactly he understands by this concept and how he would defend it biblically. We have argued (2.4) that the distinction between *missio Dei* and *missiones ecclesiae* is indefensible.

In the preceding chapters, we have already addressed Recker's judgment that the Confession portrays a church speaking with itself, or that its nature is *inter nos*. Recker's critique at this point reveals more about his own ecclesiology than it does about the Belgic Confession and its view on mission and particularly the objects of mission. He writes of the Confession "speaking to the various sections of the household of faith," but de Brès and other sixteenth-century Reformed ministers would vociferously protest including Rome or the Anabaptists in this way. Further, we have seen that their protest would have a biblical basis.

Recker takes issue with the Confession regarding the marks of the false church. He argues that the Confession does not say anything in article 29 about the falseness of a church which is not outward-looking in its administration of the gospel. This is a weak criticism because it fails to take into account the structure of this article. The article first lays out the marks of the true church, and the first is the faithful proclamation of the gospel. Given the historical context, it is not unreasonable to see this as referring to preaching both inside and outside the church walls.[28] The order of the marks is also significant. The preaching of the gospel is that which creates faith, the administration of the sacraments strengthens faith, and the exercise of church discipline preserves faith. When the article proceeds to deal with the false church, it follows the pattern of the marks of the true church, framing them in the negative. So, the inverse of the first mark becomes, "The false church assigns more authority to itself

---

28. This was not clear, however, in the CRC edition then in use. See further 7.2.1.

and its ordinances than to the Word of God. It does not want to submit itself to the yoke of Christ." One could understand this to refer primarily to matters of ethics or polity, and those are certainly in view. Nevertheless, the "yoke of Christ" includes the faithful preaching of the gospel both in established churches and on the mission fields. When one considers that the "yoke of Christ" has a gospel-oriented character, one cannot but conclude that Recker's judgment is hasty and ill-considered.[29]

Something similar must be said for his approach to discipline as mentioned in article 29. Recker's issue is with the expression that speaks of church discipline being used for the "punishing of sin." As mentioned above, he does recognize that this criticism is related to a translation problem with the CRC edition in use at the time, and an extensive footnote compares the early French, Latin and Dutch editions on this point. But strangely, Recker still insists that this is "a deficient concept of the intent of church discipline." He wants to see church discipline as a "missionary vehicle." Recker seems to be saying that discipline somehow functions to bring unbelievers to repentance and faith in Jesus Christ. In a sense this *may* be true. When a brother or sister is brought under the steps of discipline, it is because he or she is not showing the fruits of faith with a Christian life. Their spiritual state is in question. However, they formally remain a brother or sister and member of the church until excommunication. In this sense, discipline is not a missionary activity of the church. In the sense that it preserves the integrity of the witness of the church, one can speak of a missionary element to church discipline. But that does not seem to be what Recker has in mind here.

Recker's insistence that the mediatorial work of Christ needs to be referenced to the ongoing church-gathering work of Christ is something worthy of further reflection. Recker wants to ask whether Christ prays for those who are not yet gathered in. Is there a message for the animists, Muslims, etc. who are yet-to-believe? For that matter, in the original context of the Confession, is there a message here for the Roman Catholics and Anabaptists who are yet to come to a saving belief in the gospel revealed in Scripture? These are good questions and not easy to answer. The heart of the matter is what the Bible says about this. Does Scripture speak anywhere about the Lord Jesus interceding for those who have yet to come to faith in him? Scripture does speak this way in John 17:20 where the Lord Jesus prays saying, "I do not pray for these alone, but also for those who

---

29. See G. Van Rongen, *The Church*, 96-100, 161.

will believe in me through their word." It is reasonable to conclude that the Lord Jesus did not only make this intercession here at this moment, but also continues to do so at the right hand of God in heaven. However, we must be clear that this prayer was and is and will be uttered by the Son of God only for those who will believe, or in other words, the elect.[30] That complicates the missionary use of such a concept. We cannot tell individual unbelievers about what has not been revealed to us. We simply do not know which unbelievers the Lord Jesus is praying for, any more than we know which unbelievers he died for. The identity of the elect is unknown to us. So, while the truth that the Lord Jesus prays for and intercedes for elect unbelievers is something worthy of further missiological reflection, it is questionable whether such a concept belongs in a missionary confession of faith as a message for these unbelievers. After all, the doctrine of election has not been revealed for unbelievers, but for believers. It has been given for their comfort and their praise-filled devotion to God the Sovereign Redeemer.

In conclusion, Recker's analysis raises some good questions at certain points. But the overall tenor of his essay is unsympathetic to the Confession. This can be attributed to Recker's failure to account for the historical (and biblical) view of mission out of which the Confession originally speaks.[31] While he is correct in identifying the apologetic and polemical purposes of the Confession, he does not recognize that these purposes are oriented to the mission of the church. In the Confession we see a church speaking to the world of wrong belief and unbelief, to a world plagued by idolatry and false religion — a world not so unlike our own.

7.2 THE CHRISTIAN REFORMED CHURCH IN NORTH AMERICA

Like other Reformed churches, the CRC traces its roots back to the Reformation of the sixteenth century and particularly to the Netherlands.

---

30. For a refutation of a universalistic approach to this passage and its context, see John Owen, *The Death of Death in the Death of Christ: A Treatise in which the whole controversy about Universal Redemption is fully discussed* (London: Banner of Truth Trust, 1959), 84-85.

31. This assessment is different from that of Harvie Conn in *Eternal Word and Changing Worlds*, 245. Conn found Recker's judgment on the Belgic Confession to be accurate, adding that the length of time that Reformed churches have held to it has only contributed further to a fading evangelistic focus. Conn added references to a number of authors (Piet, De Ridder, Bosch) who allegedly support Recker's conclusion. These authors, however, simply argue that the Belgic Confession emerges from a *Corpus Christianum* perspective — a point that has already been disputed in the first chapters of this book.

In 1834, a further Reformation took place known as the Secession or *Afscheiding*. Following this Secession, large numbers of Dutch immigrants flooded to the United States. First joining the Reformed Church in America, many of them later seceded in 1857 to form the True Dutch Reformed Church. This would later become known as the Christian Reformed Church. The CRC would later itself be divided in secessions producing the Protestant Reformed churches, the Orthodox Christian Reformed churches and the United Reformed churches. Headquartered in Grand Rapids, Michigan, the CRC today consists of over 1000 congregations and over 268,000 members.

Writing in 1990, J. D. Bratt identified three characteristics of the CRC:
- heartfelt conversion and piety, although cast in covenantal rather than revivalistic terms

- confessionalism and orthodoxy, as set by its three standards — the Belgic Confession, the Heidelberg Catechism, and the Canons of Dort

- Christian cultural engagement[32]

For our purposes, the second characteristic is especially important. In principle, the CRC has always been a confessional church. Yet, as we shall see, the place and value of the confessions has been a subject of discussion over the last six decades.

7.2.1 BACKGROUND: 1950S & 1960S

Robert Recker's 1972 article in *Calvin Theological Journal* presented a few new particular criticisms, but the general tenor of what he was saying about the Belgic Confession had been heard at least twenty years earlier in the CRC. Samuel Volbeda, who taught mission at Calvin Seminary from 1926 to 1952, insisted that the creeds of the CRC were "practically devoid of missionary material. They are mum on the matter of missions. Missions are still an extra-creedal affair."[33] This would set the tone for discussions in years following.

---

32. J. D. Bratt, "Christian Reformed Church," in *Dictionary of Christianity in America*, ed. Daniel G. Reid et al. (Downers Grove: Intervarsity Press, 1990), 260.

33. Quoted in Kevin Allen Schutte, "The Missional Church and New Church Development in the CRCNA," (MA thesis for Calvin Theological Seminary, March 2003), 5.

Late Twentieth-Century Judgements 237

In the Acts of Synod 1952, we find the following in article 143:

IX. CREEDAL FORMULATION FOR MISSIONS

Material: Overture No. 38.
The Consistory of Prospect Park, Holland, petitions Synod to forward its overture to the Reformed Ecumenical Synod to draw up a creedal statement concerning Christian Missions.

Recommendation:
Your advisory committee does not recommend acting favorably on this overture.

Ground:
The work of Missions is included in the connotation of the first mark of the church, namely "the faithful preaching of the Word."

Adopted.[34]

So far as can be determined, this is the first official instance of an indication of dissatisfaction in the CRC with the current confessions regarding mission. Interestingly, the response of the advisory committee, taken over by the Synod, appeals to article 29 of the Belgic Confession. Speaking through its synod, the CRC in this era considered that the Belgic Confession spoke to the missionary task of the church.

However, not all in the CRC shared that perspective. In November 1952, *The Reformed Journal* published Harry Boer's response to Synod 1952. In "Missions and the Creeds," Boer gives particular attention to the Belgic Confession since it is the most detailed of the confessions and is also more theological in character. He finds only three statements in the Confession that may be understood as having missionary value. All three statements are found in the ecclesiological articles:

1. Art. 27, par. 3. "Furthermore, this holy church is not confined, bound or limited to a certain place or to certain persons, *but it is spread and dispersed over the whole world.*"

2. Art. 28, par. 2. "And that this [the Christian life and doctrine] may be the more effectually observed, it is the duty of all believers, according to the Word of God, to separate themselves from all those who do not belong to the Church, and to join themselves to this congregation, *wheresoever God has established it.*"

---

34. *Acts of Synod 1952*, article 143, 81.

3. Art. 30. "We believe that this true Church must be governed by the spiritual polity which our Lord has taught us in His Word . . .that by these means the true religion may be preserved, *and the true doctrine everywhere propagated.*"[35]

Boer asserts that these three statements exhaust the missionary relevance of the Belgic Confession.

Interacting with the 1952 Synod, Boer points out that the CRC edition of the Belgic Confession then in use does not support the grounds for the decision to deny the overture of Prospect Park. Article 29 in that edition says, "The marks by which the true Church is known are these: If the pure doctrine of the Gospel is preached therein." Boer builds his case on the word 'therein.' He notes that the earlier Dutch and Latin translations did not have that word. While he does not mention the first French editions of 1561-62, we can add that they do not have that word either. It was something added later on by the CRC. Yet, interestingly, Boer maintains that "there can be little doubt that the English translation quite conveys the spirit of the original creedal statement."[36] This is interesting because Boer simply does not prove that the Reformed churches of the Lowlands or Guido de Brès believed that the first mark was limited to preaching done in the church. Nevertheless, Boer is emphatically correct in drawing attention to a problem with the CRC edition of the Confession — this would be corrected in a much later edition (1985).

Like Recker twenty years later, Boer's assessment regarding the Belgic Confession (and the other creeds and confessions) is that they are inward-looking. The fathers have a "limited vision" of the missionary task of the church.[37] Boer concludes, "It is obvious that the Belgic Confession has little appreciation for the missionary witness of the Church and therefore provides little stimulation for its execution. Its best expressions on this score are ambiguous to say the least . . .The loud silence in the Belgic Confession on the missionary task may serve our day by calling forth reflection on the subject by the church at large."[38] It is clear that Boer was dissatisfied with the Belgic Confession. In his estimation, the church

---

35. Harry R. Boer, "Missions and the Creeds," *The Reformed Journal* 11.11 (November 1952): 15. Italics have been added by Boer.
36. Boer, "Missions and the Creeds," 15.
37. Boer, "Missions and the Creeds," 15.
38. Boer, "Missions and the Creeds," 16.

would be well-served by the drafting of a new confession with a deeper missionary consciousness.

As an aside, Boer was serving as a CRC missionary in Nigeria at this time. Serving alongside him was none other than Robert Recker. Some of Boer's thoughts are reflected in what Recker would later write. The questions of influence and interaction between these two are interesting, but unfortunately cannot be pursued further in this work.

In 1955, John Harold Bratt authored a Th.D. dissertation entitled, "The Missionary Enterprise of the Christian Reformed Church of America." In the first chapter, Bratt surveyed the confessions of the CRC with an eye to missionary significance. Regarding the Belgic Confession, Bratt echoed Boer's assessment: it is "marked by the 'inward look,' and is concerned in the main with development within the Church rather than with its expansion."[39] While he acknowledged that there were some statements that imply mission, in the main, the Belgic Confession, along with the other Forms of Unity, is characterized by paucity when it comes to mission.[40]

He observed that this paucity could be accounted for in the fact that the original context was not known for its missionary zeal. "In point of fact, the sense of evangelistic obligation was notoriously absent at that particular juncture of history."[41] Bratt goes so far as to characterize this period as being one of "evangelistic lackadaisicism." A second factor is the apologetic and polemical stance of the Reformation churches. This is particularly evident with the marks of the church found in article 29 of the Confession. These marks are "introvertively beamed and no mention is made of the responsibility to the outside world."[42]

Bratt went on to make two — more positive — observations. He noted that the concept of "confession" embodies the idea of open profession and, as such, "involves intrinsically the assumption of the missionary obligation."[43] Finally, Bratt noted that the Calvinism of the Christian Reformed Church is itself not a deterrent to the missionary endeavour. Rather, it stimulates it, and this has been well-illustrated throughout history. Thus, Bratt concludes that the Reformed believer could do more and his confessions could

---

39. John Harold Bratt, "The Missionary Enterprise of the Christian Reformed Church of America" (Th.D. diss. for Union Theological Seminary, May 1955), 25.
40. Bratt, "The Missionary Enterprise," 41.
41. Bratt, "The Missionary Enterprise," 42.
42. Bratt, "The Missionary Enterprise," 45.
43. Bratt, "The Missionary Enterprise," 46.

be more explicit about mission "but his theology impels him to go to the ends of the earth with the saving gospel of the grace of God."[44]

Meanwhile, other discussions about the Belgic Confession were also taking place in the CRC. These had to do with the question of an editorial revision. There was a growing recognition that the text of the Confession in use by the CRC in the 1950s was deficient in certain respects. Since the CRC held to strict confessional subscription at this time, this created difficulties for some office bearers. The June 9, 1961 issue of the official CRC publication *The Banner* featured some roundtable discussion on this matter. One of the contributions was from a proponent of the majority report (Paul G. Schrotenboer), advocating for a revision. The other was from a proponent of the minority report (Gordon J. Spykman), advocating the status quo. Finally, there was also a third contribution (Peter G. Berkhout) that also came down in favour of revision.[45]

From this discussion, it becomes readily apparent that there were at least two ways of thinking about this issue in the CRC of the early 1960s. One party (the majority report) wanted a revision so that there could be clear, complete, and honest subscription to the confession by the office bearers of the church. The other party wanted to keep the confession in its historical form "as a historical statement of faith."[46]

For our purposes, the article of Berkhout is especially relevant. After identifying some areas that he sees as theologically problematic in the Belgic Confession, he added: "In addition to all this, leaders have been writing about expansion of the Confession for years. For example, the Confession under the task of the church mentions nothing about its missionary function, nor does it have anything to say about the modern conflicts in theology."[47] Berkhout claimed that because of the Belgic Confession's many problems, it had become a "rubber Confession." Consequently, he insisted that the need was great to either write a new confession or thoroughly rework the existing one.

---

44. Bratt, "The Missionary Enterprise," 51.
45. Paul G. Schrotenboer, "Editorial Revision of Belgic Confession — A Majority Opinion," *The Banner* 96.23 (June 9, 1961): 18; Gordon J. Spykman, "Revision of Belgic Confession — The Minority Opinion," *The Banner* 96.23 (June 9, 1961): 18-19; and Peter G. Berkhout, "The Belgic Confession at the Crossroads," *The Banner* 96.23 (June 9, 1961): 19, 22, 23.
46. Spykman, "Revision of Belgic Confession," 19.
47. Berkhout, "The Belgic Confession," 23.

Another important development in this period was the discussion about missionary and evangelistic zeal in the CRC. In his dissertation, John Bratt had already indicated that one of his chief concerns was interacting with those who charged the CRC with having a lack of enthusiasm for mission and outreach.[48] In two articles in 1962 and 1964, Harold Dekker (professor of missions at Calvin Theological Seminary) also dealt with this lack of missionary zeal in the CRC. He attributed it to a widespread misunderstanding of the doctrine of limited atonement or particular redemption.[49] As a result of these discussions, a study committee was appointed by Synod 1964. In 1966, the committee reported that missionary apathy was indeed a problem in the CRC, but this was to be attributed to:

- spiritual apathy due to material possessions
- a feeling of inferiority and fear to speak to others
- a lingering immigrant mentality
- weariness because of poor results in evangelization
- not enough individual prayer for the unconverted
- a preoccupation with theological correctness during the twenties, which hindered compassionate interest in people outside the church.[50]

The Synod of 1967 made no statement or decision on this issue, so the question remained unanswered. Harvey Smit came back to this question fifteen years later (1982) and proposed that the most striking cause of the CRC's lack of missionary zeal in the preceding decades was not actually a lack of zeal, but zeal projected in the wrong direction. The CRC had been concerned with preserving correct doctrine, and it understood this to be the essence of what it means to be a true church. Self-maintenance was

---

48. Bratt, "The Missionary Enterprise," vi.
49. Harold Dekker, "God So Loved — ALL Men!," *The Reformed Journal* 12.11 (December 1962): 5-7; Harold Dekker, "Limited Atonement and Evangelism," *The Reformed Journal* 14.5 (May-June, 1964): 22-24.
50. *Acts of Synod 1966*, 504. Cited in Harvey A. Smit, "Mission Zeal in the Christian Reformed Church: 1857-1917," in *Perspectives on the Christian Reformed Church: Studies in Its History, Theology and Ecumenicity Presented in Honor of John Henry Kromminga at His Retirement as President of Calvin Theological Seminary*, ed. Peter De Klerk and Richard R. De Ridder (Grand Rapids: Baker, 1983), 229.

far more important than witnessing to unbelievers.[51] While Smit does not say it explicitly, it would appear that his target here is again the allegedly inward-looking ecclesiology of the Belgic Confession, particularly what it says in article 29 about the marks of the true church. This discussion also appears to provide the background to Recker's statement that if he were to look for a document to stir up missionary passion, he would not look to the Belgic Confession.

Nevertheless, there were some voices in the CRC that saw more missionary value in and missiological relevance to the Belgic Confession. When then-Calvin seminary student Verlyn Verbrugge explored missionary ecclesiology in 1967, he worked sympathetically with the Confession.[52] In particular, he worked with article 29 and not only the marks of the church, but also the marks of Christians. He argued that a missionary ecclesiology would be better served by emphasizing the latter (the subjective marks) rather than the former (the objective marks). While one may take issue with Verbrugge's approach, for our purposes we can note that there were those who sought to use the Confession positively for missiological reflection.

To summarize this section, in the period from 1950 to 1970, there were numerous developments taking place with regard to the Belgic Confession and mission in the CRC. There were some explicit discussions about the missiological relevance of the Confession and these tended to emphasize its inadequacies and failings. However, the discussions of the revision of the Confession and the lack of zeal for mission in the CRC are also important here. Some placed part of the blame for this missionary lukewarmness at the feet of the Three Forms of Unity, even singling out the Belgic Confession as being especially responsible. Moreover, there seems to have been a polarization developing in the CRC during this era, especially between those wanting confessional revision (along with full, strict, and honest subscription) and those desiring to retain the status quo (and whose position on subscription was ambiguous at best). These background developments culminate in several discussions at CRC Synods in the 1970s and '80s. It is to those that we now turn.

---

51. Smit, "Mission Zeal," 240.
52. Verlyn Verbrugge, "Suggestions for A Missionary Ecclesiology," *Stromata* 13.2 (December 1967): 9-13.

7.2.2 Development of the Contemporary Testimony: Our World Belongs to God

The journey to the Contemporary Testimony (CT) began in 1971 with an overture to Synod from Classis Chatham. The Classis requested Synod to declare that a new confession was both necessary and desirable. This new confession would replace the existing Three Forms of Unity. As grounds, Classis Chatham indicated that the Three Forms were helpful historically, but today "need the interpretation of theological and historical experts; they cannot serve as an adequate expression of the faith of the ordinary members of Christ." Further, since the Synod of Dort, the Holy Spirit has brought new insights to the church, and evil spirits have introduced new heresies. The new insights are not specified, nor are the new heresies. Since every church member is expected to agree with the confessions and share in them, they should be "more obviously relevant." Fourth, because of their antiquity and our ignorance, the Three Forms of Unity are in danger of veneration. Finally, Classis Chatham argued that "a paralyzing unbelief keeps telling us that the Church of the living God cannot do today what it was called to do in the times of the Reformation." The Classis concluded by asking the Synod to further declare that the existing confessions would continue to be binding until the adoption of this proposed new confession.[53]

Classis Alberta North interacted with this overture and presented its own overture to Synod 1971. This Classis agreed in general with the proposal to draw up a new confession. Still, they added, "We do not endorse that part of the overture which reads 'which will replace the Belgic Confession, the Heidelberg Catechism and the Canons of Dordt as a statement of the truth and as our standard of unity." The ground was that such a judgment would be premature at this particular point in time.[54]

Meeting on June 17, 1971, the Synod discussed these overtures. In analyzing the overtures, the advisory committee felt that the first four grounds of Classis Chatham were "more negative than positive in their thrust" and were more supportive of replacement rather than augmentation. The fifth ground was also found wanting since it assumed that unbelief is what paralyzes the church today and that the church has the same confessional calling in all eras. The advisory committee decided, therefore, not to adopt the grounds. However, the general thrust of the

---

53. *Acts of Synod 1971*, Overture 5, 624-625.
54. *Acts of Synod 1971*, Overture 77, 672-673.

overture from Classis Chatham, together with the amendment of Classis Alberta North, was found amenable. The Synod adopted these recommendations of the advisory committee:

1. That synod, recognizing that it is desirable for the church to confess its faith in contemporary ways, and recognizing that at times it becomes necessary for the church to augment its confession, appoint a committee to study

    a) How the church can confess its faith in contemporary ways today

    b) Whether the churches consider it necessary to augment their confessions at this time, and if so,

    c) In what areas the church desires to augment its confession.

2. That synod request this committee, on the basis of this study to present recommendations to the Synod of 1972.

3. That synod declare this to be its answer to overtures 5 and 77.[55]

In its first iteration, the committee came to be known as the "Committee on a New Confession." Appointed to the Committee were: Dr. L. Oostendorp, Rev. L. Schalkwyk, Mr. Morris N. Greidanus, Mr. H. Arens, and Dr. J. H. Kromminga.

In 1972, the Committee on a New Confession brought a report to that year's synod. The committee sent out a questionnaire to each consistory in the CRC. It was also sent to those active ministers not currently serving a regular church. A total of 367 churches responded to the survey, approximately 55% of the aggregate. A total of 116 ministers not serving regular congregations responded, approximately 50% of the aggregate.

Of 367 consistories, 135 responses (37%) considered it necessary for the church to augment its confession at that time. Of those 367, 213 (58%) did not consider it necessary. Among the 135 who considered it necessary, 129 believed that the need for augmentation was strongly felt in the function of a confession as a "witness to the world." This was the highest number. Furthermore, 90 respondents among the churches thought that it was urgently desirable to augment the confession in the area of "the mission of the church." Again, this was the highest number. A further 45 maintained that it was desirable to do this.[56]

---

55. *Acts of Synod 1971*, article 140, 109-110.
56. *Acts of Synod 1972*, Report 38, 403.

Among the responses from the 116 ministers, 96 (83%) considered it necessary for the church to write an additional confession; 18 (17%) did not consider it necessary. Of those 96, 88 thought that the need for augmentation was acute in the function of a confession as a "witness to the world." This was the highest number. Moreover, 77 respondents among these active ministers not serving a church believed that it was urgently desirable to augment the confession in the area of mission — the highest number again. A further 19 felt that it was desirable to do this, resulting in a total of 96. When reflecting on this set of statistics, one must remember that many of these active ministers not serving a congregation were either missionaries, evangelists, chaplains, or professors.[57]

In its concluding analysis of this survey, the committee wrote, "Among those who favor augmenting the confession, there was near unanimity on the desirability of augmenting the confession in the area of 'the mission of the church.'" The committee also noted the enormous discrepancy between the churches and the ministers not serving churches. Next, the committee concluded, "The affirmative answer by 135 churches and many ministers indicates a significant sense of need for augmenting the confession in some way, particularly in the areas of the mission of the church, the doctrine of the Holy Spirit, and Christian address to human need."[58]

The committee went on to present "Observations on the Confessional Task of the Church." For our purposes, part of the discussion on "When is a New Confession Necessary?" is particularly pertinent. The report states that the Three Forms of Unity assume a situation where nearly all of Europe is "at least formally Christian." The Confessions are therefore not entirely speaking to the world, but rather to other Christians:

> While the attitude of the church to the unbelieving world is not absent from their language, their definitions and pronouncements are made in distinction from other confessions, churches, and theologies, all of which profess to be Christian. The kind of threat which rival theologies pose to the church is not absent from our situation. But the question may well be asked whether this continues to be the major crisis which the true church faces today. The writers of these confessions could hardly have been expected to read the situation otherwise than they did. But the

---

57. *Acts of Synod 1972*, Report 38, 404.
58. *Acts of Synod 1972*, Report 38, 406.

question is whether the situation has changed enough to make their formulations insufficient.[59]

The report unwittingly reveals an ecclesiology at this point which departs from that of the Belgic Confession.

The report attempts to identify some kind of new crisis facing the churches. This notion of a major, contemporary crisis will reappear throughout the development and reception of the CT, even into the new century. The crisis is secularization. Christendom no longer exists. There is no longer a situation "in which there are only varieties of the one faith."[60] Everywhere one looks, the church's voice is being muted. Instead, there is an increasing and uninhibited focus on man and what he can accomplish. Says the report, "The faith of man is a faith in himself, his hope is a mundane hope, and his love, even at best, limited by earthly horizons. Whatever label — e.g. 'post-Christian' — one wishes to attach to this, it constitutes a drastic change in the situation of the Christian faith. This state of affairs is with us, and apparently not to be reversed. Probably it has been with us longer than we have suspected."[61] This is the modern crisis. But the modern challenge is the missionary task of the church in this milieu. The report concludes that the church must speak clearly and exhaustively in this context. "The church must maintain its identity with the purpose of fulfilling its mission. Such speaking, whatever name may be given it, is a confession."[62]

The committee recommended, first, that the Synod judge that the CRC was not ready for a supplemental confession. The second recommendation was that the Synod recognize that the churches need to pay attention to their confessional task at this time. Third, the committee recommended that the committee be continued to promote further study among the churches regarding this confessional task. Fourth, there was a recommendation to encourage study and reflection among the different institutions and agencies of the CRC "in order to discover together which aspects of our biblical heritage need special emphasis in a confessional statement in our time." Finally, the committee recommended that the Synod make no further commitments regarding a new confession at this moment.[63] These

---

59. *Acts of Synod 1972*, Report 38, 411.
60. *Acts of Synod 1972*, Report 38, 412.
61. *Acts of Synod 1972*, Report 38, 412.
62. *Acts of Synod 1972*, Report 38, 412-413.
63. *Acts of Synod 1972*, Report 38, 413-414.

recommendations were all adopted by Synod 1972. The Synod also decided to add two new members to the committee.[64] Those two members were S. DeYoung and F. Van Houten.

In their report to the 1973 Synod, the committee made some notes and observations. For instance, they indicated their gratitude to the faculty of Calvin Seminary for "providing the churches with informative articles about the confessions in the *Calvin Theological Journal* of November 1972."[65] This was the issue that included Recker's article on the Belgic Confession and mission. From this we know that Recker's article did have the attention of this committee — however, we cannot definitively state what their reaction to it was.

The committee also made an observation on confession writing taking place in other churches. "There is evidently a growing feeling, particularly in Reformed churches, that something needs to be done to confess the faith in our time."[66] They also offered some reflection on making a more effective use of the existing confessions — one of the more significant items was the need to have the creeds and confessions in more contemporary English.

The Synod agreed that greater and more effective use could be made of the Three Forms of Unity and mandated the committee to explore those means. The Synod of 1973 also decided to continue the New Confession Committee with the mandate "to assist the churches in further study of our confessional task and to watch confessional developments that are under way in other churches." The Committee was therefore reappointed to continue with its work.

The Committee did not report again until Synod 1975. That year the committee reported on its activities in assisting the churches in studying their confessional task. Two articles were written and one of the committee members led two workshops. The committee also observed ongoing developments in other churches, specifically the Gereformeerde Kerken in Nederland and the Reformed Church of America — both of which were developing new confessions. Discussions and consultations were also held regarding the translation of the existing Three Forms of Unity and also on the project to versify parts of the Heidelberg Catechism for singing. Finally, the committee also explored "new methods of com-

---

64. *Acts of Synod 1972*, article 26, 30-31.
65. *Acts of Synod 1973*, Report 35, 496.
66. *Acts of Synod 1973*, Report 35, 497.

munication." But at the end, there was no clarity on "how the church should stimulate and coordinate multi-media confessing of the faith on a denominational and local level."[67]

The recommendations to Synod 1975 were that a new translation of the Canons of Dort be prepared, that the Synod appoint a committee to investigate whether they might adopt the translation by Dr. Anthony Hoekema, and that the churches give suggestions regarding new means of confessing and communicating the faith.[68] There was nothing at this Synod about the Belgic Confession or about formulating a new confession, although the committee continued to be called the "New Confession Committee."

1977 was a watershed year for the development of the Contemporary Testimony. The New Confession Committee presented a report to that year's Synod that made the recommendation that finally provided the impetus for this project. In their report, the committee observed that the Reformed Presbyterian Church of North America was working on a contemporary testimony "to bring the Westminster Confession up to date." They also observed the ongoing developments in the Reformed Church in America with their contemporary testimony, "Our Song of Hope."[69] While the committee appreciated the style and concept of this testimony, the conclusion was that its poetic form resulted in a lack of precision, and therefore the CRC would not be well served in adopting this document for itself.[70] Interestingly, this exact criticism would later be brought to bear upon the Contemporary Testimony of the CRC. The report also featured discussion about the translation of the existing confessions and the beginning of nearly thirty years of discussion about Question and Answer 80 of the Heidelberg Catechism.

For our purposes, the most important part of Report 45 to Synod 1977 was the section on "The Confessional Task of the Churches." The committee argued that the time was right to engage in renewed consideration of the need for a new confession. The committee emphasized that this was not to replace any of the existing confessions, but rather to supplement in order to cover vital topics and issues not covered by them. Four grounds were given for this proposal:

---

67. *Acts of Synod 1975*, Report 42, 541.
68. *Acts of Synod 1975*, Report 42, 542.
69. *Acts of Synod 1977*, Report 45, 654-656.
70. *Acts of Synod 1977*, Report 45, 656.

1. There is a great crisis confronting the church in the pervasive secularization of modern life...the classical confessions of the Reformation do not address this crisis directly, since it has arisen after the time in which they were written.
2. We are living in a vastly different age from that which the Reformation-age confession writers experienced . . . The upshot of all this is a secularized society and a radically changed position in the world . . . We live in an age of uninhibited emphasis upon man and his capabilities.
3. The response of Protestantism to the pervasive secularization of life has been one of accommodation.
4. The confessions written in the sixteenth and seventeenth centuries do have some implications for this situation, but do not speak directly to it. Every one of them bears the marks of the times in which they were written. Particularly pertinent is an assumption which they all held in common. Their concentration was on Europe, and their assumption was that all of Europe was Christian. While the stance of the Christian Church with respect to the unbelieving world can be detected in their language, their definitions and pronouncements were made in distinction from other churches, confessions, and theologies, all of which professed to be Christian. The need for distinctions between Christian theologies still exists. But it is eclipsed by the need for defining the stance of the Christian Church in a world in which the living God is not necessarily or even probably a presupposition of thought and action.[71]

It should be readily apparent that much of the argument here, especially in the fourth point, is directly taken over (almost word for word) from Report 38 to Synod 1972.

The committee went on to identify several areas in which a supplementary confession could be of profit to the CRC. They stated that the relationship between church and state needed a positive statement. Also, they indicated that the nature of Christian hope required augmentation, especially since the existing confessions say so little about eschatology. For our purposes it is the third item that is especially important: "The *mission of the church in the world* is a subject approached only indirectly in our present confessions, but it is perhaps the central question

---

71. *Acts of Synod 1977*, Report 45, 659-660.

facing the church in its contemporary life. On this score also there are a host of views and approaches which cannot all be harmonized with each other or with a Reformed view of Scripture."[72] Given the background we surveyed earlier, the first sentence here is not surprising. However, the second sentence does give evidence of some distinction between various approaches to mission. This seems to be saying that it is important to have a confession in which the church echoes the true teaching of Scripture on this matter.

The relevant recommendations of Report 45 to Synod 1977 were that the assembly should declare "that there is need to move in the direction of a testimony which addresses itself to the secularization of modern life." Secularization was perceived as the major new crisis which required a confessional address. Building on that ground, the committee also recommended that a new committee be established with a mandate to make recommendations on these questions:

- the specific areas to be covered by the testimony
- the procedure to be followed in producing the testimony
- the advisability of cooperating in this work with other churches closely related to our own
- the qualifications desired in the members of a committee appointed to draft the testimony[73]

The New Confession Committee would continue, but only with the mandate to complete their assignment with regard to translating the Canons of Dort. These recommendations were adopted by Synod 1977, and the Contemporary Testimony Committee was appointed.[74] The first iteration of the committee consisted of Dr. G. Spykman, Rev. A. Kuyvenhoven, Rev. J. Eppinga, Rev. M. Greidanus, Rev. T. Hofman, Dr. R. Mouw, and Rev. C. Tuyl.[75]

Continuing the bi-annual pattern of the previous committee, the Contemporary Testimony Committee did not report until 1979. The committee communicated its understanding of its mandate, viz., that they were a preliminary or procedural committee laying the ground work for the

---

72. *Acts of Synod 1977*, Report 45, 660. Italics belong to the original document.
73. *Acts of Synod 1977*, Report 45, 661.
74. *Acts of Synod 1977*, article 59, 89-90.
75. *Acts of Synod 1977*, article 81, 150.

appointment of another committee which would actually formulate the Contemporary Testimony.[76] The committee also indicated its full conviction of the need for this testimony. They went on to identify four features that they desired to characterize the new testimony:

- boldly orthodox
- an expression of Reformed piety
- articulate the kingdom vision of our unique strand of Calvinism, insisting on the inseparable connection between "that which is to be believed" and "that which is to be done"
- an ecclesiastical confession that addresses current issues[77]

At this point, there was some reason to be hopeful. After all, the committee did want to see the formulation of a Reformed testimony that would not only address contemporary issues, but also be "basic and orthodox, so that it commands the agreement of all Bible-believing Christians."[78]

The report went on to recommend the areas to be addressed in the CT. A number of issues were identified being broadly classified under the headings of the Church, Basic Issues in Human Relations, Fundamental Human Needs, and Issues in Larger Public Domain.[79] The committee also isolated several areas where the existing confessions give inadequate guidance. One of these areas is *missio Dei*. Before proceeding, we should note that this is the first time that this concept appears in the development of the CT. The committee does not define or explain *missio Dei* in the report. According to the committee, "Our classic confessions say nothing on this topic." There are some incidental references in the Heidelberg Catechism and "the Canons of Dort has a curiously un-missionary line in III, IV, Art. 15." There is no mention of the Belgic Confession. The committee asserted that there is a lack of confessional guidance in this area.[80]

The committee then presented two possibilities for the structure of a testimony. The one would involve a "full-perspective" approach oriented to the classic Reformed motifs of creation, fall, and redemption. This was the preferred approach of the committee. However, they also presented an "issue-oriented" approach, noting that "this is the form which most Re-

---

76. *Acts of Synod 1979*, Report 32, 521.
77. *Acts of Synod 1979*, Report 32, 523-524.
78. *Acts of Synod 1979*, Report 32, 523.
79. *Acts of Synod 1979*, Report 32, 524-525.
80. *Acts of Synod 1979*, Report 32, 527.

formed church testimonies have taken over the past 300 years."[81] Examples include the Conclusions of Utrecht of 1905 and the Three Points on Common Grace of 1924. The committee provided three samples of how this might work in a contemporary testimony. The first two had to do with poverty and education. The third was regarding mission: "Mission: repenting of our lack of diligence in missions, for our failure to make the gospel believable because of inconsistent ways of living it out, and for our tendencies to pour the gospel in the molds of western ideologies; and recognizing that increasingly our mission fields lie near to home as well as far away; we reaffirm the world's need of the renewing power of God's Word; and rededicate ourselves to proclaiming the gospel in all its fullness, in word and deed, to our fellowmen in all their life-relationships."[82] Of course, this was not even a proposal, but just a sample. There is no direct or obvious formal connection to what the committee wrote here and what would later appear in the CT, although there is some conceptual identification. It does give some indication of how the committee was thinking about what needed to be said concerning mission. The lack of zeal issue reappears. The gospel also needs to be proclaimed in "word and deed," possibly reflecting a more comprehensive approach to the definition of mission.

The report goes on to reflect on the relationship between the proposed testimony and the existing Three Forms of Unity. The committee was insistent that "it would be well to bear in mind that this task is not being undertaken because we find fault with the Three Forms of Unity."[83] There was no desire to criticize the work of the fathers, but simply to build on what they had done. Then the issue is raised of the status of the CT when completed. Should it be received immediately as a confession on equal footing with the Three Forms of Unity? The committee argued that it should be given time and that it should be regarded initially as subordinate to the Three Forms. But yet the hope of the committee was that it "might eventually gain confessional standing."[84]

It is worth noting that the committee based their approach to the status of the proposed CT on the history of the Belgic Confession:

> The Belgic Confession was written by one individual as a contemporary testimony. Within ten years it received creedal

---

81 *Acts of Synod 1979*, Report 32, 528.
82 *Acts of Synod 1979*, Report 32, 529.
83 *Acts of Synod 1979*, Report 32, 530.
84. *Acts of Synod 1979*, Report 32, 531.

status when the Synod of Emden (1571) required its member churches to adhere to this document. Other classes and "particular synods" followed suit. But it was not until the closing session of the Synod of Dort (May 6, 1619) that the three creeds became "doctrinal standards of the church." Unanimously that synod declared that the Belgic Confession and the Heidelberg Catechism were "agreeable to the Word of God;" and the Canons, which that synod had adopted, were judged to be "in agreement with the Word of God and the Reformed confession."[85]

This recounting of the history of the authority of the Belgic Confession is incorrect.[86] The Confession was already adopted and had ecclesiastical authority before its publication in 1561. Ecclesiastical assemblies in the years following simply reaffirmed their existing commitment to it. The proposed approach of the committee (which was later adopted, as we shall see) cannot be grounded on the precedent of the early history of the ecclesiastical authority of the Belgic Confession.

Responding to the recommendations of the report, Synod 1979 decided to continue working towards a contemporary testimony. A committee would be appointed to work on this and they were expected to have a draft prepared for the synod in 1983. The goal of 1986 was set as the year that this testimony would be finally approved and adopted.[87] Appointed to this new iteration of the committee were G. Spykman, M. Greidanus, R. Recker, L. Den Besten, C. Hoogendoorn, R. Mouw, B. Nederlof, H. De Moor and G. Vander Velde.[88] Some of these individuals had served on previous iterations. For our purposes, the addition of Robert Recker and George Vander Velde are significant since both were prominent CRC missiologists and Recker in particular had expressed himself clearly on the inadequacies of the Belgic Confession.

The 1981 report of the Committee for Writing a Contemporary Testimony was brief. The committee gave notice that it was working towards its goal of producing a draft document in 1983. Members were writing drafts of various sections. The working theme was identified as "Our world belongs to God!" It seemed to the committee that this would be

---

85. *Acts of Synod 1979*, Report 32, 530-531.
86. See Gootjes, *The Belgic Confession*, 93-115.
87. *Acts of Synod 1979*, article 65, 75-76.
88. *Acts of Synod 1981*, Report 37, 562-563.

the best way to most directly address the secularism of this era. A summary statement of the CT was provided and it included these key lines:

> God uses those he has found to keep reclaiming the world as his: His church worships him and goes to all nations with his message. His people follow their Lord in homes and schools, in work and recreation, in national and international affairs, seeking his justice and peace.[89]

From this summary, it is evident that mission was to be an important feature in this document. The definition of the mission and message of the church is, however, ambiguous.

A brief report was also presented by the committee to the 1982 Synod. This time the committee simply gave an update of where things stood with regard to their work. There was also a reminder of the rationale for the CT: "Our classic Reformed confessions are several centuries old. During these centuries great changes have taken place in the church and in the world. The church, for instance, has been led to see its mission more clearly and to understand the Spirit's gifts more flexibly. The world has become more secular: many do not believe in God; many more act as if he has little to do with daily life."[90] Once again, we can note that mission was front and centre as something missing in the Three Forms of Unity and something that was going to be included in the CT. Yet, exactly how the church has improved its mission vision since the sixteenth century is not specified. This report was received for information by the Synod of 1982.

The Synod of 1979 had mandated the committee to have its draft ready for the Synod of 1983. The committee met this deadline and presented the first draft of the Contemporary Testimony: Our World Belongs to God. The committee indicated that it took the "full-perspective approach." They formulated the CT in a poetic style reminiscent of the Reformed Church in America's Song of Hope. Structurally, it consisted of a brief preamble, followed by the longer testimony constructed along the lines of creation, fall, redemption, and new creation. There are several subheadings and 62 stanzas. The committee also wrote a commentary on the CT to expand on the issues raised.[91]

Strikingly, despite what one might have expected based on the 1981 report, there was nothing explicit about mission in the preamble. How-

---

89. *Acts of Synod 1981*, Report 37, 563.
90. *Acts of Synod 1982*, Report 34, 576.
91. *Acts of Synod 1983*, Report 32, 409.

ever, the theme did appear elsewhere in the CT draft. For instance, in the section on the Spirit:

> The Spirit breathes life
> into the mission of the church
> using young and old,
> men and women,
> to send out the Good News of God's grace.
> In state and school,
> science and art,
> media and marketplace,
> we may declare the saving acts of him
> who called us out of darkness into his marvelous light.[92]

Then in the section on the Church:

> Following the apostles, the church has been sent —
> Sent to tell the news that the world belongs to God,
> To call disciples from all nations,
> To offer the cup of cold water,
> And to proclaim the assurance that in the name of Christ
> There is forgiveness of sin and new life now and forever.
> In a time when billions do not know God,
> This mission is central to our being.
> We repent of leaving this work to a few,
> And we rejoice that the Spirit
> Is waking us to see
> Our mission in God's world.[93]

Intrinsic to this statement is the union of word and deed in Christian mission. Already at this point we can recognize that mission here involves the sending of the church for this task. There is no hint of *missio Dei*. While the commentary states that missions "spring out of the saving work of God," there is a clear understanding that *the church* has been sent out with a definite and limited task.[94]

Synod 1983 gave provisional approval to this draft, and it was sent to the churches "for use in worship, education, and outreach and for discussion." Comments were to be sent to the secretary of the committee and

---

92. *Acts of Synod 1983*, Report 32, 417.
93. *Acts of Synod 1983*, Report 32, 419.
94. *Acts of Synod 1983*, Report 32, 443.

then the committee was to report back with a final draft to Synod 1986. The Board of Publications was also instructed to "seek ways of ensuring wide circulation of the Contemporary Testimony among the churches."[95]

Synod 1986 was presented with a final draft and the CT was approved and adopted. According to a news item in the official CRC magazine, it "easily won synod's approval."[96] This was despite the fact that two classes (Hudson and Zeeland) had overtured to delay approval of the CT and not include it in the new Psalter Hymnal.[97] Synod made clear, however, that the CT was not on an equal footing with the Three Forms of Unity. Mission not only remained in the final draft, it was even strengthened. The subject was revised in the section on the Spirit to read:

> The Spirit thrusts
> God's people into worldwide mission.
> He impels young and old,
> men and women,
> to go next door and far away
> into science and art,
> media and marketplace
> with the good news of God's grace.
> The Spirit goes before them and with them,
> convincing the world of sin
> and pleading the cause of Christ.[98]

The final draft omits the mention of the church and instead, at least at this point, seems to indicate that mission is a matter of individual Christians being sent out by the Spirit. Moreover, although this was also present in the first draft, here the sphere of mission is envisioned as wide and comprehensive, encompassing all areas of human life. From this statement, one certainly finds grounds for maintaining the idea that all Christians are missionaries.

---

95. *Acts of Synod 1983*, article 74, 707.
96. RR, "Contemporary Testimony Passes Final Test," *The Banner* 121.25 (June 30, 1986): 16.
97. Patricia Alderden, Carol Flietstra, and MM, "Classes Seek to Retain Hymnal Forms, Exclude Contemporary Testimony," *The Banner* 121.10 (March 17, 1986): 24.
98. *Our World Belongs to God: A Contemporary Testimony (Study Edition)*, Christian Reformed Church in North America (Grand Rapids: CRC Publications, 1987), 22.

However, a different voice is heard elsewhere in the CT. In the adopted version, mission receives its own heading, "The Missions of God's People." This section begins with a revision of the statement we noted before:

> Following the apostles, the church is sent —
> Sent with the gospel of the kingdom
> To make disciples of all nations,
> To feed the hungry,
> And to proclaim the assurance that in the name of Christ
> There is forgiveness of sin and new life
> For all who repent and believe —
> To tell the news that our world belongs to God.
> In a world estranged from God,
> Where millions face confusing choices,
> This mission is central to our being,
> For we announce the one name that saves.
> We repent of leaving this work to a few,
> We pray for brothers and sisters
> Who suffer for the faith,
> And we rejoice that the Spirit
> Is waking us to see
> Our mission in God's world.[99]

Again, this is a comprehensive vision of what mission involves, but it does certainly involve the sending out of the church. The comprehensive character is emphasized by the stanzas that follow this one. Here the "missions of God's people" include protesting and resisting the abuse and harm of life, protecting a biblical view of sexuality, singleness, family and marriage, education, work, science and technology, government, and peace making.

In a moment, we will survey reactions to the CT in the CRC. But first it must be noted that the CT underwent yet another revision in 2008. The article regarding the Holy Spirit and mission was revised to make it clear that it is the church which is sent out by the Spirit. Further, believers are sent into all different areas to point "to the reign of God with what they do and say."[100] Finally, the last section is now "The Mission of God's People"

---

99. *Our World Belongs to God* (1987), 25.
100. *Our World Belongs to God*, Christian Reformed Church in North America (Grand Rapids: Faith Alive Christian Resources, 2008), 18.

(note the singular). The opening stanza begins explicitly with *missio Dei* and goes on to exhibit a classically comprehensive understanding of what mission involves: taking care of the poor and sick and freeing prisoners.[101]

From this overview of the history of the development of the CT in the CRC, it is apparent that there was dissatisfaction with the existing confessions regarding mission. From the survey presented to Synod 1972 we discover that this was more among ministers without a church, than among the churches themselves. Furthermore, where dissatisfaction was expressed, the Belgic Confession was again singled out in certain instances. The CT was developed to address perceived inadequacies in the Three Forms of Unity; most prominent among these was the missionary task of the church. Along the way, there was also a slow drift away from the classical definition of mission towards a more comprehensive definition oriented to and grounded on *missio Dei*.

7.2.3 Reception of the Contemporary Testimony: Our World Belongs to God

As might be expected, there was some critical interaction in the CRC with both the CT and the process leading up to it. While it is not clear whether he was reacting to the development of the CT, Timothy Monsma argued on the basis of its ecclesiological articles that the "missionary thrust of the Belgic Confession is clear and compelling."[102] Sounding as if he might be interacting with the CT development process, Monsma concluded: "The Belgic Confession makes provision for missions both in its definition of the Church and in its description of civil government. Were we to write the confession today, we would wish to make this provision more explicit. But this should not blind us to the fact there is provision for missions both in the Heidelberg Catechism and the Belgic Confession as these documents now stand. The question that individual Reformed Christians must ask themselves is this: Do I take *this part* of the creeds seriously?"[103] Monsma appears to be arguing that, rather than develop a new confession, more attention should be given to the existing confessions and what they say regarding mission.

---

101. *Our World Belongs to God* (2008), 24.
102. Timothy Monsma, "Mission Themes in the Belgic Confession," *The Outlook* 30.2 (February 1980): 21. Monsma was contacted about the rationale/background for his writing this article, but he could not remember.
103. Monsma, "Mission Themes," 22. Italics have been added by Monsma.

The first explicit interaction with the CT in the CRC press was positive. Writing in May 1983, A. James Heynen related the history of the CT and the process by which it developed. Heynen reported some of the thoughts of the committee members regarding the CT. Gordon Spykman related how speaking of a new "confession" aroused much antipathy in certain corners of the CRC. To mollify this antipathy, "testimony" became the preferred (and eventually adopted) term. The hope of the committee that the CT would eventually receive confessional status on par with the Three Forms of Unity was also expressed. Finally, Richard Mouw was reported as being satisfied with the work of the committee and commenting, "I hoped we could draft a confession that would embarrass a white Afrikaner, that our daughters could read with joy twenty years from now, and that Kuitert couldn't sign. And I think we have."[104] There was no mention of mission anywhere in this article.

The following year, *The Banner* published a critique of the CT by Jacob Binnema. Binnema's critique of the CT is essentially the same as that of Report 45 to Synod 1977 regarding the Song of Hope of the Reformed Church of America. In other words, Binnema found that the prose-poem format limits the theological precision needed. He illustrated his concern with a number of points, but none of them had to do with mission. Binnema stated his assessment of the CT, "I hope it remains very temporary. Its purpose, to speak out against secular trends is excellent, but this Testimony does not reach the high standards of our church's confessions."[105]

An important development before, during, and after the writing of the CT was the emergence of a conservative wing of concerned members in the CRC. These members would eventually depart because they observed the erosion of biblical authority, especially evidenced in matters like the ordination of women to ecclesiastical office. Among these members, the CT came to be known informally by the derogatory moniker "The Contemptible Testimony."

The concerned members of the CRC roundly panned the CT. In two articles, Jelle Tuininga critiqued the CT on a number of points (including theological imprecision), but nothing explicitly to do with mission.[106] Cornelis Venema echoed some of Tuininga's concerns, but was

---

104. A. James Heynen, "The Making of a Confession," *The Banner* 118.20 (May 23, 1983): 15-16.
105. Jacob Binnema, "Beef It Up," *The Banner* 119.43 (November 26, 1984): 11.
106. Jelle Tuininga, "Critique of the Contemporary Testimony," *The Outlook*

also apprehensive about the confessional or quasi-confessional status that the CT was beginning to take on even before it was officially adopted. He also stated that the CT does not "strike one as the common expression of a self-consciously Reformed church." Further, he could find "no compelling reason why a universalist could not embrace it as a statement of his own faith."[107] Of course, as we have seen in an earlier chapter (5.1.5), the question of universalism does fall under the rubric of mission.

In the same month the final draft was approved by Synod 1986, two more critical articles appeared. Timothy Turngren interacted with the final draft. He noted that the CT presented a deficient view of the gospel, diminishing it to God's ownership and love for the world. Turngren asked, "Is this what the Gospel is about? Is this what Paul and Guido de Brès, author of the Belgic Confession, died for? It is not."[108] This weak view of the gospel necessarily entails a weak view of sin, according to Turngren. When the necessity for redemption is weak, sanctification is also negatively impacted. As an example of this, Turngren pointed out the statement of the CT about the Spirit "thrusting" God's people into global missions. He noted that the CT appears to be saying that the Holy Spirit forces believers into missions against their will. Wrote Turngren, "What a difference between this and the Catechism or Canons II.5!"[109] Finally, Turngren noted that the need for the CT arose because of secularization. He asked, "But is the church today facing an essentially different crisis than the church of the 16th and 17th centuries? 'Secularization' simply means 'relating to the worldly or temporal.' How is this any different from the time in which the creeds were written?"[110] His conclusion was that if the challenge was the same, the mission of the church simply remains the same: preach the gospel of Christ crucified.

The second article from June of 1986 was by T. Hoogsteen. Hoogsteen critiqued the CT as being neo-Kuyperian, transformationalist, and

---

34.6 (July/August 1984): 10-11; Jelle Tuininga, "The Contemporary Testimony," *The Outlook* 35.6 (June 1985): 20.

107. Cornelis P. Venema, "The Contemporary Testimony: A New Confession," *Christian Renewal* 4.13 (March 3, 1986): 6-7.

108. Timothy Turngren, "The Contemporary Testimony," *The Outlook* 36.6 (June 1986): 14.

109 Turngren, "The Contemporary Testimony," 15.

110. Turngren, "The Contemporary Testimony," 15.

oriented towards the social gospel. According to this author, the CT essentially confuses church and kingdom. "With the focus on pertinent social issues and in the interest of transformationalism, the Social Gospel concentrates attention downwards into the world."[111] While Hoogsteen did not explicitly mention mission, it was there in the background of this critique. He argued that the church needs to be clear on what its task and calling is: to proclaim the gospel.

In the scheme of things, the CT was a lesser issue in the struggles of the concerned members of the CRC in the 1980s and 1990s. Therefore, after 1986 nothing is heard from these members again about it. However, the CT continued to be promoted in the official CRC press. For example, one of its framers, Morris Greidanus, took up his pen when the 1988 edition of the Psalter Hymnal came off the press — the first edition to include the CT. Greidanus asserted several times that the CT was written with a view not only to building up the church from within, but also as a witness to the world. He noted further that the CT deals with modern issues not found in the Heidelberg Catechism or the other confessions. One of those modern issues is mission.[112] Here Greidanus was popularly recapitulating what he had written four years earlier in *The Reformed Ecumenical Synod Theological Forum*, viz., that the CT fills some crucial gaps in the doctrinal statements of the CRC, a leading one of which is mission.[113]

By way of summary, we may note both positive and negative reactions in the CRC to the CT around the time of its approval. The positive reactions were found among members content with the general trajectory of the CRC in this era. The negative reactions came from the concerned members, members who were more strongly committed to the Three Forms of Unity. Reactions on both sides dealt with the missionary character of the document and some also recognized that it was a reaction to perceived failings in the existing confessions, especially regarding mission.

---

111. T. Hoogsteen, "A Debatable Testimony: One That Ought Not to Have Seen the Light of Day," *Christian Renewal* 4.19 (June 9, 1986): 16-17.
112. Morris N. Greidanus, "A Voice for Today: A Contemporary Testimony," *The Banner* 123.18 (May 9, 1988): 14-15.
113. Morris N. Greidanus, "Case Study No. 4: 'Our World Belongs to God: A Contemporary Testimony of the Christian Reformed Church in North America," *The Reformed Ecumenical Synod Theological Forum* 11.4 (March 1984): 36.

7.2.4 Evaluation

As we engage in some critical reflection on this history and its relevance for our topic, we have the benefit of a little historical distance. As this is being written, more than twenty years have passed since the original CT was adopted by the CRC. In those twenty years, we are able to observe some trends and patterns in missiological thinking in the CRC. The question is whether these trends and patterns can be related to the CT and its relationship with the Belgic Confession since 1971.

The understanding of the gospel expressed in the Three Forms of Unity has been influential in shaping the identity of the CRC. Yet, Craig Van Gelder was not certain that this has been for the better. He argued that these confessions have their own culture-shaped emphases peculiar to the sixteenth and seventeenth centuries. Meanwhile, biblical interpretation has continued to develop. With regard to mission, we now see the importance of "engaging mission in terms of the mission of God (*missio Dei*)." This might be implied in the confessions, but we are moving beyond their emphases. Van Gelder argued that typically the confessions are only used in a defensive mode "as a litmus test of orthodoxy" and such a use diminishes their intention and worth. On this point he concluded, "Let the forms provide for us a partial entryway into our understanding of the Bible, but let us continue to hear the voice of the Spirit through the living Word instruct [sic] us into a deeper understanding of God's truth."[114] Van Gelder, as others before him in the CRC, continues to regard the historical confessions as inadequate when it comes to mission. The key example is in regard to the concept of *missio Dei*. This concept, crucial for Van Gelder, is missing in the Belgic Confession and the other Forms of Unity. While this appears to be a sympathetic-critical stance insofar as the historic confessions are not expected to speak with language from later developments, there is a definite sense that significant progress has been made in thinking about mission since the sixteenth century. But the question may be asked: is this really progress or regress? Did the Belgic Confession (and the other Forms of Unity) emerge from a context where Reformed believers had a better (more biblically-based) understanding of the gospel and the missionary task of the church than some of the influential figures in the CRC of the late twentieth century? Based on what we determined in chapters 1 and 2, we would argue that this is indeed the case.

---

114. Craig Van Gelder, "Revisioning the CRC," in *Together We Gather: Understanding the Mission of the Church* (Grand Rapids: Christian Reformed Home Missions, 1994), 81.

Another central feature in the development of the CT and the (attempted) marginalization of the Belgic Confession was a chronic misunderstanding of the sixteenth-century conception of the relationship between the church and the world. This feature returns in a document prepared by the CRC "Classical Renewal Facilitation Team," entitled *Rethinking Ministry: From Church-Shaped Missions to a Mission-Shaped Church*. Discussing the marks of the true church as formulated by article 29 of the Belgic Confession, the Facilitation Team noted that these marks developed within a Christendom worldview identical to that of the Roman Catholic Church. In this worldview, all are Christians to some degree. As a result, "later Reformed Christians focused so much attention on using the marks to distinguish the true church from the false church that they neglected to pay careful attention to the mission of the church itself." The Team granted that there were a few modest efforts, but nothing of substance. The focus of the church was on Christians, not on unbelievers.[115] When it comes to church government, the principles of the Belgic Confession also reflect its contemporary circumstances and a belief that its surroundings comprise 'Christendom.' According to this document, the reality today is often different and these principles may no longer be sufficient: "An increasingly secular and hostile environment may lead the church to identify additional principles that bear on its structure and work."[116] Here we see the theme of secularization reappear as well as the marginalizing of the Confession by referring to its alleged conception of the (non-)relation between the church and the world. By way of interaction, we can point back to our discussions in earlier chapters (1.1.3 and 3.2) on this point. Reformed believers in the Low Countries of the mid-sixteenth century had a clear understanding of the difference between the church and the world. While there may have been some isolated remnants of the "Christendom" view, many understood that unbelief and wrong belief were rampant in western Europe.

In this regard, Turngren was somewhat correct to identify secularization as an omnipresent challenge for the Christian church.[117] If we

---

115. Classical Renewal Facilitation Team, *Rethinking Ministry: From Church-Shaped Missions to a Mission-Shaped Church* (Grand Rapids: Christian Reformed Home Missions and Christian Reformed World Relief Committee, 1999), 15.
116. *Rethinking Ministry*, 24.
117. See also R. C. Janssen, *By This Our Subscription: Confessional Subscription*

define secularization as a longing for emancipation from organized religion, the sixteenth century featured large numbers of people who were glad for the Reformation simply because they wanted to break free from the Roman Catholic Church, but had no interest in becoming Protestants of any stripe. In this sense, secularization is not a late-twentieth century development, nor was it or is it the greatest challenge for Christians in North America.

However, secularization is often understood as theoretical and especially practical irreligiosity. In this sense, secularization never happened, is not happening, and never will happen. Herbert Schlossberg and others have pointed out the religious nature of the challenges facing Christianity on this continent.[118] It has been observed by many that there has rarely been an age in which people have been more religious. Most of these people want to be religious on their own terms, but there are also growing numbers of adherents of organized non-Christian religions. Rather than secularization, we see a growing trend toward religious pluralism. This is not something that began recently; this trend dates back decades.

Consequently, the forecast of the victory of secularization that was issued in the 1960s to 1980s has been definitively cancelled. Paul Visser provides some helpful insights: "To the amazement of the predictions of Enlightenment philosophers who forecasted the decline of religion — according to the secularization theory that human self-confidence and rational ability would free people from religious superstition — religion did not fade away during the twentieth century but began to explode in both intensity and variety. The world has become massively religious. It is nothing like the secularized world that was predicted by so many analysts of modernity."[119] Secularization theory comes from social science of the 1950s and 1960s. The theory states that modernization inevitably results in the decline of religion, both societally and individually.[120] This theory

---

in the Dutch Reformed Tradition Since 1816 (Kampen: Theologische Universiteit, 2009), 176. Janssen notes that concerns about secularization were already expressed in the 1920s in both the CRC and the Gereformeerde Kerken in Nederland.

118. Herbert Schlossberg, *Idols for Destruction: The Conflict of Christian Faith and American Culture* (Wheaton: Crossway Books, 1990).

119. Paul J. Visser, "Religion in Biblical and Reformed Perspective," *Calvin Theological Journal* 44.1 (April 2009): 9.

120. Peter L. Berger, "The Desecularization of the World: A Global Overview," in *The Desecularization of the World: Resurgent Religion and World Politics*, ed. Peter

has now been widely discarded. For our purposes it is important to note that the CT was predicated upon the acceptance of this theory. It was assumed that secularization was the greatest challenge facing the CRC in this era. But if secularization was not the challenge facing the CRC (or any church), then the CT was the wrong response. If unbelief and wrong belief continue to be the challenge faced by the CRC, then a case can be made that the Belgic Confession continues to be an appropriate confessional response.

We could go through the CT and analyze it in detail. However, we want to limit our analysis and evaluation to the document as it developed in relation to the Belgic Confession. More recent interactions with both are helpful. In this respect, Kevin Schutte's 2003 MA thesis is revealing. Schutte interviewed three CRC church-planting pastors. There was some discussion with each pastor about the Belgic Confession and its relation to their work. All three pastors were insistent on the need either to re-articulate or dismiss the paradigms of the creeds and confessions, including — and especially — the Belgic Confession.[121] Schutte himself was more appreciative of the Confession, even arguing that the marks of article 29 "can be understood as being missional."[122] He went on to state that the very writing of the confessions and the time at which they were written is "evidence of missional behavior and action."[123] Schutte concluded with gratitude for the "missional spirit" of the Reformed confessions.[124] The interesting thing about this thesis is that the CT is not mentioned at all. While the Belgic Confession is still being discussed and there is debate and disagreement about its missiological relevance, the CT is the document that has been marginalized. At least in this instance, this would seem to indicate that the CT is not functioning in the CRC as originally envisioned. When reflecting on the missionary task of the church, these CRC pastors at least did not turn to the CT for guidance.

In summary, the CT grew out of a number of intertwined developments. Among an influential and vocal minority, there was a dissatisfaction with the existing confessions and quite often the Belgic Confession was singled out. Some of this dissatisfaction had to do with the inferior

---

L. Berger (Washington: Ethics and Public Policy Center, 1999), 2.
121. Schutte, "The Missional Church," 68-69.
122. Schutte, "The Missional Church," 83.
123. Schutte, "The Missional Church," 83.
124. Schutte, "The Missional Church," 84.

edition of the Confession then in use in the CRC and this brought out debate about revision and subscription. Confessional dissatisfaction was also expressed in regard to the missionary task of the church. The Belgic Confession was regarded as irrelevant on this score, but only because the definition of mission was beginning to shift, and CRC missiologists were emphasizing the concept of *missio Dei*. While this concept remains in ascendance today, there is much reason to question it. In addition, the state of Reformation historiography was such that sixteenth-century history was not read or understood in its own terms and context. Newer historiography has remedied this situation in many regards, but it has yet to filter down to how most mission historians portray the sixteenth century. Finally, the perceived need for a new confession was directly linked to the uncritical acceptance of the secularization theory. Certain key figures recognized that a new confession would not be possible unless the CRC was *in statu confessionis*. Secularization provided the rationale to argue for this, even though the acceptance of this theory would later prove to have been premature. Today, so far as our research can determine, the CT does not function in CRC missiological discussions, whereas the Belgic Confession continues to receive some limited (and sometimes negatively critical) attention.

7.3 Conclusion

In the late twentieth century, the CRC felt the need to augment its confessions because these existing confessions were regarded by some as inadequate in certain areas, including and especially mission. As we have noted, the Belgic Confession was identified as being particularly problematic. Robert Recker's 1972 article emphatically underlined this point. The CT developed in response to this perceived need to fill doctrinal gaps. Recker's article was part of this development, and Recker himself would eventually be involved with the process of writing the CT. Looking to the present, despite the intentions of its framers, the CT continues to have a subordinate status to the Belgic Confession and the other Forms of Unity

We may applaud the CRC for giving such concentrated attention to the missionary task of the church in the late twentieth century. This was an important discussion, even if there were shortcomings and limitations. We may note the historiographic limitations that prevented or discouraged a more sympathetic reading of the Confession (and its context). Next, there were social scientific limitations that prevented or discouraged a more accurate reading of the culture. Finally, we may note the missiological limitations that disallowed or discouraged critical analysis of the concept of *missio Dei* and its corollary, the comprehensive approach. These notes help *us* to give a more sympathetic-critical reading to the history of the CT. We are all children of our time and context.

Recognizing these things, one can say that the development of the CT and the attempted marginalization of the Belgic Confession vis-à-vis mission was almost inevitable. It was ultimately unnecessary, unsuccessful and lamentable, but seemingly unavoidable. If we may conclude this chapter on a more positive and certain note, this history does not inevitably have to be repeated.

Chapter Eight
Confession and Reformed Missiology

8.0 Introduction

As we draw to the close of this study, it is worthwhile to consider the relationship between the Reformed confessions and missiology. How do these two relate to one another? Closely connected with that question is something that was mentioned in the last chapter dealing with the Christian Reformed Church in North America: under what conditions might a new confession become desirable or necessary? Or what about a confessional revision? Further, if such a new confession or revision is developed at some point, what sorts of contributions might Reformed missiology make?

To consider these questions, we begin with a brief exploration of the relationship between the confessions and Reformed theology. Then we draw the circle tighter with Reformed missiology. Finally, we consider the question of what it means for a church to be in a state where a confession is necessary (*in statu confessionis*), and how one might determine whether one is in such a state.

8.1 The Confession and Reformed Theology

The relationship between the confession and Reformed theology has often been explored. One can easily speak of a broad consensus about the contours of this relationship. But before we explore those contours, we need to be clear about our definitions.

By "the confession" we simply mean the collection of creeds and confessions adopted by Reformed and Presbyterian churches. In the nature of the case, we specifically have in mind the Ecumenical Creeds (Apostles', Nicene, and Athanasian) and the Three Forms of Unity (Belgic Confession, Heidelberg Catechism, and Canons of Dort), though our conclusions could easily be extended to apply to churches with other confessions.

"Reformed theology" is theology in the broadest sense of the term, not in the sense of systematic theology or dogmatics. Rather, what we mean is the study of God and his revelation under which all the different departments are subsumed. According to one taxonomy in Reformed seminaries, those departments are the bibliological, dogmatological, ecclesiological, and diaconiological. We qualify this term with "Reformed" to indicate that those engaged in this study emerge from a certain history and doctrinal commitment which can be traced back to the Protestant Reformation, particularly in its Calvinistic wing.

Next we need to consider the question of priority. Logically and historically, theology always takes priority over the confession.[1] Confessions are the ecclesiastical fruit of theological (especially, but not exclusively, dogmatic) reflection and investigation in the Word of God. Our confessions were produced by theologians working carefully with the Scriptures and then, as deftly and faithfully as possible, reproducing the key teachings of Scripture in a document for the church. In this sense, the making of creeds and confessions can be described as a scientific procedure — not in the sense of the modern scientific method, but in that they are the product of meticulous theological science.[2]

All of that means that confessional documents at the same time are and are not theological documents. They are theological in the sense that one can speak of them as containing theological statements — things which have to do with the study of God and of his revelation. One could even speak of, for instance, "the theology of the Belgic Confession." However, they are not theological in the sense of being produced by academics for academia.[3] In this sense, the confessions are not theological documents, but ecclesiastical; they belong not to academia, but to the church. In them, it is the church — not the academy — that speaks and confesses her faith, albeit in a theologically responsible manner.

---

1. This has been a matter of debate in Reformed circles. For one example, see the debate between Daubanton and Bavinck described by Janssen, *By This Our Subscription*, 171.

2. Paul Woolley, "What is a Creed For? Some Answers from History," in *Scripture and Confession: A Book About Confessions Old and New*, ed. John H. Skilton (Phillipsburg: Presbyterian and Reformed Publishing Co., 1973), 97, 124.

3. Norman Shepherd, "Scripture and Confession," in *Scripture and Confession*, 21.

Confessions were developed by theologians, but then adopted by the church. We see this, for instance, with the Belgic Confession. Written by de Brès, who was not only a pastor, but also a capable theologian, the Confession was likely adopted by the Reformed churches in Belgium even before its publication.[4] The Confession quickly received ecclesiastical sanction so that it could meaningfully use the first person plural — not only at the beginning, but throughout. Thus it could be said: "We all believe with the heart and confess with the mouth..."

As confessions receive ecclesiastical sanction as faithful summaries of the Word and are received as doctrinal standards, they in turn become touchstones or even rules of faith (*regula fidei*) for further theological reflection and investigation, but also are subject to that investigation. On the one hand, Reformed theologians subscribe these confessions and make them their own and often have them guide their work either overtly or in a presuppositional manner. Jaroslav Pelikan asserts that an important function of creeds and confessions is that they define rules of biblical hermeneutics.[5] However, this has been more true of the relationship between the Roman Catholic Church and its creeds than those churches descended from the Protestant Reformation. Nevertheless, after over four hundred years, eventually even in Reformed theology the confession inevitably creates a presuppositional framework for biblical hermeneutics. Especially for those born and raised in Reformed churches, the confession naturally informs our preunderstanding of how to read the Bible before we even read the Bible.

In principle, Scripture has been rightly described in classical Reformed theology as the epistemological or cognitive foundation (*principium cognoscendi*). To put it a different way, Scripture is the norming norm (*norma normans*) for theology, whereas the confession is the normed norm (*norma normata*). Theology and the confession are always subject to Scripture and Scripture is also the source, root, and foundation for both.[6]

---

4. Gootjes, *The Belgic Confession*, 115.
5. Jaroslav Pelikan, *Credo*, 142.
6. Richard A. Muller, *After Calvin: Studies in the Development of a Theological Tradition* (New York: Oxford UP, 2003), 52. Speaking of seventeenth-century Reformed theology, Muller writes, "... the large-scale dogmatic projects of the day were consistently conceived within the creedal and confessional boundaries — not out of undue deference to these secondary authorities but on the assumption that these churchly standards had been framed and tested by the study of Scripture and were, therefore, sound guides to the limits of theological formulation."

Theology is not above being critiqued by the Word of God and neither is the confession.

Therefore, we can speak of a reciprocity between the confession and Reformed theology. Each informs and develops the other. Theology has given the confession to the church. Theology serves the church and does so on the foundation of the Word of God, also looking to the summary of the Word of God in the confession. Theology not only builds on and is guided by the confession, but also, where necessary, humbly suggests places where the confession may be improved. In so doing, it also serves the church. The confession and theology need each other. The confession is the voice of the church and the church and theology have a responsibility towards one another.[7] Herman Ridderbos said it well when he pointed out that theology serves the church; theology which places itself outside or above the confessions, places itself outside the church, loses its servant character, and will ultimately become unfruitful (or worse) for the church.[8] Consequently, it is imperative that Reformed theology be confessional — which means that Reformed theology must be respectfully, sympathetically, and symbiotically engaged with the confession.

8.2 The Confession and Reformed Missiology

In chapter 2, we defined mission as "the official sending of the church to go and make disciples by preaching and witnessing to the good news of Jesus Christ in all nations through the power of the Holy Spirit" (2.2). We then defined missiology as the study of this mission in all its various aspects (2.5). However, at that point, we did not place missiology within the framework of theological encyclopedia. Obviously, it is a field within theology, but where do we place it? Different answers have been given to that question. For our purposes, it is adequate to place it within the diaconiological department, or what some have labelled "practical theology."[9]

More important, but less considered in the literature, is the relationship between the confession and Reformed missiology. Some thought has gone into the relationship between the confession and theology in general, and even more into the relationship between the confession and dog-

---

7. Dr. J. Van Genderen, *Confessie en theologie* (Apeldoornse Studies) (Kampen: J. H. Kok, 1975), 26.

8. Quoted in Van Genderen, *Confessie en theologie*, 26-27. "De theologie, die zich buiten of boven de confessie stelt, stelt zich buiten de kerk, verliest haar dienend karakter en wordt voor de kerk onvruchtbaar, zo niet erger."

9. See Bavinck, *An Introduction to the Science of Missions*, xx.

matics.¹⁰ Yet, it is virtually impossible to find anyone who has given any careful reflection on the relationship between the Reformed confessions and missiology, especially in the English speaking world. For instance, J. H. Bavinck gives no consideration to this question in *An Introduction to the Science of Missions*. The confession does not seem to function at all in his missiology.¹¹ While Harvie Conn extensively argues that Western creeds have little to no value on foreign mission fields, he also does not engage the question of what positive function the confession might have in missiology.¹² It seems this is a discussion which still needs to take place, and what can be offered here is only a small beginning contribution.

We noted that the confession is the product of theological reflection and investigation in the Word of God. That was "theology" in general. But what about missiology? Is the Reformed confession a fruit of *missiological* reflection? This must be regarded as an anachronistic question, since missiology as a field is a much later development in theology. We might regard Guido de Brès as a theologian in some sense, but there is no sense in which we may properly regard him as a missiologist. He did not systematically or carefully study the missionary task of the church, nor could we reasonably expect him to have done so. However, as we have seen, he did have a missionary perspective in his theology and that perspective has been transmitted into the Belgic Confession. Therefore, one can say that the Belgic Confession is a fruit of theological reflection which included a missionary perspective.

What was just considered was a question of history. Bringing matters into the present, we ought also to explore how the confession informs missiological reflection and investigation today. In chapter 5, we reflected on some ways in which the Belgic Confession might provide a doctrinal foundation for the further development of Reformed missiology. Here we want to take a methodological step back and consider the way in which the confession (in general) relates to missiology.

As for theology in general, Scripture must be the cognitive foundation (*principium cognoscendi*) for missiology. While missiology makes use of

---

10. See, for instance, Herman Bavinck, *Reformed Dogmatics* (Vol.1: Prolegomena), ed. John Bolt, trans. John Vriend (Grand Rapids: Baker Academic, 2003), 31, 88-89.

11. This is confirmed by reference to Paul Visser's *Heart for the Gospel, Heart for the World*. Visser makes no mention of Bavinck's use of the confession in his missiology or any consideration of the relationship of the confession to missiology.

12. Conn, *Eternal Word and Changing Worlds*, 211-260.

insights from other fields (even non-theological ones such as anthropology), the foundation of missiology (the norming norm — *norma normans*) must always be Scripture alone (as noted in 5.1.5). Everything must be evaluated according to the norm of God's Word. Like a dogmatician, a Reformed missiologist will both begin and end with Holy Writ. Whence then the confession?

It may be argued that, since it has been proven to be faithful to Scripture and ecclesiastically sanctioned as such, the confession forms an ancillary component of the *principium cognoscendi*. The confession is a reliable compendium of biblical truths. Still, it is ancillary; as a human document it must remain subordinate to Scripture. Furthermore, we must also remember that in the confession, the church speaks out of Scripture, and missiology, like theology in general, exists to serve the church and its outreach. As a corollary of its servant character, Reformed missiology must listen to the church's voice.

From a practical perspective, this means that the Reformed missiologist must turn to Scripture as he seeks to develop his science. But at the same time, since both he and his science are servants of the church, he will turn to the confessions of the church — also because that confession is something he has made his own. He will ask, "What have I confessed about this from the Scriptures, together with my brothers and sisters in the church? What is the bearing of my confession, of *our* confession, on this subject or this point that I am studying?" Those insights should be capitalized upon and incorporated into Reformed missiology.

The symbiotic character of the relationship between theology and the confession is recapitulated at this point. As the missiologist studies the confession *and* Scripture, he might discover places in the confession where a scriptural missionary consciousness is lacking. He would serve the church by drawing attention to these places. In his studies, a missiologist may discern and highlight places where a scriptural missionary perspective is latent in the confession, but could be developed and expanded. He could further be of service to the church and its confession by bringing his scriptural insights to the table if and when a new confession (either supplementary or a replacement) is deemed necessary.

This study has established that the Belgic Confession holds continuing relevance for the study of Christian mission in all its various aspects. Not only is it relevant, it also continues to be more than adequate. It addresses the church's task to preach the gospel of Christ to the unbelieving world. It is especially strong on reminding us of the missiological significance of martyrdom and persecution, a message we need to hear in our affluent and secure Western societies. It can be argued that the Belgic Confession is a relatively unplowed field that will, as it is further worked in the years to come, bear a greater harvest for Reformed missiology.

However, that conclusion makes one key assumption: that things will remain much the same for the foreseeable future. Our Reformed churches will continue to exist in relative peace and prosperity. We will maintain our comfortable and prosperous lives. Yet what if that assumption is wrong? Given the patterns of history, quite likely it is wrong. If it is wrong, will the Belgic Confession continue to be relevant and adequate for guiding the church's study of mission, not to mention other areas?

That leads us to some thoughts about the question of *status confessionis*.

8.3 STATUS CONFESSIONIS?

In surveying the development of new confessions since 1945, Eberhard Busch enthusiastically concluded that there was "an unmistakable, living, new *confessional eagerness*" among "members of the world Reformed family."[13] He noted that Lukas Vischer's 1982 anthology *Reformed Witness Today* contained more than thirty new confessions from Reformed churches worldwide. Engaging in some possible hyperbole, Vischer is cited as saying there has been "no time in which . . . so many confessions have been compiled as in the last three decades."[14] Meanwhile, many Reformed churches have not been part of this "new confessional eagerness," but have been content with the existing Reformation-era confessions and early church creeds. These developments may lead us to question whether we perhaps are *in statu confessionis*. Have all these other churches around the world noticed something that we have not? Is this the time to supplement or replace our existing confessions?

Before answering that, we need to examine more carefully the terminology. Despite its Latin garb, the term *status confessionis* does not have a

---

13. Eberhard Busch, "The Closeness of the Distant: Reformed Confessions after 1945," in *Toward the Future of Reformed Theology: Tasks, Topics, Traditions*, ed. David Willis and Michael Welker (Grand Rapids: Eerdmans, 1999), 518. Italics are original.

14. Busch, "The Closeness of the Distant," 512-513. Vischer's statement may either be hyperbole or simply incorrect. Pelikan notes that the age of the Reformation featured the proliferation of confessions: "For the Dutch Reformation alone, and only for the sixteenth century, the detailed bibliography of William Heijting comes to two substantial volumes" (*Credo*, 460).

lengthy pedigree in Protestant theology. According to D. J. Smit, the term itself was probably used for the first time in 1927 by Horst Stephan in an article on 'confession' for *Die Religion in Geschichte und Gegenwart*.[15] A form of the concept may, however, be detected in the Lutheran Formula of Concord of 1577. The Formula of Concord article 10 speaks of times "when a confession is called for" and times "when a clear-cut confession of faith is demanded of us."[16] The concept emerges from German Protestantism, and the terminology eventually also appears in this context. It becomes an important term in the struggle of the confessing church in Germany against the "German Christians" and the Third Reich — a struggle which resulted in the production of the Barmen Declaration of 1934. One of the key figures involved with the development of the Barmen Declaration was Karl Barth, and in his *Church Dogmatics* he gave some attention to the contours of *status confessionis*.[17] We will interact with some of his insights in 8.3.3.

Following the Second World War, the concept appears to have been relatively dormant for a number of years. It reappears in the late 1960s and early 1970s in the writings of men such as D. K. Wielenga and G. C. Berkouwer.[18] It receives the greatest prominence in the discussions in South Africa leading up to and following the development of the Belhar Confession. The Belhar Confession was a response from the Dutch Reformed Mission Church to the socio-political issue of apartheid. This confession emerges from an ecumenical perspective informed by liberation theology. In the later part of the twentieth century, *status confessionis* becomes a common term in circles influenced by this theology. As we noted in the last chapter, it also featured in the discussions in the Christian Reformed Church in North America in the development of the Contemporary Testimony.

Surprisingly, most theological dictionaries and encyclopedias do not have an entry for *status confessionis*. An exception is Paul Hinlicky's ar-

---

15. D. J. Smit, "What does *Status Confessionis* Mean?" in *A Moment of Truth: The Confession of the Dutch Reformed Mission Church, 1982*, ed. G. D. Cloete and D. J. Smit (Grand Rapids: Eerdmans, 1984), 9.

16. *The Book of Concord: the Confessions of the Evangelical Lutheran Church*, trans. and ed. Theodore G. Tappert (Philadelphia: Fortress Press, 1959), 492-493.

17. Karl Barth, *Church Dogmatics* III/4, ed. G. W. Bromiley and T. F. Torrance (Edinburgh: T. and T. Clark, 1961), 73-86.

18. D. K. Wielenga J. Dzn., *De akker is de wereld* (Amsterdam: Uitgeverij Ton Bolland, 1971), 31-72;   G. C. Berkouwer, *The Church*, trans. James E. Davison (Grand Rapids: Eerdmans, 1976), 299-309.

ticle in *The Encyclopedia of Christianity*.[19] He defines the term as follows: "The Latin term *status confessionis* means the stance of a witness summoned to testify. In the 20th century the term acquired the technical sense among Protestants of a binding doctrinal stance on socio-political questions."[20] The emphasis on the socio-political is worth noting. Robert McAfee Brown writes in a similar vein: "every now and then the issues become so clear, and the stakes so high, that the privilege of amiable disagreement must be superseded by clear-cut decisions, and the choice must move from 'both/and' to 'either/or.' Such a time is called a *status confessionis*, a 'confessional situation.'"[21] As Brown formulates it, there are moments when the Church must take a stand, and typically this is in regards to social and political issues. Milan Opocênsky defines it thus: "*Status confessionis* refers to a radically challenging situation — a *Grenzsituation* [a water-shed moment]. It is a matter of life and death. Such a declaration stems from the conviction that in an alarming situation of oppression, exploitation, hypocrisy, and heresy, when the boundaries between right and wrong, between good and evil are blurred, the integrity of the gospel and its proclamation are stake."[22]

Can this concept be appropriated? It is clear that the concept, as it has been formulated in the last century, carries a substantial amount of heterogeneous baggage that should concern confessionally Reformed theologians. However, if we clarify that our use of this term is limited to what Hinlicky describes as "the stance of a witness summoned to testify," then this concept and terminology may be used. To clarify further, when the church is in a place where the call to confess what is believed becomes undeniable, that is a *status confessionis*. This might have reference to socio-political questions, but it does not have to necessarily.

Framing the issue in this way, a church can be *in statu confessionis* because of its young age. A recently established church on a mission field may be in a situation where it is called to formulate its beliefs in its own

---

19. Paul R. Hinlicky, "Status confessionis," in *The Encyclopedia of Christianity* (Vol.5), ed. Erwin Fahlbusch, Jan Milič Lochman, John Mbiti, Jaroslav Pelikan, and Lukas Vischer (Grand Rapids: Eerdmans, 2008), 198-201.
20. Hinlicky, "Status confessionis," 198.
21. Robert McAfee Brown ed., *Kairos: Three Prophetic Challenges to the Church*, (Grand Rapids: Eerdmans, 1990), 7.
22. Milan Opocênsky, "Processus Confessionis," in *Reformed Theology: Identity and Ecumenicity*, ed. Wallace M. Alston Jr. and Michael Welker (Grand Rapids: Eerdmans, 2003), 394.

words, language, and cultural setting. This confession becomes a testimony to the unbelieving world. This was exactly the situation that the churches in the Low Countries found themselves in the early 1560s. This is a situation that repeats itself throughout history.

Yet, there is also the question of whether older churches may find themselves *in statu confessionis*. As with the younger churches, this may also be related to the missionary task of the church in a given situation. This is worthy of some further investigation and to facilitate that, it will be helpful to consider the thoughts of two figures: Abraham Kuyper (1837-1920) and Robert Bertram (1921-2003).

8.3.1 Abraham Kuyper

The name of Abraham Kuyper is still well-known in Reformed and Presbyterian circles. He was a Dutch pastor, theologian, author, educator, and statesman in the late nineteenth and early twentieth centuries. Kuyper led the Doleantie movement out of the Nederlands Hervormde Kerk in 1886. He was a widely respected leader not only in the church but also in education and politics. He established the Free University of Amsterdam in 1880 and served as Prime Minister of the Netherlands from 1901 to 1905. His theological influence would be felt in Reformed circles in the Netherlands and North America well into the twentieth century.

Abraham Kuyper
(1837-1920)

Although the term *status confessionis* does not appear to have existed in the time of Abraham Kuyper, the concept certainly did. In the early 1890s, there was a discussion about confessional revision in American Presbyterianism. This was not so much a matter of producing a new confession but amending the existing confessions to better address the pressing issues of the day. Such discussions had also taken place in the Netherlands dating back to the 1860s.[23] Kuyper interacted with the American developments in a lengthy article published in *The Presbyterian and Reformed Review* in 1891.[24]

---

23. Janssen, *By This Our Subscription*, 136, 156.
24. Abraham Kuyper, "Calvinism and Confessional Revision," trans. Geerhardus Vos, *The Presbyterian and Reformed Review* 7 (July 1891): 369-399.

In the course of his reflections, Kuyper outlined what would for us amount to four conditions necessary for an established church to be *in statu confessionis*. In the first place, Calvinism does not endeavour to devise its confession apart from some kind of pressing circumstance which reaches into its very soul. As examples, Kuyper mentions the Reformation-era confessions in France, Switzerland, the Netherlands, Scotland, and England. Furthermore, he says, "The impulse giving birth to such a confession did not come from the spirit of man, but from the Spirit of the Lord." The Holy Spirit led these churches to a point where they were not able to do anything but confess. This work of the Spirit also leads Kuyper to state, probably with some rhetorical exaggeration, that the words of these confessions "spontaneously suggested themselves."[25] We assume this is rhetorical, because in the case of the Belgic Confession, it is clear that de Brès did not spontaneously produce this document apart from careful thought and preparation. The use of various sources (Calvin, the Gallican Confession, etc.) is evidence enough that spontaneity was not a factor in the production of the Belgic Confession.

In the second place, Kuyper maintains a close connection between exegesis and confession. The Holy Spirit satisfies the desire for a confession through the exposition of the Word: "From the Holy Spirit the impulse proceeds, from the Word the contents are taken in which it finds utterance."[26] Reformed churches simply wish to echo in their own words and language what God himself has said in Scripture.

Third, in its method of developing a confession, Calvinism consistently excludes individualism and sectarianism. Calvinists never issue an official confession of faith without the assurance that the same voice has been spoken by other Reformed believers in other places. Kuyper writes:

> Only after perceiving that the one Spirit has by means of the one Word everywhere produced the same conviction in the hearts of all that move in the same current, they feel warranted to make a public profession in the name of the Church and to formulate in writing that same faith which has been sealed with the blood of their brethren at the stake. Hence it is that Calvinists always and everywhere have struck the same keynote in their confessions; that they subscribed each other's symbols; that in draw-

---

25. Kuyper, "Calvinism and Confessional Revision," 385.
26. Kuyper, "Calvinism and Confessional Revision," 386.

ing up and revising their Standards they always solicited one another's advice; and that in point of fact in their various creeds they have professed one and the same faith.[27]

In other words, according to Kuyper, no Reformed church can recognize its *status confessionis* or proceed to produce a new confession without taking seriously its ecumenical relationships and seeking the advice of brothers and sisters elsewhere. There must be an ecumenical consensus for there to be a true *status confessionis*. Although he did not mention this, it may be noted that Kuyper's position here was not unique; Hendrik De Cock had held a similar position some decades earlier.[28]

Finally, the work of the Holy Spirit returns in Kuyper's fourth point: "We must observe that the Calvinists never proceeded to formulate their confession until after and only so far as the Holy Spirit had clearly given them to understand the meaning of the divine Word on disputed points."[29] The writing of confessions requires a sufficient level of theological maturity and development. For a church to be *in statu confessionis*, it is necessary that her theologians be able to provide leadership in plain and clear speaking on whatever matters are pressing upon her. Although Kuyper does not mention this, it would seem that this would also be a prerequisite for young churches on mission fields as well.

Being the main subject of his article, Kuyper also comes to several points regarding confessional revision. He began by noting that this question came up in the context of the debate between the orthodox Reformed and the Remonstrants at the beginning of the seventeenth century. There was a definite difference of opinion between the Reformed and the Remonstrants regarding the confessions. According to Kuyper, the Remonstrants viewed the confessions exclusively as products of human study and, as such, subject to regular review and revision. On the other hand, the Calvinists stated that "our confession did not originate from man alone, and shall not be treated as a bare product of human study."[30] Unfortunately, Kuyper does not provide primary source material to support these statements. He went on to state that the confessions are a gift from God to the church — and not just for one generation, but for all future generations until the end of the age. The church is therefore bound to submit to this truth and to keep this

---

27. Kuyper, "Calvinism and Confessional Revision," 386.
28. See Janssen, *By This Our Subscription*, 58.
29. Kuyper, "Calvinism and Confessional Revision," 386.
30. Kuyper, "Calvinism and Confessional Revision," 392.

treasure untarnished. So, when the Synod of Dort ultimately dealt with the Remonstrants, no one was allowed to contribute to the discussion about the existing confessions unless he had first unconditionally and unreservedly subscribed them. From this sympathetic standpoint, questions about the confessions would be resolved by recourse to the Scriptures.[31] In the nature of the case, this resulted in the strengthening of the Belgic Confession on a number of points.

It is readily apparent that the era of the Synod of Dort was one of grave crisis in the Reformed churches. This crisis led not only to a new confession (the Canons of Dort), but also to revision of the existing confessions, especially the Belgic. Kuyper then asked himself whether his day was also an era of crisis. He acknowledged that "in these very days our Churches are passing through a crisis of the most serious character." He highlights the growing chasm dug by Schleiermacher and others between subjective convictions and the objective confessions.[32] Yet, was the crisis of such a nature that a confessional revision was required? Kuyper was not convinced. He stated that four conditions were necessary before this could take place.

First of all, the development would have to serve the church and be a richer unfolding of what Kuyper called "the Calvinistic principle." By that principle, he means the "knowledge of God almighty," or the profession of God's expansive sovereignty.[33] Second, there must be complete unanimity in all the churches regarding this unfolding. Third, "Calvinistic theology must have made sufficient progress to furnish the churches with adequate means for formulating this development." Finally, looking to ecumenical relationships, foreign churches must have also developed similar convictions.[34]

According to Abraham Kuyper, none of those conditions were met in 1891. In fact, he stated that to engage in confessional revision in that day would have been detrimental to the Reformed churches in the Netherlands, though he did not presume to speak for American Presbyterians. In the Dutch context, Kuyper stated that producing a revision at this time would have resulted in only more revisions in the near future and that, instead of strengthening faith, it "would be turned into

---

31. Kuyper, "Calvinism and Confessional Revision," 393.
32. Kuyper, "Calvinism and Confessional Revision," 394.
33. Kuyper, "Calvinism and Confessional Revision," 379.
34. Kuyper, "Calvinism and Confessional Revision," 394-395.

a very hurtful instrument for injuring the faith of our people to an ever-increasing extent." He also stated that a confessional appendix along the lines of the Canons of Dort was also not desirable at that time. It would first be necessary to purge the atmosphere of the Reformed churches of certain heterogeneous elements.[35]

In this article, there is no missionary perspective or consciousness. Kuyper does not entertain the notion that the existing Reformed confessions are somehow lacking in the area of mission, nor does he interact with those who might be of that mind. Furthermore, some of his idiosyncrasies are in evidence here and need to be carefully pruned away.[36] Nevertheless, Kuyper does have something to contribute to this discussion, and in 8.3.3 we will come back and evaluate his contribution and appropriate some of his more helpful insights.

8.3.2 Robert Bertram

Our discussion now turns to a figure from American Lutheranism. In the 1960s and 1970s, a struggle developed within the Lutheran Church — Missouri Synod (LCMS). The LCMS had long been known for its confessional orthodoxy among Lutheran bodies. However, the confessional commitments of the LCMS eventually came into question, specifically on issues of biblical authority and interpretation, as well as the ecumenical relationships with other Lutheran and non-Lutheran churches. In 1974, this controversy came to a head with a major development at the official seminary of the LCMS in St. Louis, Missouri. The majority of students and faculty left Concordia Seminary and established a "Seminary in Exile" (or "Seminex"). These developments also led to the formation of the Association of Evangelical Lutheran Churches, which itself would soon be folded into the Evangelical Lutheran Church of America (ELCA).

Robert Bertram was one of the professors who left Concordia Seminary in 1974. He was an influential teacher and lecturer, although only

---

35. Kuyper, "Calvinism and Confessional Revision," 398.

36. With the language of "the Calvinistic principle," Kuyper appears to adhere to the central dogma theory made popular in the eighteenth century by Alexander Schweizer and others. He also appears to make John Calvin the measure of all things Reformed. For discussion on the problematic nature of these positions, see Richard A. Muller, *Post-Reformation Reformed Dogmatics* (Vol. 1: Prolegomena to Theology, Second Edition) (Grand Rapids: Baker Academic, 2003), 39; and especially Muller, *After Calvin*, 47-63. Janssen also identifies Kuyper's ecclesiology functioning in this article, as well as his view of confessional documents as "graces of providence." See *By This Our Subscription*, 158.

one book of his was published, and that posthumously. He was regarded highly as a theologian in the ELCA.

The battles in the LCMS form the background to his discussions of *status confessionis* in his book *A Time for Confessing*. While the term is often applied to situations of socio-political turmoil, here it is applied to a situation of intra-ecclesiastical polemics. It was Bertram's position that the alleged heavy-handedness and theological rigidity of the LCMS bureaucracy forced the church *in statu confessionis*.

Bertram defined *status confessionis* forensically and he linked it to the biblical notion of μαρτυρες (*martures*; witnesses). Accordingly, "the confessors are on trial for their faith before a superior critical tribunal from whose higher authority they must nevertheless dissent."[37] Edward Schroeder summarized Bertram's definition in his Foreword, saying that it "means being on the witness stand, on trial, out in public, before the authorities. You are in the dock, accused of 'bad' faith and under orders to 'fess up,' to testify (*martyria* in Greek, with the overtones included), seeking to show your critics that the faith they call bad is indeed the faith that Christ commends."[38] In that particular situation, "the authorities" were the establishment of the LCMS. He does provide other examples throughout *A Time for Confessing*; for instance, the American civil rights movement (American government authorities), apartheid (South African authorities) and the German confessional church in the time of the Third Reich.

To develop his understanding of this concept, Bertram appealed to the Formula of Concord and the elements of article 10 that were mentioned above in the introduction to this section. He also appealed to the Augsburg Confession.[39] In these old Lutheran symbols, Bertram found his paradigm for what it means to be a confessing church in the face of opposition and even persecution.

There are a number of clues, says Bertram, as to when a church may find itself in a *tempus confessionis* or *in statu confessionis*.[40] The first

---

37. Robert W. Bertram, *A Time for Confessing*, ed. Michael Hoy (Grand Rapids: Eerdmans, 2008), 2.
38. Bertram, *A Time for Confessing*, xi.
39. Bertram, *A Time for Confessing*, 1-22.
40. We will look at five here. According to Schroeder (xii), there are six. The sixth is "ambiguous certitude." Bertram himself says (1) that there are a half dozen clues from the Lutheran symbols, but only deals with five in chapter 1. "Ambiguous certitude" is discussed in chapter 7, but it is not clear that this is a clue.

is when an answer is demanded by those in authority. These authorities can be either political or ecclesiastical. Bertram speaks of this as "confessing as *martyria*."[41] Second, there is "confessing as protesting gospel-plus." This envisions a time in which those in authority are subverting the gospel by "embellishing, reinforcing, [and] safeguarding." It also includes points at which the authorities are imposing adiaphora as necessities.[42] Next, there may be a *status confessionis* when ecumenical interests are at stake. Times for confessing are "also in their dissent, moves towards reunification."[43]

In the fourth place, Bertram says that confessing may be required in order to redefine authority. A *tempus confessionis* is one in which those in authority need to be put in their place and reminded of the proper contours and limits of their power.[44] Confessing is also necessary as an appeal for and to those who are oppressed. Confession is required when false brethren are secretly bringing in a yoke of slavery to burden poor consciences and to demoralize people. This is oriented *for* them, but there is also an orientation *to* them. The oppressed need to be taken seriously as responsible agents. Writes Bertram, "Their justification, their divine revaluing on account of Christ, is not some remote transaction conducted behind their backs, but on the contrary involves them quite directly as participating agents."[45]

As with Kuyper, there is no explicit missionary perspective in this summary presentation of the clues for *status confessionis*. It may be argued that it is implicit, especially in the first two clues. Yet, through all of this discussion it is clear that Bertram's main concern is the struggle within and against the LCMS. This is not so much a case of the church witnessing to the world with its confessing, but rather the faithful church confessing to and against the unfaithful church. Nevertheless, Bertram did endeavour to build his understanding of *status confessionis* from the Lutheran symbols and some aspects of his study will prove helpful.

8.3.3 Evaluation

In both Kuyper and Bertram, we find an emphasis on a serious crisis as a criteria for a church being *in statu confessionis*. Confronted by grave

---

41. Bertram, *A Time for Confessing*, 2-4.
42. Bertram, *A Time for Confessing*, 4-8.
43. Bertram, *A Time for Confessing*, 8-12.
44. Bertram, *A Time for Confessing*, 12-19.
45. Bertram, *A Time for Confessing*, 21.

doctrinal concerns or the demands of hostile authorities, a church may find itself required to confess its faith. This is a helpful emphasis that contains an incipient missionary perspective — it accords with what the Lord Jesus told his disciples in Matthew 10:18-20: "You will be brought before governors and kings for my sake, as a testimony to them and to the Gentiles. But when they deliver you up, do not worry about how or what you should speak. For it will be given to you in that hour what you should speak; for it is not you who speak, but the Spirit of your Father who speaks in you." This would appear to be what Kuyper had in mind as he spoke of spontaneity in the formulation of confessions — however, while this passage is relevant to our topic, it must be acknowledged that what was envisioned in Matthew 10 is not the writing of ecclesiastical confessions per se. Nevertheless, the point remains that a *status confessionis* is not something that we do create or place ourselves in; it is something to be recognized. While Karl Barth was wrong on many things, he did get this right and he is worth quoting at length:

> That Daniel had to spend some time in the lion's den was a quite extraordinary situation. And even in this situation he was not expected to pull the animals' tails. Similarly, the first disciples of Jesus were not asked to provoke anyone by their behaviour merely in order to have an opportunity to confess. It was when men delivered them to the courts, scourged them in the synagogues and led them before governors and kings for Jesus' sake that they were to confess, and then they were to do so without the slightest care or anxiety (Mt. 10:17ff.). Correspondingly, the confessions of Paul in Acts are characterized as solemn actions of a special type in special situations which he had not engineered. Above all we may recall the accounts of Jesus' own confession before the Sanhedrin (Mk. 14:60ff. and parallels) and before Pontius Pilate (Jn. 18:37ff., 1 Tim. 6:13). Here also and particularly it is not a matter of everyday occurrence but of special and outstanding events which he had not provoked.[46]

The production of a new confession of faith, then, is something imposed upon the church by circumstances of one sort or another, usually because of political persecution, but sometimes also because of the external or internal threat of false doctrine. There is a role for missiology here. While the circumstances should be clear, they may not necessarily be equally

---

46. Barth, *Church Dogmatics* III/4, 79.

clear to everyone. It is conceivable that the eyes and ears of a Reformed missiologist will be more sensitive to the existence of a *status confessionis*, and then the missiologist has a responsibility to serve the church with a persuasive case for a new or revised confession.

Historically, the impulse to confess is always something that involves three parties: the body of believers compelled to confess, those to whom the confession is to be made, and God. Consequently, confession takes the form of a serious protest. It is not to be done lightly. As mentioned earlier, Barth was involved in the production of the Barmen Declaration, so he addresses this topic out of personal experience:

> We now assume that the confession demanded of us occurs in a particular situation not created by us but to be perceived by us, and that it occurs when it is given us to confess. We can thus proceed to say that it consists in a protest against the various judgments of unbelief, superstition and heresy. We know that it can be only a protest to the honour of God and therefore without ulterior aim. But it must have the character of a protest. Confession has nothing to do with lyricism or pure meditation. Confession is always the protest against the utterance of a false faith that contradicts the glory of God . . .
>
> . . . We may note that all confession which lacks this character and is outside this opposition and threat cannot be the required pursuit but only a forbidden sport of empty luxury. Confession is a serious and stringent matter. If it becomes beautiful and ceremonious (liturgical), there is cause to mistrust its genuineness.[47]

When reading these paragraphs, one cannot but help think not only of the CRC Contemporary Testimony, but also the dozens of other contemporary confessions. Do these confessions give the impression of being "serious and stringent"? Do they emerge from situations of grave crisis where the church's very existence or the truth of the Scriptures is in question? To ask these questions is to answer them. The church in the Low Countries of the sixteenth century was *in statu confessionis* — of that there can be no doubt. Yet, doubts *can* be raised about Reformed churches in North America and whether today's situation or the situation of the last three or four decades constitutes a *status confessionis*. We question

---

47. Barth, *Church Dogmatics*, III/4, 80-81.

Berkouwer's assertion that "even the tensions of the modern world can force the Church into a *status confessionis*."⁴⁸ Historically, scripturally, and confessionally, such an assertion appears indefensible.

Both the authors surveyed above also spoke of the ecumenical aspects of this issue. Bertram's approach was to see confession as a means to achieve consensus and reunion. Kuyper's emphasis was on the necessity for Reformed churches to have consensus before proceeding to develop new confessions or engage in confessional revision. There is no dilemma between these two perspectives — both are necessary and helpful. Ecumenical concerns might lead to efforts for a new confession, and here we think especially of the long-standing differences between Presbyterians and the Reformed whose heritage is on the European continent. Perhaps organizations such as the North American Presbyterian and Reformed Council (NAPARC) or the International Conference of Reformed Churches (ICRC) will be instrumental in developing such a new confession. Such a new confession would also serve the missionary task of the church, providing the world with a message that is readily perceived as unified.⁴⁹

Reformed missiology could be involved with this process by bringing more recent insights from the Scriptures to the table, as well as more recent concerns from our context. For instance, we noted in 5.2.2 that the Belgic Confession has a limited perspective on world religions. A new ecumenical Reformed confession should have a global perspective which includes what the Bible teaches on how believers stand with regard to Buddhism, Sikhism, and especially Islam. Reformed missiology can contribute the fruits of its investigations and reflections with regard to these world religions and others.

Kuyper insisted that the writing of new confessions and also the revision of older ones requires a certain maturity of theological development. This was not a factor for Bertram, but it is something worth considering. On the one hand, it can be difficult to gauge maturity of theological development from within in any sort of objective way. On the other hand, Kuyper is correct insofar as saying that ideally churches should not rush

---

48. Berkouwer, *The Church*, 302.
49. R. Scott Clark noted that attempts at contemporary confessions by both the CRC and the RPCNA were idiosyncratic and that any new efforts at creedal formulation in our day should be done under the auspices of NAPARC. See *Recovering the Reformed Confession: Our Theology, Piety and Practice* (Phillipsburg: P&R Publishing, 2008), 188-191.

into confession-writing. There needs to be time for careful reflection, discussion, and definition.

Abraham Kuyper wrote in 1891 that it was not the right time for the Reformed churches in the Netherlands to produce a new confession. In 1936, J. Gresham Machen argued that because of "intellectual and moral indolence," his was not a creed-making age. Besides, he was of the opinion that it was unlikely that improvements could be made upon the existing creeds and confessions.[50] In his 1987 book *The Doctrine of the Knowledge of God*, John Frame also entertained the question of whether new creeds and confessions should be written. His answer was the same as that of Kuyper and Machen, although his reasons were different. According to Frame, serious creeds require broad consensus, and this is unattainable at this time. Frame wrote, "For in the present context, new creeds are *obstacles* to union and therefore, ironically, obstacles to really significant creedal work."[51] All of this is despite the fact that he sees a need for new creeds which would deal with modern heresies.

Janssen is one contemporary author who would dissent from those just mentioned. He argues that "a serious attempt should be made to reassess the Reformed confessional heritage and update it."[52] This updating should take the form of creating new confessions. Further, Janssen believes "that substantial mutation of confessional substance should be an ongoing activity of the church. New confessing is part of being the church. I believe the church is always up to the task: if it is not, is it up to the task of being the church?"[53] Janssen is arguing his case in the context of a discussion regarding confessional subscription. He identifies a series of problems associated with a stricter subscription to the Three Forms of Unity, and part of his solution for those problems is to advocate for new confessions. It is beyond the scope of this study to interact with what he writes about confessional subscription and how that relates to new confessions. Still, his statement about the church always being up to the task of confessing is worthy of some consideration. The question is whether the church, by its very nature, is always capable of

---

50. J. Gresham Machen, "The Creeds and Doctrinal Advance," in *Scripture and Confession*, 156.
51. John M. Frame, *The Doctrine of the Knowledge of God* (Phillipsburg: Presbyterian and Reformed Publishing Company, 1987), 306. Italics are original.
52. Janssen, *By This Our Subscription*, 367.
53. Janssen, *By This Our Subscription*, 369.

creating new confessions. In principle, this would seem to indeed be the case. Janssen rightly draws our attention to 1 Timothy 3:15 and the fact that the church "proclaims and preserves the divine Word" as the "pillar and bulwark of the truth."[54] Thus, there is always, in some sense, new confessing taking place.[55] However, that is not the same thing as writing formal, official confessions and what is true in principle, and what is true at some level, is not always necessarily true in practice and at other levels. The church is what it is by grace, and seldom is it what it should be. Perhaps this is nowhere more true than on mission fields with younger churches (Janssen does not directly deal with the missionary aspect of this question). Therefore, we can conclude that there may be periods in which it is inadvisable for a church, whether older or younger, to be engaged in the preparation of official written confessions of faith. Not every age finds every church *in statu confessionis* also when it comes to the capacity to confess.

Excepting Janssen's dissent, it is apparent that there is a consensus, at least among many confessionally Reformed/Presbyterian writers in the English-speaking world, that Reformed churches have not been *in statu confessionis* in the last century. We would agree and add that neither are these churches in that situation today. The time is not right for the production of a new confession of faith, nor even for substantial revisions to the existing confessions. The most important consideration here is that there is no discernible large scale crisis threatening our churches at this point. Confession is not being demanded of established Reformed churches in North America. We can easily grant that perhaps such a time is coming and Reformed missiology ought to play a role in discerning such a time. Should such a time come, the witness produced ought to have a sharper missionary character because of developments in Reformed missiology over the last century. As mentioned above, perhaps the interests of ecumenicity will also bring us to the production of a new confession and, here too, we can expect a symbol that reflects more recent missiological concerns and insights.

---

54. Janssen, *By This Our Subscription*, 301.

55. Janssen identifies "layers of confessing" in Reformed churches. The first layer consists of the church's explicit confessions ("that confessed by the church"). The second layer consists of the church's liturgical forms, church order, sermons, and official church pronouncements ("that applied by the church"). The third layer consists of such things as private discussions and publications ("that discussed in the church"). See *By This Our Subscription*, 343-345.

Finally, we must also be open to the development of new confessions in younger churches on our mission fields.[56] These churches are more convincingly *in statu confessionis* than the established churches, at least as far as North America is concerned. Such new confessions may not be *demanded* of these younger churches by the established churches or their missionaries. In many situations, younger churches will be content to adopt the confessions of the established churches from afar. This should not be discouraged. If younger churches are content to appropriate the sixteenth- and seventeenth-century confessions of the Reformation, we should be glad and respect their wishes. Perhaps they may even see things in those confessions that speak to their situation in ways that we have not considered. Moreover, in due time, the circumstances of the mission field combined with a growing theological acuity may lead to the natural development of new confessions.

8.4 Conclusion

We want to conclude with two related points. The first is a helpful analogy proposed by Jaroslav Pelikan. He compared confessions of faith to compact disks. When CDs are stored, whether in stores or in the home, they are inert and static. They can be shipped and stored. They can be handed down from parents to children without ever being used or heard. Yet, says Pelikan, it is their inertness that allows them to suddenly become dynamic when they are placed in a CD player and the sounds of beautiful music issue forth from the speakers.[57] Confessions only have value as they are "played," as they are engaged and as their voice is heard through the coming generations.

On the one hand, there is a danger that confessions (including the Belgic Confession) will remain inert, and that Reformed believers will not engage them, or perhaps not engage them on the terms of the confessions themselves. Herman Bavinck drew attention to another danger on the opposite end of the spectrum. Bavinck wrote about those who "no longer

---

56. Writing about the development of "Eastern" theologies and "Eastern" confessions, Wielenga was cautious and even considered it dangerous to speak about promoting these as desirable. Some of his concern is valid (especially where syncretism is concerned), but nevertheless one must account for changing circumstances and also variations in the way different cultures prioritize the various cognitive processes (see 4.2.1). See Wielenga, *De akker is de wereld*, 56.

57. Pelikan, *Credo*, 515.

confess their faith, but only believe their confession."[58] It is theoretically possible to have the confessions function in both the church and academy as something virtually on the same level as Scripture. In such a situation, the confessions themselves are dishonoured, since they never claim such a status for themselves. Moreover, such a situation also means that the confessions become static and untouchable, and the confession of faith of Reformed believers becomes stale and directed towards words on a page rather than towards the living God and his Son Jesus Christ through the power of the Holy Spirit. Every generation must meaningfully appropriate these symbols for itself and engage them, but never at the expense of a true faith.

Reformed missiology must work along those same lines. Reformed missiology will and must be confessional. Deference is due to these symbols at every juncture in a Reformed missiologist's task. Reformed missiologists will always seek to do their work in accordance with the Reformed confessions. Yet more importantly, Reformed missiology will be biblical, finding its solid foundations on the Word of God alone. The consequence is that the Reformed confessions, including the Belgic Confession, are not beyond missiological analysis and even critique. Everything is subject to the Word of God.

In the nature of the case that has been before us, we can be thankful for our Reformed confessions. They have been proven by the passage of time and careful study to be faithful to the Scriptures. As we have seen in this study, the Belgic Confession is also a rich treasure, a gift from God to his church. We have only scratched the surface of its missiological significance. There remains much to be explored, and perhaps there are also more places where future scholarship will recognize further defects of lesser or greater significance. Yet, from our study it appears quite certain that Reformed missiology would benefit from careful

---

58. Herman Bavinck, *The Certainty of Faith*, trans. Harry der Nederlanden (St. Catharines: Paideia Press Inc., 1980), 41. Bavinck is referring here to the "orthodoxy of the seventeenth" century or Protestant scholasticism. This assessment of seventeenth-century Reformed orthodoxy is problematic. See the discussion in Muller, *After Calvin*, 90-91. "Spener and his pietist colleagues protested against the replacement of the Christian piety of the Reformation with a strict confessionalism and to the confusion of confessional adherence with a life of faith." Muller goes on to note that it is not easy to draw a line between scholasticism and pietism in the orthodox period. See also Gregory D. Schuringa, "Orthodoxy and Piety in the *Nadere Reformatie*: The Theology of Simon Oomius," *Mid-America Journal of Theology* 20 (2009): 95-103.

reflection, not only on Scripture, but also on the Church's summary of important scriptural truths in the Belgic Confession.

BIBLIOGRAPHY

Primary Sources

Augustine of Hippo. *City of God*. New York: Image Books, 1958.

Calvin, John. *A Commentary on Daniel*. London: Banner of Truth Trust, 1966.

_____. *Commentary on the Book of the Prophet Isaiah*. Grand Rapids: Eerdmans, 1948.

_____. *Commentary on the Book of Psalms*, Vol. 1. Reprint, Grand Rapids: Baker, 1979.

_____. *Commentary on a Harmony of the Evangelists: Matthew, Mark and Luke*, Vol. 3. Reprint, Grand Rapids: Baker, 1979.

_____. *Institutes of the Christian Religion*. Edited by John T. McNeill. Translated by Ford Lewis Battles. 2 vols. Philadelphia: Westminster Press, 1960. Christian Reformed Church in North America.

Acts of Synod 1952. Grand Rapids: CRC Publications, 1952.

_____. *Acts of Synod 1971*. Grand Rapids: CRC Publications, 1971.

_____. *Acts of Synod 1972*. Grand Rapids: CRC Publications, 1972.

_____. *Acts of Synod 1973*. Grand Rapids: CRC Publications, 1973.

_____. *Acts of Synod 1975*. Grand Rapids: CRC Publications, 1975.

_____. *Acts of Synod 1977*. Grand Rapids: CRC Publications, 1977.

_____. *Acts of Synod 1979*. Grand Rapids: CRC Publications, 1979.

_____. Acts of Synod 1981. Grand Rapids: CRC Publications, 1981.

_____. *Acts of Synod 1982*. Grand Rapids: CRC Publications, 1982.

_____. *Acts of Synod 1983*. Grand Rapids: CRC Publications, 1983.

_____. *Ecumenical Creeds and Confessions*. Grand Rapids: CRC Publications, 1988.

———. *Our World Belongs to God: A Contemporary Testimony.* Grand Rapids: CRC Publications, 1987.

———. *Our World Belongs to God.* Grand Rapids: Faith Alive Christian Resources, 2008.

De Brès, Guy. *Le baston de la foy chrestienne....* Geneva: Nicolas Barbier & Courtreau, 1558.

———. *Confession de foy, faicte d'un commun accord par les fideles qui conversent és pays bas.* Rouen: Abel Clemence, 1561.

———. *Confession de foy, faicte d'un commun accord par les fideles qui conversent ès pays Bas.* No publisher, 1562 (Major).

———. *Confession de foy, faicte d'un commun accord par les fideles qui conversent ès pays Bas.* No publisher, 1562 (Minor).

———. *Confession de foy, faite d'un commun accord par les fideles qui conversent és pays bas.* Lyon: Jean Frellon, 1561.

———. *La racine, source et fondement des anabaptistes....* Rouen: Abel Clemence, 1565.

Luther, Martin. *Luther's Works.* Philadelphia: Fortress Press, 1958.

Megapolensis, Johannes. *Reply of Rev. Johannes Megapolensis to a Letter of Father Simon Le Moyne.* Edited by Edward B. Coe and E. T. Corwin. Translated by Louis Bevier. New York: The Collegiate Church, 1907.

———. "A Short Account of the Mohawk Indians." In *Narratives of New Netherland, 1609-1664,* edited by J. Franklin Jameson, 168-180. New York: Charles Scribner's Sons, 1909.

Mornay, Philippe Du Plessis. *De Veritate Religionis Christianae Liber; Adversus Atheos, Epicureos, Ethnicos, Judaeos, Mahumedistas, et caeteros Infideles.* Antwerp: Christopher Plantin, 1583.

Procedures tenues a l'endroit de ceux la religion du pais bas. Geneva: Jean Crespin, 1568. A reprint was published by S. Cramer and F. Pijper, eds. *Bibliotheca Reformatoria Neerlandica* Vol. 8. 'S-Gravenhage: Martinus Nijhoff, 1911. 491-643. Available in English as *Procedures Held with Regard to Those of the Religion of the Netherlands,* author, translator and publisher unknown.

State of New York. Edwin T. Corwin. *Ecclesiastical Records of the State of New York* Vol. 1. Albany: James B. Lyon, 1901.

Taffin, Jean. *The Marks of God's Children*. Edited by James A. De Jong. Translated by Peter Y. De Jong. Grand Rapids: Baker Academic, 2003.

Van der Heyden, Gaspar. "The Minister of the infant Reformed congregation at Antwerp seeks the Advice of the Brethren at Emden, 17 December 1555." Letter translated by Alastair Duke and accessed at http://dutchrevolt.leidenuniv.nl. Source: E. Meiners, *Oostvrieschlandts kerkelyke geschiedenisse*, Vol. 1, 365-370. Groningen, 1738-1739.

Van Haemstede, Adrien. "The Witness of Calvinist Martyrs: Arnoud Diericx, Carolus de Koninck, Gillis and Anton Verdickt, Adriaan [Coreman] de Schildern, Hendrik [Snoelacke] van Boekholt, 1557-1559." Excerpt translated by Alastair Duke. Accessed at http://dutchrevolt.leidenuniv.nl. Source: *Geschiedenis der Marterlaren*, 543-681. Arnhem, 1868.

Voetius, Gisbertus. *Politica Ecclesiastica*. Vol.3. Amsterdam: Johannes Janson à Waesberge, 1676.

———. "Selectae Disputationes Theologicae." Edited and translated by John W. Beardslee. *In Reformed Dogmatics: J. Wollebius, G. Voetius, F. Turretin*. New York: Oxford UP, 1965.

———. *Selectarum Disputationum Theologicarum*. Vol. 2. Utrecht: Joannes à Waesberge, 1655.

———. F. L. Rutgers, ed. *Tractatus Selecti de Politica Ecclesiastica*. Vol. 2. Amsterdam: J. H. Kruyt, 1885.

Secondary Sources

Books and Dissertations

Althaus, Paul. *The Theology of Martin Luther*. Philadelphia: Fortress Press, 1966.

Arias, Mortimer and Alan Johnson. *The Great Commission: Biblical Models for Evangelism*. Nashville: Abingdon Press, 1992.

Bahnsen, Greg L. *Van Til's Apologetic: Readings & Analysis*. Phillipsburg: P&R, 1998.

Bakhuizen van den Brink, J. N. *De Nederlandse Belijdenisgeschriften*. Amsterdam: Uitgeverij Ton Bolland, 1976.

Barrett, David B., George T. Kurian, and Todd M. Johnson. *World Christian Encyclopedia: A Comparative Study of Churches and Religions in the Modern World*, Second Edition. Oxford: Oxford UP, 2001.

Barth, Karl. *Church Dogmatics*. III/4: Creation. Edinburgh: T. and T. Clark, 1961.

Bavinck, Herman. *The Certainty of Faith*. St. Catharines: Paideia Press Inc., 1980.

———. *Reformed Dogmatics*. Vol. 1: Prolegomena. Grand Rapids: Baker Academic, 2003.

Bavinck, J. H. *An Introduction to the Science of Missions*. Phillipsburg: Presbyterian and Reformed, 1960.

———. *Zending in een wereld in nood*. Wageningen: N.V. Gebr. Zomer en Keuning's Uitgeversmij, 1948.

Beale, G. K. *The Temple and the Church's Mission: A Biblical Theology of the Dwelling Place of God*. Downers Grove: IVP, 2004.

Benedict, Philip. *Christ's Churches Purely Reformed: A Social History of Calvinism*. New Haven: Yale UP, 2002.

Berger, Peter L. "The Desecularization of the World: A Global Overview." In *The Desecularization of the World: Resurgent Religion and World Politics*. Edited by Peter L. Berger. Washington: Ethics and Public Policy Center, 1999, 1-18.

Berkhof, Louis. *Principles of Biblical Interpretation*. Grand Rapids: Baker, 1950.

Berkouwer, G. C. *The Church*. Grand Rapids: Eerdmans, 1976.

Bertram, Robert W. *A Time for Confessing*. Grand Rapids: Eerdmans, 2008.

Boer, Harry R. *Pentecost and Missions*. Grand Rapids: Eerdmans, 1961.

Boice, James Montgomery and Philip Graham Ryken. *The Doctrines of Grace: Recovering the Evangelical Gospel*. Wheaton: Crossway Books, 2002.

Book of Praise: Anglo-Genevan Psalter. Winnipeg: Premier Printing, 1998. Bosch, David J. Transforming Mission: Paradigm Shifts in Theology of Mission. Maryknoll: Orbis, 1991.

_____. *Witness to the World: The Christian Mission in Theological Perspective*. Atlanta: John Knox Press, 1980.

Bouwman, Clarence. *The Overflowing Riches of My God*. Winnipeg: Premier, 2008.

Braaten, Carl E. *No Other Gospel! Christianity Among the World's Religions*. Minneapolis: Fortress Press, 1992.

Braekman, E. M. *Guy de Brès, I. Sa Vie*. Brussels: Editions de la Librairie des Esclaireurs Unionistes, 1960.

Bratt, J. D. "Christian Reformed Church." In *Dictionary of Christianity in America*. Edited by Daniel G. Reid, Robert D. Linder, Bruce L. Shelley, and Harry S. Stout. Downers Grove: InterVarsity Press, 1990.

Bratt, John Harold. "The Missionary Enterprise of the Christian Reformed Church of America." Th.D. dissertation for Union Theological Seminary, May 1955.

Bredenhof, Wes, ed. *Papers Presented at the First Reformed Missions Conference*. Hamilton: Theological College of the Canadian Reformed Churches, 2005.

_____. *The Whole Manner of Worship: the Sufficiency of Scripture and Worship in Article 7 of the Belgic Confession*. Edmonton: Still Waters Revival Books, 1997.

Breen, Quirinus. *John Calvin: A Study in French Humanism*. Hamden: Archon Books, 1968.

Brown, Harold O. J. *Heresies: The Image of Christ in the Mirror of Heresy and Orthodoxy from the Apostles to the Present*. Grand Rapids: Baker, 1984.

Brown, Raymond E. *The Gospel According to John* (Anchor Bible). New York: Doubleday, 1970.

Brown, Robert McAfee, ed. *Kairos: Three Prophetic Challenges to the Church*. Grand Rapids: Eerdmans, 1990.

Burgon, John W. *The Last Twelve Verses of the Gospel According to S. Mark*. Ann Arbor: Sovereign Grace Book Club, 1959.

Busch, Eberhard. "The Closeness of the Distant: Reformed Confessions After 1945." In *Toward the Future of Reformed Theology: Tasks, Topics, Traditions*. Edited by David Willis and Michael Welker. Grand Rapids: Eerdmans, 1999. 512-531.

Cameron, Euan. *The European Reformation*. Oxford: Clarendon Press, 1991.

_____. *Interpreting Christian History: the Challenge of the Churches' Past*. Malden: Blackwell Publishing, 2005.

Carson, D. A. "Christology." In *Evangelical Dictionary of World Mission*. Edited by A. Scott Moreau. Grand Rapids: Baker, 2000.

_____. *Right with God: Justification in the Bible and the World*. Grand Rapids: Baker, 1992.

_____. *The Gagging of God: Christianity Confronts Pluralism*. Grand Rapids: Zondervan, 1996.

Catechism of the Catholic Church, Second Edition. New York: Doubleday, 1997.

Clark, R. Scott. *Caspar Olevian and the Substance of the Covenant*. Grand Rapids: Reformation Heritage Books, 2008.

_____, ed. *Covenant, Justification and Pastoral Ministry: Essays by the Faculty of Westminster Seminary California*. Phillipsburg: P&R, 2007.

_____. *Recovering the Reformed Confession: Our Theology, Piety and Practice*. Phillipsburg: P&R Publishing, 2008.

Bibliography

Classical Renewal Facilitation Team. *Rethinking Ministry: From Church-Shaped Missions to a Mission-Shaped Church*. Grand Rapids: Christian Reformed Home Missions and Christian Reformed World Relief Committee, 1999.

Coakley, John. "The Reformed Church in America as a National Church." In *Church, Identity and Change: Theology and Denominational Structures in Unsettled Times*. Edited by David A. Roozen and James R. Nieman. Grand Rapids: Eerdmans, 2005.

Cochrane, Arthur C. ed. *Reformed Confessions of the Sixteenth Century*. Louisville: Westminster John Knox Press, 2003.

Collinet, Robert. *La Réformation en Belgique au XVIme Siècle*. Brussels: Editions de la Librairie des Eclaireurs Unionistes, 1958.

Conn, Harvie. *Eternal Word and Changing Worlds: Theology, Anthropology and Mission in Trialogue*. Grand Rapids: Academie, 1984.

_____. "Mission, Missions, Theology and Theological Education." In *The Urban Face of Mission: Ministering the Gospel in a Diverse and Changing World*. Edited by Harvie Conn, Manuel Ortiz and Susan S. Baker. Phillipsburg: P&R, 2002. 11-26.

Corrie, John, ed. *Dictionary of Mission Theology*. Downers Grover: Intervarsity Press, 2007.

Crew, Phyllis Mack. *Calvinist Preaching and Iconoclasm in the Netherlands, 1544-1569*. Cambridge: Cambridge UP, 1978.

Cross, F. L. and E. A. Livingstone, ed. *The Oxford Dictionary of the Christian Church* (Third Edition). Oxford: Oxford UP, 1997.

Dawkins, Richard. *The God Delusion*. Boston: Houghton Mifflin Company, 2006.

Deddens, K. "Contextualization." In *Proceedings of the International Conference of Reformed Churches*, June 19-28, 1989, Langley, BC, Canada. Winnipeg: Premier, 1989. 240-258.

DeGreef, W. *The Writings of John Calvin: An Introductory Guide* (Expanded Edition). Grand Rapids: Baker, 2008.

De Jong, Gerald Francis. *The Dutch Reformed Church in the American Colonies*. Grand Rapids: Eerdmans, 1978.

DeJong, P. Y. *The Church's Witness to the World*. St. Catharines: Paideia Press, 1980.

Deputies of Synod Amersfoort 1948. *Rapport over de verhouding van den zendingsarbeid tot medischen en onderwijs-arbeid op de zendingsterreinen (kwestie 'hoofd' —en 'hulp-diensten.') uitgebracht door de Deputaten, benoemd vanwege de Generale Synode te Amersfoort 1948 tot herziening van de K.O. (art.52) en Z.O. volgens art. 65 and 129 der Acta, aan de Kerken voorgelegd.* Kampen: Drukkerij Ph. Zalsman, 1950.

Dickens, A. G. *The German Nation and Martin Luther.* New York: Harper & Row, 1974.

Dickens, A. G. and John Tonkin. *The Reformation in Historical Thought.* Cambridge: Harvard UP, 1985.

Dillenberger, John, ed. *John Calvin: Selections from his Writings.* Scholars Press, 1975.

Drew, Charles D. *The Ancient Love Song: Finding Christ in the Old Testament.* Phillipsburg: P&R, 2000.

Duke, Alastair. "The Netherlands." In *The Early Reformation in Europe.* Edited by Andrew Pettegree. Cambridge: Cambridge UP, 1992. 142-165.

Elton, G. R. *Reformation Europe, 1517-1559.* London: Fontana, 1963.

Evans, C. F. *Saint Luke.* London: SCM, 1990.

Evers, Georg. "The Problem of Martyrdom in Missionary Countries." In *Rethinking Martyrdom.* Edited by Teresa Okure. London: SCM Press, 2003. 87-95.

Feenstra, J. G. *Onze Geloofsbelijdenis,* tweede druk. Kampen: J. H. Kok N.V., 1947.

Fesko, J. V. *Justification: Understanding the Classic Reformed Doctrine.* Phillipsburg: P&R, 2008.

Fields. Rona M., ed. *Martyrdom: The Psychology, Theology and Politics of Self-Sacrifice.* Westport: Praeger, 2004.

Frame, John M. *The Doctrine of the Knowledge of God.* Phillipsburg: Presbyterian and Reformed Publishing Co., 1987.

France, R. T. *The Gospel of Mark: A Commentary on the Greek Text.* Grand Rapids: Eerdmans, 2002.

Friedrich, Gerhard. "κηρυξ". In *Theological Dictionary of the New Testament*. Vol. 3. Edited by Gerhard Kittel. Translated by Geoffrey W. Bromiley. Grand Rapids: Eerdmans, 1964. 683-696.

Gathercole, S. J. "Justified by Faith, Justified by his Blood: The Evidence of Romans 3:21-4:25." In *Justification and Variegated Nomism*. Vol.2. Edited by D. A. Carson, Peter Thomas O'Brien and Mark A. Seifrid. Grand Rapids: Baker Academic, 2001.

Geertsema, J. "The Scriptural Foundation of Mission in its Biblical History and Normative Direction." In *Missionary Preaching: Papers Presented at the First Reformed Missions Conference*. Edited by Wes Bredenhof. Hamilton: Theological College of the Canadian Reformed Churches, 2005.

Goertz, Hans-Jürgen. *The Anabaptists*. New York: Routledge, 1996.

Goheen, Michael W. *"As the Father has sent me, I am sending you": J.E. Lesslie Newbigin's Missionary Ecclesiology*. Zoetermeer: Boekencentrum, 2000.

Gootjes, Nicolaas H. *The Belgic Confession: Its History and Sources*. Grand Rapids: Baker Academic, 2007.

Green, Anna and Kathleen Troup. *The houses of history: A critical reader in twentieth-century history and theory*. Manchester: Manchester UP, 1999.

Green, Lowell. "Melanchthon's Relation to Scholasticism." In *Protestant Scholasticism: Essays in Reassessment*. Edited by R. Scott Clark and Carl Trueman. Carlisle: Paternoster Press, 1999. 273-288.

Greenway, Roger S. *Go and Make Disciples: An Introduction to Christian Missions*. Phillipsburg: P&R, 1999.

Gregory, Brad S. *Salvation at Stake: Christian Martyrdom in Early Modern Europe*. Cambridge: Harvard UP, 1999.

Greijdanus, Dr. S. *Schriftbeginselen ter schriftverklaring: en historisch overzicht over theorieen en wijzen van schriftuitlegging*. Kampen: Kok, 1946.

Greschat, Martin. *Martin Bucer: A Reformer and his Times*. Louisville: Westminster John Knox, 2004.

Guthrie, Donald. *New Testament Introduction (Revised Edition)*. Downers Grove: IVP, 1990.

Haak, C. J. *Gereformeerde Missiologie & Oecumenica: Beknopt overzicht aan het begin van de 21e eeuw A.D..* Zwolle: De Verre Naasten, 2005.

———. *Metamorfose: Intercultureel begeleiden van kerken in een niet-christelijke omgeving.* Zoetermeer: Uitgeverij Boekencentrum, 2002.

Hendriksen, William. *New Testament Commentary: The Gospel of Luke.* Grand Rapids: Baker, 1978.

———. *New Testament Commentary: The Gospel of Mark.* Grand Rapids: Baker, 1975.

Hendrix, Scott H. *Recultivating the Vineyard: the Reformation Agendas of Christianization.* Louisville: Westminster John Knox, 2004.

Hesselgrave, David J. *Communicating Christ Cross-Culturally: An Introduction to Missionary Communication* (Second Edition). Grand Rapids: Zondervan, 1991.

Hesselgrave, David J. & Edward Rommen. *Contextualization: Meanings, Methods and Models.* Grand Rapids: Baker, 1989.

Hesselgrave, David J. *Paradigms in Conflict: 10 Key Questions in Christian Missions Today.* Grand Rapids: Kregel, 2005.

Hick, John. "A Pluralist View." In *Four Views on Salvation in a Pluralistic World.* Edited by Dennis L. Okholm and Timothy R. Phillips. Grand Rapids: Zondervan, 1995. 29-59.

Hillerbrand, Hans J., ed. *The Oxford Encyclopedia of the Reformation.* New York: Oxford UP, 1996.

———. *The World of the Reformation.* Grand Rapids: Baker, 1973.

Hinlicky, Paul R. "Status confessionis." In *Encyclopedia of Christianity* (Vol.5). Edited by Erwin Fahlbusch, Jan Milič Lochman, John Mbiti, Jaroslav Pelikan, and Lukas Vischer. Grand Rapids: Eerdmans, 2008. 198-201.

Hitchens, Christopher. *God is Not Great: How Religion Poisons Everything.* Toronto: McClelland & Stewart Ltd., 2007.

Hoogstra, J. T., ed. *John Calvin: Contemporary Prophet.* Grand Rapids: Baker, 1959.

Horton, Michael. *Putting Amazing Back into Grace: Embracing the Heart of the Gospel* (Second Edition). Grand Rapids: Baker, 2002.

――――――. *Covenant and Eschatology: the Divine Drama*. Louisville: Westminster John Knox Press, 2002.

――――――. *Covenant and Salvation: Union with Christ*. Louisville: Westminster John Knox Press, 2007.

Hovey, Craig. *To Share in the Body: A Theology of Martyrdom for Today's Church*. Grand Rapids: Brazos Press, 2008.

Hsia, R. Po-Chia, ed. *A Companion to the Reformation World*. Malden: Blackwell Publishing, 2004.

Hughes, Philip Edgcumbe, ed. and trans. *The Register of the Company of Pastors of Geneva in the Time of Calvin*. Eugene: Wipf and Stock, 2004.

Hyde, Daniel. *God With Us: Knowing the Mystery of Who Jesus Is*. Grand Rapids: Reformation Heritage Books, 2007.

――――――. *With Heart and Mouth: An Exposition of the Belgic Confession*. Grandville: Reformed Fellowship Inc., 2008.

Israel, Jonathan. *The Dutch Republic: Its Rise, Greatness, and Fall, 1477-1806*. Oxford: Clarendon Press, 1995.

Janssen, R. C. "By This Our Subscription: Confessional Subscription in the Dutch Reformed Tradition Since 1816." Th.D. dissertation for Theologische Universiteit, Kampen, the Netherlands, 2009.

Jarrel, W. A. *Baptist Church Perpetuity: Or the Continuous Existence of Baptist Churches*. Dallas: no publisher indicated, 1894.

Jongeneel, Jan A. B. *Philosophy, Science and Theology of Mission in the 19th and 20th Centuries: A Missiological Encyclopedia, Part II: Missionary Theology*. Frankfurt am Main: Peter Lang, 1997.

Joose, Leendert Jan. *Geloof in de Nieuwe Wereld: Ontmoeting met Afrikanen en Indianen (1600-1700)*. Kampen: Uitgeverij Kok, 2008.

――――――. *Reformatie en zending, Bucer en Walaeus: vaders van reformatorische zending*. Goes: Oosterbaan & Le Cointre, 1988.

Kaiser Jr., Walter C. *Towards An Exegetical Theology: Biblical Exegesis for Preaching and Teaching*. Grand Rapids: Baker, 1981.

Kidwell, Clara Sue, Home Noley, and George E. "Tink" Tinker. *A Native American Theology*. Maryknoll: Orbis Books, 2001.

Kraft, Charles H. *Anthropology for Christian Witness*. Maryknoll: Orbis Books, 1996.

Kromminga, D. H. *Article XXXVI of the Belgic Confession and the Christian Reformed Church*. Grand Rapids: Baker, 1943.

Lenski, R. C. H. *The Interpretation of St. John's Gospel*. Columbus: Lutheran Book Concern, 1942.

Lindberg, Carter. *The European Reformations*. Oxford: Blackwell Publishers, 1996.

Machen, J. Gresham. "The Creeds and Doctrinal Advance." In *Scripture and Confession: A Book About Confessions Old and New*. Edited by John H. Skilton. Phillipsburg: Presbyterian and Reformed Publishing Co., 1973. 149-157.

Marnef, Guido. "Calvinism in Antwerp, 1558-1585." In *Calvinism in Europe: 1540-1620*. Edited by Andrew Pettegree, Alastair Duke, and Gillian Lewis. Cambridge: Cambridge UP, 1994. 143-159.

Marshall, Paul. *Their Blood Cries Out: The Worldwide Tragedy of Modern Christians Who Are Dying for Their Faith*. Dallas: Word Publishing, 1997.

Matheson, Peter. "Martin Bucer and the Old Church." In *Martin Bucer: Reforming Church and Community*. Edited by David F. Wright. Cambridge: Cambridge UP, 1994.

McKim, Donald K., ed. *Encyclopedia of the Reformed Faith*. Louisville: Westminster John Knox Press, 1992.

McQuilkin, Robertson. "The Role of the Holy Spirit in Missions." In *The Holy Spirit and Mission Dynamics*. Edited by C. Douglas McConnell. Pasadena: William Carey Library, 1997. 22-35.

Merwick, Donna. *The Shame and Sorrow: Dutch-Amerindian Encounters in New Netherland*. Philadelphia: University of Pennsylvania Press, 2006.

Monter, William. "Heresy Executions in Reformation Europe, 1520-1565." In *Tolerance and Intolerance in the European Reformation*. Edited by Ole Peter Grell and Bob Scribner. Cambridge: Cambridge UP, 1996. 48-64.

Moreau, A. Scott, Gary R. Corwin, and Gary B. McGee. *Introducing World Missions: a Biblical, Historical and Practical Survey.* Grand Rapids: Baker Academic, 2004.

Moreau, A. Scott. "Mission and Missions." In *Evangelical Dictionary of World Missions.* Edited by A. Scott Moreau. Grand Rapids: Baker, 2000.

Muller, Richard. *After Calvin: Studies in the Development of a Theological Tradition.* New York: Oxford UP, 2003.

————. *The Unaccommodated Calvin: Studies in the Foundation of a Theological Tradition.* New York: Oxford UP, 2000.

————. *Post-Reformation Reformed Dogmatics.* Volume One: Prolegomena to Theology, Second Edition. Grand Rapids: Baker, 2003.

————. *Post-Reformation Reformed Dogmatics.* Volume Two: Holy Scripture, the Cognitive Foundation of Theology, Second Edition. Grand Rapids: Baker, 2003.

————. "'To Grant this Grace to All People and Nations:' Calvin on Apostolicity and Mission." In *For God So Loved the World: Missiological Reflections in Honor of Roger S. Greenway.* Edited by Arie C. Leder. Belleville: Essence Publishing, 2006. 211-232.

Murray, Iain. *The Puritan Hope: Revival and the Interpretation of Prophecy.* London: Banner of Truth Trust, 1971.

Murray, Stuart. *Post-Christendom: Church and Mission in a Strange New World.* Waynesboro: Paternoster Press, 2004.

Neill, Stephen C. *Creative Tension.* New York: Doubleday, 1959.

Nijenhuis, Willem. *Adrianus Saravia (c. 1532-1613): Dutch Calvinist, first Reformed defender of the English Episcopal Church order on the basis of the ius divinum.* Leiden: E. J. Brill, 1980.

————. *A History of Christian Missions.* New York: Penguin, 1964.

Opocênsky, Milan. "Processus Confessionis." In *Reformed Theology: Identity and Ecumenicity.* Edited by Wallace M. Alston Jr. and Michael Welker. Grand Rapids: Eerdmans, 2003. 385-397.

Owen, John. *The Death of Death in the Death of Christ: A Treatise in which the whole controversy about Universal Redemption is fully discussed.* London: Banner of Truth Trust, 1959.

Ozment, Steven. *The Age of Reform, 1250-1550: An Intellectual and Religious History of Late Medieval and Reformation Europe.* New Haven: Yale UP, 1980.

———. *The Bürgermeister's Daughter: Scandal in a Sixteenth-Century German Town.* New York: HarperPerennial, 1996.

Packer, J. I. *Evangelism and the Sovereignty of God.* Downers Grove: IVP, 1961.

Parker, Geoffrey. *The Dutch Revolt.* New York: Penguin, 1979.

Pauck, Wilhelm, ed. *Melanchthon and Bucer.* Philadelphia: the Westminster Press, 1969.

Pelikan, Jaroslav. *Credo: Historical and Theological Guide to Creeds and Confessions of Faith in the Christian Tradition.* New Haven: Yale UP, 2003.

Peters, George W. *A Biblical Theology of Missions.* Chicago: Moody Press, 1972.

Peterson, Robert A. and Michael D. Williams. *Why I Am Not an Arminian.* Downers Grove: IVP, 2004.

Peterson, Roger, Gordon Aeschliman, and R. Wayne Sneed. *Maximum Impact Short-Term Mission: the God-commanded Repetitive Deployment of Swift, Temporary, Non-professional Missionaries.* Minneapolis: STEM Press, 2003.

Piper, John. *Let the Nations Be Glad: the Supremacy of God in Missions* (Second edition). Grand Rapids: Baker, 2003.

Plass, Ewald M., comp. *What Luther Says: An Anthology.* 3 volumes. Saint Louis: Concordia Publishing House, 1959.

Platt, John. *Reformed Thought and Scholasticism: The Arguments for the Existence of God in Dutch Theology, 1575-1650.* Leiden: Brill, 1982.

Rahner, Karl. *Theological Investigations.* Vol. 5. New York: Crossroad, 1983.

Ramsey, Ann W. *Liturgy, Politics and Salvation: The Catholic League in Paris and the Nature of Catholic Reform, 1540-1630.* Rochester: University of Rochester Press, 1999.

Reymond, Dr. Robert L. *A New Systematic Theology of the Christian Faith*. Nashville: Thomas Nelson Publishers, 1998.

Rooy, S. H. "The Reformers and Missions." In *Signposts of God's Liberating Kingdom: Perspectives for the 21st Century*. Vol. 2. Edited by Bennie van der Walt and Rita Swanepoel. Potchefstroom: Potchefstroomse Universiteit vir Christelike Hoër Onderwys, 1998.

Rublack, Ulinka. *Reformation Europe*. Cambridge: Cambridge UP, 2005.

Sayers, Dorothy L. *Letters to a Diminished Church: Passionate Arguments for the Relevance of Christian Doctrine*. W Publishing Group, 2004.

Schaff, Philip. *History of the Christian Church*. 8 volumes. Peabody: Hendrickson Publishers Inc., 2002 reprint.

Schalkwijk, Frans. *The Reformed Church in Dutch Brazil (1630-1654)*. Zoetermeer: Uitgeverij Boekencentrum, 1986.

Scherer, James A. *Gospel, Church and Kingdom: Comparative Studies in World Mission Theology*. Minneapolis: Augsburg, 1987.

Schirrmacher, Thomas. *The Persecution of Christians Concerns Us All: Towards a Theology of Martyrdom*. Bonn: VK/Idea, n.d.

Schlossberg, Herbert. *Idols for Destruction: the Conflict of Christian Faith and American Culture*. Wheaton: Crossway Books, 1990.

Schmidt, Karl Ludwig. "ἔθνος" In *Theological Dictionary of the New Testament*. Vol. 2. Edited by Gerhard Kittel. Translated by Geoffrey W. Bromiley. Grand Rapids: Eerdmans, 1964. 364-372.

Schutte, Kevin Allen. "The Missional Church and New Church Development in the CRCNA." MA thesis for Calvin Theological Seminary, March 2003.

Seifrid, Mark A. *Justification by Faith: The Origin and Development of a Central Pauline Theme*. Leiden: E. J. Brill, 1992.

Senior, Donald. "Bible." In *Dictionary of Mission: Theology, History, Perspectives*. Edited by Karl Müller. Maryknoll: Orbis Books, 1997. 44-45.

Shepherd, Norman. "Scripture and Confession." In *Scripture and Confession: A Book About Confessions Old and New*. Edited by John H. Skilton. Phillipsburg: Presbyterian and Reformed Publishing Co., 1973. 1-30.

Smit, D. J. "What Does *Status Confessionis* Mean?" In *A Moment of Truth: The Confession of the Dutch Reformed Mission Church, 1982*. Edited by G. D. Cloete and D. J. Smit. Grand Rapids: Eerdmans, 1984. 7-32.

Smit, Harvey A. "Mission Zeal in the Christian Reformed Church: 1857-1917." In *Perspectives on the Christian Reformed Church: Studies in Its History, Theology and Ecumenicity Presented in Honor of John Henry Kromminga at His Retirement as President of Calvin Theological Seminary*. Edited by Peter De Klerk and Richard De Ridder. Grand Rapids: Baker, 1983. 225-240.

Smith, Lacey Baldwin. *Fools, Martyrs, Traitors: the Story of Martyrdom in the Western World*. New York: Alfred A. Knopf, 1997.

Steinmetz, David C. *Calvin in Context*. New York: Oxford UP, 1995.

———. "The Scholastic Calvin." In *Protestant Scholasticism: Essays in Reassessment*. Edited by Carl Trueman and R. Scott Clark. Carlisle: Paternoster Press, 1999. 16-30.

Stott, John R. W. *Christian Mission in the Modern World*. Downers Grove: IVP, 1975.

Strathmann, H. "Μαρτυς" In *Theological Dictionary of the New Testament*. Vol. 4. Edited by Gerhard Kittel. Translated by Geoffrey W. Bromiley. Grand Rapids: Eerdmans, 1964. 74-514.

Tappert, Theodore G., trans. and ed. *The Book of Concord: the Confessions of the Evangelical Lutheran Church*. Philadelphia: Fortress Press, 1959.

Taylor, William D. "Drawing to a close: inviting reflective, passionate and globalized practitioners." In *Global Missiology for the 21st Century: the Iguassu Dialogue*. Edited by William D. Taylor. Grand Rapids: Baker Academic, 2001.

Thomas, Norman E., ed. *Classic Texts in Mission & World Christianity*. Maryknoll: Orbis Books, 1995.

Tippet, Alan. *Introduction to Missiology*. Pasadena: William Carey Library, 1987.

Tracy, James D. *Europe's Reformations, 1450-1650*. Lanham: Rowman and Littlefield, 1999.

Trelease, Allen W. *Indian Affairs in Colonial New York: the Seventeenth Century*. Ithaca: Cornell UP, 1960.

Trueman, Carl R. and R. Scott Clark, ed. *Protestant Scholasticism: Essays in Reassessment*. Carlisle: Paternoster Press, 1999.

Tucker, Ruth A. *From Jerusalem to Irian Jaya: A Biographical History of Christian Missions* (Second Edition). Grand Rapids: Zondervan, 2004.

Vallensis, Lepusculus. *The Belgic Confession and Its Biblical Basis*. Neerlandia: Inheritance Publications, 1993.

Van Andel, H. A. *De Zendingsleer van Gisbertus Voetius*. Kampen: J. H. Kok, 1912.

VanBruggen, J. *The Ancient Text of the New Testament*. Winnipeg: Premier, 1976.

VanBruggen, J. *The Church Says Amen: An Exposition of the Belgic Confession*. Neerlandia: Inheritance Publications, 2003.

Van Engen, Charles. *Mission on the Way: Issues in Mission Theology*. Grand Rapids: Baker, 1996.

Van Gelder, Craig. "Revisioning the CRC." In *Together We Gather: Understanding the Mission of the Church*. Edited by Craig Van Gelder. Grand Rapids: Christian Reformed Home Missions, 1994. 72-91.

Van Genderen, J. *Confessie en theologie* (Apeldoornse Studies). Kampen: J. H. Kok, 1975.

Van Henten, Willem and Friedrich Avemarie. *Martyrdom and Noble Death: Selected Texts from Graeco-Roman, Jewish and Christian Antiquity*. London: Routledge, 2002.

Van Hoozer, Kevin. "The Trials of Truth: Mission, Martyrdom and the Epistemology of the Cross." In *To Stake a Claim: Mission and the Western Crisis of Knowledge*. Edited by J. Andrew Kirk and Kevin Vanhoozer. Maryknoll: Orbis, 1999. 120-156.

Van Langeraad, Lambregt Abraham. *Guido de Bray: zijn leven en werken*. Zierikzee: S. Ochtman & Zoon, 1884.

Van Rongen, G. *The Church: Its Unity in Confession and History*. Neerlandia: Inheritance Publications, 1998.

Van't Spijker, W. " 'Den Hals Buygende Onder Het Jock Jesu Christi,' Oorsprong en zin van een uitdrukking in art. 28 en 29 van de Nederlandse Geloofsbelijdenis." In *Bezield Verband: Opstellen aageboden aan prof. J. Kamphuis.* Edited by J. Douma. Kampen: Van den Berg, 1984. 206-219.

Van Til, Cornelius. *Common Grace and the Gospel.* Phillipsburg: Presbyterian and Reformed, 1972.

Von Campenhausen, Hans. "Das Martyrium in der Mission." In *Kirchengeschichte als Missionsgeschichte.* Band I: Die Alte Kirche. Edited by Heinzgünter Frohnes, Hans-Werner Gensichen, and Georg Kretschmar. Munich: Chr. Kaiser Verlag, 1974. 71-85.

Vonk, C. *De voorzeide leer: de Nederlandse Geloofsbelijdenis Art. 1-21 en 25-26.* Barendrecht: Drukkerij "Barendrecht", 1955.

_____. *De voorzeide leer: de Nederlandse Geloofsbelijdenis Art. 22-24 en 27-37.* Barendrecht: Drukkerij "Barendrecht", 1956.

Verkuyl, Johannes. *Contemporary Missiology.* Grand Rapids: Eerdmans, 1978.

Visser, Paul J. *Heart for the Gospel, Heart for the World: The Life and Thought of a Reformed Pioneer Missiologist, Johan Herman Bavinck [1895-1964].* Eugene: Wipf and Stock, 2003.

Wallace, Daniel B. *Greek Grammar Beyond the Basics: An Exegetical Syntax of the New Testament.* Grand Rapids: Zondervan, 1996.

Walton, Steve. "Acts: Many Questions, Many Answers." In *The Face of New Testament Studies: A Survey of Recent Research.* Edited by Scot McKnight and Grant R. Osborne. Grand Rapids: Baker Academic, 2004. 229-250.

Warneck, Gustav. *Outline of a History of Protestant Missions from the Reformation to the Present Time.* New York: Fleming H. Revell Company, 1901.

Weston, Paul, comp. *Lesslie Newbigin: Missionary Theology, A Reader.* Grand Rapids: Eerdmans, 2006.

Wielenga, D. K. *De akker is de wereld.* Amsterdam: Uitgeverij Ton Bolland, 1971.

Williams, Joel F. "Mission in Mark." In *Mission in the New Testament: An Evangelical Approach.* Edited by William J. Larkin Jr. and Joel F. Williams. Maryknoll: Orbis, 1998.

Woolley, Paul. "What is a Creed For? Some Answers from History." In *Scripture and Confession: A Book About Confessions Old and New*. Edited by John H. Skilton. Phillipsburg: Presbyterian and Reformed Publishing Co., 1973. 95-124.

Wright, D. F., trans. and ed. *Common Places of Martin Bucer*. Appleford: the Sutton Courtenay Press, 1972.

Young, Edward J. *Thy Word is Truth: Thoughts on the Biblical Doctrine of Inspiration*. Grand Rapids: Eerdmans, 1957.

Zwemer, Samuel M. *Into All the World, The Great Commission: A Vindication and an Interpretation*. Grand Rapids: Zondervan, 1943.

Articles

Alderden, Patricia, Carol Flietstra, and MM. "Classes Seek to Retain Hymnal Forms, Exclude Contemporary Testimony." *The Banner* 121, no. 10 (March 17, 1986): 24.

Berkhout, Peter G. "The Belgic Confession at the Crossroads." *The Banner* 96, no. 23 (June 9, 1961): 19-23.

Binnema, Jacob. "Beef It Up." *The Banner* 119, no. 43 (November 26, 1984): 11.

Blaser, Klauspeter. "Should we stop using the term 'mission'?" *International Review of Mission* 301 (Jan. 1987): 68-71.

Blue, J. Ronald. "Go, Missions." *Bibliotheca Sacra* 141, no.564 (October/December 1984): 341-353.

Boer, Harry R. "Missions and the Creeds." *The Reformed Journal* 11, no.11 (November 1952): 14-16.

Bosch, David J. "Mission and Evangelism: Clarifying the Concepts." *Zeitschrift für Missionswissenschaft und Religionswissenschaft* 68 (1984): 161-191.

Bredenhof, Wes. "De Brès vs. Simons: A Sixteenth-Century Debate that Still Matters." *Clarion* 57, no. 24 (Year-End Issue): 638-641.

_____. "Johannes Megapolensis: Pioneer Reformed Missionary to the Mohawks." *The Confessional Presbyterian* 5 (2009): 161-169.

_____. "Martyrdom, Mission, and the Belgic Confession." *The Confessional Presbyterian* 4 (2008): 109-121.

Chaney, Charles. "The Missionary Dynamic in the Theology of John Calvin." *The Reformed Review* 17, no.3 (March 1964): 24-38.

Cloud, David. "Calvinism on the March Among Evangelicals." *Friday Church News Notes* 7, no. 38 (Sept. 29, 2006): 1.

Cortez, Marc. "Context and Concept: Contextual Theology and the Nature of Theological Discourse." *Westminster Theological Journal* 67, no.1 (Spring 2005): 85-102.

Corwin, Charles. "Efforts of the Dutch-American Colonial Pastors for the Conversion of the Indians." *Journal of the Presbyterian Historical Society* 12, no. 4 (October 1925): 225-246.

_____. "The First Dutch Minister in America." *Journal of the Presbyterian Historical Society* 12, no. 3 (April 1925): 144-151.

De Jong, Gerald Francis. "Dominie Johannes Megapolensis: Minister to New Netherland." *The New York Historical Society Quarterly* 52, no. 1 (January 1968): 7-47.

DeJong, J. "Even So I Send You — Some Reflections on the Current Missionary Task of the Church — (2)" *Clarion* 45, no.21 (October 18,1996): 471-474.

DeJong, James. "John Calvin in Mission Literature." *Pro Rege* 4, no.1 (Sept. 1975): 6-17.

Dekker, Harold. "God So Loved — ALL Men!" *The Reformed Journal* 12, no. 11 (December 1962): 5-7.

_____. "Limited Atonement and Evangelism." *The Reformed Journal* 14, no. 5 (May-June 1964): 22-24.

Faber, J. "The Civil Government in Article 36 B.C." *Clarion* 28, no. 24 (December 1, 1979): 510-512.

_____. "De Brès Versus Calvin? Early History of the Belgic Confession." *Clarion* 28, no.17 (August 25, 1979): 354-356.

Gensichen, Hans-werner. "Were the Reformers Indifferent to Mission?" *Verbum SVD* 25 (1984), no. 1: 3-10.

Gootjes, Nicolaas H. "Calvin on Epicurus and the Epicureans: Background to a Remark in Article 13 of the Belgic Confession." *Calvin Theological Journal* 40, no. 1 (April 2005): 33-48.

———. "The Earliest Report on the Author of the Belgic Confession (1561)." *Nederlands archief voor kerkgeschiedenis* 82, no.1 (2002): 86-94.

Greidanus, Morris N. "Case Study No. 4: 'Our World Belongs to God: A Contemporary Testimony of the Christian Reformed Church in North America." *The Reformed Ecumenical Synod Theological Forum* 11, no. 4 (March 1984): 33-36.

———. "A Voice for Today: A Contemporary Testimony." *The Banner* 123, no. 18 (May 9, 1988): 14-15.

Haak, Cornelis J. "The Missional Approach: Reconsidering Elenctics (Part 1)." *Calvin Theological Journal* 44, no. 1 (April 2009): 37-48.

———. "The Missional Approach: Reconsidering Elenctics (Part 2)." *Calvin Theological Journal* 44, no. 2 (November 2009): 288-305

Heynen, A. James. "The Making of a Confession." *The Banner* 118, no. 20 (May 23, 1986): 15-16.

Hoogsteen, T. "A Debatable Testimony: One That Ought Not to Have Seen the Light of Day." *Christian Renewal* 4, no. 19 (June 9, 1986): 16-17.

Irving, Justin A. and Karin Klenke. "Telos, Chronos and Hermeneia: The Role of Metanarrative in Leadership Effectiveness through the Production of Meaning." *International Journal of Qualitative Methods* 3, no. 3 (September 2004).

Jongeneel, Jan. "The Missiology of Gisbertus Voetius: the First Comprehensive Protestant Theology of Missions." *Calvin Theological Journal* 26, no. 1 (April 1991): 47-79.

Kolb, Robert. "God's Gift of Martyrdom: The Early Reformation Understanding of Dying for the Faith." *Church History* 64, no. 3 (September 1995): 399-412.

Koranyi, Andras. "Mission as Call to Metanoia and Witness to Hope: A Historical Survey." *International Review of Mission* 88 (July 1999): 267-279.

Kuyper, Abraham. "Calvinism and Confessional Revision." *The Presbyterian and Reformed Review* 7 (July 1891): 369-399.

Kvalbein, Hans. "Go therefore and make disciples...The concept of discipleship in the New Testament." *Themelios* 13, no.2 (Jan./Feb. 1988): 48-53.

Matheson, Peter. "Martyrdom or Mission? A Protestant Debate." *Archiv für Reformationsgeschichte* 80 (1989): 154-171.

McGavran, Donald. "A Missionary Confession of Faith." *Calvin Theological Journal* 7, no. 2 (November 1972): 133-145.

Monsma, Timothy. "Mission Themes in the Belgic Confession." *The Outlook* 30, no. 2 (February 1980): 21-22.

Recker, R. "An Analysis of the Belgic Confession as to its Mission Focus." *Calvin Theological Journal* 7, no.2 (November 1972): 158-180.

Richter, Daniel K. "Some of Them . . . Would Always Have a Minister with Them: Mohawk Protestantism, 1683-1719." *American Indian Quarterly* 16, no. 4 (Autumn 1992): 471-484.

RR. "Contemporary Testimony Passes Final Test." *The Banner* 121, no. 25 (June 30, 1986): 16.

Schrotenboer, Paul G. "Editorial Revision of Belgic Confession — A Majority Opinion." *The Banner* 96, no. 23 (June 9, 1961): 18.

Schuringa, Gregory D. "Orthodoxy and Piety in the *Nadere Reformatie*: The Theology of Simon Oomius." *Mid-America Journal of Theology* 20 (2009): 95-103.

Shenk, Wilbur R. "Recasting Theology of Mission: Impulses from the Non-Western World." *International Bulletin of Missionary Research* 25, no. 3 (July 2001): 98-107.

Sinnema, Donald. "The Origin of the Form of Subscription in the Dutch Reformed Tradition." *Calvin Theological Journal* 42, no. 2 (November 2007): 256-282.

Spykman, Gordon J. "Revision of Belgic Confession — The Minority Opinion." *The Banner* 96, no.23 (June 9, 1961): 18-19.

Strauss, S. A. "John Calvin and the Belgic Confession." *In Die Skriflig* 27, no. 4 (December 1993): 501-517.

Trites, Allison. "Martuj and Martyrdom in the Apocalypse: A Semantic Study." *Novum Testamentum* 15, no.1 (January 1973): 72-80.

Tuininga, Jelle. "Critique of the Contemporary Testimony." *The Outlook* 34, no. 6 (July/August 1984): 10-11.

———. "The Contemporary Testimony." *The Outlook* 35, no. 6 (June 1985): 20.

Turngren, Timothy. "The Contemporary Testimony." *The Outlook* 36, no. 6 (June 1986): 14-16.

Van den Berg, J. "Calvin's Missionary Message: Some Remarks About the Relation

Between Calvinism and Missions." *The Evangelical Quarterly* 22 (1950): 174-187.

Van der Merwe, Dirk. "Perseverance through Suffering: A Spirituality for Mission." *Missionalia* 33, no.2 (August 2005): 329-354.

Venema, Cornelis. "The Contemporary Testimony: A New Confession." *Christian Renewal* 4, no. 13 (March 3, 1986): 6-7.

Verbrugge, Verlyn. "Suggestions for a Missionary Ecclesiology." *Stromata*. Vol. 13, no. 2 (December 1967): 9-13.

Visser, Paul J. "Religion in Biblical and Reformed Perspective." *Calvin Theological Journal* 44, no. 1 (April 2009): 9-36.

Wallace, Daniel B. "The Majority-Text Theory: History, Methods and Critique." *Journal of the Evangelical Theological Society* 37, no.2 (June 1994): 185-215.

INDEX

PEOPLE AND PLACES

A

Albany 210, 211, 214, 294
Alsted, J. H. 150
Althaus, Paul 17, 161, 296
Alva, Duke of (fernando Alvarez de Toledo) 13
Antwerp 13, 15, 21, 24, 56, 101, 102, 116, 294, 295, 304
Aquinas, Thomas 128, 135
Aristotle 131, 181
Arminius, Jacobus 175, 198
Augustine of Hippo 98, 134, 155, 156, 174, 293

B

Backerus, Johannes 210
Bahnsen, Greg 165, 296
Barrett, David 140, 146, 296
Barth, Karl 132, 161, 276, 285, 286, 296
Bavinck, J. Herman 29, 57, 67, 129, 148, 149, 177, 178, 270, 272, 273, 290, 291, 296, 310
Beale, G. K. 32, 33, 296
Berkhout, Peter G. 240, 311
Berkouwer, G. C. 276, 287, 297
Bertram 278, 282, 283, 284, 287, 297
Beza, Theodore 23, 59, 122, 327
Biel 125
Biel, Gabriel 125
Binnema, Jacob 259, 311
Boer, Harry 54, 55, 224, 237, 238, 239, 297, 311
Boniface VIII, Pope 108
Bosch, David 29, 47, 48, 49, 51, 56, 67, 158, 169, 170, 171, 177, 183, 194, 235, 297, 311
Bouillon, Duke of 86

Bouwman, Clarence 121, 195, 297
Braaten, Carl 160, 161, 162, 164, 297
Braekman, E. M. 79, 80, 81, 82, 83, 86, 87, 88, 139, 297
Brainerd, David 208
Bratt, J. D. 236, 240, 241, 297
Bratt, John Harold 239
Breen, Quirinus 8, 298
Brown, Robert McAfee 35, 114, 277, 298
Brunain 88
Brussels 14
Bucer, Martin x, xviii, 26, 50, 51, 52, 53, 54, 55, 56, 57, 58, 91, 94, 95, 96, 97, 99, 116, 301, 303, 304, 306, 311
Burgon, John 40, 298
Busch, Eberhard 275, 298

C

Calvin, John viii, ix, x, xviii, xxii, 3, 4, 8, 10, 13, 17–23, 50, 51, 59, 83, 91, 95, 97, 98, 99, 113, 114, 122–128, 135, 138, 139, 143, 148, 156, 159, 174, 178, 197, 224, 225, 236, 241, 242, 247, 264, 271, 279, 282, 291, 293, 298, 299, 300, 302, 303, 305, 307, 308, 312– 315, 327
Cameron, Euan 9, 90, 298
Carey, William xi, xii, xiii, 46, 57, 168, 176, 177, 304, 308
Carson, D. A. 35, 150, 160, 161, 298, 301
Castro, Emilio 47
Charles Van Engen 11, 12, 16, 156, 157
Clemence, Abel 82, 83, 84, 86, 104, 194, 294

Cloud, David 176, 312
Coakley, John 193, 194, 299
Conn, Harvie 66, 133, 235, 273, 299
Cordelier 108
Crespin, Jean 81, 82, 87, 89, 106, 294
Crew, Phyllis Mack 17, 81, 87, 99, 100, 101, 102, 104, 137, 299
Cyprian 155

D

Dawkins, Richard 164, 299
de Brès, Guido i, ii, iii, iv, vi, x, xviii, xxi, 8, 13, 21, 22, 23, 24, 50, 63, 79, 80, 81, 82, 83, 84, 85, 86, 87, 88, 89, 90, 91, 96, 97, 102, 103, 104, 105, 106, 107, 108, 109, 110, 111, 112, 113, 114, 115, 116, 117, 118, 124, 127, 128, 135, 136, 137, 138, 139, 140, 149, 151, 153, 155, 161, 172, 181, 188, 189, 194, 205, 233, 238, 260, 271, 273, 279, 297
Deddens, Karel ix, 132, 299
DeJong, J. 35, 36, 49
DeJong, James viii, 4
DeJong, P. Y. 82, 119
Dekker, Harold 241, 312
de la Grange, Peregrin vi, 87, 88
Dickens, A. G. 9, 81, 300
Drews, Paul 18
Drisius, Samuel 216, 217
Duke, Alastair 13, 79, 82, 84, 86, 88, 101, 111, 295, 300, 304

E

East Indies 197, 198, 206
Edward VI 51, 55, 56, 80
Eliot, John xi, xii, 208
Elton, G. R. 7, 8, 9, 300
Emden 15, 101, 253, 295
Erasmus, Desiderius 8
Esch, Johann 14

F

Faber, Jelle 22, 152, 153, 154, 155, 193, 312
Faukelius, Herman 221
Frame, John 288, 300
France, R. T. 38
Francis I 22, 83, 97
Frankfurt 81, 167, 303

G

Geneva ix, 14, 23, 56, 59, 81, 87, 98, 99, 100, 103, 106, 122, 294, 303
Gomarus, Franciscus 198
Gootjes, Nicholas xxii, 21, 22, 23, 24, 56, 81, 82, 89, 91, 96, 104, 113, 138, 175, 253, 271, 301, 312
Greenway, Roger 20, 178, 190, 191, 301, 305
Greidanus, Morris 244, 250, 253, 261, 313
Greijdanus, Seakle 31, 301
Grenier, Nicholas 80, 102

H

Haak, C. J. 27, 48, 132, 133, 148, 302, 313
Heidelberg ix, 1, 46, 51, 63, 138, 159, 196, 204, 206, 216, 221, 226, 236, 243, 247, 248, 251, 253, 258, 261, 270
Hendrix, Scott 3, 51, 55, 90, 91, 93, 94, 99, 302
Hesselgrave, David 49, 129, 130, 132, 133, 134, 135, 136, 137, 185, 186, 187, 221, 302
Heurnius, Justus 206
Heynen, A. James 259, 313
Hick, John 162, 163, 164, 302
Hinlicky, Paul 276, 277, 302
Hitchens, Christopher 164, 302
Hoekema, Anthony 226, 248
Hoffmann, Melchior 14, 151, 181

INDEX

Holsten, Walter 51
Hoogsteen, T. 260, 261, 313
Horton, Michael 150, 156, 157, 158, 176, 303
Hyde, Daniel xxii, 84, 110, 116, 121, 122, 123, 124, 152, 303, 327

I
Ikenga-Metuh, Emefie 183, 184

J
Janssen, R. C. 263, 264, 270, 278, 280, 282, 288, 289, 303
Jogues, Isaac 217
Jongeneel, Jan x, 167, 177, 178, 197, 198, 199, 200, 201, 202, 203, 303, 313
Joosse, L. J. iii, x, xxi, 51, 54, 116, 202, 210, 211, 215, 222

K
Klooster, Fred ix, 226
Kuhn, Thomas 170
Kuitert, H. M. 259
Küng, Hans 170
Kuyper, Abraham xx, 148, 149, 278, 279, 280, 281, 282, 284, 285, 287, 288, 313

L
Lasco, John A. 80
Lausanne 81, 96, 138
Leiden, John of 14
Le Moyne, Simon 211, 216, 217, 218, 219, 220, 294
Lille 14, 80, 81, 82, 87
Lombard, Peter 125, 126, 127, 128, 135
London xi, 7, 15, 18, 43, 66, 68, 80, 100, 177, 235, 293, 300, 305, 309
Lull, Raymond 131
Luther, Martin viii, 9, 13, 16, 17, 18, 19, 20, 23, 50, 51, 77, 91, 92, 93, 94, 95, 97, 98, 99, 126, 150, 294, 296, 300, 306
Lystra 129, 130

M
Maccovius, Johannes 198
Machen, J. Gresham 288, 304
Manhattan 214, 217
Margaret of Parma 6, 12, 13, 82
Marnef, Guido 101, 304
Matheson, Peter 95, 96, 304, 314
Matthijs, John 14
McGavran, Donald 143, 144, 145, 152, 191, 314
McGovern, Terry 176
McLuhan, Marshall 136
Megapolensis, Johannes ii, xix, 197, 208, 210, 211, 212, 213, 214, 215, 216, 217, 218, 219, 220, 221, 222, 223, 294, 311, 312
Melanchthon, Philip viii, 51, 94, 126, 301, 306
Michaelius, Jonas 210, 212
Moded, Herman 100
Mons 79, 82
Monsma, Timothy 258, 314
Monter, William 79, 304
Mouw 250
Mouw, Richard 250, 253, 259
Muller, Richard 20, 98, 118, 119, 125, 126, 127, 128, 271, 282, 291, 305
Munster 14, 104, 105

N
Neill, Stephen vii, 28, 131, 208, 305
New Amsterdam (New York City) 211, 214, 216, 218, 221
Newbigin, Lesslie 178, 179, 301, 310
New Netherland xv, xix, 197, 208, 209, 210, 211, 212, 213, 214,

215, 216, 217, 221, 222, 294, 304, 312
Nijenhuis, Willem 56, 57, 58, 305
Nineveh 33

O
Opocënsky, Milan 277
Ozment, Steven 8, 15, 16, 174, 189, 306

P
Pannikkar, Raimundo 160
Parker, Geoffrey 12, 13, 306
Pelikan, Jaroslav 185, 271, 275, 277, 290, 302, 306
Peters, George 38, 49, 306
Philip II, King of Spain 6, 10, 11, 12, 13, 16, 83, 110, 204
Piper, John xviii, 71, 72, 73, 74, 75, 76, 78, 176, 306
Platt, John 159, 306
Propst, Jakob 13

R
Rahner, Karl 163, 164, 306
Ramon, Catherine 81
Ramsey, Ann 16, 306
Recker, Robert xix, 3, 50, 158, 182, 224, 225, 226, 227, 228, 229, 230, 231, 232, 233, 234, 235, 236, 238, 239, 242, 247, 253, 266, 314
Rensselaerswyck 211, 212, 213, 217
Reu, Countess du 105
Ricci, Matteo 131
Richardot, Francois 108, 109
Rommen, Edward 129, 130, 132, 133, 134, 302
Rooy, Sidney viii, xi, 19, 20, 307
Rotman, Bernard 104, 105
Ryland, John 176, 177

S
Saravia, Adrian xviii, 21, 22, 50, 56, 57, 58, 59, 305
Sayers, Dorothy 141, 142, 307
Schalkwijk, Frans ii, x, xiii, 221, 307
Schenectady 214
Schilder, Klaas 88, 158
Schirrmacher, Thomas 68, 70, 77, 78, 146, 307
Schleiermacher, F.D.E. 281
Schlossberg, Herbert 264, 307
Schrotenboer, Paul G. 240, 314
Schutte, Kevin 236, 265, 307
Scotus, John Duns 174
Senior, Donald 169, 307
Shenk, Wilbur 173, 314
Simons, Menno 104, 114, 151, 152, 172, 181, 182, 311
Smit, D.J. 276, 308
Smit, Harvey 241
Smith, Lacey Baldwin 66, 185, 308
Socrates 70, 71
Spykman, Gordon J. 240, 250, 253, 259, 314
Steinmetz, David 125, 174, 308
Stephan, Horst 276
Stott, John R.W. 28, 30, 34, 308
Strasbourg 23, 51
Strauss, S.A. 22, 124, 314

T
Taffin, Jean 21, 88, 100, 295
Taylor, William D. 67, 68, 308
Tertullian 67, 77, 88
Tesschenmaeker, Peter 214
Tillich, Paul 161
Tippet, Alan 168, 308
Titelmans, Pieter 14
Tournai vi, 14, 22, 23, 24, 81, 82, 86, 87, 88, 100, 204
Tracy, James 10, 13, 14, 15, 16, 134, 308

INDEX

Tuininga, Jelle 259, 260, 315
Turngren, Timothy 260, 263, 315

U
Utrecht x, 198, 202, 207, 252, 295

V
Valenciennes 13, 82, 87, 88, 89, 105, 106, 107, 108
Vallensis, Lepusculus 145, 309
Van Andel, H.A. x, 202, 309
Van Bruggen, J. 39, 40, 121, 194, 195
Van den Berg, J. 19, 20, 116, 310, 315
Vander Heyden, Gaspar 101
Vander Velde, George 253
Van Engen, Charles 156, 157, 158, 309
Van Gelder, Craig 262, 309
Van Haemstede, Adrien 88, 101, 102, 295
Vanhoozer, Kevin xviii, 68, 69, 70, 71, 72, 74, 75, 76, 309
Van Langeraad, L.A. 139, 309
Van Rensselaer, Kiliaen 211, 215, 220
Van Til, Cornelius 165, 296, 310
Van Wingen, Godfried 24
Venema, Cornelius 259, 260, 315
Verbrugge, Verlyn 242, 315
Verdickt, Anton 88, 101, 295
Verdickt, Gillis 88, 101, 295
Verkuyl, J. 47, 310
Viret, Pierre 81, 96, 122
Vischer, Lukas 275, 277, 302
Visser, Paul ii, 67, 149, 177, 264, 273, 310, 315
Voes, Heinrich 14
Voetius, Gisbertus x, xix, 148, 177, 178, 179, 197, 198, 199, 200, 201, 202, 203, 204, 205, 206, 207, 208, 215, 220, 222, 223, 295, 309, 313
Volbeda, Samuel 236
Vos, Geerhardus 156, 278

W
Warneck, Gustav 3, 57, 170, 310
Weston, Paul xxi, 178, 310
Wielenga, D.K. 276, 290, 310
William of Orange 12

Z
Zwingli, Huldrich viii, 138

Subject

African culture, theology 183, 184
Amsterdam consistory 198
Anabaptists 10, 11, 12, 14, 101, 102, 104, 105, 114, 116, 138, 149, 151, 152, 172, 180, 181, 233, 234, 301
Anonymous Christians 164
Anticlericalism 15
Antichrist 77, 95, 98, 105, 117, 194, 219
Arminian/Remonstrant party, Arminianism 175, 176, 306
Athanasian Creed 113, 151
Atheism 164–165

Barmen Declaration of 1934 276
Belgic Confession
    Article 1 112
    Article 2 159, 164
    Article 3 30
    Article 4 30
    Article 6 112
    Article 7 113
    Article 8 113
    Article 9 116
    Article 10 171, 173, 186, 276, 283
    Article 12 85, 174, 222
    Article 13 85, 113, 187, 227, 312
    Article 14 227
    Article 15 227
    Article 16 174, 175, 176, 177, 179, 202, 207, 208
    Article 17 182
    Article 18 114, 172, 173, 180, 181, 182, 184
    Article 20 182, 228
    Article 21 182
    Article 22 114, 150, 176, 187, 190, 191, 228
    Article 24 176, 229
    Article 26 114, 115, 128, 229
    Article 27 22, 85, 115, 119, 154, 186, 188
    Article 28 85, 115, 116
    Article 29 85, 115, 203, 219, 230, 233, 234, 237, 238, 239, 242, 263, 265
    Article 30 230
    Article 31 151
    Article 32 115, 167
    Article 35 187
    Article 36 2, 17, 117, 121, 192, 193, 195, 202, 206, 215, 312
    Article 37 23, 117, 121, 122, 124, 231
    Structure of 121
Belhar Confession 276
Buddhism/Buddhists 147, 161, 189, 287

Calvinism/Calvinists vii, xi, 10, 11, 14, 19, 79, 101, 102, 176, 177, 213, 239, 251, 278, 279, 280, 281, 282, 296, 304, 312, 313, 315
Calvin Theological Journal ix, x, 3, 113, 138, 143, 148, 178, 197, 225, 236, 247, 264, 312, 313, 314, 315
Calvin Theological Seminary xxii, 225, 236, 241, 307, 308
Canadian Reformed Churches xxii, 1, 31, 167, 297, 301
Candlestand Statement 191
Canons of Dort 1, 63, 179, 196, 216, 226, 236, 248, 250, 251, 270, 281, 282
Catholicity 152
Chambers of Rhetoric 99, 136
Chanteries (see Psalm-singing)

INDEX

Christendom 18, 56, 92, 93, 94, 95, 246, 263, 305
Christian Reformed Church ii, xx, 143, 192, 193, 225, 226, 235, 236, 239, 241, 256, 257, 261, 269, 276, 293, 297, 304, 308, 313
Christology 35, 114, 173, 174, 180, 181, 184, 298
Civil Government xix, 121, 123, 192, 193, 312
Classis Alberta North (CRC) 243, 244
Classis Amsterdam 209, 211, 215, 216, 221
Classis Chatham (CRC) 243, 244
Compendium of Faukelius 221
Committee on a New Confession 244
Conclusions of Utrecht 1905 252
Concordia Seminary 282
Confession of 1967 144
Confucianism 189
Contemporary Testimony ii, xx, 243, 248, 250, 251, 253, 254, 256, 258, 259, 260, 261, 276, 286, 294, 311, 313, 314, 315
Contextualization xviii, 129, 130, 132, 133, 134, 183, 299, 302
Conventicles 101, 102
corpus Christianum 92, 200
Council of Trent 150
cuius regio, eius religio 16

Diet of Regensburg 95, 96
Doleantie (1886) 278
Dutch Revolt xvii, 11, 12, 13, 306
Dutch West India Company 208

Ecclesiology 202, 203, 220, 233, 242, 246, 282
Ecumenical Creeds 193, 269, 293
Election, doctrine of 114, 175, 176, 177, 178, 179, 199, 202, 207, 208, 228, 235
Elenctics 148, 149, 313
Emergent 171
Epicureans 113, 312
Eschatology 156, 303
Evangelical Lutheran Church of America 282
Evangelism viii, xvii, 29, 39, 45, 47, 176, 241, 296, 306, 311, 312

Fifth Lateran Council of 1516 108
Formula of Concord 276, 283
French (Gallican) Confession of 1559 22

Great Commission iii, 32, 34, 36, 37, 39, 42, 43, 44, 49, 54, 55, 56, 57, 59, 64, 104, 177, 190, 296, 311

Heidelberg Catechism ix, 1, 46, 63, 138, 159, 196, 204, 206, 216, 221, 226, 236, 243, 247, 248, 251, 253, 258, 261, 270
Hinduism, Hindus 147, 161, 190
Holy Spirit, the person and work of iii, xix, xxi, 30, 35, 36, 37, 38, 42–47, 49, 50, 123, 128, 143, 144, 149, 176, 177, 179, 180, 181, 190–192, 196, 227, 228, 243, 245, 257, 260, 272, 279, 280, 291, 304
Homiletics 167

Iconoclasm 13, 102
Idolatry 17, 95, 100, 108, 117, 144, 152, 189, 192, 194, 195, 219, 235
incarnational sonship, doctrine of 172, 173
Incarnation, doctrine of 180
Institutes of the Christian Religion 22, 83, 97, 122, 293

International Conference of Reformed Churches 132, 287, 299
Islam, Muslim 146, 163, 189, 202, 287

Jainism 190
Jodo Shinsu 161
Judaism, Jews 33, 164, 189, 202
Justification, doctrine of 150, 298, 300, 301, 307

Kingdom of God, of Christ 52, 55, 94, 117, 212

Labyrinth 98
La racine 87, 102, 104, 105, 114, 189, 294
law and gospel, distinction 167, 172
Le baston 80, 102, 103, 104, 127, 139, 140, 294
liberation theology 173, 180, 183, 188, 276
liturgics 167, 168
locus method 125, 126, 127, 139, 140
Lord's Supper, the 89, 100, 107
Luddites 136
Lutheran Church — Missouri Synod 282
Lutherans 10, 116

Magistrates 204
Marcionites 114
marriage 80, 98, 99, 257
martyrdom iii, 14, 15, 59, 63, 66, 67, 68, 69, 70, 71, 72, 74, 75, 76, 77, 78, 79, 80, 81, 83, 85, 86, 87, 88, 89, 90, 95, 96, 109, 111, 119, 137, 145, 146, 147, 148, 275
metanarrative, historical tool 141, 148
Missio Dei 158
Missiology, definition of x, xvii, xix, xx, 36, 47, 49, 50, 60, 68, 158, 168, 178, 197, 198, 199, 200, 201, 202, 203, 269, 272, 308, 310, 313
missionary historiography 118
Mission, definition of 4, 5, 20, 27, 28, 29, 30, 48, 50, 59, 60, 119, 155, 232, 252, 258, 266
missiones ecclesiae 48, 233
Mission, short-term 28, 306
mission, sixteenth-century understanding of 232
Mission, the church and ii, iii, vi, vii, viii, x, xiii, xvii, xviii, xix, xxi, 3, 4, 18, 20, 27–34, 39, 45, 46, 47, 48–51, 56, 59, 63, 66–68, 78, 90, 92, 95, 96, 133, 157, 158, 167, 168, 169, 170, 171, 173, 177, 183, 199, 201, 208, 225, 241, 242, 252, 256–258, 262, 263, 276, 296, 297, 298, 299, 301, 303–315
Mission, the Holy Spirit and 257
Mohawk creation narrative 222
Mohawks ii, xix, 210, 212, 213, 214, 217, 218, 221, 222, 311
Mystery 152, 303

Nadere Reformatie 197, 211, 291, 314
Narrative theology 157
Nederlands Hervormde Kerk 278
norma normans, norma normata 271, 274
North American Presbyterian and Reformed Council (NAPARC) 287
Ottoman Empire 189
Our Song of Hope 248
Pentecost 42, 52, 54, 297
Pentecostalism 174
Persecution ii, 2, 12, 14, 15, 63, 65, 66, 67, 74, 76–87, 90, 115, 122, 137, 146–148, 200, 205, 206, 207, 209, 275, 283, 285, 327

principium cognoscendi 128, 271, 273, 274
principium essendi 128, 135
Psalm-singing 13, 82, 101

Reformed Church in America 193, 236, 248, 254, 299
Reformed Presbyterian Church of North America i, 248
Regulative principle of worship 167
religious pluralism 160, 162, 163, 264, 327
Roman Catholics, Roman Catholicism x, 99, 116, 140, 141, 146, 149, 151, 152, 181, 183, 199, 202, 207, 208, 234

Sacraments 104, 115, 117, 187, 230, 233
Saints, veneration of 96, 115
Scholasticism 125, 126, 159, 197, 301, 306, 308, 309
Secession (Afscheiding) of 1834 236
Second Helvetic Confession 139
Secularization 250, 260, 264, 266
Sikhism 190, 287
Singing of Psalms 13, 82, 101
Social Gospel 261
Status confessionis 277, 302
Synod of CRC, 1952 237–238
Synod of CRC, 1958 192
Synod of CRC, 1964 241
Synod of CRC, 1967 241
Synod of CRC, 1971 243–244
Synod of CRC, 1972 244
Synod of CRC, 1973 247
Synod of CRC, 1975 247–248
Synod of CRC, 1977 248–250
Synod of CRC, 1979 254
Synod of CRC, 1982 254
Synod of CRC, 1983 254
Synod of CRC, 1986 256

Synod of Dort 1618–19 153, 175, 198, 243, 253, 281
Synod of French Reformed Churches, 1559 22, 24, 29, 122, 124, 153, 175, 192, 198, 241, 243, 244, 247, 253, 254, 281
Synod of Liberated (Vrijgemaakte) Reformed Churches, 1948 29
Synod of Reformed Churches of the Netherlands, 1905 117

Taoism 189
Theological Education Fund 131, 132
theological encyclopedia 272
Third Reich 78, 276, 283
Three Forms of Unity 1, 2, 192, 196, 225, 242, 243, 245, 247, 252, 254, 256, 258, 259, 261, 262, 269, 288
Three Points on Common Grace (Kalamazoo) 1924 252
Trinity, doctrine of the xxii, 22, 59, 113, 152, 174, 189, 190
Turks 93, 98

Unam Sanctam (papal bull) 108
United Pentecostal Church 174
United Presbyterian Church 144
United Reformed churches 236

Walcheren classis 198
Westminster Confession 2, 40, 248
Westminster Standards 2
witchcraft 100
Word of God ii, 3, 30, 40, 78, 83, 85, 98, 103, 104, 115, 153, 154, 159, 161, 162, 166, 171, 184, 193, 218, 228, 234, 237, 253, 270, 272, 273, 291
World Council of Churches (WCC) 131

Recommended Reading

FAITHFULNESS UNDER FIRE:
The Story of Guido de Bres

William Boekestein

Illustrated by Evan Hughes

A true story of faith and Perseverance for children

DESCRIPTION:
The life of Guido de Bres teaches us that we can find enduring hope in the gospel of Jesus Christ, even during persecution. Author William Boekestein sensitively tells the story of de Bres for children, guiding them through his turbulent life and times— from his birth in 1522 in a small Belgium town, to his call to the ministry and study under Reformers such as John Calvin and Theodore Beza, to his authorship of the Belgic Confession and a life of suffering, to his martyr's death in 1567. Skillfully crafted illustrations and an easy-to-understand narrative combine to capture the interests— and admiration—of the entire family for this amazing Reformation hero.

ENDORSEMENTS:
"Bill Boekestein shows his pastor's heart and desire to make the riches of our Reformed heritage known in a simple way in *Faithfulness under Fire*. Men like de Bres lived in a tumultuous time, and their example of total commitment is needed in today's world of religious pluralism, tolerance, and moderation. Our children need to learn this devotion and parents need to teach it with all their heart."
— DANIEL R. HYDE, Oceanside United Reformed Church, Carlsbad/Oceanside, CA

Hardcover, 32 pages • Page Size: 5.5 x 8.5 inches
ISBN: 978-1-60178-102-4 • Retail Price: $10.00

Reformation Heritage Books
Order from: www.heritagebooks.org or your local bookstore

www.ingramcontent.com/pod-product-compliance
Lightning Source LLC
Chambersburg PA
CBHW060551230426
43670CB00011B/1781